Cooking Through Rose-Colored Glasses

PUBLISHED

BY

THE JUNIOR LEAGUE

OF

TYLER, INC.

TYLER, TEXAS

Since it would be impossible to acknowledge individually the many people who gave freely of their time to contribute recipes, test them for accuracy and excellence, and edit them for publication, the Junior League of Tyler expresses heartfelt thanks to our Active and Sustaining members, their relatives, and their friends who made this cookbook a reality.

Additional copies of COOKING THROUGH ROSE-COLORED GLASSES may be obtained by sending $18.50 + $3.00 postage and handling to the address below. For your convenience, an order blank has been included in the book.

Junior League of Tyler, Inc.

1919 South Donnybrook Avenue

Tyler, Texas 75701

Copyright 1975, THE JUNIOR LEAGUE OF TYLER, INC ., Tyler, Texas
ISBN 0-9697122-0-8

First Printing	April, 1975	5,000 Copies
Second Printing	September, 1975	10,000 Copies
Third Printing	August, 1977	10,000 Copies
Fourth Printing	October, 1980	10,000 Copies
Fifth Printing	July, 1983	5,000 Copies
Anniversary Edition	August, 1989	1,000 Copies
Seventh Printing	October, 1993	1,000 Copies
Eighth Printing	June, 1999	7,500 Copies

Printed in the United States of America
TOOF COOKBOOK DIVISION

STARR ★ TOOF

670 South Cooper Street
Memphis, Tennessee 38104

PREFACE

The Junior League of Tyler is proud to introduce Rosie, our charming friend who will tempt you with culinary creations throughout COOKING THROUGH ROSE-COLORED GLASSES. Rosie is the personification of the many lovely ladies whose varied talents and interests blend to become the gracious traditions of East Texas. Her recipes range from exotic party fare to penny-wise, efficiently-prepared family dishes.

Rosie's accomplishments are not limited to her kitchen. Her garden is a show place to delight the many visitors who view the splendor of the Azalea Trail each spring. Complementing myriad banks of azaleas are flowering trees and spring bulbs which turn the verdant landscape into a breath-taking display of color.

In October Rosie joins hundreds of community-spirited citizens to present the Texas Rose Festival, a salute to the rose-growing industry of Tyler and vicinity. The fame of our roses has spread around the globe, and thousands come to celebrate the harvesting of the rose bushes and enjoy the pageantry of our Festival.

Culture, education, and welfare are of prime concern to Rosie, and she recognizes the invaluable contributions of volunteers in creating a progressive community. Her own service commitments have been through the projects of the Junior League of Tyler, an organization which strives to demonstrate the effectiveness of trained volunteers by developing the potential of its members for voluntary participation in community affairs. The proceeds from the sale of this volume will be used to fund these projects.

We hope you will find Rosie as helpful as she is enchanting, and that you will introduce her to many new friends.

TABLE OF CONTENTS

WEIGHTS AND MEASURES

Standard

3 teaspoons = 1 tablespoon
4 tablespoons = ¼ cup
5-1/3 tablespoons = 1/3 cup
8 tablespoons = ½ cup
10-2/3 tablespoons = 2/3 cup
12 tablespoons = ¾ cup
16 tablespoons = 1 cup
1 cup = 8 fluid ounces
1 cup = ½ pint
2 cups = 1 pint
4 cups = 1 quart
4 quarts = 1 gallon
8 quarts = 1 peck
4 pecks = 1 bushel
16 ounces = 1 pound

Metric

WEIGHT

1.1 ounces = 30 grams
3.6 ounces = 100 grams
9.0 ounces = 250 grams
1.1 pounds = 500 grams
2.2 pounds = 1 kilogram

VOLUME

1 teaspoon = 5 milliliters
1 tablespoon = 15 milliliters
1 fluid ounce = 30 milliliters
1 fluid cup = 236 milliliters
1 pint = 473 milliliters
1 quart = .946 liters
1 gallon = 3.8 liters
1 milliliter = .03 fluid ounces
1 liter = 2.1 fluid pints
1 liter = 1.06 fluid quarts
1 liter = .26 gallons

Appetizers

ANTIPASTO

1 c. catsup
1 c. salad oil
1 small can tomato sauce
1 bay leaf
2 cans [2 oz.] anchovy
   fillets
1/4 t. garlic salt
Pepper to taste
1 t. Accent

1 t. chili powder
1/2 c. chopped celery
1 can [6 oz.] tuna, flaked
1 c. sweet pickle relish
1 bottle [5 oz.]
   pickled onions
1 small jar stuffed olives
1 small can sliced
   mushrooms

In 3 quart saucepan, combine catsup, salad oil, tomato sauce, bay leaf, anchovies (cut in halves), garlic salt, pepper, Accent and chili powder. Bring to a boil and cook 2 minutes, stirring constantly. Remove from heat.

Cook chopped celery in small amount of water until barely done, drain and add to above mixture. Add tuna, pickle relish, onions, olives and mushrooms.

Bring to a boil and simmer for about 5 minutes, stirring gently. Cool and store in refrigerator. Delicious with a variety of crackers as a dip.

Mrs. E. D. Ftizpatrick

APPETIZER DIP

1 small glass Roka
   cheese spread
1 pkg. [3 oz.] Philadelphia
   cream cheese

1 T. Wilson BV
1 small onion, grated
1 pt. Hellman's
   mayonnaise

Mix cheese spread, cream cheese, BV and onion. Add to the mayonnaise a little at a time. Serve with raw vegetables (carrots, celery, cauliflower, etc.) or Fritos.

Mrs. Moliere Scarborough, Jr.

HOT BROCCOLI DIP

1 pkg. chopped broccoli
1/3 c. finely chopped onion
1/3 c. finely chopped celery
8 mushrooms, chopped

1 can cream of mushroom
   soup
1 pkg. [6 oz.] garlic cheese
Juice of 1/2 lemon

Cook broccoli and drain well. Saute' onion, celery, and mushrooms. When tender, add drained broccoli, soup, cheese, and lemon juice. Warm until cheese is melted. Serve with Fritos.

Mrs. A. Y. Lewis

BROCCOLI AND CHEESE DIP

4 pkgs. frozen broccoli,
  chopped
1 lg. onion, chopped
1 stick butter

4 rolls garlic cheese
2 cans mushroom soup
Red pepper to taste

Cook broccoli according to directions on box and drain completely. Saute onion in butter. Combine cheese and mushroom soup and heat, stirring until melted. Add onion, broccoli and red pepper to taste. Serve with Melba rounds.
Freezes well.

Mrs. A. W. Riter, Jr.

CAULIFLOWER SALAD OR APPETIZER

1 envelope Good Seasons
  bleu cheese salad
  dressing mix
1 head cauliflower, broken
  into pieces

1 jar artichoke hearts,
  drained
1 can mushroom buttons
1 jar stuffed green olives

Prepare salad dressing according to directions on envelope. Combine all other ingredients and marinate in dressing. May be served with toothpicks as an appetizer or may be used as a salad.

Mrs. William C. Smyth

CHEDDAR CHEESE QUICHE

1 unbaked 9-inch pastry in
  pyrex dish
1/2 lb. sausage
1/2 lb. Cheddar cheese [sharp],
  thinly sliced

2 eggs, slightly beaten
1 c. cream
1/2 t. salt
1/8 t. pepper

Fry sausage in skillet; drain well and crumble. Lay sliced cheese in bottom of pyrex dish (on pastry). Scatter the sausage on top of cheese. Beat eggs and cream together. Season with salt and pepper. Pour over sausage. Bake in a preheated 400 degree oven for 30 to 40 minutes or until a knife inserted in center of custard comes out dry. Serves 4 for lunch; 8 as an hors d' oeuvre.

Mrs. Wilbert Lasater

Good cold weather supper dish.

ONION TART OR QUICHE

6 medium onions, minced
4 T. butter
1 t. salt
2 T. cumin seed
3 eggs

1/2 to 1 pt. sour cream
[according to taste]
1 9-in. unbaked pie shell
1/2 c. Parmesan cheese

Sauté onions in butter until golden. Add salt and cumin seed and set aside to cool for 15 minutes. Beat eggs slightly before adding the sour cream to them and beating together. Add this mixture to the onions and pour into the unbaked pie shell. Sprinkle Parmesan cheese over the top and bake at 400 degrees for 35 to 40 minutes until the top forms a brown crust. Serves 4 to 6. Freezes beautifully.

Mrs. William Rowe

QUICHE LORRAINE

4 eggs
1 c. cream
Cayenne pepper
Salt and white pepper
Nutmeg

6 slices crisply fried bacon
or 1/2 c. diced ham
6 slices Gruyere or Swiss
cheese
Slightly baked pie shell

Beat eggs and cream with seasonings. Use pepper and salt to taste. Place crumbled bacon or ham on top of pie crust with cheese slices on top. Pour egg and cream mixture over this and bake in preheated oven at 350 degrees for 40 minutes.

Mrs. Robert E. Knox, Jr.

CHEESE PUFF SOUFFLÉS

1 lb. butter or margarine
4 jars Old English Cheddar
cheese
1 t. Tabasco
1 t. onion powder
1 1/2 t. Worcestershire
Dash cayenne

Dash hot sauce
1 t. Beau Monde seasoning
powder
2 T. dill weed
2 1/2 loaves thinly sliced
bread

Soften butter in mixer bowl. Add cheese and beat well with mixer. Add remaining ingredients and mix well. Make "sandwiches" by spreading cheese mixture between slices of bread, using 3 slices bread per sandwich ("double-decker"). Trim crust from sandwiches; then quarter each sandwich. "Ice" tops and sides of sandwiches with cheese mixture. (Place on waxed paper on cookie sheet. Quick freeze, then place in plastic bags to store in freezer.) Bake on cookie sheet at 350 degrees for 25 minutes or until brown on edge. Use toothpick in center of each sandwich to keep from sliding.

Mrs. Harold Cameron

CHEESE-OLIVE PUFFS

1/4 lb. Cheddar cheese
  grated [1 cup]
1/4 c. soft margarine
1/2 c. sifted flour

1/4 t. salt
1/2 t. paprika
Jar of stuffed olives

Blend the cheese, margarine, flour, salt and paprika. Shape around the stuffed olives. Bake on ungreased cookie sheet at 400 degrees for 10 to 15 minutes. Makes about 2 dozen. These can be frozen before baking.

Mrs. Charles Clark

 Excellent served for a morning coffee!

CHEESE RING

2 stalks celery
1/2 onion
1/4 green pepper
Small jar green stuffed
  olives
6 pkgs. [3 oz.] Philadelphia
  cream cheese

1 T. gelatin
1/4 c. water
2 T. catsup
Dash red pepper
1/2 pt. cream, whipped

Chop (fine) celery, onion, green pepper and olives. Cream the cheese and soften gelatin in water. Mix all ingredients with catsup and red pepper. Fold in whipped cream.

Pour into ring mold. Refrigerate. Unmold and serve with currant jelly and crackers (Triscuits, Melba rounds, etc.).

Mrs. Upton Beall

CHEESE SOUFFLÉ SANDWICHES

1 lb. butter
1 lb. brick processed Old English Cheese
1 to 1 1/2 large loaves sandwich bread

Allow butter and cheese to warm to room temperature. Whip together for 5 minutes in electric mixer. Decrust bread, stack 3 slices together, and cut stacks into 4 sections. Ice each layer and frost top and sides like small 3-layer cakes. Bake at 350 degrees for about 15 minutes. Makes about 40. Sandwiches can be frozen or stored in refrigerator until ready for baking.

Mrs. Henry M. Bell, Jr.

CHEESE MOLD

1 c. whipped cream	2 T. Knox gelatin,
1 lb. grated American cheese	dissolved in
1/2 c. mayonnaise	1/2 c. hot milk
Paprika, cayenne pepper,	1 t. Worcestershire sauce
salt to taste	Almonds or pecans

Whip cream. Add all other ingredients and mix well. Pour into slightly greased 1 quart mold. Chill. Unmold and serve with crackers.

Mrs. Gates Brelsford

COCKTAIL CHEESE BALLS

1/4 lb. margarine	1/2 t. salt
1/2 lb. sharp cheese, grated	1 pkg. onion soup mix
1 c. flour	1/4 c. parsley

Warm the margarine and cream with the grated cheese. Add remaining ingredients and roll into small balls. Bake about 10 minutes at 400 degrees. These may be frozen before baking.

Mrs. Lynn F. Cobb

CHILI CHEESE ROLL

1/2 lb. sharp Cheddar cheese	2 T. chili powder
1 pkg. [8 oz.] cream cheese	1 c. finely chopped pecans
1/4 t. instant garlic powder	

Grate cheese. Cream the Cheddar and cream cheese together. Add other ingredients except 1 tablespoon chili powder. Form into ball and roll in remaining tablespoon chili powder. Refrigerate until ready to serve.

Mrs. Glenn Collins
Mrs. Charles Fenn
Dayton, Texas

CHEESE STRAWS

3 c. grated sharp cheese	1 1/4 t. cayenne pepper
2 sticks margarine	3 c. sifted flour
1 t. salt	

Cream cheese and margarine together until soft. Add salt and pepper. Slowly work in enough flour to make a stiff dough. Roll, cut in strips, and bake slowly in oven about 300 degrees about 15 minutes.

Mrs. Elam Swann

CHEESE WAFERS

2 sticks butter
2 c. grated sharp Cheddar
cheese
2 c. flour

Pinch of salt
2 dashes Tabasco
2 c. Rice Krispies

Allow butter and grated cheese to soften. Work them together by hand. Add flour, salt, Tabasco and Rice Krispies. Shape by hand into wafers the size of a silver dollar. Bake at 325 degrees on ungreased cookie sheet about 12 to 15 minutes until lightly browned.

Mrs. Upton Beall
Mrs. Watson Simons

CHEESE BALLS

6 pkgs. [8 oz.] cream cheese
3 lb. Velveeta cheese
6 wedges bleu cheese
4 lb. sharp Cheddar cheese
6 t. garlic juice [bottled]
Choice of: chopped parsley, curry powder, paprika, chili powder, chopped nuts [pecans or walnuts, etc.]

2 dashes red pepper
2 t. Tabasco sauce
3 T. Worcestershire sauce
8 c. pecans

Have cream cheese at room temperature. Grate other cold cheeses and mix all together. (Use a large pan for this). Add the seasonings and nuts and mix well. Shape balls about the size of large oranges or grapefruit. Wrap in waxed paper, then in foil, until time to serve. When cold and firm, roll in any of the following: chopped parsley, curry powder, paprika, chili powder, chopped nuts. Yields approximately 7 grapefruit-sized balls.

Mrs. James Fair

PINEAPPLE CHEESE BALL

2 pkgs. [8 oz.] cream cheese, softened
1 can [8 oz.] crushed pineapple, well-drained
2 c. finely chopped pecans or Stuckey's pecan meal
    [reserve 1/2 c. to coat outside of ball]
1/4 c. green bell pepper, finely chopped
2 T. onion, finely chopped
1 T. Lawry's seasoning salt
Dash of Worcestershire sauce
Dash of Tabasco sauce

Beat cream cheese until smooth. Add pineapple, 1 1/2 cups pecans, bell pepper, onion and seasonings and mix well. Chill mixture in refrigerator until workable. Shape into ball and roll in reserved 1/2 cup pecans. Serve with Ritz crackers. The ball may be reshaped and rolled in additional pecans after it has been served. It freezes well.

Mrs. Fred Haberle

CHEESE BALL QUICKIE

1 sm. pkg. bleu cheese
2 sm. pkgs. Philadelphia
  cream cheese
1 jar Old English sharp cheese

2 T. chopped onion
1 t. Worcestershire sauce
1/4 c. chopped pecans
1/4 c. parsley flakes

Mix well first five ingredients. An electric mixer can be used. Form into a ball and roll in pecans and parsley until covered. This keeps well in the refrigerator and can be frozen.

Mrs. William H. Starling

TROPICAL CHEESE BALL

3 large pkgs. Philadelphia
  cream cheese
1/2 jar Major Grey's chutney
1/2 c. chopped pecans

1/2 t. curry powder
  [more if desired]
Shredded coconut

Allow cream cheese to reach room temperature. Blend in chutney, pecans and curry powder. Form into round ball and roll in coconut. Refrigerate until one hour before serving time. Serve with snack crackers.

Mrs. Earl Bateman
New Orleans, Louisiana

CHICKEN FOLDOVERS

2 sticks margarine,
  softened
2 c. flour
1 pkg. [8 oz.] cream
  cheese, softened

1 can boned chicken
1/2 can mushroom soup

Mix margarine, flour and cream cheese. Chill. Roll and cut with biscuit cutter into rounds.

Combine chicken and soup to make filling.

With finger tips gather just enough filling for one round of dough. Place on round and fold in half. Seal edges. Prick top with fork. Sprinkle with paprika for color and flavor. Bake at 375 degrees for 15 or 20 minutes. Makes 65 to 70 foldovers.

Foldovers can be frozen, thawed briefly and baked. Or, they can be made the day before, refrigerated and baked the next day. For a party, they can be baked, put in roasting pan and kept in warm oven until time to use.

Mrs. Tom Pollard, Jr.

ORIENTAL CHICKEN WINGS

2 lbs. chicken wings
1/2 c. catsup
1/4 c. soy sauce

1/4 c. honey
1/4 c. lemon juice

Separate chicken wings into 3 pieces. Put tips aside to use for soup. Combine the catsup, soy sauce, honey and lemon juice and use as a marinade for the remaining pieces of chicken wings. Marinate at least 3 hours. Place wings on a foil covered cookie sheet, making sure that pieces do not touch. Bake at 275 degrees for 45 minutes to 1 hour.

Mrs. Robert E. Knox, Jr.

MARINATED CRAB CLAWS

2 T. olive oil
2 bouillon cubes
3/4 c. water
1/4 c. Worcestershire sauce
1/4 c. Pickapeppa sauce
8 whole cloves
3 drops Tabasco
2 T. lemon juice

1 T. sugar
2 T. salt
1 onion, sliced
1 or 2 garlic cloves,
   not crushed
1 pkg. Bouquet Garni
   [bay-celery-thyme-parsley]
1 c. white wine

Combine all ingredients and simmer until spices blend. Strain and pour over crab claws. Marinate for several hours. Recipe makes 2 cups and will cover 2 pounds of claws, closely packed.

Mrs. James B. Owen

CRABMEAT-BROCCOLI CASSEROLE OR DIP

1 pkg. frozen chopped
   broccoli
1 can crabmeat, flaked
1/2 pt. sour cream
1 can cream of mushroom
   soup

1/4 c. chili sauce
1 small onion, chopped
1 roll garlic cheese
2 T. fresh lemon juice
1 T. grated lemon peel
Salt and pepper to taste

Cook broccoli as directed on package in skillet until tender. Mix in crabmeat, sour cream, soup, chili sauce, onion, cheese, lemon juice, lemon peel, salt and pepper. Put into a shallow buttered casserole. Bake for 20 minutes at 350 degrees.

To serve as a dip, leave in skillet until cheese melts, then transfer to chafing dish. Serves 6 as a casserole, more as a dip.

Mrs. R. B. Shelton

CRAB SPREAD

1 pkg. [8 oz.] cream
  cheese, softened
1 T. pickle relish
1 T. chopped green onions
1/3 c. sour cream

1 can [6 1/2 oz.] white
  crabmeat, well-drained
1/3 to 2/3 c. seafood cocktail
  sauce [bottled or your
  own recipe]

Mix cream cheese, relish, onions and sour cream and shape into dome formation in small bowl. Chill.

Add drained crabmeat on top of cheese mixture. Then add cocktail sauce on top to taste.

Spread on Triscuits or any crackers.

Mrs. C. J. Helling, Jr.
Dallas, Texas

HOT CRABMEAT DIP

1 T. onion
3 T. green pepper
3 T. butter
3 1/2 T. flour
1 c. well-drained tomato
  pulp [2 cans]

1/2 T. mustard
1/4 t. salt
1/2 c. cheese, grated
1/2 c. milk, scalded
1 egg, slightly beaten
1 can [6 oz.] crabmeat

Saute' onion and green pepper in butter. Stir in flour, tomatoes, mustard, salt and grated cheese. In another pan, heat milk just to boiling point and add slightly beaten egg. Then add milk and egg to first mixture. Stir in crabmeat and cook over low heat until mixture thickens. Serve hot from a chafing dish with Melba rounds.

Mrs. Henry M. Bell, Jr.

HOT CRAB SQUARES

1 can [8 oz.] crab, drained
1 pkg. [8 oz.] Philadelphia
  cream cheese
1/2 t. garlic salt
1/2 t. dry mustard

5 T. mayonnaise
1 c. [or more] sharp
  Cheddar cheese, grated
Sliced white bread
Stuffed olives

Combine crabmeat, cream cheese, garlic salt, mustard, mayonnaise and Cheddar cheese and mix all together thoroughly. Trim crusts off slices of white bread and cut each in four "squares". Toast bread very lightly on both sides, but do not brown. Spread squares with crab mixture, top with paprika and a slice of stuffed olive. Broil for 5 to 10 minutes until hot and bubbly.

Mrs. David Boice

HOT CRAB DIP

3 green onions
1 can King crabmeat
1 pkg. [8 oz.] cream cheese

1 carton [8 oz.] sour cream
1 t. horseradish
Slivered almonds

Chop green onions and drain all liquid from the crabmeat. Allow cream cheese to soften at room temperature before mixing with other ingredients. Combine all ingredients except almonds. Place in buttered baking dish and top with almonds. Bake at 375 degrees for 10 minutes, then broil for 5 minutes. Serve in a chafing dish and keep warm.

Mrs. Sterling Moore

CRABMEAT APPETIZER

1 pkg. [8 oz.] cream cheese,
  softened
2 T. grated onion
1 1/2 c. flaked crabmeat,
  [6 1/2 oz. can]
1 T. milk

1/2 t. horseradish,
  cream style
Salt and pepper to taste
1/3 c. toasted almonds,
  sliced

Combine softened cheese and all other ingredients except almonds. Mix well and pour into 9-inch glass pie plate. Sprinkle with toasted almonds. Bake at 375 degrees for 15 minutes. Remove to chafing dish or leave in pie plate and place plate in silver liner. Serve with Melba toast rounds.

Mrs. Moliere Scarborough, Jr.

CRANBERRY-TURKEY SPREAD

1/2 c. chopped cranberries
1 T. sugar
2 t. grated orange rind
1 c. chopped cooked turkey
1/4 c. finely chopped unpeeled
  apple

1/4 c. chopped walnuts
1/4 c. chopped parsley
1/4 c. mayonnaise
1/2 t. salt
1/4 t. pepper
1/4 t. poultry seasoning

Mix cranberries, sugar and orange rind together and refrigerate overnight or for at least 5 hours.

Mix other ingredients together, combine the two mixtures and refrigerate until used. Makes 2 cups of spread.

Mrs. Joe Huffstutler

SMOKED TURKEY SPREAD

Smoked turkey [pieces of
  leftover turkey are fine]
Sweet pickles, chopped
  very fine

Ground pecans
Onion juice
Celery, chopped very fine
Mayonnaise

Grind turkey with pecans and add other ingredients according to taste. Serve with Ritz crackers.

Mrs. L. R. Rhine

CURRY NIBBLES

3 c. shelled pecan halves
1 c. almonds
1 1/2 sticks margarine

Salt
2 T. curry powder
2 boxes seasoned croutons

Mix pecans, almonds, margarine and salt in shallow pan to toast in 250 degree oven. Stir now and then. Add curry powder and stir. Add croutons and mix. Cool before serving! Eat by handfuls!

Mrs. Tippitt Kay
Palestine, Texas

DILL DIP

1 pkg. [3 oz.] cream cheese,
  softened
1 T. finely chopped stuffed
  green olives
1 t. grated onion

1/4 t. dill weed
Dash salt
1 to 2 T. light cream
Raw zucchini, cut in sticks

Combine cream cheese, olives, onion, dill weed and salt. Stir in cream to make mixture of dipping consistency. Chill. Serve with zucchini sticks as an appetizer or relish. Makes about 2/3 cup.

Mrs. George Echols
Lafayette, Louisiana

DILL SEED DIP

2/3 c. mayonnaise
2/3 c. sour cream
1 T. chopped onion

1 T. chopped parsley
1 T. dill seed
1 t. Beau Monde seasoning

Mix all ingredients and refrigerate for several hours.

Mrs. James E. Bass

CUCUMBER SANDWICHES OR DIP

4 cucumbers
2 pkgs. [8 oz.] Philadelphia
  cream cheese
1 garlic clove, grated
Dash paprika
1 T. onion juice

1/2 c. chopped nuts
1 t. sugar
1 t. salt
Pinch celery salt
1/4 t. Worcestershire sauce
1/2 c. mayonnaise

Grind cucumber in food grinder or blender. Mix in the other ingredients. Let sit at least 24 hours before serving. It is best not to combine the cucumber and the other ingredients in the blender. Filling will become too thin. This makes 24 sandwiches or a large amount of dip. Sandwiches will freeze.

Mrs. Frank Agar

DILL SPICED CARROTS

8 small carrots
1 c. dill pickle juice
2 T. fresh cut dill
  [or 1 T. dried dill]

1 T. minced chives
1 c. sour cream

Scrape and trim carrots. Quarter lengthwise. Simmer carrots in dill juice until they can be pierced with a fork, 20 to 25 minutes. Carrots will soften, but will stay crunchy. Chill overnight in pickle juice.

To serve, drain off liquid and sprinkle herbs on carrots. If used as garnish on dinner plate, place dab of sour cream on top. Or carrots can be used as a pick-up food at a cocktail party and dipped in sour cream.

Mrs. Tom B. Ramey, Jr.

Unusual and very good!

DIP

1 pkg. Hidden Valley Ranch
  Party Dip
1 carton [8 oz.] sour cream
2 pkgs. [3 oz.] Philadelphia
  cream cheese

1 pkg. [12 oz.] shrimp,
  cooked and cut-up

Mix party dip and sour cream. Soften cheese and mix in. Add shrimp. Serve with Melba rounds or crackers.

Mrs. Jake Patton

EGG ROLLS

1 c. water chestnuts, minced
1 c. bamboo shoots, minced
1 c. onion, minced
1 c. mushrooms, minced
1 c. celery, minced
2 lbs. bean sprouts [fresh are best but canned may be used]
1/2 lb. shrimp, diced
1 T. salt
1 T. sugar
1 T. Accent
2 T. peanut butter
1 c. cooked chicken, diced
1 lb. egg roll wrappers [can be purchased at a Chinese grocery store]

Put chestnuts, bamboo shoots, onion, mushrooms, celery, bean sprouts and shrimp in boiling water, and cook until tender. Allow to cool. (If you use canned water chestnuts, bamboo shoots, mushrooms, bean sprouts and cooked shrimp, they do not need to cook with the celery and onion.) Drain. Add salt, sugar, Accent, peanut butter and chicken. Mix well.

Place a rounded tablespoonful in center of egg roll wrapper and fold up. Dip the roll in unbeaten egg white and deep fry until golden brown.

Serve with sweet and sour sauce. Any type jelly or marmalade mixed with a little catsup and ginger will make a sweet sauce. Hot mustard can be purchased for a sour sauce.

This makes about 14 large egg rolls. If used as appetizer, cut into pieces. Should be served hot.

These are best if made and fried fresh. However, they can be made early in the day and fried later or frozen before frying.

Mrs. A. M. Limmer, Jr.

GREEN CHILE DIP

1 box [2 lb.] Velveeta cheese
1 pt. Miracle Whip
1 large onion, grated
5 cloves garlic, grated
2 sm. cans green chiles, chopped

Mix in electric mixer about 30 minutes. Chill. Makes a large bowl of dip.

Mrs. Barney Johnson
Midland, Texas

GUACAMOLE SALAD OR DIP

4 avocados, mashed
1/4 c. finely chopped onion
2 tomatoes, diced
2 T. Mexican hot sauce
1 T. lemon juice
1/4 t. garlic salt
Salt to taste
1/4 c. mayonnaise

Combine all ingredients. Serve on lettuce leaf or with chips. When using as dip, mix ingredients in blender. (When fresh tomatoes are not in season, canned salad tomatoes may be substituted.)

Mrs. Lionel Riley

HOT CHEESE DIP

1/4 c. chopped onion
1 T. butter
1 pkg. [8 oz.] cream cheese
1 c. milk
1 jar dried beef

1 can [3 oz.] sliced
 mushrooms, drained
1/4 c. shredded Parmesan cheese
2 T. chopped parsley

Saute' onions in butter. Add cream cheese and milk, stirring constantly. Add other ingredients. Serve hot in chafing dish with Melba toast rounds (flavored crackers detract from the dip). This may be frozen. Serves 8.

Mrs. Harry Hudson

ENGLISH MUFFIN PIZZA

1 pkg. English muffins
1 can [4 1/2 oz.] deviled ham
1 can [8 oz.] tomato sauce
1 T. minced onion [or 2 T.
 finely chopped onion]

1 t. oregano
3 T. Parmesan cheese
Strips of Mozzarella
 cheese

Slice and toast English muffins. Combine remaining ingredients except Mozzarella cheese. Spread mixture on muffins and top with strips of Mozzarella cheese. Broil until cheese is bubbly.

Mrs. Truman J. Pace
Austin, Texas

 A favorite for children's parties.

HORS D' OEUVRE DELIGHT

1 c. sour cream
1 c. creamed cottage cheese
1 clove garlic, pureed
1/4 t. white pepper
1 t. Worcestershire sauce

1 envelope unflavored gelatin
1/4 c. sherry
1/4 c. water
1 jar [4 oz.] red caviar
2 T. lemon juice

Combine sour cream, cottage cheese, garlic, pepper and Worcestershire sauce in blender and mix until smooth. Soften gelatin in sherry and water and place over hot water until gelatin dissolves. Add to cheese mixture and mix well. Pour into lightly greased 1 1/2 pint mold and refrigerate for several hours. When ready to serve unmold and fill scooped out section on top with caviar that has been mixed with lemon juice. Serve with saltine crackers.

Mrs. Randall D. Klein

HOT BEEF DIP

1/4 c. chopped onion
1 T. butter
1 c. milk
1 pkg. [8 oz.] cream cheese
1 can [3 oz.] sliced
   mushrooms, drained

1 c. chopped dried beef
2 c. sharp Cheddar cheese,
   grated
6 T. parsley flakes
Toasted rye bread or
   bread sticks

Saute' onion in butter until tender. Stir in milk and cream cheese, mixing until well-blended. Add remaining ingredients except bread. Serve hot in chafing dish with toasted bread rounds and bread sticks. Makes 2 cups.

Mrs. Joe Huffstutler

HOT CLAM DIP

1 pkg [8 oz.] cream cheese
1 can [4 to 6 oz.] clams,
   [save juice]
1 T. lemon juice

1/4 garlic clove,
   finely chopped
Dash Worcestershire sauce

Blend all ingredients in mixer using juice as needed. Heat in double boiler. Serve warm with chips.

Mrs. H. Don Smith

HOT HAM SPREAD

1/2 lb. lean cooked ham,
   ground
1/2 lb. American cheese,
   grated
1 green pepper [if desired]

10 crackers, soaked in
1 1/4 c. cold milk
2 eggs, beaten
1 T. Worcestershire sauce

Mix all ingredients well. Bake in a well-greased casserole at 325 to 350 degrees for 40 minutes or until lightly browned. Serve on silver tray surrounded by toasted party rye breads and assorted crackers. Use 2 butter spreaders to spread on crackers, etc. Makes about 1 quart. Serves 20. Recipe may be doubled.

By omitting 1/4 cup of milk in above recipe, this makes a good ham loaf for lunch or dinner. Bake in well-greased loaf pan at the same temperature. Good served with horseradish sauce.

Mrs. Ralph R. Hanson

This is a good way to use leftover baked ham. Do not use green pepper if planning to freeze.

HOT OYSTERS

1 pt. oysters, drained
Salt and pepper
Flour
Butter

Sauce: 3 T. butter
2 t. lemon juice
2 T. A-1 sauce
1 T. Worcestershire sauce
1 jigger sherry

Drain oysters, salt and pepper them and roll in flour. Brown in melted butter. Combine sauce ingredients and pour over oysters. Serve from chafing dish.

Mrs. Harold Cameron

SWEET-'N-SOUR MEAT BALLS

Meat Balls:

1 lb. ground beef
1/2 c. bread crumbs
1 egg
2 T. grated onion
1 t. salt
1/8 t. nutmeg
2/3 c. milk

Sauce:

1 jar [10 oz.] currant jelly
1 jar [6 oz.] prepared mustard

Meat Balls: Mix together lightly all meat ball ingredients. Gently form into small balls and cook until done in skillet with oil. Drain meat balls on paper towels. Makes approximately 20. Meat balls may be frozen.

Sauce: (Prepare the same day it is to be used.) Mix jelly and mustard in saucepan over low heat until smooth. Pour over meat balls and serve in chafing dish.

Mrs. Robert D. Jones
Midland, Texas

SWEDISH MEAT BALLS

1 lb. ground beef
1 c. fine bread crumbs
1 egg
1/2 c. milk
2 T. minced onion

1 t. salt
1/8 t. pepper
1/8 t. nutmeg
Bacon drippings
Flour

Mix beef, crumbs, egg, milk, onion and seasonings. Mold into very small balls, and brown in very hot drippings. Stir a sprinkling of flour into drippings for thickening. Add 3/4 cup hot water. Cover and simmer until meat balls are cooked through, approximately 20 minutes. Meatballs and gravy may be frozen separately after cooking.

Mrs. Henry D. McCallum

HUNGARIAN MEAT BALLS

Meat Balls:

1 lb. ham, ground [no fat]
1 1/2 lb. pork, Boston butt
   [have butcher grind the two
   meats together only once]

2 eggs, beaten
2 c. toasted bread crumbs
1 c. milk

Sauce:

1/2 c. vinegar
1/2 c. water

1 c. brown sugar

   Mix ingredients for meat balls and form into 1 to 1 1/2 inch thick balls. Chill at least 6 hours or overnight.
   Mix ingredients for sauce and bring to a boil. Stir to dissolve sugar.
   Place meat balls in a roasting pan and pour sauce over. Bake at 350 degrees for 1 hour and 15 minutes. Baste and turn often so they will form a glaze while cooking. Do not cover.
   Make additional recipe of sauce to serve with meat balls. These may be made ahead of time, stored in the refrigerator and heated with sauce in chafing dish or electric skillet. Makes 120 to 125 meat balls.

Mrs. H. Kelly Ireland

PARTY MEAT BALLS

1 lb. ground lean beef
1/2 c. corn flake crumbs
1/2 c. evaporated milk
1/4 c. finely cut onion

1/4 c. catsup or chili sauce
1 T. Worcestershire sauce
1 t. salt
1 T. pepper

   Mix all ingredients well in a 2 quart bowl. With wet hands shape meat ball mixture in 36 small meat balls using about a teaspoonful for each. Place in 13 x 9 x 2 inch pan. Bake in 400 degree oven for 12 to 15 minutes or until brown. Serve with sauce.

Sauce:

8 oz. can tomato sauce
1/2 c. catsup
2 T. brown sugar
2 T. finely cut onion

2 T. pickle relish, drained
2 T. water
1 T. vinegar
Few grains pepper

   Mix all ingredients in a 2 quart saucepan. Heat until steaming.

Mrs. C. R. Hurst

Mrs. Joe D. Clayton adds 2 tablespoons Worcestershire to the sauce.

TAMALE BALLS

1 lb. ground beef
1 lb. ground pork
1 1/2 c. corn meal
3/4 c. tomato juice

1/4 c. flour
3 cloves garlic, crushed
1 T. chili powder
2 t. salt

Grind beef and pork together twice. Add all other ingredients and form into small balls, about 150. Drop in sauce and simmer 2 hours.

Sauce:

3 cans [#2] tomatoes
2 t. salt
1 T. chili powder

Heat ingredients together in large roaster. (May use electric). Let sauce come to a boil and drop in balls. Simmer.
To serve keep hot in chafing dish and pick up with toothpicks.
Mrs. Tom Ramey, Sr.

COCKTAIL MEAT PATTIES

5 lbs. hamburger meat

Sauce I:

2/3 c. oil
2/3 c. catsup
1/4 t. Tabasco
2 T. Worcestershire sauce
2/3 c. water
1 jigger liquid smoke
2 t. sugar
2 t. flour
Juice of 1 lemon
2 t. salt
1/2 t. pepper
1/4 t. garlic powder

Sauce II:

1/2 c. A-1 steak sauce
1/2 c. cider vinegar
1/2 c. catsup
3 large onions, grated
1/2 c. brown sugar
1/2 t. celery seed
1 1/2 t. salt
1/2 t. pepper
1 t. nutmeg
1/2 t. cloves

Combine Sauce I ingredients and add to hamburger meat; mix thoroughly. Let stand in refrigerator 24 hours. Shape into dollar size patties and broil or fry.
Mix Sauce II ingredients and heat. Put cooked patties in sauce. Serve with biscuits or dollar size hamburger buns. Patties may be frozen before being put in Sauce II. Sauce may be made several days ahead and stored in refrigerator. Makes 85 dollar size patties.
Mrs. Frank Fite

JALAPENO DIP

1 lb. Velveeta cheese
1 can [7 oz.] jalapeno
  peppers and juice
1/2 small onion

1 T. lemon juice
1 c. Hellman's
  mayonnaise

Grate cheese in large mixing bowl. (Suggestion: set bowl in hot water in sink.) Remove stems from peppers and put peppers and onion in blender to pulverize. (May use food chopper.) Add pepper and onion mixture, lemon juice and mayonnaise to cheese and mix well.

Mrs. Joe Max Green
Nacogdoches, Texas

JALAPENO JELLY [GREEN]

1/4 c. green bell pepper, ground [3 medium sized peppers]
3/4 c. fresh jalapeno peppers, ground
1 c. cider vinegar
5 c. sugar
1 bottle pectin

Seed peppers and grind. Combine green peppers, jalapeno peppers, vinegar, and sugar in large saucepan. Bring to a boil. Boil 4 minutes. Remove from heat and let cool 1 minute. Add pectin and a few drops of green food coloring. Pour into hot sterilized jelly glasses and seal. Makes 5 glasses (6 oz.) of jelly. Serve with cheese and crackers.

Mrs. James C. Wynne, Jr.

HOT PEPPER JELLY [RED]

1/3 c. jalapeno peppers
2/3 c. red bell peppers
  [3 medium sized]

1 1/2 c. vinegar
6 1/2 c. sugar
1 small bottle pectin

Seed peppers and chop. Mix peppers, vinegar, and sugar in a saucepan. Boil for 1 minute. Cool 5 minutes. Add pectin and a few drops of red food coloring. Pour into hot sterilized jelly glasses and seal. Makes 7 glasses (6 oz.) of jelly.

Be sure to use gloves when grinding or chopping jalapeno peppers as they burn the hands.

Mrs. James C. Wynne, Jr.

Whipped cream cheese centered with jelly and surrounded with crackers makes an elegant snack tray.

JALAPENO APPETIZER

1 lb. sharp Cheddar cheese
6 eggs
Jalapeno peppers

Grate cheese. Place sliced peppers in greased oblong casserole dish. Beat eggs and mix with cheese. Pour over peppers. Bake at 350 degrees for 30 minutes. When done, cut into squares and serve as appetizers. Serves 6 to 8.

Mrs. Glenn Collins
Mrs. Clifford G. Swift
Houston, Texas

JALAPENO SPREAD

5 jalapeno peppers
1 lb. sharp Cheddar cheese
1 large onion

2 cloves garlic
1 1/4 c. mayonnaise

Remove tops and seed from peppers. Put peppers, cheese, onion and garlic through food grinder. Mix in mayonnaise. Store in covered crock in refrigerator until ready to serve.

Mrs. David Boice

This can be made in a blender (about a half of the recipe at a time). The result is an excellent dip for chips.

JAILHOUSE CHILI DIP

3 lbs. ground meat
Salt, pepper, or garlic salt [to taste]
1 can [4 oz.] chili powder
2 medium size onions, chopped
1 can beef consomme'

1/2 t. oregano
1/2 t. cumin
1/2 c. flour [to thicken]
10 ozs. grated Longhorn
    Cheddar cheese

Brown meat and season. Add chili powder, onions, consomme, oregano and cumin. Simmer about 30 minutes. Add flour (this is optional and depends on how fat the meat is.) This recipe can be frozen at this point. Add cheese to meat mixture and heat until melted. Serve in chafing dish. Use Fritos for dipping.

Mrs. Patrick Thomas

LEEK PIE

*1 pkg. [1 7/8 oz.] dry cream
   of leek soup mix
2 c. milk
1 c. light cream
4 eggs
2 1/2 c. [1/2 lb.] grated
   natural Swiss cheese

1 t. dry mustard
1 t. salt
1/2 t. pepper
2 cans [4 1/2 oz.] deviled
   ham
3 T. bread crumbs
10-inch unbaked pie shell

*Dry onion soup mix may be substituted with little change in taste.

In a medium skillet or saucepan, with wooden spoon, blend soup mix with milk. Over medium heat, bring to boiling, stirring. Remove from heat; cool slightly. Stir in cream. Refrigerate 20 minutes or until cold. Meanwhile, preheat oven to 375 degrees. With rotary beater, beat eggs in large bowl with soup mixture. Mix in cheese, mustard, salt and pepper. Mix deviled ham with bread crumbs. Spread ham mixture evenly in bottom of pie shell. Pour in filling. Bake 50 minutes, or until set (sharp knife inserted in center comes out clean). Cool pie slightly before serving. Makes 6 large servings.

This may also be prepared in 2 pizza pans and cooked 30 minutes (or until knife inserted comes out clean).

Mrs. John Simpson

For cocktail parties, make in tiny pastry shells.

MOLDED CHEESE PINEAPPLE

1 lb. strong New York
   Cheddar cheese
1/2 lb. Roquefort cheese
2 pkgs. [3 oz.] Philadelphia
   cream cheese
1/2 lb. imported Swiss cheese
1/2 lb. California Monterey
   Jack cheese

1/2 c. melted butter
Juice of 2 small limes
1/2 c. dry sherry
2 T. Worcestershire sauce
1 t. cayenne pepper
1 t. MSG
1 t. Beau Monde seasoning
Paprika

Grate or mash all cheeses and mix together in large bowl. Add melted butter, lime juice, sherry and seasonings except paprika. Work the mixture together with your hands and mold into a pineapple shape. Make a hole in the top big enough for the leafy top of a fresh pineapple to fit into. Roll the molded cheese in paprika until completely covered. With the end of a teaspoon, indent lines on surface to make it resemble a pineapple skin. Indentations should look like half moons.

Cut the green top off a fresh pineapple leaving enough "stem" at the bottom to trim and fit into the hole at the top of the cheese mold.

Serve on a round platter, ringed by assorted crackers. Serves about 50.

Mrs. Jack M. King

MAVIS' LIVERWURST PATÉ

15 medium mushroom caps
  [fresh]
Butter
2 T. grated white onion
3 t. mustard [prepared]
1 t. Mr. Mustard or Zatarain
  mustard

2 t. Worcestershire sauce
Dash of Tabasco
1 pkg. [8 oz.] Oscar Mayer
  liverwurst
2 pkgs. [3 oz.] Philadelphia
  cream cheese with chives

Saute' mushrooms in butter until soft. Put mushrooms and remaining ingredients in blender and mix. Put into a 20 ounce crock (one that has had cheese in it is great) and chill. Serve with Melba rounds.

Mrs. Frank Fite

ONION PIE

1 unbaked pie shell,
  [8 or 9-inch]
2 large onions, sliced thin
3 T. butter
1 egg

1/2 c. cream
Salt and pepper to
  taste
Nutmeg
1/3 c. Parmesan cheese

Pat unbaked pie shell with small amount of cream and chill. Saute' onions in butter until transparent. Bake pie shell at 400 degrees for 2 minutes. Remove from oven and add onions. Beat egg and cream together and pour over onions. Sprinkle top of pie with salt, pepper and nutmeg. Cover with Parmesan cheese. Bake at 350 degrees for about 30 minutes.

Mrs. John Hicks
Houston, Texas

ORIENTAL DIP

2 c. sour cream
3/4 c. mayonnaise
1 clove garlic, minced
1/4 c. chopped parsley
1 c. water chestnuts, chopped

3 T. soy sauce
1 t. salt
6 T. candied ginger,
  chopped

Combine all ingredients and mix well. This is best made the day before serving. Serve with chips or raw vegetables.

Mrs. George Oge

PECANS MONCRIEF

1/2-inch pat butter
10 dashes Tabasco sauce
1/3 c. Worcestershire sauce

4 c. large shelled pecans
Salt to taste

Melt butter on low heat. Pour into a bowl all but the milky part of the melted butter. Add Tabasco and Worcestershire sauce and mix well. Add pecans and stir so that all nuts are well coated with butter. Put on cookie sheet and heat at 270 degrees for 15 minutes. Stir, salt, and return to oven until nuts are crisp. Watch the last few minutes of the baking period for they burn very fast. Cool and store in covered container.

Mrs. Jack M. King

PICO DE GALLO

1 1/2 c. chopped avocado
[1 large avocado]
2 T. chopped onion
2 T. chopped tomato
1/4 c. Italian salad dressing

1/4 c. liquid from can of
jalapenos
1 or 2 chopped jalapenos
[This depends on how hot
you like it.]

Toss avocado, onion and tomato together lightly. Make sauce with remaining ingredients and blend well. Pour over avocado mixture. Leave avocado seed in mixture until ready to serve. This will keep the avocado from turning brown. Serve with warm soft tortillas, or if desired, put mixture in tortilla and roll.

Mrs. Tom Solether
Weslaco, Texas

Chopped chicken may be added for variety.

PRAIRIE FIRE SPREAD

1 can Ranch Style beans,
drained and mashed
1/4 lb. butter or margarine
1/2 lb. grated sharp Cheddar
cheese

2 jalapeno peppers
[a little juice]
1 onion, minced
1 clove garlic, crushed

Combine beans, butter and cheese in top of double boiler (or heavy saucepan) and heat slowly until cheese is melted. Add remaining ingredients and mix well. Serve warm in chafing dish with toasted tortillas.

Mrs. Harold Cameron

RED DEVIL BALLS

1 pkg. [8 oz.] cream cheese
1 can [4 1/4 oz.] deviled ham
1 c. chopped pecans

Blend cream cheese and deviled ham. Refrigerate until easy to handle. Shape into 30 small balls. Roll in chopped pecans. Refrigerate long enough to firm up. Serve on toothpicks. Makes 30.

Mrs. Jud Adams

FABULOUS SHRIMP DIP

1/3 c. canned milk
2 T. lemon juice
1/4 t. onion juice
Dash Worcestershire
Dash Tabasco

Dash cayenne
Garlic salt to taste
1 pkg. [8 oz.] cream cheese
1 c. cut-up shrimp
[may use canned]

Mix milk, lemon juice, onion juice, Worcestershire, Tabasco, cayenne and garlic salt. Gradually add cream cheese that has been softened. Add shrimp. Serve with chips and Fritos.

Mrs. Patrick Thomas

PICKLED SHRIMP

2 lbs. shrimp
2 medium onions, sliced in
rings
1 1/2 c. vegetable oil
1 1/2 c. white vinegar

1/2 c. sugar
1 1/2 t. salt
1 1/2 t. celery seed
4 T. capers with juice

Place peeled and deveined shrimp in boiling salted water for 3 to 5 minutes. Drain and rinse with cold water, then chill. Make alternate layers of shrimp and onion rings in a sealable container. Mix remaining ingredients and pour over shrimp and onions. Seal and refrigerate overnight, shaking occasionally. Remove shrimp from marinade and serve.

Mrs. Richard Grainger

Mrs. J. Ernest Alexander, Jr. prepares her Pickled Shrimp by boiling the shrimp with celery tops and 1/4 cup mixed pickling spices. Her marinade calls for 1 cup vinegar, omits the sugar, uses 2 1/2 tablespoons capers and a dash of Tabasco. She also layers bay leaves over the top of dish before adding the marinade.

Mrs. M. Earl Davis boils her shrimp with a package of crab boil, celery tops and a lemon, cut in slices. To marinate, she uses 3/4 cup vinegar, omits sugar, adds celery salt instead of celery seed and uses 2 1/2 tablespoons capers and 7 or 8 bay leaves.

CANLIS' SHRIMP

1 oz. olive oil
2 lbs. large shrimp,
   shelled
1 oz. butter
1 sm. whole garlic
   clove, crushed

1/4 t. salt
1/4 t. fresh ground pepper
Juice of 2 lemons
2 oz. dry vermouth

Place olive oil in large skillet. When simmering, add shrimp and allow to cook until golden brown. Reduce heat and add butter, garlic, salt and pepper. When well-blended, raise fire to very hot. Add lemon juice and dry vermouth and cook for about one minute, constantly stirring or shaking. Serves 4 as entrée, 8 as hors d' oeuvres.

Mrs. Wilbert Lasater

From Canlis Restaurant in Honolulu.

MARINATED SHRIMP

3 lbs. cooked shrimp
1 c. Good Seasons [oil type]
   French dressing
1/2 c. finely chopped green
   pepper
1/2 c. finely chopped onion

1/2 c. finely chopped parsley
1 lg. clove garlic, crushed
2 T. dry mustard
3 T. lemon juice
1 T. salt
Ground pepper

Mix all seasonings and vegetables; pour over shrimp in a large bowl. Chill for at least 24 hours. Turn with a spoon several times. Before serving, sprinkle with additional chopped parsley.

Mrs. William C. Lust

Try marinating this in a glass gallon jar that can be turned often.

SHRIMP BALLS

1 lb. shrimp, cooked
3 T. cream cheese
1 T. chili sauce
1 t. Worcestershire sauce
2 t. horseradish
2 t. green pepper, diced

1/4 c. celery, diced
1 boiled egg, chopped
1 T. onion, grated
1 T. parsley
3/4 t. salt
Black pepper and cayenne

Chill shrimp. Mash very finely with fork or blender. Add all other ingredients and mix well. Roll into small balls the size of large marbles. Roll lightly in finely chopped parsley. Chill. Makes 2 1/2 dozen.

Mrs. William Marsh

PINK SHRIMP DIP

1 pkg. [3 oz.] Philadelphia
  cream cheese
1/2 c. mayonnaise
1/3 c. red chili sauce
2 T. lemon juice
1 T. onion juice or 1/2 small
  onion, finely chopped

1 t. Worcestershire sauce
1 can shrimp [wash well in
  clear water] or 1/2 lb. fresh
  boiled and cleaned shrimp

Mix well all ingredients except shrimp (can use blender). Add shrimp, cut into small pieces. Serve as dip with crackers.

Mrs. James L. Gulley

SHRIMP CHEESE DIP

1. can frozen or canned cream
  of shrimp soup [undiluted]
1 can sliced mushrooms and
  liquid

1 roll garlic cheese
2 t. lemon juice
2 t. Worcestershire sauce
1 can deveined shrimp

Place all ingredients in double boiler and heat over medium heat until cheese melts and mixture is well-blended. Serve in chafing dish sprinkled with paprika. Use Fritos to dip. Serves 8-10. May be frozen.

Mrs. George Oge

SHRIMP DIP HELEN

1 pkg. [8 oz.] cream cheese
1/2 c. mayonnaise
1/2 c. celery, chopped fine
1 can [4 oz.] shrimp, diced
  or broken

1 1/2 T. dry minced onion
1 1/2 T. lemon juice

Blend cheese well with mayonnaise. Add remaining ingredients. Mix well and refrigerate several hours before serving.

Mrs. Helen Reed
Dallas, Texas

SHRIMP DIP

12 oz. shrimp
1 carton [8 oz.] sour cream
1 pkg. [8 oz.] cream cheese

3 T. lemon juice
1 envelope Italian salad
   dressing mix

Cook shrimp and chill. Cut into small pieces. Mix sour cream, cream cheese, lemon juice and salad dressing mix. Add cold chopped shrimp. Chill. Serve with chips or crackers as desired.

Mrs. Hunter Brush

SIRLOIN HOUSE DIP

1 egg
1/2 t. dry mustard
4 oz. salad oil
1/4 t. Tabasco
Juice of 2 lemons
1 t. Worcestershire sauce
1/2 t. salt
1/2 t. white pepper

2 avocados
3 fresh shallots
   [tops only]
Garlic
1 oz. anchovy fillets
4 oz. mayonnaise
1/2 t. saffron

Blend egg and mustard. Add oil and mix in well. Add Tabasco, lemon, Worcestershire sauce, salt and pepper, and blend. Peel avocados and add with shallots, garlic and anchovies. Blend to a smooth paste. Add mayonnaise and saffron, mix well. Chill. Leave avocado seed in dip and it will not turn dark.

Mrs. John Simpson

STROGANOFF DIP

1/2 c. chopped onion
1 clove garlic, diced
1 lb. ground round steak
1/4 c. butter
2 T. flour
2 t. salt
1/4 t. Accent

1/4 t. pepper
1 can chopped mushrooms
1 can cream of chicken soup
1/4 c. chopped parsley [or
   2 T. dried parsley]
2 T. A-1 sauce
1 c. sour cream

Saute' onion, garlic and meat in butter until meat is done. Add remaining ingredients and heat for several minutes. Serve warm with chips.

Mrs. R. Wilson Cozby, Jr.

May be made ahead and frozen but leave out sour cream. Just before serving, add sour cream and heat.

STUFFED MUSHROOMS I

36 large mushrooms
Butter or margarine
6 T. chopped dry parsley
6 t. grated onion

3 t. anchovy paste
1 pkg. frozen spinach
souffle', baked

Wash and chop stems of mushrooms. Saute' mushrooms, including stems, in butter. Remove mushrooms and stems and add parsley, grated onion and anchovy paste and cook 3 minutes. Mix with frozen spinach souffle' that is almost done. Fill caps and run under broiler for 5 minutes before serving. Serves 36. These may be prepared hours ahead and run under broiler at last minute.

Mrs. Robert D. Rice

STUFFED MUSHROOMS II

12 fresh mushrooms, washed
and dried
1/4 c. melted butter
1/2 lb. sausage
1 onion, finely chopped
1/4 c. dry sherry
1/2 c. fine, white bread
crumbs

1/2 t. thyme
1/4 t. crushed sage
1/4 t. salt
1/8 t. freshly ground black
pepper
3 T. fresh parsley
2 T. heavy cream

Remove mushroom stems and reserve. Brush caps with melted butter and place, hollow side up, in a buttered baking dish. Reserve unused butter for later use.

Saute' the sausage and onion slowly until both are cooked and lightly browned. Add the sherry and simmer mixture to evaporate liquid. Add bread crumbs, thyme, sage, salt, pepper and parsley. Toss lightly. Chop and add mushroom stems. Add enough cream to mixture to make it moist but still hold its shape in a spoon.

Fill caps with stuffing. Drizzle reserved butter over top. Bake at 375 degrees for 20 minutes or until mushrooms are tender and stuffing is lightly browned on top.

This can be served as a side dish or appetizer but needs to be served with a plate and fork.

Mrs. Ronald N. Schoenbrun

VEGETABLE DIP

1 qt. mayonnaise
1 bottle chili sauce

1 raw grated onion
Red pepper to taste

Mix well and chill. Makes a large amount of dip for vegetables or chips.

Mrs. Joe Herrington

Especially good with all sorts of vegetables.

SWISS FONDUE

1/4 c. butter	1/2 c. coffee cream
1/4 c. flour	1/2 c. milk
1 lb. shredded Swiss or Gruyere	1/2 c. sauterne
cheese	2 T. Kirsh

Melt butter; add flour; cook until bubbly. Add cheese, cream, milk, and sauterne. Cook until thick, stirring constantly. Add Kirsh; stir and serve. Keep hot in fondue dish.

Serve over thick slices of hot French bread. Serves 6.

Mrs. Bob Buford

TOAST FINGERS

40 toast fingers	2 T. dry mustard
2 c. Hellman's mayonnaise	2 T. grated onion
1/2 c. Parmesan cheese	

To prepare toast fingers, remove crusts from each slice of bread and cut into 3 "fingers". Bake until crisp in 250 degree oven.

Mix mayonnaise, cheese, mustard and onion together thoroughly and pile on toast fingers. Run under broiler until lightly browned. Serve immediately.

Mrs. Glenn Flinn

WATER CHESTNUTS AND BACON

2 cans water chestnuts	1 t. fresh ground pepper
Thin sliced bacon	1 t. paprika
1/3 c. white vinegar	1 t. salt
1 c. sugar	2 T. cornstarch
1/2 c. water	1 T. water

Wrap chestnuts with 1/3 to 1/2 slice bacon. Secure with toothpick. Be sure ends of bacon overlap to allow for shrinkage during cooking. Broil on lowest shelf of oven until bacon is crisp. Combine vinegar, sugar, 1/2 cup water, pepper, paprika and salt. Bring to a boil and boil for 5 minutes. Mix cornstarch with 1 tablespoon water and add to sauce. Cook until thickened. Pour over chestnuts and bacon and serve in chafing dish.

Mrs. Jack Smithson
Ft. Smith, Arkansas

NOTES AND EXTRA RECIPES

Beverages

BEVERAGES

BANANA JULEP

1 1/2 c. sugar	1 1/2 c. bottled lemon juice
5 bananas [puree in blender]	6 c. cold water
2 pkgs. raspberry gelatin	1 qt. ginger ale
2 c. hot water	
1 large can orange juice	
1 large can pineapple juice	

Add sugar to bananas. Dissolve gelatin in hot water. Combine all ingredients. Mix well and chill. Serve with ice ring or ice cubes.

Mrs. C. R. Hurst

CRANBERRY FRAPPÉ

Cranberry juice - 3 parts	Lemon juice - 1 part
Pineapple juice - 2 parts	Sugar to taste

Combine ingredients and freeze solid in ice trays or ice cream cartons.

Just before serving, chop into small pieces and whirl in blender, adding small amounts of ginger ale to make a frozen "mush" consistency. Serve in pretty glasses (like champagne glasses).

Mrs. Malcolm Hammett

This is excellent during the Christmas holidays.

HOT CRANBERRY PINEAPPLE PUNCH

3/4 c. brown sugar	2 cans [1 lb.] jellied
1 c. boiling water	cranberry sauce
3/4 t. ground cloves	3 c. water
1/2 t. allspice	1 qt. pineapple juice
1/2 t. cinnamon	2 to 3 T. butter
1/4 t. nutmeg	

Dissolve brown sugar in 1 cup boiling water and add spices. In another container, bring cranberry sauce and 3 cups water to boil and beat smooth with mixer or wire whisk. Combine all with pineapple juice; heat. Serve very hot with butter bits (1/4 to 1/6 of a pat) in cup. An added festive (but expensive) touch is cinnamon stick stirrers.

Makes 3 quarts to serve about 20 to 24 in punch cups. This may be frozen in ice cube trays. Turn out into plastic bags for storage. Use cubes as needed to reheat for use.

Mrs. Sherroll Neill

CHRISTMAS COCOA

1 lb. pkg. instant cocoa
1 c. sifted powdered sugar
1 jar [7 oz.] non-dairy
   coffee creamer

1 pkg. [1 lb. 9.6 oz.]
   instant non-fat dry milk
Marshmallows
Peppermint sticks

Combine first 4 ingredients.
To serve, combine 1/3 cup dry mix to 1 cup (8 ounces) hot water. Top each serving with marshmallow and use peppermint stick as stirrer. Serves 48.

Peggy Unfried
Dallas, Texas

 In decorated canisters, this is a lovely Christmas gift, and it can easily be made by children!

COFFEE PUNCH

1 gal. milk
3 1/2 T. instant coffee dissolved
   in 1 c. boiling water
3 T. vanilla

2 T. sugar
2 qts. vanilla ice cream,
   broken up in punch

Combine and serve to 25.

Mrs. T. Carlton Billups

HOT VEGETABLE PUNCH

1 1/2 qts. water
2 t. salt
2 t. sugar
Juice of 2 lemons
Celery leaves [from 3 stalks]
1 onion, sliced
6 whole cloves

5 beef bouillon cubes
3 cans beef consomme'
1 large can tomato
   juice
3 T. Worcestershire
Dash Tabasco

Bring first 7 ingredients to a boil and boil 20 minutes. Pour mixture through strainer; remove and discard all solids. Dissolve bouillon cubes in consomme' over medium heat - add to seasoned water. Add remaining ingredients and heat. Serve hot. Yield: approximately 1 gallon.

Mrs. J. W. Birdwell

HOT MADRILENE

1/4 c. [1/2 stick] butter
1/4 c. chopped onion
2 cans [18 oz. each] tomato
  juice
1 bay leaf

2 cans [10 1/2 oz. each]
  beef broth or
  bouillon
Grated Parmesan cheese
Parsley

In a 3 quart saucepan, melt butter and saute' onion. Add tomato juice, bay leaf and broth. Heat just to boiling point; reduce heat and simmer for 5 minutes. Serve in cups, garnished with cheese and parsley, to 10 to 12.

Mrs. R. Randall Cape

MRS. CROSS'S TOMATO DRINK

1 c. beef bouillon
2 c. tomato juice
1/2 c. lemon juice

Chives
Seasoning salt

Mix together and serve cold.

Mrs. S. W. Brookshire

An excellent "cocktail" for non-drinking friends.

TOMATO JUICE COCKTAIL

1 large onion
1 c. celery and leaves

3 c. V-8 juice

Chop vegetables and soak in juice for at least 3 hours. Strain and add:

2 T. catsup
1/4 c. orange juice
2 T. sugar

1/2 c. vinegar
Dash cayenne

Chill.

Mrs. Luther Kay, Jr.

PARTY PUNCH

1 small can frozen orange
  juice
Enough water to make
  2 qts.

1 pkg. raspberry Koolaid
1 c. sugar [or sweeten
  to taste]

Mix above ingredients together and chill.

Mrs. Hoyt Berryman, Jr.

PERCOLATOR PUNCH

1 qt. apple cider
1 pt. cranberry juice
1 c. orange juice
3/4 c. lemon juice

1 c. sugar
1 t. whole allspice
1 t. whole cloves
3 sticks cinnamon

Place first 4 ingredients in the bottom of a percolator and place last 4 ingredients in top. Perk. Makes 12 cups.

Mrs. Norman Bishop
Longview, Texas

STRAWBERRY PUNCH

1 c. boiling water
1 pkg. [3 oz.] strawberry
   Jello
1 qt. cold tap water

2 T. instant tea
1 can [6 oz.] frozen
   lemonade
Strawberry slices

Add boiling water to Jello; stir until dissolved. In a pitcher, pour cold water over tea. Stir until dissolved. Add dissolved Jello and lemonade. Chill in refrigerator. When ready to serve, pour over ice in punch bowl. Garnish with strawberry slices. Small, fresh strawberries frozen in ice cubes make it pretty. Serves 10 to 12.

Mrs. Billy Hall

INSTANT SPICE TEA

1 jar Tang [1 lb. 2 oz.]
   or less to taste
1 c. sugar
1/2 c. instant tea with lemon

1 t. cinnamon
1/2 t. cloves

Mix all together. Store in airtight container. When ready to serve, mix 2 teaspoons of mix in 1 cup hot water.
For iced tea, mix 2 teaspoons of mix in 1 glass of ice water.

Mrs. James E. Bass

This makes a lovely gift when presented in an attractive container.

DELICIOUS TEA

3 pts. water
3 t. tea
Handful of mint

1 1/4 c. sugar
Juice of 3 lemons
Juice of 3 oranges

Combine water, tea, mint and sugar; boil 1 minute. Remove from heat and leave covered 10 minutes. Strain; add lemon juice and orange juice. Serve over ice to 10 or 12.

Mrs. Hunter Brush
Mrs. Jack M. King
Mrs. Tom B. Ramey, Jr.
Mrs. Moliere Scarborough, Jr.

TEA

1 family size tea bag
1 small can pink lemonade

1 c. sugar
1 c. pineapple juice

Steep tea bag in saucepan of water for 15 minutes.
Mix all other ingredients in large pitcher. Add tea and enough water to make 1 gallon.
Serve over ice with a sprig of mint.

Mrs. James E. Bass

HOT GRAPE TEA

24 whole cloves
3 qts. plus 1 pt. water
4 small tea bags

1/2 c. lemon juice
2 c. sugar
1 pt. grape juice

Boil cloves and half water. Make tea with other half water; combine and add other ingredients. Serve hot to approximately 24. May be kept in refrigerator and reheated.

Mrs. Frank Budde

APRICOT BRANDY

1 pkg. dried apricots
1 lb. rock candy

1 bottle vodka
1 fresh peach pit

Combine all ingredients, cover and let stand for 3 months.

Mrs. Frank Fite

Makes a great Christmas gift.

BUBBLING JADE PUNCH

1 pkg. [3 oz.] lime Jello
1 c. hot water
1 c. cold water
1 can [6 oz.] frozen
    lemonade

1 c. pineapple juice
1 bottle [4/5 qt.]
    champagne

Dissolve Jello in hot water. Add cold water, lemonade concentrate and pineapple juice. Blend well. Before serving, add champagne. Serves 15 to 20.

Mrs. William D. Lawrence, Jr.

CHAMPAGNE PUNCH

10 lemons
Powdered sugar
1/2 pt. cherries
1/2 pt. curacao

1 pt. brandy
3 qt. champagne
4 cans 7-Up

Juice lemons and add enough powdered sugar to sweeten. Chill ingredients before mixing. Mix all ingredients well. Garnish with fruit. Makes 5 quarts or 40 punch cups.

Mrs. Arnold Allen
Midland, Texas

You may add the strained contents of a pot of tea, if desired.

CHRISTMAS MORNING MILK PUNCH

8 eggs
2 c. sugar
1 bottle [4/5 qt.] rum
1 bottle [4/5 qt.] brandy
2 1/2 qts. milk [some prefer
    skimmed milk]

OR

1 egg
1/4 c. sugar
2 ozs. rum
2 ozs. brandy
1/2 pt. milk

Break eggs in large bowl; add sugar gradually. Beat well. Add whiskey and milk, stirring thoroughly.

If prepared the night before used, place in empty milk cartons and whiskey bottles and refrigerate. When ready to serve, fill blender 2/3rds. full; add 1/2 cup ice and blend. Serve from cold container with ice around it.

If smaller recipe is used, all ingredients may be placed directly into blender and served immediately.

Mrs. Henry M. Bell, Jr.

COFFEE PUNCH

1 gal. strong coffee
1 qt. cream, whipped
5 T. sugar

5 t. vanilla
2 qts. vanilla ice cream
1/3 c. brandy [optional]

Chill coffee. Whip cream. Add sugar and vanilla. Place ice cream and whipped cream in punch bowl and pour coffee (and brandy, if desired) over it. Mix well before serving. If block ice cream is used, slice it into thin slices before placing in punch bowl. Serves 50 to 60.

Mrs. C. C. Coulston

FROZEN PINK DAIQUIRI

3 boxes frozen strawberries
1 can frozen limeade
2 cans frozen lemonade

1/2 c. grenadine
1 bottle light rum
[4/5 qt.]

Whirl berries in blender; then add "ades". Add grenadine and rum and add water to make 1 gallon. Freeze. Freezes and keeps a limited time.

Mrs. W. F. Bridewell, Jr.

KAHLUA

1 vanilla bean
2 c. cheap brandy
2 oz. jar instant coffee

2 c. water
2 c. sugar

Combine ingredients in jar. Close tightly and shake once a week for 1 month. Serve as after dinner drink.

Mrs. Frank Fite

MT. VERNON PUNCH

2 bottles claret or
  sauterne
4 jiggers apricot brandy
2 cans [6 oz.] frozen orange
  juice concentrate

2 cans [6 oz.] frozen
  lemonade concentrate
1 qt. sparkling water

Mix wine with fruit concentrates and brandy. Add sparkling water and ice just before serving. Serves 20 to 25.

Mrs. Gordon Brelsford

HARVARD PUNCH

1 c. lemon juice
1 can [46 oz.] pineapple juice
1 can [46 oz.] grapefruit juice
1 qt. bourbon

1 qt. rum
1 qt. champagne or
   pale dry ginger ale

Mix, pour over block of ice and serve. Makes 6 quarts.

Mrs. William C. Lust

WHISKEY SOUR PUNCH

1 1/2 bottles [4/5 qt.] bourbon
1 1/2 qts. orange juice

1 qt. lemon juice
3 qts. soda

Mix together and serve over ice ring containing fruit. Makes approximately 6 quarts or 50 four ounce servings.

Mrs. C. Aubrey Smith, Jr.

HOT MULLED CLARET

1 c. sugar
2 c. water
2 c. bottled cranberry juice
   cocktail
Peel of 1/2 lemon
6 allspice berries

12 whole cloves
2 cinnamon sticks
2 bottles [4/5 each] New
   York State Claret. [In
   large amount substitute
   Burgundy for economy]

Combine sugar, water and cranberry juice in large pan. Add lemon peel, allspice berries and cloves. Stir over medium heat until sugar dissolves; bring to boil and add cinnamon sticks and simmer for 15 minutes. Add wine; heat but do not boil. Strain and serve hot in mugs or cups. Makes about 3 quarts or 12 servings. This is a pretty burgundy color.

Mrs. Gordon Brelsford
Mrs. Arthur Cunningham

HOT TODDY

1/4 c. water
1 T. sugar
1/2 T. [1 1/2 t.] lemon juice

Dash ground cloves
1/4 c. bourbon
2 maraschino cherries

Combine all ingredients except bourbon and cherries. Heat until very hot and sugar is dissolved. Add bourbon; garnish with cherries. Serve immediately. Serves 2. (Decrease bourbon if a weaker toddy is preferred.)

Mrs. Michael Hatchell

HOT APPLE RUM

Per Serving:

1/2 c. apple juice
1 or 2 inch strip orange peel
1 t. [heaping] brown sugar
1/2 jigger rum
1 stick cinnamon

2 dashes nutmeg
2 dashes cloves
2 dashes allspice
Thin slice lemon

Heat apple juice to boiling.

Put orange peel, brown sugar and rum in each serving cup. Set afire (don't be concerned if it fails to blaze - it's only for "show" and doesn't affect the taste).

Add spices, apple juice and lemon.

Mrs. John D. Glass, Jr.

HOT BUTTERED RUM

1 1/4 c. cider [sugarless]
1/2 t. lemon juice
1 T. sugar

1/2 cinnamon stick
1/4 c. dark rum

Heat the first 4 ingredients to boiling, then add rum. (Do not boil again.)

Serve in mugs with a slice of lemon and a "spot" of butter (remove cinnamon stick). Makes 2 servings.

To double or make in quantity: increase all ingredients proportionately except cinnamon stick. One cinnamon stick should do for up to 8 servings.

Mrs. Jack Harper

RUM PUNCH

1/2 pt. [1 c.] lemon juice
1/2 pt. [1 c.] lime juice
1 pt. [2 c.] orange juice
*1/2 pt. [1 c.] sugar syrup
  [see recipe below]

2 ozs. grenadine
1 qt. soda [may use
  one fifth]
2 qts. rum [may use
  two fifths]

*Sugar syrup - combine 1 c. sugar and 1/2 c. water. Bring to boil and cook until sugar dissolves.

Mix all ingredients in large container. Serve chilled or over ice. You may wish to combine juices ahead of time and add soda and rum immediately before serving. The quantity of rum may be lessened without affecting taste of punch. This does pack a PUNCH if you are not careful. Serves 30.

Mrs. C. Aubrey Smith, Jr.

SANGRIA

8 lemons
6 oranges
1 c. sugar
Fruit to float according
   to season [1 box strawberries with stems nice]

2 bottles dry red or
   white wine, chilled
1 qt. soda, chilled

Juice 6 of the lemons and slice the other 2 in round slices. Then add the juice from 2 of the oranges. Cut the remaining oranges in thin slices. Add 1 cup sugar to the juice and stir until well-dissolved. (Leave for several hours, if possible, then chill).

Place fruits and juice in a large punch bowl or 2 glass pitchers. Add 2 bottles wine and soda. Stir with wooden spoon. Taste for sweetness and right blend and serve.

Mrs. Jack M. King

SUPER RICH EGG NOG

6 egg yolks
5 T. sugar
4 jiggers brandy
1 jigger light Jamaican
   rum [use 4 to 1 pro-
   portion brandy and rum]

1/2 pt. heavy whipping
   cream
3 or 4 egg whites,
   beaten stiff

Beat egg yolks well; add sugar very slowly, beating constantly until all sugar is completely dissolved. Slowly add a jigger of brandy (this cooks the egg) then a jigger of rum and the rest of the brandy. Fold in whipped cream, then the stiffly beaten egg whites (to which about 1 tablespoon sugar has been added). Serve immediately. Serves 10.

Mrs. Russell B. Watson, Jr.

Soups

SOUPS

ANTI-COMMUNIST BORSCHT

2 T. butter
1/2 c. chopped onion
1 can [1 lb.] beets, cut
in strips
1/4 c. red wine vinegar
2 tomatoes, chopped
1 t. sugar
2 t. salt
Dash of pepper
2 qts. beef stock [or 3 cans
beef consomme' with water
to make 2 qts.]

1/4 to 1/2 lb. ham, cubed
3/4 lb. brisket or lean
beef, cubed
2 sprigs parsley
1 bay leaf
1 large potato, diced
1 clove garlic, chopped
1 or 2 ribs celery with
some leaves, chopped
1/2 small cabbage, shredded

Melt butter in large kettle and saute' onion until soft. Add all ingredients except cabbage and cook for 1 hour. Add cabbage and cook 30 minutes more. Serve topped with sour cream (if desired) and garnish with parsley or dill. Makes 6 to 8 servings.

Rowland Baldwin, Jr.

BEAN SOUP

2 c. dried pinto beans
1 lb. ham, cubed
1 qt. water
1 can [22 oz.] tomato juice
4 c. chicken stock
3 onions, chopped
3 cloves garlic, minced
3 T. chopped parsley
1/4 c. chopped green bell
pepper
4 T. brown sugar
1 T. chili powder
1 t. MSG

1 t. salt
1 t. crushed bay leaves
1 t. oregano
1/2 t. cumin seeds, ground
1/2 t. rosemary leaves,
crushed
1/2 t. ground thyme
1/2 t. ground marjoram
1/2 t. sweet basil
1/4 t. curry powder
4 whole cloves
1 c. sherry

Wash beans and soak overnight. Drain and place in large saucepan. Add all other ingredients except sherry. Cover with water and bring to a boil, cooking slowly until beans are tender. Add sherry. Serve in soup bowls topped with chopped green onions. Serves 10 to 12. Freezes well.

Mrs. J. Donald Guinn

BLACK TURTLE BEAN SOUP

3 c. black turtle beans
   [dried]
2 T. B.V. meat extract
3 stalks celery
1 bay leaf
1/2 lb. lean cured ham
2 T. chopped parsley

1 t. Italian seasoning
1 green pepper
2 onions
1 clove garlic
1/3 lb. salt pork
1 t. cracked pepper
1 c. dry sherry

Wash beans and soak overnight well-covered with water in which 1/2 teaspoon baking soda is dissolved. After soaking, wash beans and drain. Place in a pot with 4 pints of water and the meat extract. Chop and add celery, crumbled bay leaf, cubed ham, parsley and Italian seasoning. Brown cut up green pepper, chopped onion, garlic, chopped salt pork and cracked pepper in butter. Add to pot. Cover and simmer for 4 hours or longer.

Cool and blend in electric blender. Add sherry. Heat and serve. Freezes well.

Mrs. Frank Fite

CLAM CHOWDER

1/2 c. green pepper, chopped
1 onion, chopped
3 stalks celery, chopped
2 T. bacon drippings
2 large [or 3 small] potatoes,
   diced

3 cans [8 oz.] minced
   clams
2 cans cream of mushroom
   soup
3 c. milk
1 t. marjoram

Saute' green pepper, onion and celery in bacon drippings. Add diced potatoes. Cover with water and simmer until done. Add clams and their juice, soup, milk and marjoram. Salt to taste. Simmer 1 hour, stirring occasionally.

Mrs. Nelson Clyde

Children like this one.

CRABMEAT BISQUE

3 cans crabmeat
Italian salad dressing
Lemon juice
Coarse black pepper
2 cans cream of tomato
   soup

2 cans green pea soup
1 can Cheddar cheese soup
4 to 5 soup cans light cream
   [half and half]
Sherry to taste

Marinate the crabmeat (checked carefully for shell pieces) in Italian dressing, lemon juice and pepper for several hours. Blend soups and cream together and add marinated crabmeat and sherry. Serves 8.

Mrs. W. F. Bridewell, Jr.

CALIENTE TORTILLA SOPA

1 small onion, chopped
1 jalapeno pepper, seeded
 and chopped
2 cloves garlic, crushed
2 lbs. stew meat
2 T. vegetable oil
1 can stewed tomatoes
1/2 can Rotel tomatoes
1 can beef bouillon
1 can chicken broth
1 can tomato soup

1 1/2 c. water
1 t. ground cumin
1 t. chili powder
1 t. salt
Lemon pepper to taste
2 t. Worcestershire sauce
1 T. Pickapeppa sauce
4 tortillas, cut in 1/2 inch
 strips
1/4 c. shredded Cheddar
 cheese

Saute' onion, pepper, garlic and meat in oil. Add tomatoes, soups, water and seasonings and bring to a boil; lower heat and simmer covered for 1 hour. Add tortillas and cheese and cook 10 minutes more. Serves 6.

Mrs. Brad Holmes

CREAM OF CUCUMBER SOUP

2 8-in. cucumbers [1 lb.]
2 T. butter
1/4 c. chopped shallots or
 scallions
4 c. clear chicken broth
1 t. wine vinegar
1/2 t. dried dill weed or
 tarragon

3 T. quick-cooking farina
 cereal
Salt and white pepper
1 c. sour cream
1 T. dill weed or parsley
 for garnish

Peel cucumbers. Cut 12 to 14 paper-thin slices and reserve in a bowl for decoration later. Chop rest in 1/2 inch chunks - about 3 cups in all. Melt butter in a heavy 3 quart saucepan, stir in shallots or scallions and cook over moderate heat for 1 minute. Add cucumber, chicken broth, vinegar and either dill weed or tarragon. Bring to a boil and stir in farina gradually. Boil slowly, uncovered for 20 minutes until farina is very tender. Purée through foodmill (medium disk) or coarse sieve and return soup to pan. Mixture should be consistency of vichyssoise; thin with milk if necessary. Season to taste with salt and white pepper. If to be served cold, add extra salt and beat in sour cream. Add cucumber slices, dill or parsley on top. To serve hot, bring soup to simmer and beat in sour cream just before serving. Top with cucumber slices, dill or parsley. Serves 6. May be frozen before adding sour cream.

Mrs. Harold B. Cameron

 Delicious hot or cold.

CABBAGE SOUP

1/2 medium head of cabbage
4 medium potatoes, peeled
4 cleaned leeks or 1 bunch
    spring onions with tops
    off

1/2 c. whipping cream
1/2 stick butter
Salt and pepper to
    taste

Core cabbage. Slice cabbage and potatoes in large slices. Cut leeks (or spring onions) in large sections. Put all vegetables into 1 1/2 quarts of boiling water. Cook covered until tender (about 20 minutes - test with a fork). Over very low heat, add cream and butter. Butter should be cut up in very small pieces. Season to taste and serve at once. Tasty with Parmesan toast. Serves 4 to 6 large portions.

Mrs. E. N. Kittrell, Jr.

CREAM OF OYSTER SOUP

1 c. celery, finely
    chopped
1 c. green onions and
    tops, finely chopped
1 stick butter or margarine
2 dozen oysters [retain
    oyster liquid]

3 T. flour
1 c. milk
1 c. heavy cream
1/4 t. Tabasco
Salt and pepper to taste

Saute' celery and onion in butter until golden. Add oysters and cook over low heat until the edges of the oysters begin to curl. Gradually add flour and blend to make a light roux. Slowly add oyster liquid to roux and let simmer while bringing the milk and cream to a simmer in another pan. Add the heated milk and cream and season with Tabasco, and salt and pepper to taste. Serves 4.

Mrs. William Rowe

CREAM OF POTATO SOUP

1 c. potatoes, chopped
2 carrots
1/2 c. celery
1/4 c. green pepper
1 onion

1 T. butter
1 T. flour
2 c. milk
Seasonings to taste

Chop potatoes, carrots, celery, green pepper and onion, and combine. Barely cover with water. Cook until done and mash. Make a very thin cream sauce with the butter, flour and milk. Pour the vegetables into the cream sauce and season to taste. Serves 4.

Mrs. Madison J. Lee, Jr.

GRANNY'S POTATO SOUP

6 c. diced potatoes
1 large onion, chopped fine
Water to cover
Salt and pepper to taste
Milk [enough to make soup
amount desired]

1 t. dried parsley
2 T. butter
1 c. grated Cheddar cheese

Cover potatoes and onions in soup kettle with water. Bring to boiling over medium heat. Reduce heat and cook gently until potatoes are done. Add salt, pepper and milk. Add the parsley and butter. Heat to serving temperature and serve with a sprinkling of cheese on top. Serves 6.

Mrs. R. Randall Cape

May use part evaporated milk or cream for richness.

POTATO SOUP

2 T. minced onion
2 T. minced celery
2 T. butter or margarine
3 chicken bouillon cubes
2 c. boiling water
1 c. potato flakes
1 c. light cream [half
and half]

1/4 t. salt
1/4 t. garlic salt
2 T. parsley flakes
Tabasco sauce
Paprika
1/2 c. sour cream

Saute onion and celery in butter until golden; add crumbled chicken bouillon cubes. Add boiling water and stir until cubes are dissolved. Bring to a boil, cover and simmer two or three minutes. Remove from heat and stir in potato flakes. Gradually add cream, salts, 2 drops of Tabasco, parsley flakes and paprika. Cool, then blend and add sour cream. To serve, reheat in double boiler or may be served chilled. Serves 4. Freezes.

Mrs. William Rowe

MUSHROOM SOUP

1/2 lb. fresh mushrooms
1/2 chopped onion
1 stick butter

2 cans chicken broth
1 carton sour cream

Blend mushrooms with small amount of water in blender. Saute' onion in butter, add chicken broth and mushrooms and heat. Stir in sour cream just before serving. Serves 4.

Mrs. Robert Henry

HEARTY LENTIL SOUP

1 1/4 c. dry lentil beans
5 c. water
1 onion, chopped fine
1 clove garlic, crushed
1 carrot, sliced thin
1 green pepper, chopped
1 tomato, chopped

4 slices bacon
3 T. butter or margarine
3 T. flour
1 can [10 1/2 oz.] consomme'
   or stock
2 t. salt
2 t. vinegar

    Soak lentils overnight and cook in the water in which they soaked for 1 hour. While they cook, chop vegetables fine. Cook bacon (cut in small pieces) in large skillet until crisp. Saute' vegetables with bacon and fat until they are limp (about 5 minutes). Add vegetables and bacon to cooked lentils. In same skillet, melt butter and stir in flour to a smooth paste. Add consomme', season with salt and vinegar and cook until smooth and slightly thickened. Add this sauce to lentil mixture; stir, cook over low heat for another 30 minutes or longer. May be mixed in blender for smoother consistency. Serve with crisp French bread and green salad. Serves 8.

                          Mrs. Russell B. Watson, Jr.

For variety, try slicing vienna sausage into soup before serving.

HUNGARIAN SOUP

6 bacon slices, chopped
1/2 c. chopped onion
1 1/2 lbs. ground chuck
1 can [1 lb. 12 oz.] tomatoes,
   drained
1 can [10 1/4 oz.] frozen condensed
   potato soup [may use canned
   potato soup]

1 can [10 1/2 oz.] condensed
   beef consomme'
2 c. water
3 carrots, sliced 1/4 in.
1 c. celery leaves
1 1/2 t. salt
1/4 c. cornstarch
1/2 t. pepper

    In large kettle, saute' bacon until fat is transparent. Add onion and cook until golden. Add beef. Cook and stir over medium heat until browned. Add tomatoes, soups, water, carrots, celery leaves and salt. Bring to a boil, reduce heat, cover and simmer 45 minutes, stirring occasionally. Blend cornstarch to a smooth paste with a little cold water and add to soup. Stir and bring to a boil. Add pepper. (If desired, sprinkle with Parmesan cheese when serving.) Serves 8 to 10.

                          Mrs. Marshall McCrea

Quick and easy for a busy day.

CREAM OF ONION SOUP

1/4 c. margarine
1 large onion, sliced
   finely
1/4 t. curry [optional]
3 T. flour

2 c. water
4 beef bouillon cubes
Salt to taste
2 c. milk

Melt margarine and saute' the onion with curry. Add the flour and then the water, stirring constantly. Add the bouillon cubes and salt and finally, the milk. Simmer until the onion is completely tender. If necessary, thin with light cream or more milk. Serves 4 to 6.

Mrs. William R. Clyde

SOUPE A L'OIGNON [ONION SOUP]

3 T. butter
4 large onions, sliced
2 t. browned flour
1/2 t. salt
1/8 t. pepper
1 clove garlic, crushed
Sprig of parsley

Pinch of thyme
1 qt. chicken stock
1 c. dry white wine
1 t. cognac
French bread
Parmesan cheese

In a deep saucepan, melt butter and saute' onions until yellow and soft. Add flour, salt, ground pepper and garlic. Cook until mixture is brown but not burned. Add parsley, thyme, chicken stock and wine and simmer for 45 minutes. Add cognac and serve in ovenproof individual bowls.

Bake sliced French bread spread with garlic butter and sprinkled with Parmesan cheese in a slow oven until crisp. Just before serving, put one slice of the toasted French bread on top of full bowl of onion soup, sprinkle with more grated cheese; run under the broiler and heat until cheese is bubbly. Serves 6.

Mrs. Bruce Brookshire

SMOKED TURKEY SOUP

Carcass and skin from a
   smoked turkey
1 large or 2 small
   onions

5 or 6 ribs of celery
1 lb. dried split green
   peas, washed, but not soaked
Salt and pepper to taste

Cover bones and skin with water in large kettle. Add chopped onions and celery. Bring to a boil; add peas and simmer for 2 to 3 hours. Remove bones and put the soup mixture through a colander. Return to heat and stir until smooth. Season to taste. For thicker soup, make a roux of 1 tablespoon flour and 1/2 cup milk, and gradually stir into soup before serving.

Mrs. Tony Spitzberg

SOPA MAJORCA

1 can [8 oz.] cream of tomato
   soup
1 c. sour cream
1 bottle [12 oz.] clam juice

1 t. Cavender's Greek
   seasoning
1 T. chopped chives

Combine all ingredients and chill. Garnish with chives or dill weed and float a slice of cucumber on each serving. Serves 3 to 4.
Mrs. James B. Owen

GAZPACHO [COLD SPANISH SOUP]

1/2 green pepper, cut in
   1-inch pieces
1 c. onion, chopped
1/2 cucumber, unpeeled in
   1-inch slices
1 stalk celery in 1-inch
   slices
Water
1 beef bouillon cube

1 c. hot water
1/2 clove garlic, peeled
2 ripe tomatoes, quartered
Dash Tabasco
1 sprig parsley
1 t. salt
1/4 c. Wishbone Italian
   dressing
2 c. canned tomato juice

Place green pepper, onion, cucumber and celery in blender container with water to cover. Blend at low speed for 3 seconds. Drain and place in a large bowl. Soften bouillon in hot water a few minutes and place in blender with garlic, tomatoes, Tabasco, parsley, salt, dressing and tomato juice. Cover and blend at high speed about 1 minute. Pour over drained vegetables in bowl and stir. Refrigerate covered at least 4 hours, preferably overnight. Serves 8.
Mrs. Nelson Clyde

SQUASH SOUP

3 T. chopped onion
2 T. butter
1 c. cooked squash
2 c. chicken broth [may use
   bouillon cubes or canned
   chicken broth, if desired]

1 T. flour
Salt and pepper to taste
1 T. sugar
2 c. half and half cream

Saute' onion in butter until browned and place in blender with squash and chicken broth and blend together. Add flour and blend again. Place mixture in a saucepan, season, add sugar and fold in cream. Bring to a boil over medium heat, stirring constantly. Serve hot.
Mrs. Marvin T. Evans
Austin, Texas

TOMATO BOUILLON

3 1/2 lbs. soup bone with
    some meat
5 onions, cut in large
    pieces
1/2 bunch of celery, cut in
    large pieces

3 bay leaves
3 cans tomatoes
Juice of 3 lemons
2 to 3 T. Worcestershire
Few drops Tabasco sauce
Salt to taste

Simmer meat in water for 1 hour in a deep kettle. Add onions, celery, bay leaves and canned tomatoes, and simmer 1 hour longer. Remove from fire and strain. Cool and refrigerate several hours or overnight. Skim fat from soup mixture. Add lemon juice, Worcestershire sauce, Tabasco and more salt if necessary. Reheat. Serve in small cups with a slice of avocado in each cup. Serves 12 to 20. Freezes up to one month.

Mrs. Tom Ramey, Sr

COLD TOMATO SOUP

1 can tomato soup
1 soup can half & half
1/4 c. lemon juice
2 medium stalks celery

2 green onion tops
Few drops Tabasco sauce
Few drops Worcestershire
    sauce

Place all of this in electric blender and mix. Pour into a refrigerator jar and chill for several hours. Serve in chilled cups to 8.

Mrs. Dan C. Woldert

TOMATO-LIMA BEAN SOUP

1 lb. large dry lima beans
1 large onion, chopped
2 T. butter
2 T. olive oil
2 cans [2 lb. 3 oz.]
    tomatoes, chopped
    [save liquid]

1 can [7 oz.] green
    Mexican sauce
1 1/2 t. salt [or more to
    taste]

Place lima beans in a large bowl and cover with water 2 inches above level of beans. Soak overnight. Drain and remove skins. In a large saucepan, saute' the onion in the butter and oil until golden. While the onion is cooking, put the beans through the fine blade of a food mill, then add to onion. Chop the canned tomatoes in medium-small pieces and add to beans and onions. Then add tomato liquid and green Mexican sauce. Mix well and salt to taste. Simmer the soup, stirring occasionally for 30 minutes. Serves 10. Freezes well.

Mrs. William Rowe

HEARTY VEGETABLE SOUP

3 1/2 lb. chuck roast
2 cans [1 qt. 14 oz.] tomato
   juice
1 pkg. frozen mixed vegetables
1 large onion, finely chopped
2 stalks celery, finely chopped

1/2 c. okra, chopped
1/2 c. chopped parsley
Tabasco to taste
Salt to taste
1 c. spaghetti, broken
   in small pieces

    Cut chuck roast into small pieces removing all gristle and fat. Place in a very large pot and add all ingredients except spaghetti. Cover and simmer slowly for 3 hours. Add spaghetti and simmer another hour. Serves 12 to 14. Freezes.

Mrs. Allen Pye

WEEKEND VEGETABLE SOUP

2 lbs. stew meat, trimmed
   of fat and cut into bite
   size pieces
1 large onion, chopped
1 1/2 qts. water
3 bay leaves
2 large pinches Bouquet
   Garni [Spice Islands]

2 cans [15 1/2 oz.] tomatoes
2 c. sliced carrots
4 c. diced potatoes
1 stalk celery, diced
2 cans kidney beans
Salt and pepper to taste

    Gently saute' meat in a little cooking oil until lightly browned. Add onion, water, bay leaves and Bouquet Garni (crush between fingers as added to water). Simmer until very tender - about 2 hours. Add vegetables and simmer for additional 2 hours or more. Excellent additions to this soup are shredded cabbage and any other vegetable leftover in the refrigerator. Remove bay leaves before serving.

Mrs. Randall Cape

Keep this simmering "on the back of the stove" for a busy weekend when the family members are in and out on different schedules.

COLD AVOCADO SOUP

4 c. chicken broth
2 large avocados, chopped
Juice of 3 limes
Cracked salt to taste

    Combine all ingredients in blender and blend until smooth. Serve chilled in cups or small bowls with any garnish desired. Serves 6 to 8. Freezes.

Mrs. William Rowe

Salads

SALADS

AMBROSIA MOLD

1 pkg. [3 oz.] orange Jello
1 T. sugar
1 c. boiling water
3/4 c. cold water
1 c. whipped cream or prepared Dream Whip Dessert
Topping

1 c. mandarin orange slices
1 1/2 c. seeded, halved red
grapes or 1 banana, sliced
and quartered
2/3 c. Baker's Angel Flake
coconut

Dissolve Jello and sugar in boiling water. Add cold water. Chill until slightly thickened. Fold in whipped cream, then remaining ingredients. Spoon into 1 1/2 quart mold or 8 individual molds. Chill until firm. Unmold, garnish with additional whipped cream, coconut and fruit if desired. Serves 8.

Mrs. Louie Cobb, Jr.

AVOCADO SALAD

1 pkg. [3 oz.] lime Jello
1/2 c. hot water
2 T. lemon juice
1 small can crushed
pineapple

1/2 t. salt
1 c. whipping cream
1/3 c. mayonnaise
1 c. thin sliced avocados

Dissolve Jello in water; add lemon juice, pineapple and salt. Refrigerate until slightly thickened. Whip cream and add mayonnaise and avocados. Fold into Jello mixture. Cover and refrigerate until congealed.

Mrs. Hunter Brush

CHERRY SALAD SUPREME

1 pkg. [3 oz.] raspberry
Jello
1 can [22 oz.] cherry pie
filling
1 pkg. [3 oz.] lemon Jello
1 pkg. [3 oz.] cream cheese

1/3 c. mayonnaise
1 small can crushed pineapple
1/2 pt. heavy cream, whipped
1 1/2 c. miniature marshmallows
Chopped pecans [optional]

Dissolve raspberry Jello in 1 cup boiling water. Stir in pie filling. Turn into a 2 quart pyrex dish. Chill until partially set.

Dissolve lemon Jello in 1 cup boiling water. Beat cream cheese and mayonnaise until smooth. Gradually add to lemon Jello. Stir in undrained pineapple. Fold in whipped cream and add marshmallows. Spread on top of cherry mixture already set. After lemon mixture sets, sprinkle with chopped pecans if desired. Serves 12.

Mrs. Tom Tatum

COKE SALAD

2 pkg. [3 oz.] black cherry
   Jello
2 c. hot water
1 can [#2] crushed
   pineapple

1 can bing cherries
1 small Coke
1/2 c. pecans

Dissolve Jello in hot water. Add crushed pineapple and sliced bing cherries, drained and pitted. Add Coke and pecans and refrigerate. Serves 12.

Mrs. Sam Adams
Henderson, Texas

CONGEALED SALAD

1 large pkg. lemon Jello
1 1/2 c. hot water
1 pkg. [8 oz.] cream cheese,
   softened
1/2 c. Miracle Whip
1 pkg. Dream Whip [follow
   directions on package]

1/2 c. pineapple, well
   drained, [reserve juice]
1/2 c. nuts, chopped
1 large pkg. lime Jello
1 1/2 c. hot water
2 1/2 c. pineapple juice
   and 7-Up

Dissolve lemon Jello in hot water. Chill until partially set. Remove from refrigerator and whip until foamy. Beat in cream cheese, Miracle Whip, Dream Whip, pineapple and nuts. Pour in buttered dish (large pyrex baking dish). Refrigerate until firm.

For top layer, dissolve lime Jello in hot water. Combine pineapple juice (drained from pineapple used in first layer) and 7-Up to make 2 1/2 cups liquid. Add to lime Jello. Pour this on congealed first layer and refrigerate. This is a pretty green salad which serves about 16.

Mrs. C. R. Hurst

FESTIVE CONGEALED SALAD

1/2 c. cinnamon red hots
2 c. boiling water
1 large pkg. [6 oz.]
   strawberry gelatin
Juice of 1/2 lemon

2 c. applesauce
1 pkg. [8 oz.] cream cheese
1/2 c. salad dressing
1/2 c. finely diced celery
1/2 c. chopped nuts

Dissolve red hots in boiling water. Add gelatin and stir until dissolved. Add lemon juice and applesauce. Put one-half mixture in buttered mold to congeal. (1st. layer)

Soften the cream cheese and blend with salad dressing. Add celery and nuts and mix thoroughly. Spread this on top of gelatin in mold. Chill until firm. Add remaining gelatin mixture and congeal. Unmold for serving. Serves 12.

Mrs. C. R. Hurst

BERRY HOLIDAY RING

1 pkg. [8 oz.] dates, cut up
3 T. lemon juice
1 T. water
1 pkg. [6 oz.] raspberry
  Jello

2 c. boiling water
1/2 c. plain yogurt
1 lb. can whole cranberry
  sauce
Pinch of salt

Combine dates, lemon juice and water in a saucepan. Cook over medium heat, stirring constantly, until dates begin to soften (about 3 minutes). Remove from heat and cool the mixture. Place Jello in large mixing bowl, pour boiling water over and stir until Jello is dissolved. Chill until partially set, whirl in blender until the mixture is light and airy, then beat in yogurt. Stir in cooled date mixture and add cranberry sauce and salt. Return to refrigerator and chill for about 15 minutes. Stir and place in 5 cup ring mold or in individual molds. Chill until firm. Serves 8.

Mrs. E. B. Yale

CRANBERRY FRUIT SUPREME

1 c. raw cranberries, ground
1 c. winesap apples,
  ground or finely chopped
1 c. sugar
1 pkg. [3 oz.] lemon Jello
1 c. boiling water

1/2 c. pineapple or
  orange juice
1/2 c. purple grapes,
  peeled and seeded
1/2 c. pecans, chopped

Blend cranberries, apples and sugar and set aside. Dissolve Jello in boiling water; add juice. Chill until it just begins to jell, then add all ingredients. Place in individual salad molds or can be made in one pyrex dish and cut in squares. Chill until firm. Serve on lettuce with a bit of mayonnaise on top.

Mrs. H. L. Gist, Jr.

CRANBERRY MOLDED SALAD

1 pkg. [3 oz.] cherry Jello
1 c. boiling water
1 can whole cranberry sauce
1 small can crushed
  pineapple

1 grated orange rind
[grapes, pecans,
celery optional]

Dissolve Jello in boiling water. Add cranberry sauce, pineapple, orange rind, etc. Pour into mold greased with mayonnaise. Serve molded or cut in squares.

Mrs. Wilton J. Daniel

GRAPEFRUIT SALAD

4 small grapefruit, should
  be pink and sweet
1 pkg. [6 oz.] lemon Jello
1 1/2 c. hot water
1 can [8 1/2 oz.] crushed
  pineapple

2 sliced avocados,
  sprinkled with lemon juice
2 pkgs. [3 oz.] cream
  cheese, softened
3 T. half-and-half
Poppy seed dressing

Cut grapefruit in halves lengthwise and scoop out inside with a spoon. Separate and peel grapefruit. Do not use any pulp as it is bitter. Set shells aside. Dissolve gelatin in hot water and add pineapple and grapefruit sections. Use half of gelatin and fruit mixture and fill shells half full. Place in refrigerator to congeal. Peel and slice the avocados; sprinkle with lemon juice, salt lightly and set aside. Combine cream cheese and half-and-half, blending until smooth. Spread this over mixture in shells when it has congealed and pour remaining gelatin-fruit mixture over cream cheese. Chill until firm. To serve, arrange avocado slices in wheel fashion over top, pour 2 tablespoons of poppy seed dressing over this. Serves 8.

Mrs. William Rowe

GREENGAGE PLUM SALAD

1 pkg. [3 oz.] lime Jello
2 pkgs. [3 oz.] cream cheese
1/2 c. chopped nuts

1 c. mayonnaise
1 large can greengage
  plums

Dissolve Jello in one cup heated juice from plums. In remaining juice beat cream cheese. Mix together and refrigerate. As mixture thickens, fold in nuts, mayonnaise and plums, cut in pieces. Congeal. Serves 8 to 10.

Mrs. Randall Klein

MANGO SALAD

2 pkgs. [3 oz.] lemon
  Jello
2 c. hot water

1 large can mangos,
  including juice
1 pkg. [8 oz.] cream cheese

Dissolve Jello in hot water, add mangos and cream cheese and mix well in blender or electric mixer. Pour into large mold and congeal.

Mrs. Dwight James
McAllen, Texas

LIME SALAD

2 pkgs. [3 oz.] lime Jello
2 c. boiling water
2 c. 7-Up
1 can crushed, drained
    pineapple [save juice]
1 c. miniature marshmallows
2 or 3 large bananas

Topping:

1/2 c. sugar
2 T. flour
1 c. pineapple juice
1 egg, beaten
2 T. butter
1/2 pt. whipped cream
1/2 c. grated American cheese

Dissolve Jello in boiling water. Add 7-Up and refrigerate until partly congealed. Fold in pineapple, marshmallows and bananas. Chill until firm.

For topping, mix sugar and flour. Stir in juice and egg. Cook over low heat until thickened. Remove from heat and add butter. Chill. Fold in whipped cream. Spread on Jello mixture and sprinkle with cheese. Serves 10 to 12.

Mrs. Billy Hall

LIME SALAD MOLD

2 pkgs. Knox gelatin [2 T.]
1/2 c. cold water
1 c. boiling water
1/2 t. salt
1/2 c. sugar
1/2 c. lime juice
Few drops green food
    coloring

3 T. horseradish
1 c. evaporated milk
1 c. cottage cheese
1 c. crushed pineapple,
    drained
1 c. chopped nuts [pecans]
1 c. mayonnaise

Sprinkle gelatin in cold water and soften. Add boiling water, salt and sugar, and stir until dissolved. Add lime juice and green food coloring and chill until syrupy. Add horseradish and evaporated milk. Refrigerate again until almost congealed. Add cottage cheese, pineapple, nuts and mayonnaise. Refrigerate. Serves 18.

Mrs. James Scurlock

LIME JELLO AND COTTAGE CHEESE SALAD

1 large can crushed
    pineapple
1 pkg. [3 oz.] lime Jello

1 carton cottage cheese
1 pkg. Dream Whip
1/2 c. chopped pecans

Heat the crushed pineapple. Dissolve the Jello in the hot pineapple. Let cool. Add cottage cheese and chill until partly congealed. Prepare Dream Whip according to the directions on the package. Fold in the Dream Whip and pecans. Pour into 2 quart dish. Congeal. Serves 12.

Mrs. Gene Caldwell

FROSTED FRUIT SALAD

2 pkgs. |3 oz.| cherry
   Jello
2 c. hot water
1 1/2 c. cold water
Juice of 1 lemon
1 large can crushed
   pineapple, drained
1 or 2 bananas
1 c. miniature marshmallows

Topping:

2 T. flour
1/2 c. sugar
1 egg, slightly beaten
1 c. pineapple juice
1 T. melted butter
1 pkg. Dream Whip

    Dissolve Jello in hot water. Add cold water and lemon juice. Chill until slightly thickened. Add pineapple, bananas and marshmallows and congeal until firm.

    For topping, mix flour, sugar, egg, pineapple juice and melted butter. Cook over medium heat until sauce is thickened. Cool. Prepare Dream Whip according to directions on package and fold into topping mixture. Spread over top of gelatin mixture. Serves 12.

Mrs. Harold Beaird

ORANGE CREAM SALAD

2 pkgs. |3 oz.| orange Jello
2 c. boiling water
1 large can crushed
   pineapple, drained
   |reserve juice|
10 marshmallows, diced

Topping:

2 T. butter
2 T. flour
1/2 c. pineapple juice
1/2 c. apricot nectar
1/4 c. sugar
1 egg, beaten
1 c. whipping cream

    Dissolve Jello in boiling water. Add drained crushed pineapple. Pour into 1 1/2 quart oblong baking dish. Cover top with marshmallow pieces. Refrigerate until set.

    For topping, melt butter in heavy saucepan (or top of double boiler), add flour and cook until bubbly. Add pineapple juice and apricot nectar slowly, stirring vigorously (use wire whisk if you have one). Add sugar and egg and cook over low heat until thickened. Cool to room temperature. Whip cream until stiff and fold into juice mixture. Pour over Jello mixture and refrigerate at least 3 hours. Cut in squares and serve. Serves 12.

Mrs. Joe D. Clayton

EASY ORANGE SALAD OR DESSERT

1 carton [8 oz.] small curd
  cottage cheese
1 small can crushed
  pineapple, drained

1 small carton Cool Whip
1 can [11 oz.] mandarin
  oranges, drained
1 pkg. [3 oz.] orange Jello

Mix all ingredients together. Toss dry Jello with other ingredients and place in mold and refrigerate.

Mrs. Max Freeman

An excellent quickie!

ORANGE-APRICOT SALAD

2 pkgs. [3 oz.] orange Jello
1 1/2 c. boiling water
1 1/2 c. apricot nectar
2 c. apricot pulp [drain 2
  cans apricot halves and
  mash or blend in blender]

2 T. lemon juice
1 c. chopped pecans

Dissolve Jello in water; then add remaining ingredients. Pour into 2 quart dish and refrigerate until firm. Serves 12.

Mrs. Gene Caldwell

ORANGE DELIGHT

2 pkgs. [3 oz.] orange Jello
1 c. boiling water
1 pt. orange sherbet

1 pt. heavy cream, whipped
1 c. mandarin orange
  sections, drained and cut

Dissolve Jello in water. Add sherbet and set aside to partially congeal. This will happen almost instantly. Fold in whipped cream and orange sections. Chill. Serves 12.

Mrs. Gene Caldwell

ORANGE-PINEAPPLE SALAD

1 large can crushed
  pineapple
1 pkg. [3 oz.] orange-
  pineapple Jello

1 pkg. [3 oz.] cream cheese
1 pt. heavy cream, whipped
1 c. chopped nuts

Heat crushed pineapple to boiling, add Jello and softened cream cheese. Cool this mixture and fold in whipped cream and chopped nuts. Mix well and freeze. Serves 10.

Mrs. Raymond Cozby
Grand Saline, Texas

GOLDEN GLOW SALAD

1 pkg. orange Jello
1/2 t. salt
1 1/2 c. hot water
1 can [9 oz.] crushed pineapple or 2/3 c. pineapple
  and 1/3 c. pineapple juice

1 T. lemon juice
1 c. grated raw carrots
1/3 c. chopped pecans

Dissolve Jello and salt in hot water. Add pineapple and lemon juice and refrigerate until slightly thickened. Fold in carrots and chopped pecans and pour into six individual molds.

Mrs. Jack Skeen

PARTY PINEAPPLE SHERBET SALAD

1 can [8 oz.] pineapple
  tidbits
1 pkg. [3 oz.] raspberry
  gelatin

1/2 pt. pineapple sherbet
1 banana, sliced
1/4 c. toasted slivered
  almonds

Drain pineapple, retaining liquid. To this, add enough water to measure 1 cup liquid. Heat to boiling. Add gelatin, stirring to dissolve. Stir in sherbet and cool. When mixture begins to thicken, add the banana, almonds, and pineapple tidbits. Chill in mold until firm. Serves 8.

Mrs. Scott Evans

PINEAPPLE FRUIT SALAD

2 pkgs. [3 oz.] lemon
  Jello
4 c. water [2 hot and
  2 cold]
3 T. sugar
Dash salt
2 red apples, cut in small
  cubes
3 bananas, cut in
  small cubes
1 can [#2] crushed
  pineapple, drained

Topping:

1 egg, beaten
2 T. flour
1/2 c. sugar
1/2 c. pineapple juice
1 box Dream Whip Topping
  Mix
Slivered almonds [optional]

Dissolve Jello in 2 cups hot water. Add 2 cups cold water, sugar and salt. Refrigerate and when partially congealed, stir in apples, bananas and pineapple. Chill until firm.

For topping, combine beaten egg, flour, sugar and pineapple juice in a small saucepan. Cook over medium heat until mixture is thickened. Remove from heat and allow to cool. Prepare Dream Whip as directed on package and fold into cooled topping mixture. Spread on congealed gelatin mixture and sprinkle with almonds, if desired.

Mrs. William H. Starling

RASPBERRY SALAD MOLD

1 pkg. [6 oz.] raspberry Jello
2 c. boiling water
1 box frozen raspberries
3 bananas, mashed

1 small can crushed pineapple, drained
1/2 pt. sour cream

Dissolve Jello in boiling water; add raspberries, bananas, and pineapple. Pour one-half of this mixture into 8 x 12 inch dish. Refrigerate to congeal (leave remaining mixture out of refrigerator). After first mixture has firmly set, spread 1/2 pint of sour cream across top and then pour remaining Jello mixture over this. Congeal firmly and serve on fresh lettuce leaves topped with a touch of mayonnaise. Serves 8 to 10.

Mrs. E. B. Yale

STRAWBERRY CREAM SQUARES

1 pkg. [3 oz.] strawberry Jello
1 c. boiling water
1 box [10 oz.] frozen strawberries

1 small can crushed pineapple, drained
1 carton [8 oz.] sour cream

Dissolve Jello in boiling water. Add strawberries and drained crushed pineapple. Pour half Jello mixture into 8-inch square pan and refrigerate until firm. Spread with sour cream and add the rest of the Jello mixture. Refrigerate until firm.

Mrs. Linda Chambless
Dallas, Texas

Mrs. William Rowe adds one large banana, diced.

STRAWBERRY SALAD

1 pkg. [3 oz.] strawberry Jello
1 1/2 c. boiling water
1 dozen marshmallows
1/2 c. pineapple juice
1 pkg. [3 oz.] cream cheese

1 c. crushed pineapple, drained
1/2 c. nuts, chopped
3 T. salad dressing
1 c. heavy cream, whipped

Dissolve Jello in boiling water. Add marshmallows and pineapple juice. While this mixture is cooling, mix the softened cream cheese, crushed pineapple, nuts and salad dressing. Add these to the cooled mixture. Refrigerate and when partly congealed, fold in whipped cream. Serves 12.

Mrs. Watson Simons

SALAD DELIGHT

2 pkgs. lemon or raspberry
   Jello
2 c. hot water
2 c. cold water
2 small cans pineapple
   tidbits, drained
4 bananas, sliced
2 c. small marshmallows

Topping:

Pineapple juice [drained
   from canned pineapple
   used in Jello]
4 rounded T. flour
1 c. sugar
2 eggs, beaten
Dash salt
1 c. whipping cream
Grated cheese

Combine 2 packages lemon or raspberry Jello with 2 cups hot water. When dissolved, add 2 cups cold water. Let partially set. Add drained pineapple tidbits, sliced bananas and marshmallows. Put in large flat 9 x 12 inch baking dish and congeal.

For topping, add enough water to pineapple juice to make 2 cups. Add flour mixed with sugar, beaten eggs and salt. Cook until mixture is thickened. Chill. Fold in cream which has been whipped. Spread on congealed Jello mixture. Grate cheese lightly on top and refrigerate.

Mrs. John W. Turner
Kilgore, Texas

SEAFOAM SALAD

1 can [#2 1/2] pears, mashed
1 c. pear syrup
1 pkg. [3 oz.] lime Jello
2 pkgs. [3 oz.] cream cheese

2 T. cream
1/2 t. ginger
1 c. heavy cream, whipped

Drain pears. Heat pear syrup, add lime Jello and pour over cream cheese which has been softened with cream. Beat thoroughly. When cool and slightly thickened, add pears (mashed with fork), ginger and whipped cream. Pour into pyrex dish and refrigerate. Serves 8.

Mrs. William F. Turner

FROZEN CRANBERRY SALAD I

1 can [1 lb.] whole
   cranberry sauce
1 flat can crushed pineapple,
   drained

1 mashed banana
1 large carton Cool Whip

Mix all ingredients and freeze, either in a mold or in paper lined muffin tins. Serves 12.

Mrs. Hunter Brush

FROZEN CRANBERRY SALAD II

1 can whole cranberry sauce,
  slightly mashed
1 can [#2] crushed
  pineapple

3 bananas, mashed
1 c. chopped pecans
1/2 pt. heavy cream,
  whipped

Mix all ingredients. Put in cake pan (9 x 12 inch). Freeze. Cut into squares. Serves 12.

Mrs. Harold Cameron

FROZEN FRUIT COCKTAIL SALAD

2 pkgs. [3 oz.] cream cheese
1 c. mayonnaise
1 can [#2 1/2] fruit
  cocktail, well drained

1/2 c. maraschino cherries,
  quartered
2 1/2 c. miniature marshmallows
1 c. heavy cream, whipped

Soften cream cheese and blend with mayonnaise. Stir in fruits and marshmallows. Fold in whipped cream. Pour into freezer trays or shallow pan and freeze overnight. Let stand out a few minutes before serving. Serves 10 to 12.

Mrs. J. W. Hammett
Ruston, Louisiana

This may be varied by adding different fruit or nuts, if desired.

FROZEN FRUIT DELIGHT

1 can [8 oz.] crushed
  pineapple, drained
2 or 3 bananas, mashed
3/4 c. sugar

2 T. lemon juice
2 T. chopped cherries
2 c. sour cream
1/2 c. pecans

Combine pineapple and bananas and blend in sugar. Add remaining ingredients. Freeze and cut in squares. Can be frozen in muffin papers or fruit can. If can is used, push frozen salad through and slice as needed. Serves 8.

Mrs. Charles Clark
Mrs. Jack Norwood

FROZEN FRUIT SALAD

2 T. sugar
2 T. vinegar
2 egg yolks
16 regular size marsh-
mallows, cut up

1 can [#2 1/2] fruit
cocktail, well-drained
1/2 pt. heavy cream,
whipped

Mix sugar and vinegar in top of double boiler. Beat egg yolks and stir into the mixture, cooking until thick. Add marshmallows, stirring constantly until marshmallows melt. Cool and add the fruit cocktail. Fold in whipped cream and spoon into 1 1/2 quart mold. Freeze overnight and cut in squares and garnish. Serves 8.

Mrs. Louie Cobb, Jr.

FROZEN PEAR LIME SALAD

1 large can Bartlett pears
3 pkgs. [3 oz.] Philadelphia
cream cheese

1 pkg. [6 oz.] lime Jello
1/2 pt. whipping cream

Drain pears, reserving juice. Press pears and cheese through colander or blend together in electric blender. Dissolve Jello in heated pear juice and cool slightly. Stir pear and cheese mixture into Jello. Add whipped cream and, if desired, about 2 drops green food coloring. Freeze.

Mrs. W. F. Bridewell, Jr.

FROZEN SALAD

1 can [8 1/2 oz.] crushed
pineapple
1/2 can water
1 t. butter or margarine

1/2 c. sugar
1 pkg. [3 oz.] lime Jello
1 pkg. [3 oz.] cream cheese
1/2 pt. heavy cream, whipped

Combine pineapple, water, butter and sugar. Heat to boiling point. Add lime Jello and stir until dissolved. Chill until partly congealed; fold in cream cheese which has been softened with a little milk and whipped until smooth. Fold in whipped cream and freeze, covered. Thaw slightly before serving. Serves 8.

Mrs. Glenn Collins

CURRIED FRUIT

1 can [#2] fruits for salad
1 can [#2] bing cherries
1 small can pineapple chunks
2 bananas, sliced

1/4 c. margarine
1/4 c. brown sugar
2 T. cornstarch
1 t. curry powder [or less]

Arrange fruit in buttered casserole dish. Melt and pour margarine over fruit. Blend brown sugar, cornstarch and curry powder and sprinkle over fruit.

Bake at 350 degrees until bubbly, about 10 minutes. Serves 6.

Mrs. James Boring

CURRIED FRUIT BAKE

1/3 c. butter
3/4 c. brown sugar
1 t. curry powder
1 can [#2] pear halves
1 can [#2] peaches

1 can [#2] apricots
1 can [#2] bing cherries
1 can [#2] pineapple slices
6 maraschino cherries

Heat oven to 325 degrees. Melt butter, sugar and curry. Drain fruit and place in 1 1/2 quart casserole. Add butter mixture to fruit and bake 1 hour. Serve warm. This may be refrigerated and reheated.

Mrs. Harold Beaird

An excellent brunch dish with scrambled eggs and cheese grits.

FRUIT COMPOTE SUPREME

1 can [16 oz.] sliced
     peaches, undrained
1 c. dried apricots
1/2 c. brown sugar
1 t. grated orange peel

1/3 c. orange juice
2 T. lemon juice
1 can [16 oz.] dark sweet
     pitted cherries, drained

Combine all ingredients except cherries in 10 x 6 x 1 1/2 inch baking dish. Cover, bake at 350 degrees for 45 minutes. Add cherries; bake covered, 15 minutes more. Makes 6 to 8 servings.

Mrs. Robert Hood

This may also be served as a dessert. For variety, use dried apples instead of apricots and serve with whipped cream.

HOT FRUIT CASSEROLE

1 medium can sliced
   pineapple
1 medium can peach halves
1 jar apple rings
1 can pear halves
1 can seedless apricots

2 T. flour
1/2 c. brown sugar
1 stick margarine,
   melted
1 c. sherry

Drain fruit and arrange in layers in a glass ovenproof casserole.
Mix flour, brown sugar, melted margarine and sherry. Pour over fruit and place covered in refrigerator until baking time. Bake at 350 degrees until bubbly.

Mrs. C. D. Acker
Jacksonville, Texas

CRANBERRY SALAD

1 lb. cranberries
2 c. sugar, scant
1 lb. purple grapes

1/2 c. chopped nuts
1 lb. miniature marshmallows
1 pt. heavy cream, whipped

Grind cranberries and mix well with sugar. Let stand overnight in refrigerator. Halve grapes and remove seeds. This may also be done the night before and refrigerated. Chop nuts. Whip cream. Combine and mix all ingredients. Refrigerate until serving time. Serves about 24.

Mrs. T. A. Pinkerton

FRUIT DELIGHT

1 can mandarin orange segments,
   drained
1 tall can pineapple tidbits,
   drained

2 c. miniature marshmallows
1 can Angel Flake coconut
1/2 pt. sour cream

Combine all ingredients, adding the sour cream last. Chill several hours and serve on a lettuce leaf. Serves 6 to 8. This may be prepared the day before.

Mrs. Bob Buford

Mrs. Lee Lawrence prefers to use the frozen coconut and more sour cream in her very similar Mandarin Orange Salad.

Mrs. Scott Evans varies the above recipe in her Oriental Orange Salad with the addition of 2 cups of grated Cheddar cheese sprinkled over the top of salad just before serving.

FRUIT SALAD

1 egg
3 T. sugar

1 1/2 T. flour
3/4 c. pineapple juice

3 or 4 bananas
1 can [#2] chunk pineapple,
   drained [reserve juice]
Few white grapes

1 c. chopped pecans
1 c. small marshmallows
1 c. heavy cream, whipped

Beat egg well and add sugar and flour (combined together) and pineapple juice. Cook until thickened and cool. Fold cooled custard into combined fruits, nuts and marshmallows. This may be prepared ahead and refrigerated. When ready to serve, fold in whipped cream. Serves 8 to 10.

Mrs. Mickey Pfaff

MIMI'S FRUIT SALAD

2 eggs, well-beaten
2 T. vinegar
2 T. sugar
1 T. margarine
1 can Royal Anne cherries,
   drained

1 can chunk pineapple,
   drained
24 or more marshmallows,
   cut up
1/2 pt. heavy cream, whipped

Cook eggs, vinegar and sugar in top of double boiler until thickened. Add margarine and cool. Add fruit and marshmallows and fold in whipped cream. Mix well and chill.

Mrs. James M. Summers
Henderson, Texas

SPICED PEACH SALAD

1 jar [14 oz.] spiced
   peaches
1 pkg. [3 oz.] cream cheese
1/4 c. sugar
1/3 c. evaporated milk
1/2 c. liquid from spiced
   peaches

1 c. miniature marshmallows
1/3 c. chopped pecans
2/3 c. evaporated milk,
   partially frozen
1 T. lemon juice

Drain peaches, reserving 1/2 cup liquid. Discard peach stones and chop peaches coarsely. Blend cream cheese and sugar until smoothly mixed. Slowly beat in evaporated milk and peach syrup. Stir in peaches, marshmallows and pecans. Whip frozen evaporated milk until very stiff. Beat in lemon juice to blend thoroughly. Fold into cheese mixture. Turn into 2 1-quart ice cube trays and freeze until firm. Serves 10 to 12.

Mrs. Jerry Bain

Something different for Thanksgiving or Christmas.

BAKED CURRIED CHICKEN SALAD

2 1/2 c. cubed cooked
    chicken
1 1/2 c. finely chopped
    celery
1 c. shredded sharp Cheddar
    cheese
1/2 c. mayonnaise
1/4 c. chopped onion

1 T. lemon juice
1 T. margarine
1/2 c. bread crumbs
1/2 t. paprika
2 1/2 t. curry powder
Crushed peanuts
Coconut

Mix chicken, celery, cheese, mayonnaise, onion and lemon juice in 1 1/2 quart casserole. Melt margarine, stir in bread crumbs, paprika and curry powder; sprinkle over casserole. Bake at 350 degrees for 30 to 40 minutes. Just before serving sprinkle crushed peanuts over dish following with coconut. Garnish with parsley sprigs. Serves 6 to 8. Freezes beautifully before addition of peanuts and coconut.

Mrs. E. B. Yale

CELESTIAL CHICKEN SALAD

4 c. diced chicken
2 c. chopped celery
1 can [4 1/2 oz.] mushrooms,
    drained
1/2 c. pecans, toasted in
    butter

Dash salt
2 T. lemon juice
1 c. sour cream
4 [or more] strips bacon,
    fried and crumbled
Mayonnaise [optional]

Mix all ingredients together. If not moist enough, add mayonnaise to taste.

Mrs. W. H. Merrill, Jr.
Irving, Texas

HOT CHICKEN OR SEAFOOD SALAD

2 c. cut-up chicken
    [crab or shrimp]
2 c. celery, thinly sliced
1/2 c. cashews
1/2 t. salt

1 onion, grated
1 c. mayonnaise
2 T. lemon juice
1/2 c. grated sharp cheese
1 c. potato chips, crushed

Combine all ingredients, except cheese and potato chips. Pile lightly in casserole or individual baking dishes. Sprinkle with cheese and potato chips. Bake in preheated oven at 400 degrees for about 20 minutes. Serves 6.

Mrs. David Russell

CHICKEN SALAD

4 c. cooked cubed chicken
1 c. chopped celery
1 c. halved seedless
  grapes
1 pkg. toasted slivered
  almonds

1 t. salt
1/4 t. pepper
3/4 c. mayonnaise
1/4 c. sour cream

Mix all ingredients in order. Chill well and serve on lettuce leaf. Serves 4.

Mrs. Glenn Collins

HAM-AND-EGG-SALAD SANDWICH LOAF

Ham-Horseradish Filling:

1 1/4 c. cooked ground ham
1/4 c. mayonnaise
  [may need a little
  more mayonnaise]
1 T. horseradish

Curry-Egg Filling:

6 hard cooked eggs
1/3 c. mayonnaise
2 T. minced parsley
1 1/2 t. seasoned salt
3/4 t. curry powder

Icing:

1 pkg. [8 oz.] Philadelphia cream cheese with chives

Cut all crusts from 1 loaf unsliced white bread (about 12 inches). Cut horizontally into 3 slices (about 3/4 inch thick). Spread first slice (bottom slice) with ham spread. Top with next slice and spread with curry-egg filling. Top with third slice. Ice with chive flavored cream cheese, softened and thinned with mayonnaise and cream. Serves 14.

Mrs. E. E. Cornelius, Jr.

TACO SALAD

1 1/2 lbs. ground chuck
1 bell pepper, chopped
1 onion, chopped
1 T. chili powder
6 to 8 dashes cumin powder

1 lb. Velveeta cheese
1 small can Rotel tomatoes
1 head lettuce, shredded
2 tomatoes, chopped
1 pkg. [6 oz.] Fritos

Brown meat, pepper and onion together. Add spices. Melt cheese and Rotel in double boiler. Layer on platter in this order: lettuce, tomatoes, chips, meat, cheese. Serves 6.

Mrs. Joe Max Green
Nacogdoches, Texas

MEXICAN CHEF SALAD

1 onion
2 tomatoes
1 head lettuce
4 oz. Cheddar cheese, grated
8 oz. Catalina dressing
Hot sauce to taste
1 bag [6 oz.] Doritos

1 avocado
1 lb. ground beef
1 can [15 oz.] Ranch
  Style or kidney beans,
  drained
1/4 t. salt

Chop onion, tomatoes and lettuce together. Toss with grated cheese, Catalina dressing and hot sauce. Crush the Doritos and add. Slice and add avocado. Brown the ground beef, add beans and salt. Simmer for 10 minutes and mix into cold salad.

Mrs. Lonnie R. Holotik

TOSSED FRITO SALAD

1 head lettuce
1 chopped onion
2 diced tomatoes
1 medium can Ranch Style
  beans, rinsed

1 bottle Catalina salad
  dressing
1/2 lb. grated cheese
1 medium size bag Fritos

Combine lettuce, onion, tomatoes, beans, salad dressing and cheese. Just before serving add Fritos.

Mrs. Hazel A. Owens

CURRIED SEAFOOD SALAD

3/4 c. mayonnaise
2 T. lemon juice
1 t. curry powder
1 can [7 oz.] tuna,
  packed in water
2 c. cooked shrimp [small]

1/2 c. chopped celery
1 pkg. [10 oz.] frozen
  green peas, cooked
4 c. cooked rice
1/4 c. bottled Italian
  dressing

In large bowl, stir mayonnaise, lemon juice and curry powder until well-blended. Add tuna, separate into chunks, shrimp, celery and peas; toss together well.

In medium bowl, toss rice with Italian dressing and combine with shrimp mixture. Refrigerate, covered. Serves 6 to 8.

Mrs. Jack Smith

CURRIED TUNA SALAD

2/3 c. mayonnaise
1 t. curry powder
1/4 t. salt
1 T. lemon juice

1 can tuna, scalded and
   broken in chunks
1 c. chopped nuts
1 c. chopped celery

    Combine mayonnaise, curry powder, salt and lemon juice and mix well. Stir tuna, nuts and celery into the dressing and blend together. Serve over Jellied Pineapple Slices (recipe follows).

Jellied Pineapple Slices:

1 small can sliced pineapple
1 pkg. [3 oz.] orange or lime Jello
1 c. boiling water

    Drain pineapple, leaving it in the can. Dissolve Jello in boiling water and pour over slices in can. Refrigerate until congealed. At serving time, cut other end from can, slide fruit out and slice into individual servings. Makes 4 servings.

Mrs. Robert Peters, Jr.

The curried tuna also makes a wonderful filling for tea sandwiches or miniature cream puffs.

SUNDAY SALAD

Dressing:

1 c. mayonnaise
1/2 c. chili sauce
1/2 t. Worcestershire sauce

1/2 lb. shrimp, cooked
1/2 lb. frozen or fresh
   crabmeat, cooked
1/2 c. celery
1 pkg. frozen artichoke hearts
   [or canned, if frozen
   not available]

1 head Boston lettuce
1 head iceberg lettuce
1 head watercress
2 avocados
2 hard boiled eggs
1 sm. can pitted black olives

    Combine dressing ingredients and chill. Add half of dressing to cut and chilled shrimp, crabmeat, celery and artichoke hearts. Arrange chilled greens in bowl, add dressing-shrimp mixture and garnish with avocados, eggs and olives. Add remaining dressing. Serves 6.

Mrs. Robert D. Rice

SHRIMP SALAD

Dressing:

1 pt. mayonnaise
Juice of 1 lemon
1 1/2 T. grated onion
1/2 c. chili sauce
Dash red pepper
Dash Worcestershire
1 T. dried parsley

Salad:

1/2 to 3/4 head lettuce
2 tomatoes, sliced [or
    cherry tomatoes, halved]
1 lb. shrimp, cleaned
    and cooked
3 or 4 slices bacon,
    fried and crumbled
2 hard boiled eggs, diced

Combine dressing ingredients. Mix salad ingredients. Serve separately, allowing each person to add his own dressing. The proportions of lettuce, etc., do not matter, but do not skimp on the bacon and eggs. Serves 8 to 10.

Mrs. Galloway Calhoun

TOMATO-SHRIMP ASPIC

6 pkgs. unflavored gelatin
1 can [10 oz.] tomato
    cocktail [Snap-E-Tom]
2 cans [12 oz.] V-8 juice
    cocktail
2 cans [10 3/4 oz.] con-
    densed tomato soup
6 bay leaves
4 T. lemon juice
1/2 t. garlic juice
1 t. onion juice
2 T. Worcestershire sauce
1 1/2 T. seasoning salt
1/2 T. freshly ground
  . pepper

4 dashes Tabasco sauce
2 pkgs. [8 oz.] cream
    cheese
1 c. mayonnaise or salad
    dressing
24 oz. cooked shrimp,
    chopped
1 c. celery, chopped
1 c. green pepper, chopped
1 can [17 oz.] very small
    young green peas [and
    liquid]
1 c. stuffed olives,
    chopped

Dissolve gelatin in tomato cocktail and 1 can of V-8 juice, stirring until completely dissolved. Combine remaining can of V-8, soup and bay leaves and heat to boiling. Pour over gelatin mixture, stirring well. Add lemon, garlic and onion juices, Worcestershire, salt, pepper, Tabasco and set aside. Mix softened cream cheese and mayonnaise in large bowl; gradually blend in tomato-gelatin mixture, a little at a time, until all is well mixed. Add shrimp, celery, green pepper, peas and liquid and olives. Pour into mold that has been greased with mayonnaise. Chill until congealed. Unmold and serve on lettuce leaves. Serves 18 as a main dish.

Mrs. James W. Fair

SHOESTRING SALAD

1 can [6 1/2 oz.] tuna, drained [or shrimp, salmon, or chicken]
1 c. celery, diced
1 c. carrots, shredded

2 T. green onion, chopped
1/2 c. mayonnaise
2 T. milk
3 c. shoestring potatoes

Pour boiling water over tuna. Drain well and refrigerate until cool.

Combine celery, carrots, onion, mayonnaise and milk and let stand to blend. Add to tuna.

Add shoestring potatoes just before serving.

Serve on crisp bed of lettuce. Garnish with tomato wedges and wedges of hard boiled eggs. Serves 4.

Mrs. Pat White

ASPARAGUS MOLD I

1 sm. can cut asparagus
1 1/3 c. sour cream
2/3 c. mayonnaise
1 t. salt
1/3 t. white pepper

1/3 t. powdered garlic
1 t. MSG
2 T. gelatin [dissolved in 2/3 c. cold water for 5 minutes]

Drain asparagus. Bring liquid to a boil. Add all ingredients and mix well. Put in ring mold or individual molds. Refrigerate until congealed, about 2 hours.

Mrs. William Marsh

ASPARAGUS MOLD II

2 cans cream of asparagus soup
1 envelope gelatin
1/4 c. cold water
2 pkgs. [3 oz.] lime Jello
2 pkgs. [8 oz.] cream cheese

1 c. cold water
2 T. lime juice
3/4 c. mayonnaise
1 c. chopped green pepper
2 T. grated onion

Heat soup to boiling. Soak gelatin in 1/4 cup cold water. Pour hot soup over Jello. Add softened gelatin and stir until dissolved. Blend in cream cheese. Add water, lime juice and mayonnaise and blend. Add pepper and onion. Congeal.

Mrs. Russell Baldwin

Recipe makes a large salad, but it can be halved easily.

Page 71

CONGEALED BROCCOLI SALAD

2 pkgs. [10 oz.] frozen
   chopped broccoli
2 envelopes unflavored
   Knox gelatin
1 can beef consomme'
1 pkg. [3 oz.] cream cheese
1 c. mayonnaise

2 T. lemon juice
1 1/2 t. salt
1/2 to 1 t. pepper
4 hard boiled eggs, chopped
3 T. Worcestershire sauce
1 1/2 t. Tabasco
1 small jar chopped pimiento

Cook broccoli as directed, drain thoroughly and set aside. In saucepan sprinkle gelatin over consomme' and mix until gelatin is moistened. Let sit for several minutes, then dissolve over low heat, stirring and watching constantly. Cool slightly.

Soften cream cheese with a fork and gradually blend consomme' into mixture. When blended, add remaining ingredients. (This will be a soupy, unattractive mixture.) Decorate with more egg and pimiento if desired. Chill until set in a 6 cup ring mold or 10 individual molds.

Mrs. A. E. McCain
Mrs. John Turner

CABBAGE SALAD

1 qt. shredded cabbage
1/2 c. sour cream
1/2 c. mayonnaise
1 t. prepared mustard

1/4 c. chopped onion
Salt to taste
Toasted sesame seeds

Shred cabbage into a large bowl. Combine sour cream, mayonnaise, mustard, onion and salt. Just before serving, add the dressing to cabbage. Toss lightly to blend and add a generous sprinkling of hot toasted seeds. (To toast seeds, put in 300 degree oven until browned.) Serves 6.

Mrs. Charles Clark

CABBAGE AND CHEESE SALAD

1 pkg. lime gelatin
1 c. boiling water
1/2 c. mayonnaise
1 c. cabbage, grated
1 c. grated American cheese

1/2 c. pecan meats
1/2 t. salt
1 T. lemon juice
Onion juice, if desired

Dissolve gelatin in hot water. Cool. Mix mayonnaise with cabbage and fold into gelatin. Add remaining ingredients.

This is a good main course Lenten salad--very filling. Serves 8.

Mrs. T. C. Harvey

Page 72

GERMAN HOT SLAW

1 small or 1/2 large head cabbage,
   shredded and at room temperature
2 or 3 strips bacon, sliced in
   small pieces

1/2 c. vinegar
1 T. [heaping] sugar
1/4 c. water

Shred cabbage finely and put into mixing bowl. Cook bacon strips in small skillet and add vinegar, sugar and water. (Do not drain grease from bacon.) Let boil and pour hot mixture over cabbage. Let inverted skillet remain on cabbage until heat subsides. Toss and serve immediately. Serves 8 to 10.

Mrs. J. Donald Guinn

Variations: Substitute lettuce for cabbage and add 1 chopped hard boiled egg. Substitute green beans or asparagus for cabbage, using canned liquid instead of water.

SUPER COLE SLAW

1 c. vinegar
3/4 c. salad oil
1 t. mustard seed
1 t. celery seed
1 T. salt

1 1/2 t. dill weed
1 c. sugar
1 head shredded cabbage
1 sliced onion
1 green pepper

Mix vinegar, salad oil, mustard seed, celery seed, salt and dill. Sprinkle sugar over shredded cabbage and sliced onion which have been layered in a large dish. Pour dressing mixture over cabbage mixture. Slice green pepper thinly and place on top. Refrigerate for several hours or overnight before serving. This salad improves as it sits in refrigerator. May be kept for several days. Serves 10 to 12.

Mrs. Tom Ramey, Jr.

Mrs. Henry C. Holland makes the same slaw but omits the dill weed in her recipe.

Mrs. Fred C. McCoun prepares her Sweet and Sour Slaw without the green pepper and using 3/4 cup sugar. Her dressing consists of 1 teaspoon sugar, 1 1/2 teaspoons salt, 1 cup vinegar, 1 teaspoon celery seed and 1 teaspoon prepared mustard brought to boil. She adds 1 cup salad oil and brings to a boil again before pouring over layered cabbage and onions.

CUCUMBER SALAD

1 pkg. [3 oz.] lime Jello
3/4 c. hot water
2 pkgs. [3 oz.] cream cheese
1 c. mayonnaise
1 T. horseradish
1/4 t. salt

2 T. lemon juice
3/4 c. drained, shredded
   cucumber
1/4 c. thinly sliced green
   onions

Dissolve Jello in hot water. Add softened cream cheese, mayonnaise, horseradish and salt. Blend well with electric blender. Add lemon juice and chill until mixture begins to thicken. Add cucumber and onions and chill until set. Serves 10 to 12.

Mrs. Harold Beaird

MOLDED CUCUMBER AND COTTAGE CHEESE

1 pkg. [3 oz.] lime flavored
   gelatin
1 c. hot water
1 c. mayonnaise
1 pt. cottage cheese
1/2 c. finely chopped celery
1 large cucumber, peeled
   and diced

1 small onion, grated
1 t. salt
1 T. vinegar
1/2 c. chopped blanched
   almonds

Dissolve lime gelatin in hot water and let cool slightly. Stir in mayonnaise, cottage cheese, celery, cucumber, onion, salt, vinegar and almonds. Turn the mixture immediately into a 1 1/2 quart ring mold. Let chill overnight or until firm. Unmold and garnish with crisp greens. Serves 8 to 10.

Mrs. John Warner

EGG MOLD

1 pkg. unflavored gelatin
1/2 c. cold water
1 t. salt
2 T. lemon juice
1/4 t. Worcestershire sauce
1/8 t. cayenne
3/4 c. mayonnaise

1 1/2 t. onion, grated
1/2 c. celery, finely diced
1/4 c. green pepper,
   finely diced
1/4 c. pimiento, chopped
Mustard to taste
4 hard cooked eggs, chopped

Soften gelatin in cold water. Place over boiling water until dissolved. Add salt, lemon juice, Worcestershire and cayenne. Combine with mayonnaise, onion, celery, green pepper, pimiento, mustard and chopped eggs. Use ring mold and serve with crackers when used for appetizer. Use 6 1/2 cup mold when doubling the recipe. This is very good in place of deviled eggs. Serves 6 for salad and 12 to 15 for appetizer.

Mrs. O. C. Arnold

CAESAR SALAD

Dressing:

1/2 c. salad oil
1/4 c. red wine vinegar
1 clove garlic, crushed,
  [or garlic powder]
2 t. Worcestershire sauce
1/4 t. salt
Dash pepper

Salad:

Packaged croutons
1/2 c. grated Parmesan
  cheese
1/4 c. [1 oz.] crumbled
  bleu cheese
2 heads romaine lettuce,
  shredded
1 red onion, cut into rings
1 or 2 hard cooked eggs,
  chopped

For dressing, combine dressing ingredients in jar and chill overnight. Combine salad ingredients, pour dressing over and toss. Serves 4.

Mrs. Michael Hatchell

LUNCHEON SALAD

1 can tomato soup
1 1/2 T. gelatin
1/2 c. cold water
1 c. chopped celery
1 c. nuts [pecans]

1 c. mayonnaise
1/3 c. chopped green pepper
1 T. finely chopped onion
2 pkgs. [3 oz.] cream cheese,
  softened

Heat tomato soup. Dissolve gelatin in cold water and add to soup. Add remaining ingredients. Mix thoroughly and pour in greased mold. Refrigerate. Serves 8.

Mrs. Billy B. Rogers

ORANGE-AVOCADO TOSS

1 med. head lettuce, torn
  in bite-size chunks [6 c.]
1 small cucumber, thinly
  sliced [1 1/3 c.]
1 avocado, seeded, peeled
  and sliced
1 can [11 oz.] mandarin
  orange sections, drained
  [1 1/3 c.]

2 T. sliced green onions
1/2 t. grated orange peel
1/4 c. orange juice
1/2 c. salad oil
2 T. sugar
2 T. red wine vinegar
1 T. lemon juice
1/4 t. salt

In a large salad bowl, combine lettuce, cucumber, avocado, mandarin orange sections and onions. In a screw-top jar, combine orange peel and juice, salad oil, sugar, vinegar, lemon juice and salt. Cover tightly and shake well. Just before serving, pour over salad, tossing lightly. Serves 8.

Mrs. R. Don Cowan

SOUR CREAM CUCUMBERS I

3 lg. cucumbers
2 T. salt
Ice water

Dressing:

1 T. sugar
1/2 t. salt
1/2 t. dry mustard
1 t. finely chopped onion
3 T. vinegar
1 c. sour cream
Dash cayenne
Paprika

Peel and slice cucumbers. Soak for two hours in 2 tablespoons salt and ice water to cover. Drain and pat dry before combining with sour cream mixture.

For dressing, combine all ingredients and pour over cucumbers. Sprinkle with paprika before serving. Serves 12 to 16.

Mrs. Galloway Calhoun, Jr.

Try this at an outdoor Bar-B-Q.

SOUR CREAM CUCUMBERS II

1/2 t. salt
1/2 t. sugar
1/2 t. red pepper
1/4 c. garlic wine vinegar

1 c. sour cream
2 t. chopped chives
1 t. celery seed
2 or 3 medium cucumbers

Dissolve salt, sugar and pepper in wine vinegar. Whip cream until smooth and stiff. Add chives and celery seeds. Slice cucumbers and mix with sour cream sauce.

Mrs. Frank Agar

HOT GERMAN POTATO SALAD WITH BACON

2 3/4 lbs. boiling potatoes
1/2 lb. sliced bacon
1 1/4 c. chopped onions
1 c. chopped green pepper
2/3 c. beef bouillon

2 T. cider vinegar
1 1/2 t. salt
1/4 t. white pepper
1 1/4 t. sugar
Chopped parsley

Cook potatoes in boiling salted water in large saucepan until tender; drain, peel and cut into 1/2-inch slices. Dice bacon and fry in skillet until crisp, stirring occasionally. Drain on paper towel.

Pour off bacon drippings and measure 1/4 cup. Saute' onions in drippings until golden; stir in green pepper, beef bouillon, cider vinegar and seasonings; cook about 1 1/2 minutes or until green pepper is tender. Add potatoes and bacon; toss gently until combined. Cover skillet and cook over medium heat just until potatoes are hot. Just before serving, garnish with parsley. Serves 8.

Mrs. Will Knight

POTATO SALAD I

6 large new potatoes
2 hard boiled eggs,
  finely chopped
1/2 c. celery, cut in
  1/4 in. pieces
1/4 c. onion, finely chopped
2 T. dill pickle,
  finely chopped
2 T. sweet pickle,
  finely chopped
1/2 c. bell pepper,
  finely chopped

2 T. parsley [dry or
  fresh, finely chopped]
1 1/2 T. mustard
3 T. salad oil
1 T. dry Worcestershire
  powder
1 T. Lawry's seasoned salt
Hellman's mayonnaise
  to moisten
Salt and pepper to taste

Boil potatoes with skins on until tender. Peel and cut in cubes about 1/2 inch square. Mix all ingredients while potatoes and eggs are still warm. Refrigerate until chilled. Serves 8.

Mrs. William C. Stephens

POTATO SALAD II

1 t. salt
6 medium-sized potatoes
1/2 c. mayonnaise
1 t. prepared mustard
1 t. grated onion
1/4 t. sugar

1/4 t. paprika
1/2 t. salt
3/4 c. diced celery
1 small bell pepper, diced
1 jar [2 oz.] chopped
  pimiento

Add the teaspoon of salt to water and boil potatoes (in skins) about 45 minutes, just until tender. Drain, cool, peel and dice into bite-sized pieces. Mix mayonnaise, mustard, grated onion, sugar, paprika and the 1/2 teaspoon salt. Put diced vegetables and drained pimiento into large bowl. Add mayonnaise mixture and toss the vegetables carefully until coated. Refrigerate. Serves 10.

Mrs. Norman Shtofman

SALAD BY MARY FRANCES

1 c. wine vinegar
1 c. sugar
1 t. paprika
1/3 c. Wesson oil
Pinch of salt

2 c. French-cut green beans
1 c. peas
1 onion, thinly sliced
1 can chopped pimiento
Lettuce

Mix vinegar, şugar, paprika, Wesson oil and salt. Chill for 24 hours. Combine green beans, peas, onion and pimiento in large bowl and pour dressing mixture over, mixing gently. Serve on lettuce. Serves 8.

Mrs. Harold Cameron

SARA THOMPSON'S RICE SALAD

1 T. vinegar
2 T. corn oil
3/4 c. Hellman's mayonnaise
1 t. salt
1/2 t. curry powder
1 1/3 c. cooked rice

2 T. chopped onion
1 c. chopped celery
1 pkg. LeSueur frozen
English peas
[under cooked]

Mix vinegar, oil, mayonnaise, salt and curry powder. Cook rice until just done. Add rice to mixture, then add chopped onion while rice is hot. When cooled, add celery and peas. This is better the second day. Serves 6 to 8.

Mrs. F. O. Penn

FRESH SPINACH SALAD

1/2 pkg. fresh spinach
Salad Supreme seasoning
salt
1/2 c. chopped purple onion
[or onion rings or strips]
2 T. chopped pimientos

3 chopped boiled eggs
1/2 c. croutons [rye,
onion or plain]
1/2 c. Hidden Valley Ranch
Dressing

Wash spinach removing large stems. Dry. Salt well with Salad Supreme salt. Add all ingredients except croutons and dressing. Refrigerate until ready to serve. (May be mixed several hours ahead of time.) Just before serving, add croutons and dressing.

Tomato wedges may be used instead of croutons if preferred. (Use two large tomatoes, cut in wedges.) Serves 6 to 8.

Mrs. James H. Rippy

SPINACH SALAD

1 t. garlic
1/4 c. vinegar
8 slices bacon
1 lb. fresh spinach
1 c. raw cauliflower, sliced
in bite-sized pieces

1 c. American cheese, cubed
Salt and pepper to taste
1/2 c. salad oil

Mix garlic and vinegar and set aside. Fry bacon until crisp, drain and crumble. Thoroughly wash and dry spinach leaves, tear into bite-sized pieces and put in large salad bowl. Add cauliflower and cheese and sprinkle with crumbled bacon, salt and pepper. Combine garlic-vinegar with salad oil and beat to blend. Set aside to cool, then pour dressing over salad. Serve immediately.

Mrs. C. R. Hurst

SPINACH SALAD A LA GREQUE

6 c. [about 2/3 lb.] spinach,
 cut in bite-size pieces
1 small Bermuda onion,
 sliced
1/4 c. diced celery
4 hard-cooked eggs, sliced
1/2 t. salt

1 t. pepper
1 c. sour cream
1 pkg. garlic-cheese salad
 dressing mix
1 T. lemon juice
Seasoned croutons

Early in day combine spinach, onion, celery, eggs, salt and pepper in a large bowl and toss together well. Refrigerate. In separate bowl, combine sour cream, salad dressing mix and lemon juice and mix well. Refrigerate.

At serving time, toss half of sour cream mixture with spinach mixture. Add seasoned croutons. Serve immediately from bowl, or arrange on salad plates. Refrigerate remainder of sour cream mixture to use on other salads during week. Serves 4 to 6.

Mrs. John Short

WILTED SPINACH SALAD

2 c. lettuce
1 c. fresh spinach
1/4 c. diced celery
Fresh grated onion
2 T. crumbled bleu cheese
4 slices crumbled cooked
 bacon

1/4 c. bacon drippings
1/4 c. red wine vinegar
2 T. sugar
1/2 t. salt
1/2 t. Worcestershire sauce

Combine lettuce, spinach, celery, onion, bleu cheese and bacon bits in salad bowl. Heat the bacon drippings, vinegar, sugar, salt and Worcestershire together and pour over the salad ingredients. The dressing may be made ahead of time and reheated just before serving, if desired. Serves 4.

Mrs. Tom B. Ramey, Jr.

SAUERKRAUT SALAD

1 c. sugar
3 1/2 c. sauerkraut, drained
1 medium onion,
 chopped
1 medium green pepper,
 chopped

1 small can pimiento,
 chopped
1 1/2 to 2 c. celery,
 chopped

Add sugar to sauerkraut. Mix in other ingredients. Let stand 24 hours. This keeps well when refrigerated.

Mrs. O. C. Arnold

MOLDED TOMATO ASPIC RING

Aspic Mold:

2 envelopes gelatin
1/4 c. water
4 c. tomato juice [Libby's]
1 bay leaf
Red pepper to taste
1 stalk celery [about 4 in.]
2 t. salt
4 whole cloves
Onion juice to taste
1 T. lemon juice
1 T. vinegar
Finely chopped celery
[enough to line ring mold]

Dressing:

2 eggs [hard cooked]
1 sm. jar stuffed olives
1 c. mayonnaise

Soften gelatin in water. Combine tomato juice, bay leaf, pepper, celery, salt, cloves and onion juice and simmer together for 30 minutes. Strain juice and add lemon and vinegar. Dissolve softened gelatin in a small portion of the hot juice mixture, then combine with remainder of juice mixture. Pour into greased ring mold which has been lined with chopped celery. Cover and refrigerate until congealed.

For dressing, chop hard boiled eggs and slice stuffed olives. Combine eggs and olives with mayonnaise and chill. Serve dressing in center of aspic ring. Serve with lettuce or other greens surrounding the aspic. Serves 8 to 10.

Mrs. John R. Bentley

TOMATO ASPIC

1 3/4 c. V-8 juice [small can]
1 T. grated onion
Salt to taste
2 or 3 drops Tabasco
Sprinkle of ground cloves

1 pkg. [3 oz.] lemon Jello
1/4 c. vinegar
Diced avocado and celery
[about 1/4 c. combined]

Combine V-8 juice, onion and seasonings. Heat mixture and dissolve Jello in it. Add vinegar and chill until partially set (may be placed in freezer for 45 minutes to 1 hour). Add diced avocado and celery and congeal in salad molds. Diced artichoke hearts and bell pepper make good variations in this salad. Serves 6 to 7.

Mrs. C. Aubrey Smith, Jr.

TOMARTICHOKES

6 large tomatoes
6 artichokes [canned or
   frozen ones that have
   been cooked]
Salt to taste
Pepper to taste

Powdered dill [optional]
   to taste
1/2 c. mayonnaise
1/2 c. sour cream
1/2 t. lemon juice
1/2 t. curry powder

Drop tomatoes in boiling water for a minute, remove peel, cut tops off, scoop out seeds and juice. Season inside and out with salt, pepper and powdered dill. Place artichoke heart in each tomato and chill in refrigerator.

For dressing, combine mayonnaise, sour cream, lemon juice and curry powder and chill. Spoon over tomatoes before serving. Serves 6.

Mrs. Arthur L. Burch

TOMATOES PIQUANT

6 ripe tomatoes, peeled
2/3 c. salad oil
1/4 c. tarragon vinegar
1/4 c. snipped parsley
1/4 c. sliced green onions
1 t. salt

2 t. snipped fresh thyme
   or marjoram [or 1/2 t.
   dried thyme]
1/4 t. freshly ground
   pepper
1 clove garlic, minced

Place tomatoes in deep bowl. In jar, combine remaining ingredients. Shake well; pour over tomatoes. Cover and chill for several hours or overnight, spooning dressing over occasionally. At serving time, drain off dressing. Snip more parsley over tomatoes. Serves 4 to 6.

Mrs. William C. Lust

PEAR RELISH

1 qt. onions
1/2 gal. pears
6 green peppers
3 red bell peppers
1 or 2 hot peppers,
   to taste
1 T. flour

4 c. sugar
2 t. salt
1 T. mustard seed
1 qt. white vinegar
   [less 2 T.]
1 T. turmeric
2 T. celery seed

Grind first 5 ingredients and mix. Boil 5 minutes. Mix remaining ingredients and add to boiled mixture and boil 5 minutes more. Pour into sterilized jars and seal. Makes 12 pints.

Mrs. J. Harold Stringer

PEAR CHUTNEY

3 1/2 qts. pears, cut up
1 1/2 c. raisins
2 chili peppers, ground
5 garlic buttons, ground
2 onions, ground

1 1/2 c. vinegar
2 c. brown sugar
1 t. cinnamon
1 t. mustard
1/4 t. cayenne pepper

Combine all ingredients and cook until mixture thickens, about one hour.

Mrs. G. C. Clark

WINE SPICED PEARS

6 fresh pears
1/2 c. sugar
1/2 c. honey
3/4 c. muscatel or
white port

1/2 c. red wine vinegar
1 t. whole cloves
1 t. whole allspice
2 inch stick cinnamon

Wash, peel, halve and core pears. Combine remaining ingredients in a large kettle, bring to a boil and simmer for 5 minutes. Add pears, simmer for about 15 minutes more or until pears are tender. To test, pierce with a toothpick. Turn pears once during cooking and baste occasionally with the syrup. Cool, then store covered in the refrigerator. Serve as a relish with meat, especially good with ham, pork or lamb. Serves 8 to 12.

Mrs. A. B. Wilson, Jr.

The syrup that remains after serving pears is excellent for basting ham.

DILL PICKLED OKRA

2 to 3 lbs. fresh okra
Hot peppers
1 medium garlic clove
per jar

1/2 t. dill seed per jar
1 scant c. salt
1 gal. apple cider vinegar

Wash and trim tops off okra; place in large pan, cover with boiling water and let stand until cool. Pack pint jars, add 1 hot pepper, 1 medium garlic clove and 1/2 teaspoon dill seed to each jar. Bring salt and vinegar to a boil and pour over okra packed in jars. Seal immediately and store a week or two before eating.

Mrs. Brad Holmes

BREAD AND BUTTER PICKLES

Soak clean cucumbers in cold salted water overnight. To each quart of sliced cucumbers (sliced thin), add 1 medium onion, sliced.

1 c. sugar	1/4 t. celery salt
1 c. vinegar	1 t. white mustard seed
1/4 t. tumeric powder	

Mix and bring to a boil. Add cucumbers and onions and boil 3 minutes. Pack in jars and seal. Liquid covers approximately 2 quarts.

Mrs. J. Donald Guinn

A tremendous help in washing large amounts of cucumbers or turnip greens is to place them in the washing machine on the cold rinse cycle. If needed, wash twice.

QUICK SWEET PICKLES

4 qts. cucumbers, sliced thin	6 c. sugar
7 1/3 c. vinegar	2 1/4 T. celery seed
3 T. salt	1 T. allspice
1 T. mustard seed	

Simmer cucumber slices with 4 cups vinegar, salt, mustard seed, 1/4 cup sugar, celery seed and allspice. Cover for about 10 minutes. Drain and discard this liquid. Place slices in jars. Boil together remaining vinegar and sugar. Pour over cucumbers in jars and seal. Any remaining juice is good on cabbage slaw.

Mrs. J. Donald Guinn

TOMATO RELISH

1 peck tomatoes	4 T. salt
6 chopped onions	2 c. sugar
6 bell peppers	4 c. vinegar
6 hot green peppers, [increase or decrease according to taste]	

Scald tomatoes in hot water so they peel easily. Peel tomatoes and core. Cut up with chopped onions and peppers. Cook 15 to 20 minutes and add salt, sugar and vinegar. Cook over low heat for 2 hours, stirring occasionally. Place in jars and seal. For thicker relish, cook longer. May be cooked in an electric roaster. Good over East Texas peas.

Mrs. J. Donald Guinn

GREEN TOMATO RELISH

12 qts. green tomatoes,
    cut up
1/2 gal. onions, cut in
    squares
1 qt. green long hot peppers,
    cut with scissors

6 c. sugar
1/2 gal. vinegar
1 t. salt

Combine all ingredients and bring to a boil. Remove from heat and seal in hot jars. Makes 20 pints.

Mrs. James Godwin

AUNT LIL'S APPLESAUCE

Apples [6 lb., more or less]
1 1/2 c. sugar

1 1/2 c. water
2 T. lemon juice

Cut up and core apples. DO NOT peel apples. Applesauce retains more vitamins if cooked with skin. (Also gives sauce pretty pink color.) Put apples, sugar, water and lemon juice in large pan (about 6 quart Dutch oven).

Cook until soft, but not loose. Mash apples down in pan while cooking with wooden spoon.

After cooking, run apples through sieve. (This is called a Foley Food Mill.) Put about 1 cup at a time in food mill. Grind through sieve until all of apple has gone through. Only skin will be left in food mill. (Skin will be slightly transparent.) Remove some of skin before adding additional apples, and it works better. (Do not drain apples - run all through sieve.)

Makes 3 quarts of applesauce.

Mrs. L. Glenn Taylor

BLEU CHEESE DRESSING

1 1/2 oz. bleu cheese
1 oz. cider vinegar
7 oz. mayonnaise
1/8 t. onion powder

1/4 t. salt
2 T. sugar
3 oz. buttermilk
1 t. ground black pepper

Crumble bleu cheese and stir in other ingredients. Mix well and chill. Makes 1 pint of dressing.

Mrs. George B. Allen

GOLDEN DRESSING
[For Fruit Salad]

3 whole eggs, well-beaten
1/4 c. sugar
1/4 c. lemon juice
1/4 c. juice from canned
    fruit [pear or pineapple]
1 pkg. [3 oz.] cream cheese,
    diced

10 marshmallows, cut up
1/2 c. toasted pecans
1/2 pt. whipped cream
1 small can pineapple
1 fresh banana

Cook eggs, sugar, lemon juice and fruit juice in double boiler until thick. Chill and add cream cheese, marshmallows, pecans and whipped cream. Use over canned fruit (fruits for salad) but add small can of pineapple and fresh banana. Very rich. Serves 6 to 8.

Mrs. Galloway Calhoun, Jr.

GREEN GODDESS SALAD DRESSING

1 c. mayonnaise
1 clove garlic, crushed
3 anchovy fillets, minced
1/4 c. finely chopped chives or
    green onions
1/4 c. chopped parsley

1 T. lemon juice
1 T. tarragon vinegar
1/2 t. salt
Pepper, coarsely ground
1/2 c. sour cream

Combine mayonnaise, garlic, anchovy fillets, chives, parsley, lemon juice, vinegar, salt and pepper and sour cream. Put into a covered container and store in refrigerator until ready to use. Toss lightly with salad greens just before serving; or add fresh crabmeat, lobster or shrimp and serve as a main salad dish.

Mrs. Ralph Spence

This is also excellent as a dip for cold shrimp.

LEBANESE SALAD DRESSING

1 large clove garlic, mashed
3/4 c. bottled or fresh
    lemon juice
1 t. dried mint leaves
    [or fresh in season]

1 c. salad oil
1 t. dried parsley flakes
2 t. salt
1/2 t. cracked black pepper

Mix ingredients in pint jar. Shake until well-blended. Refrigerate. This will be enough dressing to serve on tossed green salad for 20 to 24 people. Dressing will keep about 2 to 3 weeks in the refrigerator.

Mrs. Joy Massad

This may also be used for marinade for cooked vegetables such as French-style green beans or asparagus. Also may be brushed on chicken before baking or broiling -- even on steak.

LIME HONEY DRESSING

2 to 3 T. lime juice
1/2 c. honey
2 eggs, well-beaten

1/2 pt. cream, whipped
stiff

Add lime juice to honey. Stir in well-beaten eggs, mixing thoroughly. Cook over simmering hot water until thickened, stirring constantly. Cool. Fold in whipped cream. Makes about 1 1/2 cups dressing.

Mrs. John B. White, III
Jacksonville, Texas

 A sweet dressing for fruit salad.

MAYONNAISE

2 egg yolks
1 t. salt
1 t. sugar
1 t. dry mustard
1/2 t. paprika
2 T. pepper sauce [or vinegar]

3 T. lemon juice
2 c. salad oil
Dash garlic salt, cayenne,
Lawry's seasoning salt
1 T. boiling water

In mixer, beat egg yolks on highest speed until creamy. Add dry ingredients, then pepper sauce or vinegar and lemon juice. Mix well, then begin adding oil, drop by drop, until about 3 or 4 tablespoonfuls are mixed into egg mixture. Gradually add the remainder of the oil. Add 1 tablespoon boiling water to "cook" the mixture. Store in jar in lower part of refrigerator.

Mrs. Russell B. Watson, Jr.

If egg yolks seem small use three for richer mayonnaise. If desired, use only one tablespoon vinegar.

POPPY SEED DRESSING I

2 t. poppy seed
1 c. sugar
1/4 t. salt
1 t. paprika
1 t. dry mustard

1/3 c. honey
1 t. onion juice
6 T. tarragon vinegar
3 T. lemon juice
1 c. salad oil

Soak poppy seed in water 2 hours; drain through cheese cloth or fine sieve. Mix dry ingredients; add honey, onion juice, vinegar and lemon juice. Add oil slowly, beating constantly, then add poppy seed. (Should be very thick).

Mrs. Jack Harper

May use Safflower oil instead of salad oil to make a lighter salad dressing.

POPPY SEED DRESSING II

2 slices onion [1 to 2 T.]   3 T. lemon juice
3/4 c. honey   2 T. vinegar
1 t. dry mustard   1 c. salad oil
1 t. salt   1 1/2 T. poppy seeds

Put first 6 ingredients in blender. Blend until onion is well chopped. Turn to low speed and gradually add oil. When thoroughly homogenized (but no longer), add poppy seeds and blend just till mixed. Refrigerate. Serve on fruit salads. Yields about 1 3/4 cups.

Mrs. William C. Lust

ROQUEFORT DRESSING

1 pkg. [3 oz.] cream cheese   1/2 t. mustard
1 triangle Roquefort cheese   6 T. mayonnaise
1/2 c. light cream or milk   2 T. sour cream
Dash salt

Blend all ingredients. Whip at high speed of mixer until smooth. Makes about 2 cups and keeps about a week in the refrigerator.

Mrs. John D. Glass, Jr.

Can be used for salad or dip. Especially good with cauliflower.

SALAD DRESSING

1 t. salt   Dash of garlic salt
1/4 t. ground pepper   Dash of celery seed
2 t. sugar   1/3 c. wine vinegar
1/2 t. dry mustard   2/3 c. oil

Shake well in a jar. Keep cold.

Mrs. Ronald N. Schoenbrun

SLAW DRESSING

1 t. dry mustard   1/4 t. salt
2 T. Miracle Whip   1/2 c. cream
5 T. [scant] sugar   1 t. celery seed
2 T. vinegar   Chopped green pepper [optional]

Mix all ingredients and pour over 5 cups shredded cabbage. (Slaw tastes better the next day.)

Mrs. A. K. Baker
McAllen, Texas

SPECIAL SALAD DRESSING

1 pt. Hellman's mayonnaise
2 hard boiled eggs, ground
3 oz. vinegar
2 t. horseradish

2 t. Worcestershire sauce
1 clove garlic, ground
1/2 t. paprika

Mix together and place in jar with tight lid. Chill until ready to use. Enough for 6 salads.

Mrs. David Russell

TEXAS FRENCH DRESSING

1/2 c. sugar
1 T. mustard
2 t. paprika
3 t. salt
1 can tomato soup
1 c. vinegar

1 c. salad oil
2 T. Worcestershire sauce
1 clove garlic, crushed
1/2 lb. Roquefort or bleu cheese

Mix at high speed of mixer for 4 minutes.

Mrs. C. C. Coulston

THOUSAND ISLAND DRESSING

1 medium green pepper
1 medium jar pimientos
1 hard boiled egg
1 small white onion

1 pt. Hellman's mayonnaise
Salt to taste
Paprika
Parsley flakes

Use hand grinder with fine blade. (Do not use blender.) Grind together pepper, pimiento, egg and onion and add to one pint of Hellman's mayonnaise. Add salt to taste. Top with paprika and parsley flakes.

This is a basic recipe to be geared to the taste of each family. For a dip, more mayonnaise may be desirable. This complete recipe should always stand 24 hours in refrigerator before being used. This will keep fresh if kept in a covered container in refrigerator.

Mrs. Alice White

This salad dressing is excellent as a vegetable dip, on cooked vegetables and is wonderful on baked potatoes.

Breads

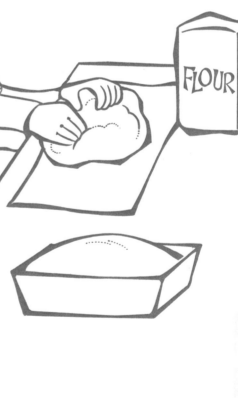

ALABAMA BISCUITS

5 c. flour
4 T. sugar
1 t. salt
1 t. soda

1 c. Crisco
2 c. buttermilk
2 yeast cakes

Mix together flour, sugar, salt, soda, Crisco. Heat buttermilk until warm and add yeast cakes. Combine the two mixtures and work like biscuits. Divide in half, roll out and cut with small biscuit cutter. Butter each biscuit and set another on top. Space in pan to give plenty of room to rise. Let rise about an hour and bake at 425 to 450 degrees for 10 to 15 minutes. (Can be frozen before allowed to rise. If frozen, remove at least 1 1/2 hours before baking).

Mrs. J. C. Bowen
Gladewater, Texas

APRICOT NUT BREAD

1 c. dried apricots
1 c. sugar
2 T. shortening
1 egg, well-beaten
1/2 c. orange juice
1/4 c. sugar

2 c. sifted flour
2 t. baking powder
1/2 t. soda
1 t. salt
1 c. chopped nuts

Cook apricots for 20 minutes. Cream sugar, shortening and egg. Stir in the orange juice mixed with 1/4 cup sugar. Add dry ingredients and blend well. Drain apricots and stir into batter with nuts. Bake in greased and floured loaf pans for about 45 minutes. Makes two loaves. Freezes well.

Mrs. Gene Caldwell

ASPHODEL BREAD

5 c. biscuit mix
1/4 c. sugar
1/2 t. salt
2 pkgs. dry yeast

2 c. warm milk
4 eggs
Pinch cream of tartar

Sift biscuit mix, sugar and salt together into a large bowl. In another bowl, sprinkle dry yeast over warm milk to soften and stir until yeast dissolves. Beat eggs with cream of tartar and combine with yeast mixture. Add to dry ingredients, stirring dough until well-mixed. Cover bowl securely with plastic wrap. Let dough stand in warm place until doubled in size.

Stir dough thoroughly and divide into 2 oiled loaf pans, 8 1/2 x 4 1/2 x 2 1/2 inches in size. Let rise in warm place until dough reaches tops of pans. Bake at 350 degrees for 25 to 30 minutes. Best served hot.

Mrs. E. D. Wilcox

BANANA NUT BREAD

3/4 c. margarine
1 1/2 c. sugar
1 1/2 c. mashed bananas
2 eggs, beaten
1 t. vanilla

2 c. sifted flour
1 t. baking soda
3/4 t. salt
1/2 c. buttermilk
1 c. nuts

Cream margarine and sugar thoroughly. Blend in bananas, eggs and vanilla. Sift flour, soda and salt together. Add to banana mixture, alternating with buttermilk. Add nuts. Bake in greased and floured 9 x 5 x 3 inch loaf pan at 325 degrees for 1 hour 15 minutes.

Mrs. Donald E. Payne

Mrs. Mack L. Hayes, Jr. uses 1/2 c. margarine, 3/4 c. sugar, 2 mashed bananas, 1 egg, 1 t. vanilla, 1 1/4 c. flour, 1 t. soda dissolved in 2 T. water, 1/2 c. nuts and 1/4 t. nutmeg (no buttermilk) and bakes at 350 degrees for 40 minutes.

KONA BANANA BREAD

2 c. sugar
1 c. shortening
6 very ripe mashed bananas
4 well-beaten eggs

2 1/2 c. cake flour
1 t. salt
2 t. baking soda

Cream sugar and shortening. Beat the eggs until well-blended and mix them with the mashed bananas. Add to sugar mixture. Sift cake flour, salt and baking soda together 3 times. Add sifted ingredients gradually, being careful not to overmix. Stir gently until all flour disappears. Batter should be very lumpy. Pour into 3 greased and floured 7 3/8 x 3 5/8 x 2 1/4 inch pans. Bake 350 degrees for 45 to 50 minutes.

Mrs. John D. Glass, Jr.

Use soft, black bananas for this recipe.

CALYPSO JAVA BREAD

3 c. biscuit mix
3/4 c. brown sugar
1/4 c. all-purpose flour
1 T. instant coffee powder
1/2 c. milk

1 c. mashed [2] bananas
1 beaten egg
1 c. snipped dates
1/2 c. chopped walnuts

In mixing bowl combine biscuit mix, brown sugar and flour. Dissolve coffee powder in milk. Add all at once to dry ingredients with bananas and egg. Beat until blended. Stir in dates and nuts.

Grease bottoms of two 1 pound coffee cans. Divide batter between cans. Bake in 350 degree oven for 50 minutes. Cool 10 minutes. Loosen sides of loaves with spatula and remove from cans.

Mrs. Pat Hightower

CARROT BREAD

4 eggs	2 t. cinnamon
2 c. sugar	1 t. nutmeg
1 1/2 c. Wesson oil	1/2 t. salt
3 c. flour	1 t. vanilla
2 t. baking powder	1/2 c. nuts
2 t. soda	2 c. grated carrots

Beat eggs. Add sugar and Wesson oil. Mix well and add other ingredients, ending with carrots.

Bake in 2 ungreased pans for 1 hour at 350 degrees. Cool thoroughly before removing from pans. Makes 2 small loaves.

Mrs. Walter P. Jones, Jr.

CHEESE-CRANBERRY BREAD

1 1/2 c. cranberries, cut in halves	1/2 c. coarsely chopped walnuts
1/2 c. sugar	1 1/2 c. finely shredded sharp Cheddar cheese
2 c. flour	
3/4 c. sugar	1 egg, slightly beaten
1 T. baking powder	1 c. milk
1/2 t. salt	1/4 c. butter, melted and cooled
2 t. grated orange peel	

Mix cranberries and 1/2 cup sugar until well-blended. Blend next four ingredients together in a large bowl. Mix in the sugared cranberries, orange peel, nuts, and cheese. Beat the egg, milk, and butter together. Add to mixture in bowl; stir just until dry ingredients are moistened (do not overmix). Butter bottom of loaf pan (9 1/2 x 5 1/4 x 2 3/4) and put batter in, being careful to spread batter evenly into corners. Bake at 350 degrees about one hour, or until a wooden pick inserted in center comes out clean. Remove from pan to cooling rack and cool completely before slicing. To store, wrap and refrigerate. This freezes very well. If preferred, this may be baked in two small loaf pans instead of one large one. Adjust cooking time for smaller loaves.

Mrs. C. Aubrey Smith, Jr.

RISEN SALLY LUNN

3 heaping T. sugar	1 cake yeast
3 heaping T. butter	3/4 c. warm milk
3 large eggs [or 4 small], beaten lightly	3 c. sifted flour
	1 t. salt

Cream sugar and butter, add beaten eggs. Dissolve yeast cake in warm milk. Add to above. Sift flour and salt together and add to above. Put in a 9-inch tube pan greased with cold lard. Let rise three hours. Bake 30 minutes at 350 degrees.

Mrs. Gates Brelsford

DILLY CASSEROLE BREAD

1 pkg. yeast
1/4 c. warm water
1 c. cottage cheese
2 T. sugar
1 T. instant onion soup
1 T. butter or margarine

2 t. dill seed
1 t. salt
1/4 t. soda
1 egg
2 1/4 to 2 1/2 c. flour

Dissolve yeast in water. Heat cottage cheese to lukewarm. Combine sugar, onion soup, butter, dill seed, salt, soda and egg in a bowl with cheese and yeast mixture. Add flour to form stiff dough. Cover and let rise until double in bulk. Stir dough down. Turn into well greased 1 1/2 quart casserole or 2 small loaf pans. Let rise 30 to 40 minutes or until double. Bake at 350 degrees for 40 to 45 minutes. Baking time may be reduced if the 2 small pans are used. Brush with butter and sprinkle with salt. Delicious sliced and toasted and spread with butter.

Mrs. Gene Caldwell

Mrs. Charles Clark varies by using 1 tablespoon finely chopped onion instead of soup, 2 teaspoons salt and 1 or 2 scant tablespoons dill seed.

FRENCH BREAD

2 c. warm water
1 pkg. active dry yeast
1/2 t. powdered ginger
2 t. salt

1 T. sugar
5 c. sifted flour
Butter
Corn meal

Pour lukewarm water into a large bowl; sprinkle yeast over water and carefully stir until dissolved. Add and mix well ginger, salt, sugar and 2 cups sifted flour. Beat with wooden spoon until smooth, then add about 3 cups sifted flour.

On a floured board, knead until dough is smooth and elastic (about 8 minutes) adding more flour if necessary. Dough should be stiff.

Cover hands with softened butter and pat dough into greased ball. Put in a large bowl, cover with towel, and let rise in warm draftless place for about 1 hour or until double in size. Break rise in dough by punching down. Turn out on lightly floured board. Shape into 1 large long French loaf or 2 smaller ones.

Lightly butter a cookie sheet and dust with corn meal. Place loaf or loaves on sheet and brush tops with cold water. With scissors make 3 or 4 diagonal slashes across top of loaves. Let rise again until double in bulk (about 1 hour).

Preheat oven to 450 degrees. For a good crust, put pan of boiling water on bottom of oven and brush each loaf with melted butter. Bake in very hot oven for 7 minutes; then reduce oven heat to 350 and bake 35 minutes longer.

Cool bread on cake rack.

Mrs. Jack M. King

This is surprisingly easy!

CRANBERRY-ORANGE NUT BREAD

3 T. grated orange rind
2 T. melted butter
3/4 c. orange juice
1 egg, well-beaten
1 c. sugar

1 c. raw cranberries, chopped
1/2 c. nuts, chopped
2 c. flour
1/2 t. salt
1/2 t. baking soda

Combine orange rind, butter and juice in mixing bowl. Beat egg and sugar and stir into orange juice mixture. Add cranberries and nuts. Sift flour, salt and soda and blend into mixture. Spoon into a 5-inch buttered loaf pan. Bake at 325 degrees for 1 hour. May be frozen.

Mrs. T. Carlton Billups

MARMALADE BREAD

3 c. sifted flour
3 t. baking powder
1 t. salt
1/4 t. soda
1 jar [1 1/2 c.]
   orange marmalade

1 egg, beaten
3/4 c. orange juice
1/4 c. salad oil or melted
   shortening
1 c. broken California
   walnuts

Sift dry ingredients together. Reserve 1/4 cup of marmalade. Combine remaining 1 1/4 cups marmalade, the egg, orange juice, and salad oil; add to flour mixture, stirring until moistened. Stir in nuts. Turn into greased 9 1/2 x 5 x 3 inch loaf pan. Bake in moderate oven (350 degrees) about one hour or until done. Remove from pan and place on baking sheet; spread top with reserved marmalade and return to oven about one minute. Cool on rack.

Mrs. F. Lee Lawrence
Mrs. A. B. Wilson, Jr.

HERB BREAD

1 pkg. yeast [dry]
1/4 c. warm water
3/4 c. milk
2 T. shortening
1 egg
2 T. sugar

1 to 1 1/2 t. salt
1/2 t. nutmeg
1 t. dried sage
2 t. caraway seed
3 to 3 3/4 c. flour

Dissolve yeast in warm water. Scald milk, put in large bowl. Add shortening, egg, sugar, salt, spices and seed. When milk mixture is lukewarm, add yeast and stir well. Gradually add flour. Mix with spoon, then with hands. Let this dough rise once. Shape into two small loaf pans which have been greased. Let rise until doubled. Bake 30 to 40 minutes at 375 degrees.

Mrs. Richard Grainger

ORANGE BREAD

Peel of 3 oranges
2 c. cold water
2 c. salted cold water

1 c. sugar
1/3 c. hot water

Batter:

1 1/2 c. sour milk
3/4 t. soda
1 egg, well-beaten

1 t. salt
4 t. baking powder
3 c. flour

Boil peel of the oranges, starting with cold water, about 20 minutes. Drain. Then put in salted water and boil until tender. Drain, remove as much of white membrane as possible, and cut up in small strips with scissors. Mix peel with sugar and hot water and boil until rather thick and syrupy.

Place in mixing bowl and add sour milk, soda, egg, salt, baking powder and flour. Pour batter into greased 9 x 5 x 3 inch loaf pan and bake at 300 degrees for 45 to 60 minutes or until brown on top. Cool and slice thin.

Mrs. William Marsh

ITALIAN HERB BREAD

1 loaf Italian or French bread [about 14 inches]
1/2 c. melted butter [1 stick]
1 t. parsley flakes
1/4 t. oregano, crushed
1/4 t. dill weed [dried]

1 clove minced garlic
1/2 t. Lawry's
seasoning salt
Grated Parmesan cheese

Cut bread diagonally into 1 inch slices. Blend melted butter, parsley, oregano, dill, garlic, and seasoning salt, and brush on both sides of bread slices. Sprinkle Parmesan cheese on top of butter into slice cuts and on top of loaf. Wrap loaf in foil and heat in hot oven (400 degrees for about 10 minutes).

Mrs. Arthur Cunningham

RAISIN BREAD

1 c. raisins
1 c. water
1 egg
1 c. sugar
1 1/2 c. flour

1 t. cinnamon
1 t. salt
1 t. soda
2 T. corn oil
1/2 c. nuts

Boil raisins and water for three minutes and set aside to cool. Beat egg and add sugar. Add remaining ingredients and stir until thoroughly mixed. Grease a large loaf pan and line the bottom with waxed paper. Bake 1 hour at 350 degrees.

Mrs. N. F. Allen

PEPPER BREAD

1 pkg. dry yeast
1/4 c. warm water
2 1/3 c. flour, unsifted
2 T. sugar
1 t. salt

1 c. sour cream
1 egg
1 c. shredded sharp
   Cheddar cheese
1/2 t. cayenne pepper

In large bowl dissolve yeast in warm water. Add 1 1/3 cups of flour and the remaining ingredients except cheese and pepper. Blend one-half minute at low speed, scraping bowl constantly. Beat 2 minutes at high speed. Stir in remaining flour by hand and add cheese and pepper. Blend thoroughly. Divide batter evenly between two greased 1 pound coffee cans. Let rise 50 minutes. Bake at 350 degrees for 40 minutes or until golden brown. Immediately remove from cans. Cool slightly before slicing.

Mrs. Jim Trotter

PUMPKIN BREAD

3 1/2 c. flour
2 t. soda
1 t. salt
1 t. cinnamon
1 t. nutmeg
3 c. sugar

1 c. cooking oil
4 eggs, lightly beaten
2/3 c. water
2 c. pumpkin
1 c. chopped nuts

Into a large bowl sift dry ingredients; mix well. Add remainder of ingredients except nuts. Mix well. Add nuts, and pour into 3 medium size loaf pans that have been greased and floured. Bake in 350 degree oven (325 degree for pyrex) about 1 hour or until done. Cool in pan for 5 minutes. Turn on rack, cool completely before storing.

Mrs. J. H. Spence

SPOON BREAD

1 pt. sweet milk
1/2 c. meal
1/2 t. salt

2 T. butter
4 egg yolks
4 egg whites

Scald milk, stir in meal. Bring to a boil. Add salt and butter. Cool. Add well-beaten egg yolks, fold in stiffly beaten egg whites. Spread in a buttered baking dish and set in a pan of hot water. Bake in a moderate oven 325 degrees, for 45 minutes.

Mrs. Henry M. Bell, Sr.

STURDY SPOON BREAD

2 1/2 c. milk
1 c. enriched white corn meal
1 t. salt

3/4 t. baking powder
2 T. butter, cut up
3 large eggs, separated

Butter entire surface of round 1 1/2 quart glass casserole (7 1/2 x 2 1/2 inch) or similar utensil (as souffle' dish).

In medium saucepan over moderate heat, scald 1 1/2 cups of milk.

In small mixing bowl, stir together corn meal, salt and remaining 1 cup cold milk; gradually stir in hot milk. Return to saucepan. Stirring constantly, cook just until thickened and sputtery -- liquid will be absorbed by corn meal. Remove from heat, stir in baking powder and butter.

In large mixing bowl, beat egg yolks until thickened and lemon-colored; gradually stir in corn meal mixture. With clean beaters, in medium bowl, beat egg whites until they hold stiff peak. Fold into corn meal mixture.

Put in casserole. Bake in preheated 400 degree oven for 15 minutes. Reduce heat to 350 degrees and bake until puffed and brown - 30 to 35 minutes. Serve at once or spoon bread will fall. Serve with pats of butter. Serves 6 to 8.

Mrs. R. Randall Cape

STRAWBERRY NUT BREAD

1 c. butter or margarine
1 1/2 c. sugar
1 t. vanilla
1/4 t. lemon extract
4 eggs
3 c. sifted flour
1 t. salt

1 t. cream of tartar
1/2 t. baking soda
1 c. strawberry jam or
  preserves
1/2 c. sour cream
1 c. broken walnuts

Cream butter, sugar, vanilla and lemon extract until fluffy. Add eggs, one at a time, beating well after each addition. Sift together flour, salt, cream of tartar and soda. Combine jam and sour cream. Add jam mixture alternately with dry ingredients to creamed mixture, beating until well-combined. Stir in nuts. Divide among five greased and floured 4 1/2 x 2 3/4 x 2 1/2 inch loaf pans. Bake 50 minutes (or until done) at 350 degrees. Cool 10 minutes in pans. Remove from pans and cool completely on wire rack.

Mrs. Watson Simons

Serve with whipped cream cheese flavored with strawberry jam.

SWEET NUT BRAID

Bread:

2 pkgs. dry yeast
1/2 c. warm water
1/3 c. butter
1/3 c. sugar
2 1/2 t. salt
1 c. scalded milk
2 unbeaten eggs
1 T. grated lemon rind
5 to 5 1/2 c. flour

Spread:

1/4 c. butter
1 1/2 c. sifted powdered sugar
1 1/2 t. milk
1 t. vanilla
1/4 t. nutmeg
1 c. chopped nuts

Soften yeast in water. Combine butter, sugar, salt and milk; stir to melt butter; cool to lukewarm. Stir in eggs, lemon rind, and the yeast. Gradually add flour to form stiff dough. Knead on floured surface until smooth. Cover and let rise until doubled.

Combine the spread ingredients, except the nuts, and cream well.

Roll out half of dough to 15 x 12 inch rectangle. Spread with half of cream mixture. Sprinkle with half the nuts. Cut in three 12 x 5 inch strips. Roll each strip starting with 12-inch side. Seal seams. Braid the rolls. Place braid in well-greased 9 x 5 x 3 inch pan. Repeat with remaining dough. Let rise until doubled. Bake at 350 degrees for 40 to 50 minutes.

Mrs. Francis Kay

WHITE BREAD

2 cakes yeast
  [or 2 pkgs. dry yeast]
1 c. tepid water
1 c. boiling water
3/4 c. sugar

3/4 c. shortening
1 1/2 t. salt
2 eggs, beaten
6 c. unsifted flour

Soften yeast for 5 minutes in 1 cup tepid water to which a little of the sugar has been added (about 1 teaspoon).

Pour boiling water over sugar, shortening and salt which have been combined in large bowl of electric mixer. Blend and cool. Add beaten eggs. Add yeast mixture. Then gradually add flour with electric mixer until dough becomes too stiff; blend in remaining flour by hand.

Cover bowl with inverted plate and place in refrigerator to rise. Let rise until double (3 to 4 hours). Separate into 4 portions and place in small (7 1/2 x 5 1/2 x 2 inch) greased loaf pans. Let rise until doubled (30 to 45 minutes). Bake at 350 degrees for about 35 minutes. If browning too fast, cover with a paper towel (it won't burn). If desired, bake in larger loaf pans and make fewer loaves; increase cooking time 5 to 10 minutes.

May be sliced, buttered and frozen. Reheat in foil to thaw. Dough may be used for rolls. This bread requires no kneading. It makes a fairly sweet white bread which is very crumbly when warm, but delicious.

Mrs. Rowland Baldwin, Sr.

EASY CORN BREAD

1 c. white corn meal
1/2 c. flour
1 T. baking powder
1 t. salt

1 egg
1 c. milk
2 T. melted butter

Mix dry ingredients; add slightly beaten egg; add milk, then melted butter. Stir until mixed and pour into greased heated muffin tin or directly into teflon tin. Bake at 400 degrees (preheated) 20 to 25 minutes or until browned.

Mrs. Edwin Simons

YELLOW CORN BREAD

1 c. corn meal, yellow
1 c. flour
1/4 c. sugar
1/2 t. salt

4 t. baking powder
1 egg
1 c. milk
1/4 c. shortening

Mix corn meal, flour, sugar, salt and baking powder. Add egg, milk and shortening. Bake at 425 degrees for 20 to 25 minutes. Makes 12 muffins.

Mrs. James E. Bass

HUSH PUPPIES

1 Jiffy corn muffin
    mix [8 1/2 oz.]
1 egg

1/3 c. milk
1 medium onion,
    coarsely chopped

Stir ingredients in order. Batter may be slightly lumpy. Spoon into deep fat. Fry until golden brown. Serves about 8.

Mrs. Joe Bill Belue

JENNIE DROP CORN CAKES

1 c. sifted corn meal
1 t. salt

Boiling water
2 eggs

Combine corn meal and salt. Pour enough boiling water over corn meal to make a mush-like consistency. Add eggs; beat well. Drop by spoonfuls into hot deep fat. Fry until golden brown. Drain on paper towels. Serve hot with butter.

Mrs. Jack Harding

MEXICAN CORN BREAD

1 c. yellow corn meal
1/2 t. salt
1/2 t. soda
1/3 c. melted shortening
   or bacon drippings
2 eggs, beaten
1 c. cream-style corn

2/3 c. buttermilk [or
   small carton sour cream]
1 c. grated sharp cheese
1 small can green chile
   peppers, drained and
   finely chopped

Combine corn meal, salt and soda. Stir in melted shortening. Add eggs, corn and buttermilk; mix well. Spoon one-half mixture into a greased 12-inch heavy skillet. Sprinkle cheese and chopped peppers over mixture and cover with remaining batter. Bake at 350 degrees for 30 to 45 minutes.

Mrs. David Boice

Mrs. Arthur Cunningham uses 1 cup of sweet milk instead of the buttermilk.

Mrs. Howard Willmann prefers the sour cream and uses 3 teaspoons of baking powder instead of soda. She used a 10 x 13 inch cake pan for thinner corn bread squares.

Mrs. F. R. Coker varies her Mexican Corn Bread by adding 1 large onion, chopped and mixed in with other ingredients. She uses 1 cup of sweet milk, 1 teaspoon soda and 2 teaspoons baking powder. She uses chopped jalapeno peppers (2 to 6 depending on preference) instead of canned green chile peppers.

BANANA MUFFINS

1/2 c. Crisco
1 c. sugar
1 egg
1 1/2 c. flour, sifted
1 t. soda
2 T. warm water
   [to dissolve soda]

1 c. crushed bananas [2]
1 t. nutmeg
1 t. salt
1 t. vanilla

Cream Crisco and sugar. Add each of the remaining ingredients in the order given. Bake at 375 degrees for 20 minutes in small greased muffin pans. After baking, roll in powdered sugar. Makes approximately 2 to 3 dozen very small muffins. If baked the day before serving, do not roll in powdered sugar until just before serving.

Mrs. Julien Moore
Waco, Texas

BROWN SUGAR BEAUTIES
[HEALTH MUFFINS]

2 c. oatmeal
2 c. All Bran
2 c. shredded wheat
1/2 c. wheat germ
1 box [1 lb.] brown sugar

4 eggs
3 t. soda
1 qt. buttermilk
5 c. flour [part
   wholewheat may be used]

Mix all ingredients together and keep in refrigerator covered. Bake muffins as needed at 350 degrees for 10 to 12 minutes. Will keep for 1 month in refrigerator. Serve with honey - a must!

Mrs. Floyd Addington
Jasper, Texas

DATE MUFFINS

3/4 c. sugar
1 box [8 oz.] dates,
   chopped
1 c. pecans, chopped

3 eggs
2 T. [heaping] flour
1 t. vanilla

Mix all ingredients together and put in greased small muffin tins. Bake at 350 degrees for 10 to 15 minutes. Dust with powdered sugar.

Mrs. Connally McKay

MOLASSES MUFFINS

1 c. sugar
1 c. butter
4 egg yolks
1 c. molasses
1 c. sour milk [to make sour
   milk, add 1 t. soda to 1 T.
   hot water and add to regular
   milk]

3 1/2 c. flour
1 t. nutmeg
2 t. ginger
1/2 t. salt
1/2 c. raisins [optional]
1 c. toasted chopped
   pecans
4 egg whites

Cream sugar and butter; add slightly beaten egg yolks and molasses. Sift dry ingredients together and add alternately with milk to the egg mixture. Add raisins and nuts. Beat the egg whites to a peak and fold into mixture. Bake at 450 degrees for 12 to 15 minutes.

Mrs. Will Mann Richardson

This amazing batter may be kept uncooked in the refrigerator for 2 weeks! Stir and place in greased muffin tins (any size) as needed. Marvelous for house guests.

ICE CREAM MUFFINS

1 1/2 c. self-rising flour [If all-purpose flour is used, add 1 T. baking powder and 1 t. salt]
2 c. very soft vanilla ice cream

Measure the ingredients in mixing bowl. Mix only until all dry particles are moistened. Fill well-greased muffin cups three-fourths full. Bake for 20 to 25 minutes at 425 degrees. Makes 8 muffins.

Mrs. Tom Connally

Let the children make this one.

ORANGE MUFFINS

1/2 c. butter	2 c. flour
1 c. sugar	1 c. raisins, ground
2 eggs	1 c. buttermilk
1 t. soda	

Cream butter, add sugar and beaten eggs. Sift soda with flour and add raisins. Add flour and milk to other ingredients. Bake in 350 degree oven until light brown - 15 to 20 minutes.

Syrup:

1 c. brown sugar   1 c. orange juice

Mix and boil 5 minutes. Let cool and dunk muffins. Turn muffins upside down and heat. Serve warm.

Mrs. Eugene Talbert

Try making these in tiny muffin pans to serve at a brunch.

PINEAPPLE YOGURT MUFFINS

2 c. biscuit mix	1/4 c. melted butter
1/2 c. coconut	1 c. pineapple yogurt
1/4 c. sugar	1 egg, slightly beaten
1/2 t. soda	1/2 c. drained, crushed pineapple

Mix biscuit mix, coconut, sugar and soda. Add remaining ingredients. Muffin batter should be slightly lumpy. Bake at 400 degrees for 15 minutes.

Mrs. T. Carleton Billups

Quick, easy, and oh so good!

POPPY SEED MUFFINS

1 1/2 c. Bisquick
1/2 c. sugar
1/2 t. poppy seeds
1 egg

3/4 c. sour cream
1 t. vanilla
3/4 c. seedless raisins
[optional]

Combine biscuit mix, sugar and poppy seeds. Add egg, sour cream and vanilla. Beat for 1 1/2 minutes. Stir in finely chopped raisins. Spoon into greased 2 1/2 inch muffin cups. Bake in moderately hot oven (375 degrees) for 20 to 25 minutes. Makes 1 dozen.

Mrs. Joe Bill Belue

Great for breakfast or drop-in coffee friends.

SIX WEEK MUFFINS

2 c. Nabisco 100% Bran [pellets]
2 c. boiling water
1 c. shortening
2 1/2 c. sugar
4 eggs
5 c. flour

5 t. soda
1 t. salt
1 qt. buttermilk
4 c. Kellogg's All Bran,
    shredded

Soak Nabisco 100% Bran in boiling water until cool. Cream shortening and sugar until fluffy. Add eggs one at a time and combine mixture with 100% Bran. Mix flour, soda and salt, and add alternately with buttermilk to above. Stir in Kellogg's All Bran. Grease muffin tins and fill half full; bake at 400 degrees for 15 to 20 minutes. Always stir before using. Cover unused batter and return to refrigerator. This will keep 6 weeks. A few raisins or blueberries may be added if desired. Wonderful and healthful on a cold morning.

Mrs. M. W. Ziemer

DINNER ROLLS

3/4 c. scalded milk
1/4 c. shortening
1/4 c. butter
1/2 c. sugar
1 1/2 t. salt

2 eggs
2 yeast cakes [dissolved
    in 1/2 c. water]
4 c. flour

Scald milk over hot water. Add shortening, butter, sugar and salt to hot milk. Beat eggs; add yeast (softened) to the eggs. Cool milk to lukewarm; mix with the eggs and yeast. Add flour and let rise until double in bulk. Punch down and place in refrigerator. Roll out in desired shapes. Bake at 375 degrees for 20 minutes. Serves 12 generously and freezes well, before or after baking.

Mrs. Sam Adams
Henderson, Texas

BRAN REFRIGERATOR ROLLS

1 c. shortening
1 c. boiling water
1/2 c. sugar
1 c. Kellogg's All Bran
2 t. salt

2 eggs, well-beaten
2 pkgs. dry yeast
1 c. lukewarm water
6 to 7 c. all-purpose
  flour, sifted

In large bowl, mix first 5 ingredients. Let stand until lukewarm. Beat eggs and add to above mixture. Stir in yeast, dissolved in the cup of lukewarm water. (It will take 5 to 10 minutes to dissolve yeast).

Add 6 cups of flour, gradually, beating as you add them. Beat thoroughly. If dough does not drop from spoon in definite lumps, add some of the seventh cup of flour until it will drop from spoon in lumps. Don't ever add more than 7 cups flour. Dough should be fairly soft, not stiff.

Cover dough tightly and place in refrigerator for several hours. Pinch off bits of dough and form balls (2 or 3) to fill well-greased muffin tins about half full. Let rise until double in size. Bake at 400 degrees for about 20 minutes. Dough will keep in refrigerator for 2 days. If not used the first day, punch down and cover with waxed paper or Handiwrap. Makes about 2 dozen rolls.

Mrs. Glenn Garvin

HOT ROLLS

2 c. milk
1/2 c. sugar
1/2 c. shortening
1 cake yeast
1/4 c. lukewarm water

6 c. flour
1 egg
2 t. salt
1/2 t. soda
1/2 t. baking powder

Heat milk, sugar and shortening until melted. Cool to lukewarm. Soften yeast cake (or package) in water 5 minutes; add to milk mixture. Add 3 cups flour, beat well, and let stand 2 hours.

Add egg, salt, soda, baking powder and stir well. Add 2 cups flour, stirring constantly. Knead in 1 more cup flour. Knead well. Grease top and refrigerate (for several days, if desired).

As needed, roll out and shape or cut, brush with melted butter, and let rise 2 hours. Bake at 350 degrees until light and brown. Makes about 7 dozen.

To freeze, make out rolls, brush with butter, and place in pans; freeze; remove from freezer about 3 1/2 hours before baking. They may be partially baked until faintly brown and then frozen immediately; then when ready to bake remove from freezer and let thaw and finish baking.

Mrs. Gene Caldwell

EASY DO HOT ROLLS

1 pkg. yeast	1 t. salt
2 c. warm water	3 T. butter
1/2 c. sugar	4 to 5 c. flour

Dissolve yeast in warm water. Add other ingredients and enough flour to make firm dough. Cover and let rise until double in bulk in warm place for 1 1/2 to 2 hours. Turn on board and roll 1/4 to 1/2 inch thick; cut with biscuit cutter; dip into melted butter; fold over and place in greased pan with sides. Let rise (covered) until double in bulk (30 to 45 minutes). Bake at 425 degrees for 15 to 20 minutes. Serves 6 to 10 generously.

Rolls may be frozen on cookie sheet after shaped, and put in plastic bag. To use, place in greased pan; cover with cloth and let rise 2 hours. Bake as above. Also, may be shaped into rolls, placed in pan and in refrigerator. Will keep for 2 or 3 days. To use; let rise 1 or 2 hours in warm spot (covered). Bake as above.

Mrs. R. Randall Cape

GRANDIE'S ROLL RECIPE

1 cake Fleishman's yeast	1 egg
2 c. warm water	6 c. flour
1/2 c. sugar	4 T. shortening
1 1/2 t. salt	

Crumble yeast into bowl with water, sugar, salt and well-beaten egg. Add half of flour. Mix well. Add melted shortening and remainder of flour. Knead lightly. Do not get too stiff. Let rise until double in size. Push it down. Cut off about 1/3 of dough for rolls. Put rest of dough in bowl, grease top, cover with plate and refrigerate. Push it down every 12 hours.

When you have pinched off amount you want for loaf or rolls, put in pan with melted shortening on bottom and top. Let rise until double in size. Then bake rolls or loaves at 350 degrees (30 to 35 minutes for loaves; 20 to 25 minutes for rolls). May be frozen after cooked. Yield: 72 rolls; 2 large loaves or 3 small loaves.

Mrs. Rowland Baldwin, Jr.

QUICK BEER ROLLS

4 c. biscuit mix	3 T. sugar
1 bottle or can of beer	

Combine all ingredients. Drop into greased muffin tins. (Fill half full). Let rise 1 hour and bake at 400 degrees 10 to 15 minutes. These are better the second day reheated sealed in foil. Makes about 24 rolls.

Mrs. J. W. Hammett
Ruston, Louisiana

MRS. GOSE'S ROLLS

1 c. boiling water	2 eggs, beaten
1 c. Crisco	2 fresh yeast cakes
3/4 c. sugar	1 c. cold water
1 to 2 t. salt	5 to 6 c. unsifted flour

Pour boiling water over Crisco, sugar and salt. Blend and cool. Add beaten eggs. Soak yeast in the cold water and add to mixture. Add flour and put in refrigerator immediately. (This dough will last for several days in the refrigerator). Try to make day before using.

About 3 hours before using, remove from refrigerator; pinch into small balls; roll in butter and put 3 small balls per muffin cup in a muffin pan for clover leaf rolls. Bake at 375 to 400 degrees for 12 to 15 minutes.

Mrs. Homer Key
Mrs. Jack M. King

Good served with Raleigh House Orange Icing of sifted powdered sugar, butter and frozen orange juice concentrate.

ROLLS

2 yeast cakes	2 eggs
2 c. lukewarm water	6 c. flour
1 c. shortening	1 t. salt
1/3 c. sugar	

Dissolve yeast in water. Cream shortening and sugar with mixer and add eggs. Mix well. Add liquid mixture. When well-mixed, add flour by hand and work well. Dough should be firm, but not stiff. Use about 5 to 5 1/2 cups and the rest will be added when kneading. Refrigerate overnight (covered with a damp cloth). Remove from bowl and knead on well-floured board. Make rolls and let rise (approximately 30 minutes). Brush tops with melted margarine before and (a little) after baking. Bake about 20 minutes at 375 degrees or until golden brown. Rolls may be made up, placed in pans and covered - then refrigerated until about 1 hour before mealtime (same day), then allow to rise and bake. Serves 16.

If you wish to freeze, it is best to bake rolls until almost browned and then freeze.

Mrs. J. B. White, Jr.
Jacksonville, Texas

REFRIGERATOR ROLLS

1 c. scalded milk
1 c. shortening
2 eggs, beaten
3/4 c. sugar
3 t. salt

1 c. cold water
2 yeast cakes
1/2 c. warm water
7 1/2 c. sifted flour

Pour hot milk over shortening and stir until it melts. In another bowl, combine eggs, sugar, salt and cold water and beat until foamy. Soften yeast in warm water. Combine the 3 mixes and add flour. Stir well. Put in large mixing bowl, cover, and chill 4 hours or more before using.

Roll out and cut into rolls. Place on buttered cookie sheet and let rise 1 to 2 hours. Bake at 375 degrees for 12 minutes or until brown. Will make enough rolls for several meals.

Mrs. Wilbert Lasater

Delicious and easy - even for the inexperienced baker.

ONION BUNS

1 1/4 c. finely chopped onion
2 T. margarine
1 pkg. hot roll mix

2 eggs
1 T. milk
1/8 t. salt

Cook onion in margarine until tender (not brown). Remove 2 tablespoons of the onions and set aside remaining. Prepare roll dough to package directions, except add one of the eggs and the 2 tablespoons onion to mixture. Cover and let rise until double in bulk (45 to 60 minutes).

Beat remaining egg slightly, add 1 tablespoon egg mixture to the remaining onion mixture, add milk and salt. With lightly floured hands, shape roll dough into 12 round buns. Place on greased baking sheet and make a large indentation in center with finger. Spoon about 2 teaspoons onion mixture into each indentation. Brush top with reserved egg. Sprinkle with poppy seed, if desired. Cover and let rise until doubled, about 45 to 60 minutes. Bake at 375 degrees for 20 to 25 minutes.

Mrs. Charles Clark

PARMESAN MELBA TOAST

1 loaf French bread   Parmesan cheese
Margarine

Slice French bread very thin - about 1/4 inch. Spread slices with margarine or softened butter; sprinkle with Parmesan cheese. Place on a cookie sheet. Bake in slow oven (325 degrees) about 20 minutes or until very crispy.

Mrs. Robert Y. Brown, Jr.

FRENCH BREAKFAST PUFFS

1/3 c. shortening	1/2 t. salt
1/2 c. sugar	1/4 t. nutmeg
1 egg	6 T. melted butter
1/2 c. milk	1/2 c. sugar
1 1/2 c. sifted flour	1 t. cinnamon
1 1/2 t. baking powder	

Mix shortening, sugar and egg thoroughly. Sift dry ingredients together and add alternately with the milk. Fill greased muffin tins two-thirds full and bake until golden brown. Immediately roll in the melted butter and then in the sugar that has been sifted with the cinnamon. Serve hot. Bake at 350 degrees 20 to 25 minutes. Makes 12 muffins.

Mrs. Wilbert Lasater

LOUISIANA YAM SPICE CUP CAKES

1/3 c. butter	1/4 t. cloves
1 c. sugar	1/4 t. salt
1 c. mashed yams	1/2 t. baking powder
1 egg	1/2 t. soda
1 c. flour	1 c. broken pecans
3/4 t. cinnamon	1/2 c. raisins
3/4 t. nutmeg	1/3 c. buttermilk
1/4 t. allspice	

Cream butter and sugar. Add mashed yams and egg and mix well. Add dry ingredients (to which raisins and nuts have been added) alternately with buttermilk. Pour into muffin tin liners, and bake 25 to 30 minutes in 350 degree oven. Freezes well.

Mrs. Nelson Clyde

Bake in small loaf pans at 350 degrees for 45 to 50 minutes.

CARAWAY PUFFS

1 pkg. dry yeast
2 1/3 c. sifted
   all-purpose flour
1/4 t. baking soda
1 c. cream-style
   cottage cheese
1/4 c. water

2 T. sugar
1 T. butter
1 t. salt
1 egg
2 t. caraway seed
2 t. grated onion

Combine yeast, 1 1/3 c. flour, and soda in a bowl. Heat together the cottage cheese, water, sugar, butter and salt until butter melts. Add to dry ingredients. Add egg, caraway seed and grated onion. Beat at low speed 1/2 minute. Beat 3 minutes at high speed. Stir in 1 cup more flour.

Grease top and let rise until doubled (about 1 1/2 hours).

Divide among 12 well-greased muffin pans. Cover. Let rise about 40 minutes. Bake 400 degrees for 12 to 15 minutes.

Mrs. Marshall Spivey

For a round loaf of bread, bake in an 8-inch round pan at 350 degrees for 40 to 50 minutes.

Vegetables

ROQUEFORT AND ARTICHOKE

1 can [14 oz.] artichoke hearts
1/2 lemon [the juice]
1 pkg. Roquefort cheese
2 t. butter or margarine

Imitation butter salt,
  to taste
Paprika

Drain artichoke hearts and place in small pyrex baking dish. In a double boiler put lemon juice, cut up Roquefort, butter and imitation butter salt. When cheese and butter have melted, spoon liquid over artichokes, sprinkle with paprika, then bake in oven for 30 minutes at 300 to 350 degrees. Marvelous with steaks instead of potatoes. Serves 3 to 4 sparingly.

Mrs. E. D. Fitzpatrick

SUE'S MARINATED ARTICHOKES

1 can artichokes
Wishbone Italian dressing

Parmesan cheese
Parsley, chopped

Marinate drained artichokes overnight in Wishbone Italian dressing. Drain on paper towel and roll in Parmesan cheese and parsley. Serve cold. Serves 4 to 6.

Mrs. James Deakins

ASPARAGUS DELORES

3 eggs
1 c. cracker crumbs
1 c. milk
1 c. grated Velveeta cheese

Pimiento, chopped
1/2 t. salt
2 c. cut asparagus
1/2 stick butter

Mix all ingredients except butter. Bake at 350 degrees in greased baking dish until firm, about 30 minutes. Melt butter and pour over it after it has begun to set.

Mrs. Fred McCoun

MARINATED ASPARAGUS OLÉ

2 cans asparagus spears
1/3 c. wine vinegar
1/4 c. sugar
1/4 c. water

1/2 t. salt
3 whole cloves
1 stick cinnamon
1/2 t. celery seed

Combine all ingredients, except asparagus, and bring to a boil briefly. Then cool, strain and pour over drained asparagus spears. Cover and refrigerate overnight before serving. Serves 6 to 8.

Mrs. Alice White

MARINATED ASPARAGUS

1 c. salad oil
1/3 c. vinegar
1 t. sugar
1 1/2 t. salt
3 T. chopped green onion

2 T. chopped parsley
4 T. chopped green pepper
2 T. chopped pimiento
2 large cans asparagus,
    drained

Combine salad oil, vinegar, sugar and salt. Shake well and add chopped onion, parsley, green pepper and pimiento. Pour over drained asparagus and marinate several hours or overnight.

Mrs. Donald Carroll
Mrs. Wilbert Lasater

ASPARAGUS CASSEROLE

1 large can English peas
1 large can asparagus
1 large can water chestnuts
Bits of pimiento

4 T. butter or margarine
1 can mushroom soup
Bread cubes
Slivered almonds

Drain peas, asparagus and water chestnuts well. Put layer of each with bits of pimiento on each layer to give color and flavor. Dot with 2 tablespoons of butter. Pour the undiluted mushroom soup over the mixture. Dip the bread cubes in the remaining 2 tablespoons of butter, then place on top. Add slivered almonds if desired. Bake in 350 degree oven until bubbly and bread crumbs are browned (about 20 minutes). Serves 6 to 8.

Mrs. Louie Cobb, Jr.

GRANNY'S ASPARAGUS CASSEROLE

2 T. butter
2 T. flour
1 large can asparagus
Milk
Salt and pepper to taste

3 hard boiled eggs
Soft bread crumbs
    [1 slice bread]
Grated cheese

Make a white sauce by melting butter and adding flour to make a paste. Drain juice from asparagus and add enough milk to make 1 cup of liquid. Mix slowly into butter and flour paste. Add salt and pepper. Dice hard boiled eggs into the sauce, reserving several slices. Line baking dish with bread crumbs and layer asparagus on crumbs. Pour sauce over, and top with grated cheese. Garnish with egg slices. Bake at 350 degrees until bubbly. Do not overcook, as eggs will be tough. Serves 4 to 6.

Mrs. F. H. Oberthier
Hereford, Texas

BARBECUED GREEN BEANS

4 slices bacon
1 can whole green beans
1 small can tomato juice
1/2 can tomato purée
1 t. prepared mustard
1 clove garlic, minced

1 t. Worcestershire sauce
1 t. grated onion
Dash of Tabasco
Dash of salt and pepper
Dash of sugar

Cut bacon slices in half. Wrap bacon around 6-7 beans and secure with toothpick. (Should have 8 "bundles" of beans). Place in shallow baking dish. Mix remaining ingredients and pour over beans. Cover dish and bake at 250 degrees for 1 hour. Remove cover during last 15 minutes of baking.

Mrs. A. E. Dennis

 Bacon may be precooked slightly before wrapping beans if crisper bacon is desired.

CHRISTMAS BEANS

1 can [16 oz.] whole
  green beans
1/2 c. olive oil
3 T. garlic vinegar
1/4 t. fresh ground pepper
1 T. chopped pimiento

1 T. sweet pickle relish
1 T. capers, chopped
1 T. chopped chives or
  green onion tops
Pinch of salt, sugar,
  paprika and red pepper

Drain beans completely and put in jar. Combine oil, vinegar, and pepper in a jar and shake together well. Pour over beans and refrigerate 24 hours. When ready to serve (either hot or cold) drain off juice (if served hot, leave a little juice). Mix pimiento, relish, capers, chives, salt, sugar, paprika and red pepper, and garnish. Serves 6.

Mrs. S. W. Brookshire

GREEN BEANS EXCELSIOR HOUSE

1/2 lb. bacon strips, cut
  in half
2 cans vertical packed
  green beans
1 c. bean juice

1/4 c. brown sugar
Dash salt
Dash pepper
1/2 t. allspice

Wrap half-slices of bacon around 10 to 12 beans; fasten with toothpicks. Mix bean juice and brown sugar together and pour over beans. Sprinkle salt, pepper and allspice over arranged beans. Bake at 375 to 400 degrees for 25 minutes. Turn once during cooking and baste. Overcooking shrivels the beans. Serves 8 to 10.

Mrs. Allen M. Burt

GREEN BEAN CASSEROLE I

2 cans green beans [long or cut Blue Lake]
Salt to taste
Bacon grease to taste

1 can golden mushroom soup
Caraway seeds
Sharp Cheddar cheese, grated
1 can fried onion rings

Heat beans in saucepan. A dash of salt and a little bacon grease may be added for flavor if desired. Drain beans thoroughly after heated and simmered a minute. Put in ungreased deep casserole dish and pour soup over beans. Spread evenly, then sprinkle caraway seeds over the top. Cover with grated sharp Cheddar cheese and bake 30 minutes at 350 degrees or until bubbly.

Sprinkle onion rings on top and replace in oven for 5 to 10 minutes until lightly browned.

Can be easily doubled for large crowd. Can be prepared ahead of time and refrigerated, without onion rings, then add onion rings after first baking as noted above.

Mrs. Lee Lawrence

Mrs. Mike Hatchell omits caraway seeds and used 2 packages frozen green beans, plus 1 can water chestnuts (sliced thin) and 1/2 cup milk.

GREEN BEAN CASSEROLE II

2 cans whole green beans
1 large [or 2 small] garlic cloves
1 can cream of mushroom soup

1 1/2 c. grated Cheddar cheese
2 T. slivered almonds [optional]

Boil beans with garlic about 5 minutes. Remove garlic, drain beans, Layer beans, soup, and cheese in 1 1/2 quart casserole, ending with cheese or, if using almonds, put them only on top. Bake at 325 degrees about 20 minutes. Serves 8.

Mrs. J. Lawrence Neill

MARINATED GREEN BEANS

2 cans green beans
Pimiento
Parsley
Italian dressing

Sauce:

1 c. sour cream
1/2 c. mayonnaise
1 t. lemon juice
1 t. anchovy paste
1/4 t. mustard
1 T. horseradish
1/4 t. onion juice

Marinate green beans, pimiento, and parsley for 24 hours in Italian dressing. After marinating, drain beans. Combine all the sauce ingredients and pour over beans.

Mrs. Luther Kay, Jr.

HERBED GREEN BEANS

3 cans French style green
  beans
4 thinly sliced onions
2 T. butter

1 T. dried tarragon
3/4 T. dried sage
2 1/2 t. salt
Liberal pinch of pepper

Drain beans and put in saucepan. Saute' onions in butter until clear. Add spices. Pour over beans. Toss and heat. Serves 8.

Mrs. Frank Fite

SWISS BEANS

1 can green beans
  [slant or French cut]
2 T. butter
2 T. flour
1/2 pt. sour cream

Salt and pepper to taste
1/2 t. sugar
1 t. grated onion [or
  dehydrated onion flakes]
1/4 lb. Swiss cheese

Drain green beans and place in a buttered dish. Melt butter, add flour and stir until blended. Blend in sour cream, stirring continuously, and then add salt, pepper, sugar and onion. Pour mixture over beans and add grated Swiss cheese. Sprinkle with paprika. Bake in moderate oven until cheese is melted and beans are bubbling hot. Serves 4 to 6. This casserole freezes fairly well for a short period of time.

Mrs. James Milstead

GREEN LIMA BEANS WITH MUSHROOMS AND CELERY

2 pkgs. frozen green lima
  beans
2 lbs. fresh mushrooms
  or 1 large can
1 medium onion
5 stalks crisp celery
1/4 lb. butter

2 T. flour
1/2 t. salt
1/2 t. nutmeg
1/8 t. pepper
1/2 c. heavy cream
1 or 2 T. sherry
Dash paprika

Cook beans according to directions. Wipe mushrooms with damp cloth (if canned, drain well). Mince onion; cut celery in 1/2 inch pieces about as thick as a match. Saute' onion and celery in butter until golden, then add mushrooms; cook gently until tender. Sprinkle in flour, salt, nutmeg and pepper. Toss until well-blended. Reduce heat and blend in cream. Add to well-drained beans. Add sherry just before serving. Dust with paprika. Serves 8 to 10.

Mrs. Joe Huffstutler

HARRY'S PINTO BEANS

1 lb. pinto beans
1 dried chili pepper, chopped
   or 1/2 T. crushed red pepper
1 clove garlic, chopped fine

1/4 lb. cut up salt pork
1 T. comino seed
1 T. salt

Soak beans overnight in enough cold water to cover them. Cook slowly for 1 hour (covered) in the water in which they soaked. Fry chili pepper, garlic and salt pork together for a few minutes. Add fried ingredients, comino seed, and salt to beans and continue cooking slowly for about three more hours. If you wish to thicken beans at end of cooking time, remove 1/2 cup of beans, mash them and fold them back into rest of beans. Add more seasonings if desired.

Mrs. C. Aubrey Smith, Jr.

Try this for a "Sunday night supper" served with salad and corn bread.

THE LOWLY BEAN

2 cans [medium size] pork
   and beans
1 c. catsup
3 T. Worcestershire sauce

1/4 lb. bacon, cut into
   strips
3/4 c. brown sugar

Mix beans, catsup and Worcestershire sauce together. Place in shallow baking dish. Cover with bacon. Spread brown sugar on top. Bake at 350 degrees for about 1 hour. Serves 6 to 8.

Mrs. Walter L. Johnson

BROCCOLI BAKE

1/4 c. finely chopped onion
6 T. butter
2 T. flour
1/2 c. water
8 oz. Old English cheese

2 pkgs. frozen chopped
   broccoli, well-drained
3 eggs
1/2 c. cracker crumbs

Saute' onion in 4 tablespoons of the butter until soft. Stir in flour, add water, cook over low heat, stirring until sauce thickens. Blend in cheese. Combine sauce and cooked broccoli (prepared according to package directions). Add well-beaten eggs. Mix until blended and turn into greased 1 1/2 quart casserole. Cover with crumbs and dot with remaining 2 tablespoons butter. Bake for 30 minutes at 325 degrees. Serves 8 to 10.

Mrs. John H. Minton, Jr.

BROCCOLI CASSEROLE I

1 small onion, chopped
1 c. rice
1 pkg. frozen chopped broccoli

1 small jar Cheez-Whiz
1 can mushroom soup

Saute' onion in small amount of butter until pale gold. Cook rice and broccoli separately. Then mix onion, butter, rice, broccoli, cheese and soup together. May be put in a casserole and kept warm until served. May be prepared in advance and reheated. Serves 6.

Mrs. Robert L. Caton, III
Mrs. W. H. Watson, Jr.

Mrs. Robert Bergfeld suggests this recipe with the addition of 1/2 cup celery (to be cooked with onion) and 1 can cream of chicken soup combined with the mushroom soup. She bakes her casserole 20 minutes at 375 degrees.

BROCCOLI CASSEROLE II

2 large onions, chopped
1 stick margarine
6 pkgs. frozen chopped
   broccoli
4 cans cream of mushroom
   soup
3 rolls garlic cheese

2 t. Accent
Dash of salt
1 large can whole mushrooms
3/4 c. chopped almonds
   [optional]
1 c. bread crumbs

Saute onions in margarine. Add broccoli (partially thawed), stir and cook 5 minutes. Add mushroom soup, cheese spread, Accent, salt, mushrooms, 1/2 cup almonds, and 3/4 cup bread crumbs. Reserve 1/4 cup almonds and 1/4 cup bread crumbs to sprinkle on top. Pour in buttered baking dish. Bake about 30 minutes at 350 degrees. Divide into 2 or 3 baking dishes for serving about 8 each. Serves about 24.

Mrs. J. Lawrence Neill

Easy to prepare, freeze, and serve to a group.

SESAME BROCCOLI

1 lb. fresh broccoli
   [or 1 frozen 10 oz. pkg.]
1 T. salad oil
1 T. vinegar

1 T. soy sauce
4 t. sugar
1 T. sesame seed, toasted

Cook broccoli in small amount of boiling water about 15 minutes, or until tender. Drain. In a small saucepan combine oil, vinegar, soy sauce, sugar, and sesame seed. Heat to boiling. Pour sauce over hot broccoli, turning spears to coat. Serve immediately. Serves 4.

Mrs. Jack Harper

CABBAGE-CELERY COMBINATION

1 1/2 c. coarsely chopped
   cabbage
1 c. celery, cut in 1 in.
   pieces
1 t. salt
1/4 c. boiling water
2 T. flour

3 T. melted margarine
2 c. milk
1 t. salt
1/4 t. pepper
1 c. grated cheese
1/2 c. buttered bread crumbs

Cook vegetables in boiling salted water for about 3 minutes; drain. Make a white sauce by blending flour with melted margarine; gradually add milk, salt and pepper. Cook until thickened, stirring constantly. Arrange cabbage and celery and white sauce in layers in a buttered casserole. Top with cheese and crumbs. Bake at 275 degrees for 1 hour. Serves 4.

Mrs. Rowland Baldwin, Sr.

 To serve more, use same amount of sauce on 1 head of cabbage and 1 stalk of celery cooked in 2 cups of water.

GERMAN RED CABBAGE

4 slices bacon, chopped
1/4 c. onion, chopped
6 T. brown sugar

3 T. vinegar
4 c. shredded cabbage
   [about 1 head]

Fry bacon. Add onion and saute' slightly. Add brown sugar and vinegar. Add cabbage and simmer over low heat 20 minutes. Makes 12 servings.

Mrs. Frank Budde

CARROT RING

1 c. shortening
1/2 c. brown sugar
1 egg
1 T. water
2 c. grated carrots
1 1/2 c. sifted flour

1/2 t. baking soda
1 t. baking powder
1/2 t. nutmeg
1/2 t. salt
1/2 t. cinnamon

Cream the shortening and brown sugar well. Mix in other ingredients and place in ring mold that has been lightly greased with butter or Wesson oil. Let set 5 to 6 hours or overnight. Remove from refrigerator one-half hour before baking. Bake 1 hour at 350 degrees or until firm. Place on platter and fill center with seasoned English peas. Serves 6.

Mrs. E. B. Yale

 Unusual, pretty and good.

DILLED CARROTS

1 bunch carrots
1/4 c. onion, chopped fine
1/4 c. Green Goddess dressing
1/4 c. Wishbone Italian
    dressing
1 t. chopped parsley

1/4 to 1/2 t. pepper
1/2 t. sugar
1 T. dill weed
1/4 t. salt

Peel and slice carrots into 3 inch sticks. Cook until just done; the carrots should be crisp. Drain and cool. Combine remaining ingredients. Add carrots and marinate overnight. Serves 6 to 8.

Mrs. Richard Grainger

GINGER CARROTS

1 med. to large onion
3 T. butter
1 1/2 bunches carrots,
    shredded or grated
3/4 c. water

1 1/2 t. lemon juice
[or more]
3/4 t. ginger
1 1/2 T. sugar
1 t. salt

Sauté onion in butter and place in a two quart casserole. Add carrots. Mix remaining ingredients and pour over carrots. Cover and bake at 350 degrees for one hour (or less, since these should be slightly crunchy). Serves 6.

Mrs. A. M. Limmer, Jr.

MUSTARD-GLAZED CARROTS

2 lbs. carrots
1 t. salt
3 T. butter

3 T. prepared mustard
1/4 c. brown sugar
1/4 c. chopped parsley

Peel and slice carrots. Cook in boiling salted water, covered, for 20 minutes. Cook butter, mustard, and sugar in saucepan until syrupy and pour over drained carrots. Sprinkle with parsley.

Mrs. Joe D. Clayton

ORANGE COMPANY CARROTS

4 c. sliced carrots
3 T. orange juice
1 t. salt
1 t. cinnamon

3 t. sugar
2 T. water
3 T. butter

Place all ingredients, except butter, in saucepan and slowly bring to a boil. Simmer covered for 30 minutes. When tender, stir in butter. Serves 8.

Mrs. Scott Evans

CARROTS GRAND MARNIER

3 lbs. carrots
1 stick margarine or butter
2 c. sugar

1 jar [10 oz.] sweet
  orange marmalade
1 1/4 c. Grand Marnier

Scrape and slice carrots, either in thin finger size or round. Cook until tender. In a large skillet, melt margarine and add 1 cup sugar and orange marmalade. Simmer until sugar is melted and not grainy, about 10 minutes. Add drained, cooked carrots, remaining sugar and 1 cup Grand Marnier. Simmer, uncovered, until carrots are shiny and candied, about 30 minutes. Add remainder of Grand Marnier. Remove from sauce to serve. Serves 6 to 8.

Mrs. Frank Fite

COPPER CARROT PENNIES

2 lbs. carrots, sliced
1 small green pepper,
  sliced into rings
1 med. onion, thinly sliced
1 can tomato soup

1 c. sugar [or less]
3/4 c. vinegar
1 t. prepared mustard
1 t. Worcestershire sauce
Salt and pepper to taste

Cook carrots in slightly salted water until tender. Cool. Alternate layers of carrots, green pepper rings and onion slices in dish. Combine the remaining ingredients. Stir until well-blended. Pour over vegetables and refrigerate at least 24 hours. Serves 8.

Mrs. Ted Chilcote
Mrs. John Warner

Mrs. Glenn Collins and Mrs. Stanley Robertson vary their Marinated Carrots by eliminating the mustard and adding 1/2 cup salad oil.

BAKED STUFFED CAULIFLOWER

1 c. salted water
1 head cauliflower
2 T. butter
2 T. flour
1 c. milk
1/2 t. salt
1/2 t. pepper

2 hard-cooked eggs, chopped
2 T. pimiento, chopped
3/4 c. green onions,
  finely chopped
1/2 c. buttered bread crumbs
2 t. Cheddar cheese, grated

Place whole cauliflower in boiling, salted water, cover and cook until tender, about 15 minutes. Remove from pan. Cool. Melt butter and add flour, then milk. Cook until thick and smooth. Add salt, pepper, eggs, pimiento and green onions. Simmer 5 minutes. Place cauliflower in greased baking dish. Remove top gently and scoop out center. Fill center with sauce and replace top. Pour remaining sauce over cauliflower. Sprinkle with crumbs and cheese. Bake in 375 degree oven for 25 to 30 minutes. Serves 4.

Mrs. Fred Bosworth

ALMOND CELERY CASSEROLE

6 c. sliced [1 inch pieces]
  celery
1 c. cream of mushroom soup
1/4 to 1/2 lb. fresh, sautéed
  mushrooms
1/2 c. milk

1 T. butter
1/2 t. salt
1/8 t. pepper
1/2 c. blanched almonds
1/2 c. bread or cracker
  crumbs

Use young inner ribs of celery and parboil until tender. Mix remaining ingredients and put in greased casserole. Bake at 400 degrees for 20 minutes. Serves 6 to 8.

Mrs. Allen M. Burt

BRAISED CELERY WITH TOASTED ALMONDS

3 1/2 c. sliced celery
1 1/2 c. chicken broth
1/4 t. salt
4 t. flour
1 1/2 T. butter or margarine,
  softened

1 egg yolk
2 T. cream
1 1/16 t. ground white
  pepper
1/3 c. toasted slivered
  almonds

Place celery, 1 cup chicken broth and salt in saucepan. Cover and cook 5 minutes or until celery is crisp-tender. Blend flour with butter. Add to celery along with remaining 1/2 cup chicken broth. Mix egg yolk with cream and white pepper. Blend into celery mixture. Cook and stir over low heat 2 to 3 minutes or until the sauce is medium thick. Serve sprinkled with almonds and garnish with chopped chives, if desired. Serves 4 to 6.

Mrs. R. Terry Graham, Jr.

ORIENTAL CELERY

4 c. celery, cut on diagonal,
  1/2 in. slices
1/4 c. pimiento, chopped
1 can [5 oz.] water chestnuts,
  sliced thin

1 can cream of chicken soup
1/4 c. blanched almonds
Cracker or bread crumbs

Boil celery until tender - about 5 minutes. Drain and add pimientos, water chestnuts and soup. Stir until well-blended. Put in casserole and top with cracker crumbs, almonds and paprika. Dot with butter or margarine. Bake in a 350 degree oven 35 to 45 minutes until top is crusty and brown. Serves 6.

Mrs. T. Carlton Billups

Mrs. Moliere Scarborough, Jr. prepares this dish using celery soup (instead of chicken) and adding 1/4 cup chopped ripe olives.

CORN CASSEROLE

1 can creamed corn
3 eggs
1 large T. butter
3/4 c. milk

1 T. sugar
3 t. flour
Salt and pepper

Mix all ingredients together and bake in 350 degree oven for 1 hour. This serves 4 generously.

Mrs. S. W. Brookshire

This is a real family favorite and easy to prepare.

CORN-CHEESE BAKE

3 c. uncooked corn cut
   from cob
2 T. finely chopped onion
1/2 t. salt
1 t. pepper

1 c. shredded Swiss cheese
6 T. butter
1/2 c. evaporated milk,
   undiluted

Dot bottom of 1 1/2 or 2 quart casserole with 3 tablespoons of butter. Combine corn, onion, salt, pepper and half the shredded cheese, and pour into casserole. Sprinkle top with remaining cheese and dot with 3 more tablespoons of butter. Add milk and bake uncovered about 30 minutes or until corn is tender and cheese has melted. Serve piping hot.

Mrs. Shirley Simons, Jr.

CORN PUDDING I

1 can cream corn
1 egg
1/2 green pepper, chopped
2 oz. pimiento, chopped
Dyhydrated or fresh onion,
   chopped

Salt
Pepper
Ritz crackers, crumbled
Margarine
Paprika

Lightly grease one quart casserole. In another bowl mix together the corn, egg, green pepper, pimiento and onion (half of small fresh onion). Season to your taste and pour in greased casserole. Cover and bake at 400 degrees until it starts to cook, then reduce heat to 325 degrees for approximately 30 minutes or until an inserted knife comes out clean. Remove from oven, allow to cool; then sprinkle heavily with cracker crumbs, dot with margarine, and sprinkle with paprika. Return to oven at same temperature until pudding is hot and lightly browned. Serves 4. This can be made 48 hours before and refrigerated.

Mrs. Alice White

CORN PUDDING II

1 can [1 lb.] cream style
  corn
Salt and pepper to taste
2 eggs
1/2 to 3/4 c. milk

3/4 c. Pepperidge Farm
  stuffing
2 T. margarine, cut in
  small pieces

Mix all ingredients and let stand uncovered in greased casserole for 1 hour or more. Sprinkle top with 1/2 cup more stuffing mix. Bake at 350 degrees for 30 minutes or until firm. Serves 4 to 6.

Mrs. Henry D. McCallum

CORN SCALLOP

1 can [17 oz.] cream style corn
2 eggs, beaten
1/2 c. crushed soda crackers
1/4 c. melted butter
1/4 c. undiluted evaporated
  milk
1/4 c. finely shredded carrot
1/4 c. chopped green pepper

1 T. chopped celery
1 T. chopped onion
6 drops Tabasco
1/2 t. sugar
1/2 t. salt
1/2 c. shredded Cheddar
  cheese
Paprika

Combine corn and all ingredients except the cheese. Mix and turn into a greased 8 x 8 x 2 inch baking dish.

Top with cheese and sprinkle with paprika. Bake at 350 degrees 30 minutes or until mixture is set and top is golden brown. Serves 6 to 8.

Mrs. Joe Herrington

CORN WITH TAMALES

1 onion, chopped
1/2 green pepper, diced
Small jar pimiento
1 can hot tamales

2 cans cream corn
Salt and pepper to taste
1 c. sharp Cheddar
  cheese, grated

Steam onion, pepper and pimiento in juice from tamales. Cut tamales into bite-size pieces. Add corn, tamales, salt and pepper to sauce mixture. Bake in 1 1/2 quart casserole at 350 degrees for 1 hour or until mixture thickens. Top with grated cheese just before serving and return to oven until cheese melts. Serves 6 to 8.

Mrs. C. Aubrey Smith, Jr.

HENRY BELL LAKEHOUSE CORN

1 large green pepper
1 large onion
3 T. bacon drippings
1 can [#2] creamed corn

1 can [#2] tomatoes,
    drained
1/4 c. tapioca
1/2 c. grated cheese

Chop pepper and onion; brown in bacon drippings. Add corn and tomatoes and blend. Add tapioca and cheese. Place in casserole and bake at 350 degrees about 20 minutes.

Mrs. Henry M. Bell, Sr.

EGGPLANT

1 eggplant
1 egg
1/4 c. milk
Cracker crumbs
Cooking oil
1 small onion

1 or 2 tomatoes
1 bell pepper
1 c. cheese [American or
    Cheddar], grated
Salt and pepper to taste

Peel and slice eggplant. Dip eggplant slices into a mixture of beaten egg and milk and then into cracker crumbs. Saute' in cooking oil until brown. Drain.

Chop onion, tomato (may use canned tomatoes) and bell pepper. Layer eggplant, onion, pepper, tomato, cheese, salt and pepper in a casserole. Top with more cracker crumbs. Bake at 350 degrees for 30 minutes. Serves 6 to 8.

Mrs. Robert Ungerecht

EGGPLANT PATRICE

1 eggplant
2 T. butter
2 T. oil
4 fresh tomatoes, sliced
1 green bell pepper, chopped
1 large onion, chopped

1 t. salt [more to taste]
1/4 t. cracked pepper
1/4 t. garlic powder
3/4 lb. Cheddar cheese,
    sliced

Slice unpeeled eggplant 1/4 inch thick. Saute' in oil and butter until partially tender. Place a layer of eggplant slices in a 13 x 9 x 3 inch casserole. Add a layer of sliced tomatoes. Fill spaces with a mixture of chopped pepper and onion. Sprinkle with salt, pepper, garlic powder; add a layer of sliced cheese. Repeat layers until casserole is filled, ending with cheese. Cover and bake at 400 degrees until mixture is steaming. Remove foil cover; reduce heat to 350 degrees and bake 30 to 45 minutes, or until eggplant is tender and sauce is thick and golden brown. Serves 6 to 8.

Mrs. James Milstead

BAKED EGGPLANT

Eggplant
Bread crumbs [3 slices bread]
1/2 green pepper
1/2 grated onion

Few drops of Tabasco sauce
2 eggs, beaten
1/4 c. milk
2 strips of bacon

Core eggplant. Boil covered in half pan of water about 30 minutes or until it is done on all sides. Turn it as it cooks. Peel and mash eggplant. Add rolled bread crumbs, green pepper (chopped fine), one-half grated onion, few drops of Tabasco sauce, beaten eggs and milk. Put in greased pyrex dish with two strips of bacon across top. Bake at 375 degrees for 30 minutes. Serves 6.

Mrs. Moliere Scarborough, Jr.

EGGPLANT CASSEROLE

1 large eggplant
1 t. sugar
1 green pepper, chopped
1 large onion, chopped
2 T. butter
Lea and Perrins sauce

Red pepper to taste
Garlic salt to taste
1 can mushroom soup
1 lb. raw shrimp
1 c. cracker crumbs
3/4 lb. cheese, grated

Peel eggplant and cut into approximately 1 inch cubes. Cook in small amount of water with sugar until tender. Drain. Saute' onion and green pepper in butter and add to eggplant. Add dashes of Lea and Perrins, red pepper and garlic salt. Add mushroom soup, shrimp, cracker crumbs and half of cheese. Place in a casserole dish and bake at 350 degrees for 1 hour. Top with remainder of cheese and melt under broiler. Serves 6 to 8.

Mrs. Upton Beall

EGGPLANT FARSI

1 eggplant
1 c. flaked crabmeat
1 small can mushrooms,
  undrained
1 small can tomatoes,
  undrained

1 T. melted butter or
  olive oil
Salt, pepper, celery seed
Garlic as desired
1/2 c. bread crumbs

Remove stem end from eggplant. Scoop out center, leaving a thin shell. Cook in boiling water until tender, but not soft, and set aside to cool. Cook pulp of eggplant in salted water until tender. Drain and add crabmeat, mushrooms, tomatoes and butter or oil. Season to taste with salt, pepper, celery seed and garlic. Fill shell with mixture, sprinkle with bread crumbs, bits of butter and green pepper or pimiento garnish if desired. Bake in greased pan at 325 degrees for 30 minutes or until brown.

Mrs. Henry M. Bell, Sr.

EGGPLANT SOUFFLÉ

1 medium eggplant
1/2 can mushroom soup
3 eggs, separated
Salt to taste

1/2 c. bread crumbs
1/2 c. grated sharp
   cheese
2 T. butter

Peel eggplant; slice and cook until tender in boiling salted water. Mash and mix in soup, beaten egg yolks and salt. Beat egg whites and fold in. Cover with buttered bread crumbs mixed with grated sharp cheese. Bake 45 minutes at 350 degrees.

Mrs. Tom Ramey, Sr.

HOMINY CASSEROLE

1 small onion, grated
1 small green pepper, minced
6 T. melted butter
6 T. flour
2 t. salt
1 t. dry mustard
Dash cayenne pepper
3 c. milk

1 1/2 c. shredded Cheddar
   cheese
1 small can ripe olives,
   sliced
2 large cans white hominy,
   drained
Buttered crumbs

Cook onion and green pepper in butter about 5 minutes. Stir in flour and seasonings. Add milk. Stir and cook until thick. Stir in cheese and add olives. Fill a large baking dish with hominy. Pour sauce over and cover with buttered crumbs. Bake at 350 degrees for 20 to 30 minutes. Serves 8 to 10.

Mrs. Foster Murphy

CREOLE HOMINY

1 chopped onion
1/2 chopped bell pepper
3 T. cooking oil
1 can tomatoes
1 t. chili powder
Worcestershire sauce

Salt
Pepper
Small amount catsup
1 can hominy
Cheddar cheese

Brown onion and green pepper in oil. Add tomatoes. Season with chili powder, Worcestershire, salt, pepper, and catsup. Simmer 10 to 15 minutes. Drain liquid from hominy and spread evenly in greased casserole. Pour sauce over hominy. Sprinkle grated cheese over top. Bake at 350 degrees for 30 minutes. Serves 6 to 8.

Mrs. Watson Simons

AUNT DOT'S HOMINY

2 large cans hominy,
  white or yellow
3 T. grated onion
1 1/2 c. Monterey Jack cheese
2 cans green chiles, cut in
  small pieces

1 1/2 c. sour cream
Salt to taste
1/2 c. buttered crumbs

Mix ingredients and put in greased casserole and bake 30 minutes at 350 degrees. Serves 12.

Mrs. Robert D. Rice

Very good and easy to fix.

OKRA AND TOMATOES

1 medium onion, diced
2 T. bacon drippings
1 lb. okra [whole pod or cut]
1 lb. tomatoes, diced
  [or 1 can 15 1/2 oz.]

2 t. Worcestershire sauce
1 T. brown sugar
1 t. salt
1/4 t. pepper

Saute' onion in bacon drippings. Add okra, tomatoes and seasonings. Simmer over low heat for about 20 minutes or until okra is tender. Serves 6 to 8.

Mrs. C. Aubrey Smith, Jr.

Two packages frozen okra may be substituted for fresh okra. Tomatoes may need to be increased by using tomato sauce or tomato juice. Tomato juice is excellent to provide liquid for reheating.

SCALLOPED ONIONS

4 c. thinly sliced sweet
  onions
2 1/2 c. milk
2 T. butter or margarine
2 T. flour

3/4 t. salt
1/4 t. pepper
Seasoned croutons
Sharp cheese, grated

Cook onions in milk, simmering until tender. Drain and reserve liquid. Make a cream sauce of butter, flour and milk from the onions. Season with salt and pepper. In a greased 2 quart casserole, put one-half the onions. Cover with a layer of croutons and a layer of cheese and one-half the cream sauce. Repeat all layers, ending with sauce. Sprinkle with paprika. Bake for 30 minutes at 350 degrees. Serves 5 or 6.

Mrs. Thomas R. Swann

An enamel pan may be used to boil the onions in milk.

FRENCH FRIED MUSHROOMS

Fresh mushrooms [not canned]
1/2 c. flour
1 t. baking powder

Pinch of salt
1 egg
Milk

Clean mushrooms with damp cloth or net and let dry. Mix flour, baking powder and salt. Blend in egg, lightly beaten, and enough milk to make a batter the consistency of heavy cream. Dip dried mushrooms (batter won't stick if they are wet) in batter and deep fry in hot grease until lightly browned. Serve with tartar sauce.

Mrs. J. Torrey Forman

FRENCH FRIED ONION RINGS

2 large Bermuda onions
2 well-beaten eggs
1 c. milk

Flour
Deep fat

Slice onions 1/8 inch thick and separate into rings. Roll each ring in flour, dip in mixture of eggs and milk, and then in flour again. Fry until brown in very hot deep fat. Remove, drain on paper towels, and hide while the steaks are broiling. Serves 6.

Mrs. Wilbert Lasater

SWEET AND SOUR ONIONS

6 onions
1/4 c. water
1/4 c. vinegar

1/4 c. sugar
1/2 stick butter
Salt and pepper to taste

Slice onions 1/4 inch thick. Place in casserole with tight lid. Add other ingredients and bake one hour covered and 1/2 to 1 hour uncovered at 350 degrees. Serves 4 to 6.

Mrs. M. B. Zeppa

ENGLISH PEA CASSEROLE

2 T. chopped onion
1 can mushroom soup
1 can tiny [LeSueur] peas
Bread crumbs

Cheddar cheese, grated
Pimiento
Mushrooms

Mix chopped onion in mushroom soup. Drain English peas. Alternate bread crumbs, peas, soup, cheese, chopped pimiento and mushrooms in a casserole and sprinkle with bread crumbs. Bake in 350 degree oven for 30 minutes or until well-heated. Serves 6.

Mrs. E. B. Yale

ENGLISH PEAS IN PATTY SHELLS

1/2 stick margarine
1 onion, chopped
1 small can button mushrooms
2 cans of peas

1 small jar pimiento, cut up
2 to 3 t. flour
Milk
12 patty shells

Saute' onion in melted margarine. Add mushrooms. Drain a little juice from cans of peas and add. Add pimiento. Thicken mixture with flour stirred into milk. When thickened to desired consistency, serve in patty shells. Serves 12.

Mrs. E. J. Mooney, Jr.
Chicago, Illinois

DELMONICO POTATOES

9 medium potatoes
1/3 c. butter
1/3 c. flour
2 1/4 c. light cream
2 t. salt

1/8 t. pepper
1 pkg. [4 oz.] shredded
    Cheddar cheese
3 T. dried bread crumbs

In large covered saucepan, cook whole unpeeled potatoes in 1 inch boiling salt water until tender (don't let water boil away - add water if needed). Drain and cool. Peel and dice potatoes. Melt butter in saucepan. Stir in flour to make smooth roux. Gradually add cream, stirring constantly until sauce is thick. Add salt and pepper. Gently add potatoes. Pour into greased baking dish. Sprinkle with cheese and bread crumbs. Bake at 375 degrees for 25 minutes. Serves 12.

Mrs. Joe D. Clayton

SCALLOPED POTATOES

4 large potatoes, sliced
1 onion, in rings
Salt and pepper to taste
1 can cream of mushroom soup

1 soup can of milk
Butter
Grated cheese

Alternate potatoes and onions. Add salt and pepper to taste. Top with mushroom soup and milk. Dot with butter. Cover and cook at 350 degrees for 1 hour. When done, grate cheese over top. Serves 8.

Mrs. Bobby Dodd

EASY SCALLOPED POTATOES

6 to 8 c. sliced potatoes
1 can Cheddar cheese soup
1 can cream of mushroom soup

1/2 to 1 white onion,
sliced
8 slices Velveeta cheese

Grease casserole dish and mix soups and onion. Stir in potatoes. Add half of potato mixture, then 4 slices cheese. Dot with butter and repeat. Cover and bake 1 hour or more at 350 degrees.

Mrs. Allen M. Burt

HOLIDAY SWEET POTATO CASSEROLE

2 cans [1 lb. 1 oz.] whole
sweet potatoes, undrained
1 can [8 3/4 oz.] crushed
pineapple, undrained
1/8 t. nutmeg

1/2 t. salt
2 T. brown sugar
1/4 c. butter or margarine,
melted

Crunchy Topping:

1/3 c. brown sugar, firmly
packed
1/2 c. butter or margarine

2 c. cornflakes

Place potatoes in large mixing bowl. Mash with electric mixer (or masher) until smooth. Add pineapple, nutmeg, salt, brown sugar and melted butter; mix with fork or mixer until well-combined. Turn into a 1 1/2 or 2 quart shallow baking dish, spreading evenly.

Make crunchy topping: Melt butter or margarine and brown sugar in large sauce pan. Add cornflakes and toss until cereal is well coated. Sprinkle evenly over sweet potato mixture.

Bake, uncovered, at 375 degrees for 30 minutes, or until topping is brown and crisp. Serves 8 to 10.

Mrs. L. Glenn Taylor

Sweet potato mixture may be prepared a day ahead and the topping added before baking.

SWEET POTATOES HAWAIIAN

4 c. [2 cans] sweet potatoes,
cooked and mashed
1 c. drained crushed pineapple

1/2 c. packed brown sugar
3 T. butter or margarine
Dash ground cloves

Combine all ingredients and turn the mixture into a 1 1/2 quart casserole. Bake in moderate 350 degree oven for 25 minutes or until bubbly hot. Serves 6 to 8.

Mrs. Paul Wick

SWEET POTATO CASSEROLE

1/2 lemon
1/2 orange
1 large can sweet potatoes
1 can [9 oz.] crushed
 pineapple

1/2 c. brown sugar
1/2 c. melted butter
 [1 stick]
1/2 t. salt
1/2 c. shredded coconut

Slice thinly the lemon and orange. Alternate layers of sliced sweet potatoes and the fruit in greased casserole. Mix the crushed pineapple, brown sugar, melted butter and salt and pour over the layered potatoes. Sprinkle coconut on top. Bake at 350 degrees for 30 minutes. Serves 6 to 8.

Mrs. Charles Clark

SWEET POTATOES SUPREME

4 c. cooked, grated
 sweet potatoes
1 1/2 T. cinnamon
2 eggs

3/4 to 1 c. sugar
Small can Pet milk
1/4 c. melted butter
1 jigger whiskey

Grate cooked sweet potatoes and sprinkle with cinnamon. Beat eggs, add sugar, Pet milk and butter. Mix well and add to potatoes. Put in a greased casserole and bake at 400 degrees until slightly brown on top. When cooked, take fork and stick holes in top of potatoes. Pour a jigger of whiskey over potatoes and serve. Serves 8.

Mrs. Robert Henry

NEW POTATOES WITH DILL

20 very small new potatoes
1 c. salt

6 stalks only, fresh dill
1 stick butter

Clean potatoes with brush, leaving skins on and drop into boiling water to cover. Add salt and dill stalks, cover and cook over low heat until the potatoes are tender, from 10 to 20 minutes, depending on the size of the potatoes. Drain and remove dill. Add the stick of butter and serve. Serves 8.

Mrs. William Rowe

The large amount of salt seems to give the potatoes a different flavor - good barbecue accompaniment on small skewers.

MAE'S NEW POTATOES

15 to 20 small new potatoes   Flour
1 stick melted butter   Salt and pepper

Boil new potatoes until just done. Slip off skin. Roll in melted butter. Roll in flour seasoned with salt and lots of black pepper; then roll quickly in butter again (just enough to wet flour).

Place on cookie sheet and bake at 400 degrees for 15 minutes or until slightly brown and crusty.

Ella Mae Tucker

GREEN RICE

3 c. cooked rice   1/2 T. grated onion
2 eggs, well-beaten   1/3 c. minced parsley
1 c. milk   2/3 c. minced spinach
1/4 c. butter   1 t. Worcestershire sauce
1/4 c. grated sharp cheese   1 1/4 t. salt

Cook rice as directed on package. Stir in the other ingredients. Pour into a greased 2 quart casserole and bake at 325 degrees for 45 minutes. Serves 8.

Mrs. George Grainger

BASIC RICE CASSEROLE

1 stick butter   2 cans broth-type soup
1 c. raw rice   1 can mushrooms

Melt butter, add rice, soup and mushrooms. Cover and bake at 350 degrees for approximately 1 hour. Serves 6 to 8. Many creative cooks have variations of this recipe as follows:

Mrs. John Noble adds 1 package blanched, slivered almonds, an extra can of mushrooms and uses 1 1/2 cans chicken broth as the soup flavoring.

Mrs. Wade Ridley doubles the rice and butter for a crowd, using 3 cans chicken consomme', 1 can of water and adding 2 teaspoons oregano.

Mrs. James R. Hicks varies the basic recipe by using 1 can onion soup and one can beef consomme', and adding 1 tablespoon Worcestershire sauce and 1 bay leaf.

Mrs. Michael Hatchell uses 2 cans beef bouillon and adds 1 chopped onion, 1 sliced green pepper and 1/4 cup chopped parsley.

Mrs. Tom Ramey, Jr. prepares her "Duffield Rice" using the basic recipe with 1 can bouillon and 1 can consomme. She adds 3 chopped small green onions, fresh mushrooms (instead of canned) and slivered almonds.

ARTICHOKE RICE

1 pkg. Uncle Ben's Chicken
   flavored rice
2 jars [6 oz.] marinated
   artichoke hearts
1/3 c. mayonnaise

3/4 t. curry powder
4 green onions, sliced
1/2 green pepper, chopped
12 green stuffed olives,
   halved

Cook rice according to package directions. Let cool. Mix liquid from artichoke hearts, mayonnaise and curry powder. Add to this mixture the onions, pepper, olives, artichoke hearts. Add this sauce to the rice and heat slowly - stirring. This casserole remains tasteful at room temperature. Serves 6 to 8.

Mrs. Alice White

HERBED RICE AND SPINACH

4 eggs
2/3 c. milk
1/4 c. butter, melted
1/2 c. finely chopped onion
2 T. chopped parsley
1 1/2 t. salt
1/2 t. thyme
1/2 t. nutmeg

1 t. Worcestershire sauce
2 pkgs. [10 oz.] frozen
   chopped spinach, cooked
   and drained
2 c. cooked rice
2 c. shredded sharp
   Cheddar cheese

Beat eggs; add milk, butter, onion, parsley, salt, thyme, nutmeg, and Worcestershire sauce, mixing well. Stir in remaining ingredients. Pour into a buttered 2 quart square baking dish. Bake in 350 degree oven for 45 minutes. If desired, sprinkle some of the cheese on top and let it remain in the oven until melted. Serves 8.

Mrs. John Warner

"ARROZ VERDE"

1 egg
1 1/2 t. instant minced onion
1/2 c. milk
1/2 c. parsley or carrot tops
1 clove garlic, crushed

2 c. cooked rice
Salt
2 slices Swiss cheese
1/2 c. Parmesan cheese

Beat egg. Moisten instant onion in milk and let stand a few minutes. Mix well all ingredients except cheeses. Top with cheese. Bake at 325 degrees until cheeses are slightly brown and bubbly, about 20 to 30 minutes. Serves 6 to 8.

Mrs. John D. Glass, Jr.

ARROZ CON JOCOQUÉ

3 c. cooked rice
Salt and pepper to taste
3 c. sour cream, salted
2 small cans peeled green
   chiles, chopped

3/4 lb. Monterey Jack
   cheese, grated or cut
   in strips
1/2 c. Cheddar cheese,
   grated

Salt and pepper rice to taste, then mix with sour cream and green chiles. In a buttered 1 1/2 quart casserole, layer rice mixture and Monterey Jack cheese, ending with rice on top. Bake for 30 minutes at 350 degrees. During the last few minutes of baking, sprinkle Cheddar cheese over the rice and allow it to melt before removing casserole from oven. Serves 8.

Mrs. William T. Read

Mrs. Galloway Calhoun, Jr. makes this by combining 3/4 c. dry rice, cooked, with 2 c. sour cream and salt to taste. Place half rice mixture in greased casserole; cut 1/2 lb. Monterey Jack cheese in 1 inch cubes and place on rice mixture along with a can (4 oz.) green chile peppers that have been seeded and chopped. Top with remaining rice mixture, followed by 1/2 c. grated Monterey Jack cheese, dotted with 1/2 stick margarine. Bake at 350 degrees for 30 minutes. Serves 4 to 6.

Mrs. Ronald Schoenbrun cooks 1 c. raw rice until just tender, then combines it with 2 c. sour cream and salt to taste. After spreading half this mixture in a buttered casserole, she tops it with 1/2 lb. Cheddar cheese, cubed, or a jar of Cheese Whiz and 1 can (6 oz.) of peeled green chiles, cut in strips. Top with remaining rice mixture, dot with butter, sprinkle with Parmesan cheese. Bake 350 degrees for 30 minutes. Serve immediately to 6.

PARTY RICE

1 box rice, cooked according
   to directions
2 c. green onions and tops,
   sliced
1 c. green peppers, sliced
2 sticks butter

3 cans water chestnuts,
   sliced
1 c. snipped parsley
3 cans mushrooms
Soy sauce

Saute' onions and peppers in butter until done. Add water chestnuts, parsley and mushrooms and cook until water chestnuts are crisp. Fold into cooked rice. Shake 1/2 bottle of soy sauce in rice (or less according to taste). Heat well and serve. Serves 12 to 15.

Mrs. Tom Ramey, Sr.

RICE POULETTE

6 T. butter
1/3 c. chopped green pepper
1/3 c. chopped onion
1/3 c. chopped celery

1 1/2 c. uncooked rice
1 large can mushrooms
2 cans beef consomme'

Melt butter in skillet. Add green pepper, onion and celery and cook until golden brown. Add rice to skillet and stir vegetables and rice together and cook on low heat for 5 minutes. Add mushrooms, juice and consomme'. Stir all throughly and place in a casserole and cover.

Bake 45 minutes at 350 degrees. Goes beautifully with roast beef. Serves 6 to 8.

Mrs. William Crawford
Baton Rouge, Lousiana

VENETIAN RICE

3 T. butter
1 medium onion, chopped
1 pkg. [10 oz.] frozen peas
3/4 c. rice [uncooked]

2 c. chicken broth
1 t. salt
Dash pepper

Melt butter. Add chopped onion and frozen peas. Cook and stir for 5 minutes. Add rice and cook until coated with butter. Add chicken broth and salt and pepper. Cover and simmer 20 to 25 minutes until broth is absorbed and rice is tender. Goes nicely with baked ham or chicken dishes. Serves 4.

Mrs. George W. Hardy, III
Baton Rouge, Louisiana

WILD RICE CASSEROLE

1 box Uncle Ben's long grain
   and wild rice
Chicken broth

2 sm. cans sliced mushrooms
1 c. pecans
1/2 c. butter

Prepare rice according to package directions, except use chicken broth instead of water called for. Saute' mushrooms and pecans in butter and mix in with the cooked rice, reserving enough for topping. Pour mixture into casserole and bake at 375 degrees until hot through and top is nicely browned. Serves 6 to 8. This recipe is more flavorful if made ahead and baked just before serving.

Mrs. Walter L. Johnson

RICE CASSEROLE

1 clove garlic, chopped
2 green onions with tops
2 T. salad oil
1 t. salt

2 c. cooked rice
2 c. grated sharp cheese
2 eggs, beaten
2 c. milk

Saute' garlic and chopped onions in oil, but do not brown. Mix this with all other ingredients and pour into a 2 quart casserole. Bake 45 minutes at 350 degrees. Serves 8.

Mrs. H. Don Smith

RICE PILAF

1 medium onion, chopped
1 clove garlic, minced
1/4 lb. butter, margarine or
   bacon drippings
1 c. raw rice

1 t. salt
1/2 t. oregano
1 can mushrooms
1 can beef consomme'
1 can water

Saute' onion and garlic in fat. Add rice and brown. Place in 2 quart casserole; add other ingredients. Bake 1 1/4 hours at 350 degrees. Serves 6.

Mrs. R. Randall Cape

MASHED RUTABAGAS WITH CHEESE

Yellow turnips [enough to
   make 3 c. hot mashed turnips]
1 t. salt
Pinch of pepper

3 T. butter
2/3 c. grated American
   cheese
1 t. thick steak sauce

Boil turnips, mash, and measure 3 cups. Add salt, pepper, butter, cheese and steak sauce. Mix and serve while hot. Serves 4.

Mrs. Frank Fite

BILL'S SPINACH CASSEROLE

1 can artichoke hearts
1/4 lb. butter
3 oz. cream cheese
1 can water chestnuts

1 pkg. frozen chopped
   spinach, cooked and
   drained

Line casserole with artichokes. Cream butter and cream cheese. Add water chestnuts, sliced thin, and spinach. Place in casserole and top with Italian bread crumbs. Bake at 325 degrees for 30 minutes.

Mrs. Joe Herrington

The artichoke hearts may be omitted for less expensive but delicious casserole; top with crumbs and Parmesan cheese.

BAKED SPINACH

2 pkgs. frozen chopped
   spinach
2 t. finely chopped onion
2 eggs
1/2 c. cracker crumbs
2 t. sugar

1 c. mushroom sauce [or 1
   can mushroom soup,
   undiluted]
Salt and pepper
Dash garlic salt

Cook spinach as directed on package and drain. Add all other ingredients. Place in a greased loaf pan and bake 45 minutes in a 325 degree oven in a pan of water. Additional mushroom sauce may be made and served beside the spinach dish to pour over each individual serving. Serves 6.

Mrs. Moliere Scarborough, Jr.

CREAMED SPINACH

2 pkgs. frozen spinach
1 pkg. [6 oz.] cream cheese
1/3 c. frozen chopped onion
4 T. lemon juice

Tabasco sauce to taste
Salt and pepper to taste
Mushrooms, if desired

Thaw spinach in top of double boiler over hot water. Stir in softened cream cheese and onions. Add remaining ingredients and cook over boiling water about one hour. To serve, garnish with slices of hard boiled eggs sprinkled with paprika. Serves 6 to 8.

Mrs. Walter P. Jones, Jr.

ITALIAN SPINACH

2 pkgs. frozen spinach
1 t. salt
Dash pepper
4 strips cooked bacon, crumbled
2 hard boiled eggs, sliced
2 c. medium white sauce
3 T. buttered bread crumbs

Sauce:

2 c. milk
4 T. flour
Dash celery salt
Dash pepper

Sauce: Heat milk and add flour until moderately thick; season.

Cook spinach according to package directions; drain. Season with salt and pepper. In a 1 1/2 quart casserole alternate layers of spinach, bacon, egg slices and white sauce; repeat layers. Sprinkle with buttered bread crumbs. Bake at 375 degrees for 20 minutes until bubbly. Serves 6 to 8.

Mrs. Edwin T. Maddox

ROSA'S CZECH SPINACH

1 pkg. fresh spinach	1/2 t. salt
[or 2 frozen pkgs.]	2 T. flour
4 pieces of fat bacon	1 c. milk
1 clove garlic	

Boil spinach until tender, drain thoroughly and finely chop; then set aside. Cook bacon over medium heat until crisp, then remove. Quarter garlic clove and put in small dish - pour salt over garlic and pulverize garlic and salt with fork. Add garlic and salt mixture to bacon drippings and cook for one minute. Stir in flour until smooth. Add 1 cup milk and stir until it thickens. After sauce has thickened, stir in chopped spinach and crushed bacon bits. Salt and pepper to taste. This is good served with ham, prime rib or pork chops.

Mrs. M. Earl Davis

SPINACH BAKE

2 1/2 lb. spinach, chopped	1/2 t. pepper
2 c. bread crumbs	1/2 T. thyme
6 scallions, minced and	1/2 t. cayenne pepper
sautéed	Salt to taste
3/4 c. butter, melted	12 thick tomato slices
1/2 c. grated Parmesan cheese	1 T. garlic salt
6 whole eggs	

Cook spinach and add all ingredients except tomatoes and garlic salt and mix well. Arrange tomato slices, seasoned with garlic salt, in buttered baking dish. Top with mounds of spinach mixture, using an ice cream scoop. Bake at 325 degrees for about 25 minutes.

Mrs. Ronald N. Schoenbrun

SUZANNE'S SPINACH

6 pkgs. frozen chopped	3 or 4 green onions,
spinach	chopped
3 pkgs. [3 oz.] cream cheese	Kellogg's seasoned croutons
3 sticks butter or margarine	

Boil spinach by instructions; drain well. While spinach is draining, soften cream cheese and half of butter or margarine over low heat. Stir in onions and spinach. Blend well. Spread in a 9 x 13 pyrex dish. Generously cover with crushed croutons on top. Sprinkle with remaining melted butter. (Water chestnuts may be added to this dish for variety.) Bake for 20 to 30 minutes in a 300 degree oven. Serves 12 to 16.

Mrs. L. Glenn Taylor

SPINACH SUPREME

2 pkgs. |10 oz.| chopped
  spinach
1 can |6 oz.| mushroom crowns
6 T. butter
1 T. flour
1/2 c. milk
1/2 t. salt
1 can mushroom pieces
Dash red pepper and mustard

1 can |1 lb.| artichokes

Sauce :

1/2 c. sour cream
1/2 c. mayonnaise
2 T. lemon juice

Cook spinach according to package directions, drain and mash. Saute mushrooms in butter. Remove mushrooms and set aside. Add flour to butter and cook until bubbly. Add milk and stir until smooth. Add salt, mushroom pieces and spinach. Add dash of red pepper and mustard to sauce. Put artichokes on bottom of buttered casserole and cover with spinach mixture. Combine sauce ingredients and pour over vegetables. Place button mushrooms on top. Bake just to heat through at 350 degrees. Serves 6 to 8. (May be made ahead and stored in refrigerator).

Mrs. James R. Perry
Odessa, Texas

BAKED SQUASH SOUFFLÉ

1 1/2 to 2 lbs. small tender yellow
  or white squash
1 large green pepper, chopped
1 c. onion, chopped
1/4 c. cream

Salt and pepper to taste
1 t. sugar
3 eggs, beaten
1/4 c. bread crumbs

Cook squash, 1/2 green pepper and onion in water until tender. Pour into a sieve and drain well. Add other half of green pepper, uncooked, and remaining ingredients and bake in casserole at 325 degrees for 40 to 45 minutes. Serve at once to 6.

Clementine Warren

MARSHA'S SQUASH SOUFFLÉ

3 c. raw squash
1/8 c. chopped onion
Salt and pepper to taste
1/4 c. margarine
3 T. sugar

2 eggs
2 T. evaporated or regular
  milk
1 c. buttered cracker crumbs
1 c. grated cheese

Boil squash, onion, salt, and pepper until tender, then drain well. Place margarine, sugar, eggs, and milk in blender. Add squash mixture and blend until well-mixed. Pour squash mixture into baking dish alternately with cracker crumbs and cheese. Bake at 350 degrees for 30 minutes.

Mrs. William E. Bertram

BAKED SQUASH

2 lbs. yellow squash	2 eggs
1 1/2 t. salt	10 saltine crackers
1 medium onion, chopped	1/2 c. milk
1 T. bell pepper, chopped	Dash pepper
1/2 stick margarine or butter	American cheese

Cook squash in small amount of salted water until tender. Saute' onion and bell pepper in margarine or butter until tender. Mix together well-beaten eggs, crackers, milk and dash of pepper and set aside. Drain squash and mash well. Add remaining ingredients and put in 8 x 12 inch buttered pyrex pan. Top with very finely grated cheese. Bake at 350 degrees for 15 to 20 minutes. Serves 6 to 8.

Mrs. J. E. Richardson

Mrs. James Milstead prepares her Zucchini Casserole (using zucchini squash) by cooking the onion and bell pepper, then adding other ingredients and baking as in the above recipe.

BAKED SQUASH CASSEROLE

1 1/2 lbs. squash, washed and sliced	3 eggs
3 onions, sliced	Green chopped onion
1 T. sugar	1/2 c. cracker crumbs
	3 T. butter

Boil squash and onions in salted water until tender. Drain well; add other ingredients and pour into greased casserole. Bake in 350 degree oven about 35 minutes or until set. Serves 6 to 8.

Mrs. E. B. Yale

SQUASH CASSEROLE

4 lbs. yellow squash	1 c. grated cheese
2 lbs. zucchini squash	[Cheddar]
1 onion, chopped	1 c. grated Velveeta
2 t. sugar	cheese
1 t. salt	1/2 c. milk
1/4 c. butter	1/2 c. cream

Cook sliced squash (both) and onion in a small amount of water, with sugar and salt, until tender. Drain. Add butter and mash well. Season to taste with salt and pepper. In a deep 2 quart casserole, make four layers of vegetables and mixed cheeses, ending with cheese layer. Combine milk and cream and pour over all. Sprinkle more cheese over top if desired. Bake at 350 degrees for 15 to 20 minutes or until bubbly. Serves 12.

Mrs. Bruce Brookshire

SQUASH SUPREME

1 can mushroom soup
1 to 1 1/2 c. chopped onion
8 to 10 medium yellow squash,
cut up

2 eggs
1 c. cracker crumbs
1 c. grated cheese

Heat soup until warm. Add onion and squash that have been parboiled. Add beaten eggs, cracker crumbs (save some to put on top) and grated cheese. Mix all together and bake uncovered until eggs are well done - about 30 to 40 minutes in 320 degree oven. Serves 6 to 8. Freezes well, and may be prepared ahead and reheated.

Mrs. Walter P. Jones, Jr.

SPANISH SQUASH

8 yellow summer squash
Velveeta or mild cheese
2 T. pimiento
1 T. chopped onion

1 T. sugar
1 T. vinegar
Salt and pepper

Boil summer squash until tender, but firm. Split lengthwise, scoop out centers and mix with equal parts grated cheese in bowl. Add remaining ingredients and mix. Stuff squash shells. Dot with butter and sprinkle with paprika. Bake at 350 degrees for 20 to 30 minutes or until hot and bubbly. This makes 16 halves and serves 8 to 10.

Mrs. Taylor Burns

STUFFED SQUASH WITH SPINACH

4 yellow squash
1 pkg. chopped frozen
spinach, cooked
1 t. chopped chives
Seasoning salt to taste

Lime juice to taste
1/2 stick butter
1/2 c. Parmesan cheese
1/4 c. cracker crumbs

Boil whole squash until tender. Cool, then halve. Remove the center. Mash the cooked spinach and add chives, seasoning salt, lime juice and butter. Stuff the squash with this mixture. Sprinkle cheese, mixed with crumbs, on top. Bake in 300 to 325 degree oven for 25 minutes. Serves 8.

Mrs. Jack King

A delightful dish and very elegant looking.

"MEXICAN" SQUASH

1 medium onion, chopped
4-6 medium yellow squash,
   sliced
4 T. cooking oil
1/2 c. milk

1 c. Rotel tomatoes and
   green chilies, drained
Salt and pepper
1 c. sharp Cheddar cheese,
   grated

Saute' onion and squash in oil until tender. Add milk, Rotel tomatoes, salt and pepper. Cover and cook over medium heat 15 minutes. Add cheese and remove from heat. Serves 8.

Mrs. John Minton

SQUASH WITH CHEESE

Butter
Yellow crookneck squash
Green onions

Salt and pepper to taste
Velveeta cheese

Melt butter in skillet. Add thinly sliced squash and thinly sliced green onions. Add salt and pepper. Cook until squash is tender. Top with small bits of cheese and cover until cheese is melted. Stir and serve.

Mrs. E. J. Mooney, Jr.
Chicago, Illinois

CREOLE STUFFED TOMATOES

3 slices bacon
1/4 c. chopped bell pepper
1/4 c. chopped onion

6 medium tomatoes
1 c. whole corn
1 t. Lawry seasoned salt

Fry bacon, drain and crumble. Leave 2 tablespoons grease in skillet and saute' pepper and onion. Core tomatoes and scoop out pulp. To onion and pepper in skillet, add pulp, corn, and salt and heat through. Add bacon and fill tomatoes. Bake at 350 degrees for 15 to 20 minutes. Serves 6.

Mrs. Galloway Calhoun, Jr.

PARMESAN TOMATOES

6 medium tomatoes
1/4 c. melted butter
1/4 c. dry bread crumbs
1/4 c. Parmesan cheese

2 T. chopped green onion
1/2 t. salt
Dash pepper

Core (scoop out) tomatoes. Combine remaining ingredients and fill tomatoes with mixture. Bake at 350 degrees for 30 minutes or until hot through. Serves 6.

Mrs. Galloway Calhoun, Jr.

Page 140

WEB'S SLICED TOMATOES

Tomatoes	**Oregano**
Red onion	**Salt and pepper**
Basil	**Italian dressing**

Slice tomatoes and sprinkle chopped red onion and other ingredients on tomatoes. Pour Italian dressing over the tomatoes and let marinate in refrigerator.

Mrs. Joe Herrington

CHEESE CASSEROLE

2 cans [4 oz.] green chiles, drained	4 egg yolks
	2/3 c. evaporated milk
1 lb. Monterrey Jack cheese, coarsely grated	1 T. flour
	1/2 t. salt
1 lb. Cheddar cheese, coarsely grated	1/4 t. pepper
	2 medium tomatoes, sliced
4 egg whites	

Preheat oven to 325 degrees. Remove seeds from chiles and dice. In a large bowl, combine the grated cheeses and green chiles. Turn into a well-buttered, shallow 2 quart casserole. In a large bowl, with electric mixer at high speed, beat egg whites until stiff peaks form when beater is slowly raised. In a small bowl, combine egg yolks, milk, flour, salt, and pepper; mix until well-blended. Using a scraper, gently fold beaten egg whites into egg yolk mixture. Pour egg mixture over cheese mixture in casserole, and using a fork, stir it through the cheese. Bake 30 minutes at 325 degrees. Remove from oven and arrange sliced tomatoes around edge of casserole. Bake 30 minutes longer, or until knife inserted in center comes out clean. Garnish with green chiles if desired. Serves 6 to 8.

Mrs. Ronald S. Smith

CHEESE AND CHILES

5 cans chiles, drained [reserve juice]	2 c. milk
	1 c. flour
1 lb. sharp Cheddar cheese, grated	2 t. salt
	1 t. pepper
4 eggs	Chile juice

Remove seeds from chiles. Butter an oblong two quart casserole. Spread half of the cheese on bottom of dish. Layer peppers on cheese. Cover with remaining cheese. Mix remaining ingredients in a bowl and pour over cheese and chiles. Bake at 325 degrees for one hour. Serves 8.

Mrs. Nelson Clyde

This is great served with steak in place of baked potatoes.

GARLIC CHEESE CASSEROLE

1 c. uncooked grits
1 roll garlic flavored cheese
1 stick margarine or butter
2 eggs, beaten

3/4 c. milk
Salt and pepper to taste
3/4 c. grated cheese

Cook grits as directed on package, and while still hot, slice garlic cheese into grits mixture, adding 1 stick butter; let cool slightly and add eggs and milk. Mix well; salt and pepper to taste. Pour into buttered casserole. Bake at 325 degrees for 35 minutes. Add grated cheese and return to oven 20 minutes more.

Mrs. James Milstead

GRITS SOUFFLÉ

2 c. cooked, cooled grits
2 eggs, separated
1/2 c. cream or evaporated
   milk

1 t. salt
1/4 t. white pepper

Beat 2 cups of cooled grits until smooth. Beat egg yolks well and stir into grits. Add cream, salt and pepper. Beat egg whites until they stand in peaks and fold into grits mixture, lightly but thoroughly. Spoon into well-greased 1 quart casserole and bake in a preheated 350 degree oven for 40 minutes or until surface is golden brown. Serve immediately. Serves 4 or 5.

Mrs. C. R. Hurst

CRACKED WHEAT PILAF

2 sticks butter or margarine
2 1/2 to 3 c. #3 [coarse grind]
   cracked wheat
2 cans beef bouillon

2 cans onion soup
1 can mushrooms [sliced,
   buttons, or pieces with liquid]

Melt butter in 3 quart casserole dish. Add remaining ingredients. Cover tightly with foil and bake covered at 350 degrees for about 45 minutes or until all liquid is absorbed. Serve during holiday season with pomegranate seeds on top - sprinkled generously. Excellent with smoked turkey, ham, roast beef or baked or broiled chicken. May be frozen if liquid is decreased so grain will not be overdone when heated. May also be prepared a day or so before. Serves 12.

Mrs. Joy Massad

Cracked wheat is available at most health food stores and at any import store. The #3 above indicates the degree of fineness.

VEGETABLE CASSEROLE

Vegetable:	2 pkgs. [10 oz.] frozen mixed vegetables
	1/4 t. garlic salt
	2 T. butter

Sauce:
1/4 c. butter	Pinch nutmeg
1/4 c. flour	Pinch thyme
1/4 t. salt	1/8 t. garlic salt
1/4 c. Parmesan cheese	1 1/2 to 2 c. half-and-half

Topping:	1/2 c. bread crumbs
	3 T. butter

Steam vegetables in 1/4 cup water for 5 minutes. Drain and save liquid. Season vegetables with garlic salt and butter, and place in greased 2 quart casserole dish.

For sauce, melt butter, add flour, salt, Parmesan cheese, spices, and garlic salt. Combine liquid drained from vegetables with half-and-half to make two cups. Add to flour mixture. Cook and stir until thickened. Pour sauce over vegetables and top with bread crumbs and dot with butter. Bake at 350 degrees for 30 to 40 minutes. This dish freezes well or may be prepared a day ahead. Serves 8.

Mrs. Nelson Clyde

The sauce could be served on any favorite vegetable.

TRIPLE CASSEROLE

Step #1:	Step #2:
2 c. mayonnaise	1 pkg. [10 oz.] frozen
4 t. olive oil	green peas
1 medium onion, grated	1 pkg. [10 oz.] frozen
Few drops Tabasco	limas
1 t. Worcestershire	1 pkg. [10 oz.] frozen
	green beans, French style
	4 hard boiled eggs

Step #1: Mix ingredients in Step #1 and chill 48 hours.
Step #2: Cook frozen vegetables according to directions. Drain well and add sauce. Top with 4 grated hard boiled eggs. Serves 10.

Mrs. Harold Beaird

Mrs. Gene Caldwell varies the sauce for these vegetables by combining 1/2 pint whipped cream and 1/2 cup mayonnaise. Fold sauce into beans and pour into a 2 quart baking dish. Sprinkle generously with Parmesan cheese. Bake in 300 degree oven until bubbly.

MARINATED VEGETABLES

1 can [16 oz.] whole green
  beans
1 can [8 1/2 oz.] whole green
  beans
1 small can sliced carrots
1 small can baby lima beans
1 jar [2 oz.] sliced mushrooms

1/2 jar [2 oz.] pimiento
1/2 medium red onion,
  chopped
1/2 medium green pepper,
  chopped
2 small stalks celery,
  diced

Marinade:

3/4 c. sugar
1/4 t. salt
1/4 t. celery seed
1/4 t. paprika

1/4 t. dry mustard
1/4 c. white vinegar
1/4 c. red wine vinegar

Combine marinade ingredients and pour over vegetables. Refrigerate at least 24 hours before serving. Gently turn in marinade several times during refrigeration to cover all vegetables. Keep in airtight container.

Mrs. Paul Brush

MIXED VEGETABLES

1 pkg. [10 oz.] frozen lima
  beans
1 pkg. [10 oz.] frozen green
  peas
1 can green beans, heated in
  own liquid

1 medium onion, grated
1 t. prepared mustard
1 t. Worcestershire sauce
3 hard boiled eggs,
  coarsely chopped
1 1/2 c. mayonnaise

Cook vegetables as directed on package. While vegetables are still hot, add other ingredients. Gently fold in mayonnaise. Put in casserole. Bake at 350 degrees for 20 to 25 minutes. Watch carefully. Serves 8 to 10.

Mrs. R. Randall Cape

If recipe is doubled, do not double mayonnaise. Add just enough to get right consistency.

ZUCCHINI

8 to 10 small zucchini
2/3 c. chopped onion
1/4 lb. mushrooms
3 T. olive oil
2/3 c. [3 oz.] Parmesan
  cheese

1 1/2 c. [2 6 oz. cans]
  tomato paste
1 t. salt
1/8 t. pepper
1/2 t. Accent
1 clove garlic

Saute' zucchini, onion, and mushrooms in olive oil. Add other ingredients and simmer until done. If needed, add water while cooking. Serves 8.

Mrs. Richard Grainger

BAKED ZUCCHINI AND TOMATOES

2 medium zucchini
2 medium tomatoes
1 medium onion
Salt and pepper

Butter
1 c. crushed buttered
crackers

Wash zucchini; do not peel unless the skin is hard. Peel the tomatoes and onion. Slice all vegetables into very thin crosswise slices. In a greased baking dish make alternate layers of zucchini, tomatoes, and onion, sprinkling each layer with a little salt and pepper and dotting with butter. Cover the top with crushed cracker crumbs. Bake at 350 degrees until vegetables are tender, about 45 minutes to 1 hour. Serves 4.

Mrs. Hunter Brush

SWISS VEGETABLE CUSTARD

1 1/2 c. zucchini, sliced
1 1/2 c. broccoli, sliced
1/2 c. butter
1 or 2 eggs, beaten
1/4 c. milk
1 t. salt

1/4 t. dry mustard
Dash cayenne
1/2 c. Swiss cheese,
shredded
Parmesan cheese

Saute' vegetables in butter until just tender. Place in casserole. Mix rest of ingredients, except Parmesan cheese, and heat until cheese is melted. Pour over vegetables. Top with Parmesan cheese. Bake uncovered at 375 degrees for 20 minutes. May be prepared ahead and heated or baked at serving time. Serves 4.

Mrs. A. M. Limmer, Jr.

ZUCCHINI AND CORN WITH DILL

1 1/2 c. whole kernel corn
[fresh is best]
1 lb. unpeeled zucchini,
sliced 1/2 inch thick
1/2 c. onion, chopped small
1/2 c. green pepper, chopped
medium
1 t. salt

2 T. water
2 T. butter
2 to 3 T. fresh dill,
snipped small [no stems]
or 1 T. dried dill weed
[fresh dill is a better
taste]

Boil corn (if using fresh) in water to cover with one tablespoon sugar, no salt, for 8 minutes. Cut off the cob and add to zucchini, onion and green pepper while still warm. Sprinkle the salt over all ingredients and add water. Cover and simmer over low heat, stirring occasionally, for 8 to 10 minutes. Drain off any liquid and add butter and dill. Serves 4 to 6.

Mrs. William Rowe

ZUCCHINI IN SOUR CREAM

3 medium zucchini
2 medium onions
2 T. butter
1 clove garlic

1 jalapeno pepper
1 t. salt
1/4 t. pepper
1 c. sour cream

Cut zucchini into small squares and onions into rings. Melt butter in a skillet and add zucchini, onions, chopped garlic, jalapeno, salt and pepper and saute' 2 or 3 minutes. Top with sour cream, then cover skillet and simmer until tender. Serves 4.

Mrs. William R. Clyde

BLENDER HOLLANDAISE

3 egg yolks
2 T. lemon juice
Pinch of cayenne

1/4 t. salt
2/3 to 1 c. butter

Place first 4 ingredients in blender. Heat butter to bubbling stage, but do not brown. Cover blender container and turn on high. After 3 seconds, remove the lid and pour the butter over the eggs in a steady stream. By the time the butter is poured in, about 30 seconds, the sauce should be finished. If not, blend on high 5 seconds.

Serve at once or keep warm by immersing blender container in warm water. This sauce may be frozen and reconstituted over hot water. This is unbelievably easy and delicious.

Mrs. Nelson Clyde

QUICK [NEVER FAIL] HOLLANDAISE SAUCE

4 egg yolks
2 sticks butter

Juice of 1 lemon
Cayenne pepper

Place egg yolks in blender and blend quickly. Melt butter in saucepan until bubbly but not brown. Pour melted butter very slowly into turned on blender. Add lemon juice and pepper to taste. Blend. Let cool and thicken in blender. Serves 4.

Mrs. Richard Grainger

ASPARAGUS OR BROCCOLI SAUCE

1/4 c. sour cream
1/4 c. mayonnaise

1 T. lemon juice
Red pepper to taste

Mix all ingredients well and chill. Serve over cold vegetables.
Mrs. Joe B. Herrington

Meats

ANNA'S BRISKET OF BEEF

4 lb. brisket, salted,
  peppered and floured
2 T. oil
2 large onions, sliced thin
1 can [1 lb.] tomatoes

1/2 c. raisins
1/4 c. sugar
1 lemon, peeled, seeded,
  and quartered
1 clove garlic, chopped

Sear meat in hot oil in heavy roaster until brown; remove from pan and saute' onions until lightly brown.

Pureé in blender the tomatoes and add them to the remaining ingredients and mix well. Pour this mixture over onions. Push to one side and place meat back in roaster. Spoon sauce over the meat until covered. Cover pan and bake at 300 degrees until very tender when pierced with fork (4 to 5 hours). Serves 6.

Mrs. A. M. Limmer, Jr.

BRISKET I

6 lb. brisket
Meat tenderizer [unseasoned]
Lawry's seasoned salt
Celery and garlic salt
Pepper

1/3 bottle Worcestershire
  sauce
1 bottle Figaro liquid
  smoke

First day: Place brisket in pan and sprinkle with tenderizer, Lawry's salt, garlic salt and celery salt and pepper. Fork it in. Pour Worcestershire and liquid smoke over it. Let stand in refrigerator overnight.

Second day: Cook tightly covered for 5 hours at 250 degrees. Cool and refrigerate.

Third day: Slice while cold into very thin slices. Heat as needed in liquid.

Mrs. J. M. Summers

BRISKET II

1 brisket that has been well-trimmed of fat

Place brisket in uncovered pan, sprinkle heavily with garlic powder, pepper and Worcestershire sauce.

Cook in a 225 degree oven for 5 hours. This will cook slowly and look ruined.

After 5 hours, remove from oven. Sprinkle again with garlic powder, pepper, Worcestershire sauce and catsup. Add a can of beer to pan and sliced peeled potatoes. Cover and return to oven at 350 degrees for 1 1/2 hours. (Be sure not to pour beer over the meat or it will wash off seasonings.)

Mrs. James E. Bass

BEEF BRISKET III

6 to 8 lb. brisket
Celery salt
Onion salt
Lawry's seasoned salt

Pepper
Garlic salt
6 oz. bottle liquid
    smoke

Place brisket in large pyrex dish. Generously sprinkle all spices over brisket and pour liquid smoke over it. Cover and refrigerate for 24 hours.

Preheat oven to 250 degrees and cook brisket for 8 hours. Refrigerate brisket. When ready to serve, skim off almost all fat, put back in oven after brisket has been sliced. Cook for 40 minutes or until hot at 350 degrees. Baste often and keep it covered between basting. Serves 4 to 6 generously.

Mrs. Floyd Cooper

Mrs. Robert Jones' variation includes a marinade of 1 T. liquid smoke, 1 T. Worcestershire, 1 T. garlic powder (or less), 1 T. celery salt, 1 T. onion salt, scant salt and pepper to taste and Woody's cooking sauce (if desired). After marinating at least 24 hours, she bakes the brisket covered at 325 degrees for 4 hours; uncovers, bastes generously with sauce, covers again and bakes another hour.

CORNED BEEF

6 lb. brisket
1/2 c. salt
2 T. sugar
1 T. saltpetre
2 cloves garlic

Brine:

1/2 box pickling spices
3/4 c. water
1/2 c. salt

Mix salt, sugar and saltpetre together. Add enough water to make a paste. Crush garlic and add to paste. Wash brisket well with cold water and rub thoroughly with paste. Combine pickling spices, water and salt to make brine. Pour over brisket that has been placed in a stone crock. It is important that the entire brisket remain under brine. The meat must be weighed down to prevent it from floating. A plate with a brick on top works nicely. Cover lightly (cheesecloth can be used). Soak for 5 days, turn and soak 5 more days. A deposit will form on the surface of the brine. This can be spooned off. On tenth day, remove from crock, rinse in cold water and cook very slowly in water with a bay leaf until tender.

Mrs. David K. Boice

BRISKET SUPREME

1/2 lb. dried apricots
1/2 lb. dried pears
1/2 lb. dried prunes
3 lb. brisket
2 t. salt
1/4 t. pepper

3 carrots, quartered
6 thin slices lemon
2 c. orange juice
4 c. water
4 T. honey
Dash of nutmeg

Wash dried fruits and soak in cold water to cover for 1 hour. Drain. Brown the meat over medium heat in a Dutch oven. Salt and pepper the meat. Arrange the fruit, carrots and lemon around it. Mix together orange juice, water, honey and nutmeg, and pour over all. Cover and bake at 350 degrees for 3 hours. Remove the cover and increase temperature to 400 degrees for 1 more hour. Add more water if necessary. Serves 8.

Mrs. George Echols
Lafayette, Louisiana

BEEF MEDLEY

3 lb. brisket, cut into
    1 inch cubes
1 c. chopped onion
3 T. brown sugar

2 cans Contadina tomato
    sauce
1 pkg. noodles

Trim fat off brisket. Heat skillet and brown meat and onion. Add brown sugar and sauce. Cover and cook until tender (about 3 hours). If it gets too thick, add water. Serve over hot noodles which have been prepared according to directions on package. Top with frozen green peas (if desired), which have also been prepared according to package directions. Freezes well; serves 12.

Mrs. Harry Hudson

BAKED STEAK

Round steak
Salt and pepper to taste
Flour
2 T. vegetable oil

1 lg. onion, thinly sliced
1/2 to 1 c. red wine
Mushrooms
Butter

Trim and cut round steak into large pieces; salt and pepper and pound in flour. Brown in oil; layer in casserole with onion. Add water to the drippings and pour over steak with red wine, 2 inches in bottom of casserole, but not covering the meat. Cover and bake in 325 degree oven until tender (about 1 hour).

Serve with mushrooms sautéed in butter. May be added to steak the last 20 minutes of cooking time.

Mrs. W. H. Merrill, Jr.
Irving, Texas

BEEF WITH ARTICHOKE HEARTS

1 1/2 lb. beef, cut
   1/4 inch thick
3 T. flour
1 1/2 t. Mei Yen Seasoning
1/2 t. garlic salt
1/2 t. onion flakes
1/2 t. [scant] black pepper
3 T. salad oil
2 stalks fresh Lemon Balm
   [optional]

1/2 c. sauterne or
   Chablis wine
1/2 c. water
1 c. fresh mushrooms
1 t. lemon juice
1 pkg. frozen artichoke
   hearts, cooked
1/2 c. sour cream
1/2 t. parsley

Cut beef into serving size pieces. Combine flour, Mei Yen, garlic salt, onion flakes and pepper. Dip meat in seasoned flour and brown in hot oil in heavy frying pan. When meat is well-browned remove from pan. Add remaining seasoned flour to drippings in pan. Stir until lightly browned. Add wine and water and stir until sauce has thickened slightly. Return meat to pan. Cover and cook slowly 30 minutes. Add sliced, fresh mushrooms. Cover and cook 15 minutes more or until meat is tender. Arrange meat on hot platter. Sprinkle lemon juice on drained artichoke hearts. Add this with the sour cream to the sauce in the pan. Stir gently for 3 minutes, then pour over meat and sprinkle with parsley. Serve immediately over rice or noodles. Serves 6.

For additional sauce, add: 1 c. water
                      1 heaping T. flour dissolved
                         in small amount of the water
                      1/2 c. wine

Mrs. John D. Glass, Jr.

Any leftover sauce is great the next morning, warmed and poured over poached, steamed or scrambled eggs.

BEEF STROGANOFF

1 stick butter
2 lb. lean steak, cut in 1/2 inch
   strips 2 inches long
4 green onions, chopped fine
2 to 3 T. flour
1 can condensed beef broth

3 t. Dijon mustard
1/2 c. sauterne or dry wine
12 oz. sour cream
12 oz. sliced mushrooms
Cooked rice

Heat butter in skillet; when hot, brown the meat in butter. Push to one side of skillet and add onions and cook until transparent. Push to one side and stir flour into the drippings; cook until thickened. Stir in beef broth and bring to a boil. Turn heat down and stir in mustard. Cover and let simmer for about 1 hour. Five minutes before serving, add wine, sour cream and mushrooms. Serve on rice. Serves 5.

Mrs. Dan C. Woldert

STEAK MADRID

1 1/2 to 2 lb. round steak
[1/2 inch thick]
Oil for browning meat
1 medium onion, chopped
1 medium bell pepper, chopped
1/2 c. chopped celery
2 cloves garlic, chopped
1/4 c. bacon fat
1 small can green chiles
chopped
1 can [10 oz.] beef gravy
1 T. Worcestershire sauce
Dash garlic salt

1/4 t. chili powder
1 can [1 lb.] peeled
tomatoes
1 can [6 oz.] tomato paste
1 can [8 oz.] tomato sauce
3 or 4 drops Tabasco
1/4 t. oregano
1/8 t. thyme
1 bay leaf, whole
Salt and pepper to taste
1 lb. grated Cheddar cheese
1 small jar sliced pimiento

Trim meat and slice in large pieces (approximately 6 inch by 6 inch pieces). Dust with flour, salt and pepper and brown in skillet. Drain meat on paper towels.

Saute' onion, pepper, celery and garlic in fat. Add all ingredients except cheese and pimiento and simmer 4 or 5 minutes. Remove bay leaf. Place half the meat pieces in a long pyrex dish, buttered. Sprinkle with all the grated cheese and pimiento. Pour a little sauce on this. Place remaining meat on top of the other meat pieces and pour on remaining sauce. Cover with foil and bake at 375 degrees for 1 to 1 1/2 hours. Serves 8.

Mrs. Robert D. Jones
Midland, Texas

SAUERBRATEN

3 T. flour
1 1/2 t. salt
1 1/2 lbs. 1 in. round steak,
cut in 1 x 3 in. strips
2 T. fat
3/4 c. sliced onion
1/2 c. cider vinegar

1 c. water
1 1/2 T. sugar
3 peppercorns
3 whole cloves
2 bay leaves
6 gingersnaps,
crumbled

Combine flour and salt; roll meat in this mixture. Brown the meat in hot fat. Add onion, vinegar, water and sugar. Tie spices in piece of cheese cloth and add to meat mixture. Cover and simmer gently about 1 1/2 hours or until meat is tender. Remove spice bag. Add gingersnaps and continue cooking about 15 minutes until gravy thickens. Serves 6 to 8.

Mrs. Brad Holmes

STEAK CHEVILLOT

3 T. butter
4 fillets of beef
[1 to 1 1/2 inches thick]
1 T. shallots, minced

1/2 c. plus 2 T. red
Burgundy wine
1 t. flour

In a skillet, heat 1 tablespoon butter and brown beef over high heat for about 3 minutes on each side according to doneness desired. Remove fillets to warm platter and keep warm. Drain fat from skillet and return skillet to moderate heat. Add 1/2 tablespoon butter and minced shallots and cook 30 seconds. Add 1/2 cup wine and cook until reduced by half. Stir in flour mixed to a paste with 1 teaspoon butter and cook, stirring for 30 seconds. Swirl in 1 tablespoon of butter; when melted, add 2 tablespoons of red Burgundy wine. Spoon 2 tablespoons of sauce over each fillet and top with a sprig of parsley and serve immediately. Serves 4.

Mrs. Bruce Brookshire

Don't overcook steak as it will cook a little while keeping warm as the sauce is prepared.

HUNGARIAN GOULASH

2 lb. beef chuck, cubed
Cooking oil [Crisco oil]
1 large onion, sliced
1 T. flour
1 t. salt
1 T. paprika
1 can [8 oz.] tomato sauce

1 #2 can [2 1/2 c.]
tomatoes, drained
1 clove garlic, minced
1 bouquet garni [bay leaves,
stalk celery with leaves,
parsley, thyme - tie in
a cheese cloth bag]

Brown beef in fat; add onion and cook to golden, but not brown. Stir in flour, salt and pepper. Add remaining ingredients. Simmer gently, covered, until meat is tender (about 1 1/2 to 2 hours). Serve goulash with hot wide noodles. Serves 4.

Mrs. Lynn F. Cobb

BEEF CHUNKS BURGUNDY

3 lbs. lean beef stew meat
2 T. butter
2 cans [8 oz.] tomato sauce
1 c. red dinner wine

2 t. onion powder
1/2 t. oregano
2 t. seasoned salt

Brown stew meat in butter until golden. Combine tomato sauce, wine and seasonings. Pour over beef. Cover and simmer 3 to 3 1/2 hours until beef is very tender. Remove excess fat, if any, from top of sauce before serving. Serve over hot rice. Serves 6 generously.

Mrs. Rolf Schroeder

Very easy, unique tasting dish that takes no fussing over!

BEEF IN WINE

3 lbs. lean stew meat
1 can cream of mushroom soup
1 can onion soup

3/4 c. red wine
1/4 c. brandy [if no brandy,
   use all red wine]

Preheat oven to 325 degrees. Place all ingredients except brandy in 3 quart casserole and cover tightly. Bake for 3 1/2 hours. Stir in brandy and cover. Bake for 30 more minutes (or until sauce thickens). Serve over rice. Serves 8 to 10.

Mrs. Glenn Collins
Mrs. Stanley Robertson

SPICY POT ROAST

3 to 5 lb. beef pot roast
2 T. fat
1/2 c. brown sugar, packed
   firmly
1/4 t. salt
1/8 t. pepper
1/2 c. vinegar
1/4 c. soy sauce

1/2 bay leaf, crumbled
4 stalks celery, cut into
   4 inch pieces
4 medium sweet potatoes
   and/or carrots, peeled
   and sliced lengthwise
   into eighths

Brown roast in hot fat in heavy skillet. Mix brown sugar, salt, pepper, vinegar, soy sauce and bay leaf together. Pour mixture over roast. Cover tightly and simmer for 1/2 hour. Add celery and sweet potatoes; cover and simmer 1 hour or more until meat and vegetables are fork tender. Remove potatoes, celery and meat and thicken broth for gravy.

Mrs. Norman Halbrooks

CORNISH PASTIES

3 lbs. tenderloin steak
4 large potatoes
4 bunches green onions or
   sliced brown onions

5 1/2 c. flour
4 T. suet

Cube meat and potatoes. Cut onions. Make a pie crust as usual using the 5 1/2 cups of flour. Also work about 4 tablespoons of suet into dough. Roll pastry in 7 inch circles. Put some meat, potatoes and onion on lower half of circle and salt and pepper. Fold over top half and seal edges as for a turnover. Cut slit in top. Cook until crust is golden brown, about 45 minutes to 1 hour at 350 degrees. Makes 9. This can be served with or without gravy.

Mrs. Robert Johnston

BURGUNDY BEEF STEW

4 lb. beef chuck
1/2 lb. salt pork
2 doz. small white onions
1 T. flour
Peppercorns
1 or 2 cloves crushed garlic
1 piece orange peel
2 pinches Bouquet Garni or
2 small bay leaves

A sprig of thyme
Pinch or two of nutmeg
Pinch of marjoram
1/2 t. oregano
1/2 bottle Burgundy wine
Mushrooms [fresh]
Parsley

Cut lean chuck into 2 inch cubes. Cut salt pork into slices 1/4 inch thick and 1 inch square. Place pork in large skillet and brown until crisp. Remove pork and saute' onions, letting them take on a lovely brown color. Do not overcook. Remove onions and place beef squares in same fat and brown on all sides. Place salt pork back in skillet and sprinkle all with flour and ground fresh pepper, liberally; add garlic, orange peel, Bouquet Garni (crushed between fingers) or bay leaves, thyme, nutmeg, marjoram and oregano. Heat 1/2 bottle of good dry red Burgundy and pour over meat mixture (should cover meat). Cover tightly and cook at 250 degrees for 3 hours. If necessary, add more wine or stock. Add onions and sautéed mushrooms 15 minutes before serving. At time of serving, add chopped parsley. Serves 8 to 10.

Mrs. Bruce Brookshire

GASTON BEEF STEW

2 lbs. stew meat
Seasoned flour
1 1/2 cloves chopped garlic
1 large chopped onion
1 bouillon cube in 1 c.
   hot water
1 can [15 oz.] tomato sauce
12 peppercorns

3 whole cloves
1/4 c. chopped parsley
   [optional]
1/2 bay leaf
6 medium potatoes
6 carrots
1 stalk celery

Cut stew meat into pieces. Saute' the meat in bacon drippings in large skillet. Sprinkle it with flour and salt and pepper. In a large pot, combine and heat until boiling all of the remaining ingredients, except vegetables. Add the meat to this mixture and simmer for about 4 hours. After 3 hours you may add 1/2 cup sherry or white wine, if you like.

Cook separately until nearly tender: 6 medium pared, quartered potatoes, 6 pared, quartered carrots and 1 stalk celery. Add these vegetables for the last 15 minutes of cooking. Serves 8 generously.

Mrs. Will Knight

CADILLAC STEW

6 lb. heavy beef chuck roast, cut in 1 1/2 to 2 inch cubes [about 5 lb. meat]
1 lb. salt pork cut into very small pieces [size of lima bean]

4 cans small white boiled onions, drained
1 1/2 or 2 bottles dry red cooking wine [Chianti may be used - 2 qts.]

Gravy:

3 T. flour
1/4 t. fresh ground black pepper
3 cloves garlic, chopped
3 t. orange peel [Spice Islands may be used]

3 bay leaves
1/8 t. thyme
1/8 t. nutmeg
3 t. parsley flakes
Dash cayenne pepper
3 large cans mushrooms

Have beef prepared at market. Chop salt pork as directed and fry until brown and crisp. Remove from fat and reserve. Brown onions in fat from salt pork. Remove onions and also reserve. Next brown beef, cubed, in same fat. (Do not flour beef). Remove beef from fat and reserve. Make gravy of remaining fat and juices in roaster adding all gravy ingredients except mushrooms. Use wine as liquid for gravy, being sure to heat wine before adding. Now add beef and salt pork to gravy and cook 3 hours covered in heavy roaster at 325 degrees. (May add more wine if needed). Add browned onions and mushrooms and cook for 20 more minutes. Serves 12.

Mrs. J. L. Gulley

FORGOTTEN STEW

2 lb. top sirloin, cut into pieces [bite size]
12 small white onions
1 c. chopped celery
2 large potatoes, cut in eighths
1 slice white bread, cubed

6 carrots, cut in 1 inch pieces
2 cans [8 oz.] tomato sauce with cheese
1 c. water
1 1/2 t. salt
1/8 t. pepper

Combine all ingredients in a heavy casserole or Dutch oven. Place in an oven preheated to 250 degrees. Cook for about 5 hours. Serves 6.

Mrs. George Echols
Lafayette, Louisiana

Excellent main dish for a busy day.

HAMBURGERS IN A SKILLET

4 slices bacon, cut in halves
1 lb. ground chuck
1 large potato
1 medium onion

2 medium carrots
1 bell pepper
Salt and pepper to season
1/4 c. water

Place slices of bacon on bottom of skillet. Make ground chuck into 4 generous patties and place over bacon. Dice all vegetables together and sprinkle over and around meat patties. Place skillet over high heat for 8 minutes. Reduce heat to low, add water, cover and cook for 45 minutes. Serves 4.

Mrs. Barbara Woldert

HAMBURGER STROGANOFF

1 lb. ground beef
1/2 c. chopped onion
1 can water chestnuts,
   sliced
1 t. salt
1/4 t. paprika

1 small can sliced
   mushrooms
1 c. sour cream
1 can mushroom soup
Cooked rice
Chinese noodles

Saute' meat and onion until meat is gray. Add remaining ingredients. Simmer 30 minutes. Serve over rice and top with Chinese noodles. Serves 6.

Mrs. Francis Kay
Mrs. Luther Kay, Jr.

Mrs. Charles Clark browns 3 slices of bacon with her meat and blends 1 1/2 tablespoons of flour with other seasonings. She omits the sliced mushrooms.

BEEF IN CASSEROLE

3 lbs. ground chuck
2 T. salt
2 T. sugar
Seasoned pepper
2 T. garlic powder
2 cans [16 oz.] tomatoes
2 cans [8 oz.] tomato sauce
2 pkgs. [10 oz.] noodles
   [medium width]

2 pkgs. [8 oz.] cream
   cheese
2 pt. sour cream
2 bunches green onion tops,
   chopped
1/4 stick butter
Longhorn cheese
   [or Cheddar]

Brown meat and seasonings; then add tomato mixture and simmer 15 minutes. Cook noodles in salted water.

Mix cream cheese, sour cream and onion tops. Add noodles and butter; stir. Add meat sauce; stir. Pour into casserole and cover with grated cheese. Cover casserole and bake at 350 degrees for 35 minutes. Serves 12. This can be frozen before cooking.

Mrs. Hunter Brush

MORE CASSEROLE

2 chopped onions
1 chopped green pepper
3/4 t. garlic purée
1 lb. ground beef
1 can [No. 2] tomatoes
1 c. water

1 can [4 oz.] mushrooms, drained
1 can peas
1 can whole kernel corn
1 or 1 1/2 pkg. spaghetti
2 c. sharp grated cheese

Brown onions and pepper in 1 tablespoon fat to which garlic purée has been added. Add ground beef and cook. Add tomatoes, water, cover and cook over low heat for 30 minutes. Add mushrooms, peas, corn and salt and pepper to taste. Let cook 15 minutes more.

Cook spaghetti. Spaghetti may be added and mixed to the above or fixed in layers: spaghetti, meat sauce, cheese, etc. and top with cheese or the entire casserole fixed with layer of cheese in middle and on top.

Grease baking dish and arrange casserole as you wish. Bake 20 to 30 minutes at 350 degrees. Serves 8 to 10. Freezes well.

Mrs. William H. Starling

The "more" you eat, the "more" you'll want.

GOOD CASSEROLE

1 onion, diced
2 T. margarine
1 1/2 lbs. ground round
Chili powder
Garlic powder
Salt

Pepper
1 pkg. spaghetti, cooked
1 can mushroom soup
1 can tomato soup
Grated cheese

Saute' onion in margarine. Add meat and cook until brown. Season to taste. Combine cooked spaghetti, soups and meat mixture. Put in baking dish and cover top with grated cheese. Cover and cook for 45 minutes in a 350 degree oven. Remove lid and cook 10 minutes more or until top browns. This dish freezes or can be made a day or so ahead. Serves 8.

Mrs. T. Carlton Billups

RANCH STYLE BAKED BEANS

~~2 T. margarine or butter~~
1 lb. ground chuck
1 pkg. Lipton onion soup mix
1 c. catsup
2 cans [1 lb.] pork and beans

~~1 can [1 lb.] kidney beans, drained~~
1/2 c. cold water
2 T. prepared mustard
2 t. cider vinegar

Ranch style beans

Preheat oven to 400 degrees. In large skillet, melt butter and brown meat. Stir in soup mix, catsup, beans, water, mustard and vinegar. Pour into a 2 1/2 quart casserole or bean pot. Bake 30 to 45 minutes until hot and bubbly. Serves 8 to 10.

Mrs. Julius Bergfeld, Jr.

EGGPLANT GREEK

1 1/2 lbs. ground chuck
1 c. onion, chopped
2 cloves garlic, chopped
1/2 T. oregano
1 t. basil leaves
1/2 t. cinnamon

Salt and pepper to taste
2 cans [8 oz.] tomato sauce
1 c. Parmesan cheese
1 c. grated cheese
2 eggplants

Cream Sauce:

4 T. butter
4 T. flour
2 c. milk

1 t. salt
1 t. pepper
2 eggs

For meat sauce, brown meat, onion, and garlic. Add seasonings and tomato sauce. Simmer while preparing cream sauce.

To prepare cream sauce, melt butter, add flour and stir. Add milk gradually. Cook and stir constantly until thickened. Add salt, pepper and beaten eggs.

Mix cheeses. Slice unpeeled eggplant crosswise, then in half (half circle). Brush with melted butter and salt lightly. Broil about 4 minutes on cookie sheet. Lay eggplant end to end on bottom of greased casserole. Layer meat sauce, cream sauce and cheese mixture. Bake 35 to 40 minutes at 350 degrees. Better the second day!

Mrs. Clyde Davis

LILLIAN'S GREEK CASSEROLE

2 lbs. ground meat
1 medium onion, chopped
1 small bell pepper, chopped
2 T. flour
2 c. water
2 T. Kitchen Bouquet

2 T. Cavender's Greek
seasoning
1 pkg. [8 oz.] medium
noodles
1 c. sour cream
Parmesan cheese

Brown meat, onion and pepper together in iron skillet. Push aside meat mixture and add flour to drippings and mix well. Add water, Kitchen Bouquet and Greek seasoning and simmer for 15 minutes. Cook noodles until almost tender. Layer noodles, meat (mixed with sour cream) and Parmesan cheese. Bake at 350 degrees for 20 minutes. Serves 8.

Mrs. Robert D. Rice

JOHNNY BRAZILIAN

9 to 10 lbs. ground beef
6 onions, chopped
6 bell peppers, chopped
4 cans whole kernel corn
8 cans tomato soup
8 cans cream of mushroom soup

6 pkgs. macaroni [any size]
1 jar [med. size] salad
   pimiento olives
2 small cans chopped ripe
   olives
4 lbs. grated cheese

Cook meat, onions and peppers until almost done. Add corn and soups and continue cooking 30 minutes. Add water, if needed, until mixture is desired thickness. Cook macaroni according to directions on the package. Gently add olives to meat sauce and fold in cooked macaroni and grated cheese, reserving enough cheese for topping the casserole. Turn into baking dish. Sprinkle on reserved cheese and bake at 350 degrees for 20 to 30 minutes or until cheese is hot and melted. Serves 30 to 40.

Mrs. James Milstead

BURGUNDY MEAT LOAF

2 lbs. medium lean ground meat
1 1/2 c. Gallo's Hearty Burgundy
1 green pepper, chopped
1 onion, chopped
1 stalk celery, chopped
Salt and pepper

1 egg
1 c. cracker crumbs
1 can [8 oz.] Hunt's
   tomato sauce
Old London bread crumbs
Parmesan cheese

In mixing bowl, soak meat in wine overnight or several hours. Mash meat down in bowl, poking holes so wine may get all through it.

Saute' in butter the green pepper, onion, and celery until tender; add small amount of water and steam them. Then mix all ingredients together. Place in baking dish. Top with bread crumbs and sprinkle with Parmesan cheese. Catsup may be added on top, if desired, or served with it. For Italian flavor, use Italian Herb Seasoning by Spice Islands. Bake at 350 degrees for 35 minutes. May be frozen (use Saran wrap and foil). Serves 6 to 8.

Mrs. Gordon Brelsford

MEAT BALLS IN BARBECUE SAUCE

1 1/2 lbs. ground beef
3/4 c. uncooked oatmeal
1 c. milk

3 T. chopped onions
1 1/2 t. salt
1/2 t. pepper

Mix the above thoroughly and form into balls. Brown on both sides and place in baking dish or casserole.

Sauce:

1 c. catsup
2 T. Worcestershire sauce
1/2 c. water

3 T. vinegar
1 T. sugar
6 T. chopped onions

Mix all sauce ingredients together; pour over meat balls and bake 300 degrees uncovered 1/2 hour. Turn occasionally. Serves 5.

Mrs. Clayton Hamilton

Meat balls may be made smaller and served in a chafing dish as an appetizer.

MARINATED CALVES LIVER

1 lb. calves liver
1/4 c. vermouth
1 c. soy sauce
1 t. salt

1/4 t. pepper
1 to 1 1/2 c. flour
1 c. vegetable oil
2 T. Worcestershire sauce

Remove all membranes and skin from the calves liver and marinate in the vermouth and soy sauce for 20 minutes. (This is one time when it does make a difference how long the meat marinates. Leaving it too long causes the meat to lose all flavor.)

Remove from the marinade and salt and pepper on both sides. Coat thoroughly with flour and brown well on both sides at medium heat. Don't overcook! Drain off any remaining oil and sprinkle the Worcestershire sauce over liver. Remove pan from heat and leave covered for a few minutes. This smothers the liver without overcooking it. Serves 4 to 6.

Mrs. William Rowe

CURRIED VEAL CUTLETS

6 veal cutlets
1/2 c. flour
2 T. curry powder
3/4 t. salt
1/4 t. pepper

1 egg, beaten
2 T. butter
1/4 c. consomme'
1/4 c. chutney

Mix flour, curry powder and seasonings together. Dip veal cutlet into flour mixture, then into beaten egg; then into flour again. Saute' in butter until brown. Add consomme', cover pan and cook slowly approximately 40 minutes. Add a little chutney on each cutlet and heat 5 minutes more. Serves 5 or 6.

Mrs. R. R. Harding

FRENCH VEAL CUTLETS

2 lbs. veal cutlets
1 T. flour
1 t. salt
3 T. fat or salad oil
1 1/3 c. minced onion
2 T. snipped parsley
1 t. paprika
2 t. prepared mustard

1 beef bouillon cube
1 c. boiling water
1 c. commercial sour
cream
1/4 t. salt
1 T. flour
1 1/2 T. cold water

Have veal flattened to 1/4 inch thick by butcher. Cut into 5 or 6 pieces. Sprinkle with 1 tablespoon flour combined with 1 teaspoon salt.

In 2 tablespoons hot fat in skillet, saute' onions until tender; remove. Add 1 tablespoon fat to skillet; brown veal until golden on both sides. Add onions, parsley, paprika, mustard and bouillon cube dissolved in boiling water.

Simmer, covered, over low heat 45 minutes, or until veal is very tender.

Remove veal to heated platter. To liquid in skillet, add sour cream; heat thoroughly. Stir together 1/4 teaspoon salt, 1 tablespoon flour, cold water; cook, stirring until thickened; pour over veal. Serves 5 or 6.

Mrs. Roy E. Tidwell

SWISS VEAL SUPREME

1 lb. veal round, 1/2 inch thick
[may substitute beef round]
4 thin slices boiled ham
[Danish ham]
8 small slices Swiss cheese
1/2 c. flour

1 egg, slightly beaten
1/4 c. milk
1 c. fine dry bread crumbs
1 stick margarine or
butter
Dry white wine

Have round steak butterfly cut and tenderized by butcher until about 1/8 inch thick (cut into 4 pieces). Place 1 slice ham and 2 slices cheese on each veal steak. Fold meat over and secure with toothpicks. Salt and pepper, cover with flour, then dip in egg and milk mixture and roll in bread crumbs until covered. Melt butter in skillet. Brown both sides until golden brown, then reduce heat to low and cook until meat is done, approximately 10 to 15 minutes. Remove meat. Swish out skillet with dry white wine and splash over meat. Serves 4.

Mrs. Robert Caton, III

VEAL BIRDS

1 1/2 lb. veal steak - have butcher trim fat and cut into 6 pieces of
uniform size.
1/4 c. flour
2 T. Crisco
1 1/2 c. boiling water

Stuffing:

1 c. bread [or cracker] crumbs
2 T. butter, melted
2 T. chopped parsley
1/2 t. onion juice

2 T. celery seed
1/2 t. salt
1/8 t. paprika

Combine stuffing ingredients. Wipe veal and spread each piece with stuffing. Roll and fasten with toothpicks. Roll birds in flour and brown in melted Crisco. Remove veal and stir in remaining flour. Add boiling water and make a smooth gravy. Place birds in covered roaster. Pour gravy over them and bake 1 hour at 375 degrees.

Mrs. Jack Harding

SAFFRON VEAL STRIPS

2 lb. veal steak
1/4 c. butter
1/8 t. garlic powder
1/2 t. Accent
1/32 t. saffron
1 t. Beau Monde seasoning
  [Spice Islands]
1/2 t. salt

1/4 t. cracked Java black
  pepper
1 T. instant minced
  onion
1/2 t. thyme, crushed
2 c. evaporated milk
1 T. arrowroot

Cut meat into strips about 1/2 inch wide. Remove bones and connective tissue. Melt butter in heavy skillet; add veal strips and brown lightly. Combine garlic powder, Accent, saffron, Beau Monde, salt and pepper. Sprinkle over veal; turn meat and stir until coated with seasonings. Add onions and thyme and sprinkle over meat. Cover and cook over low heat until veal is tender (about 45 minutes). Add milk. Moisten arrowroot with a little cold water and mix with meat. Cook, stirring constantly until sauce is thickened and smooth. Serve over noodles or rice. Serves 6.

Mrs. Norman Halbrooks

BARBECUED WIENERS

1 c. tomato catsup
3 T. Worcestershire sauce
1 T. horseradish
1 T. olive oil

1 T. vinegar
1/4 lb. butter
1 pkg. wieners

Mix all ingredients except wieners in a large skillet and cook slowly about 5 minutes, stirring well. Add boiled, split wieners and simmer in sauce until they "curl". Serve with corn bread or on buns topped with remainder of sauce. Serves 6 to 8.

Mrs. Harvey Wallender, Jr.

LEG OF LAMB

1 leg of lamb

1 onion, thinly sliced

Sauce:

Juice of 1/2 lemon
1 t. catsup

1 t. Worcestershire sauce

Place leg of lamb in roasting pan in 450 degree oven for 1/2 hour. Reduce heat to 350 degrees and add onion, sliced very thin, to the juice in the pan. Cook 20 minutes per pound of roast. Add sauce ingredients to the pan juices and onion and baste lamb with this sauce several times during duration of cooking. Add a small amount of water if necessary.

Mrs. W. Dewey Lawrence

GRILLED MINTED LEG OF LAMB

1 leg of lamb [about 7 lbs.]
1/4 c. finely chopped fresh
    mint leaves [or 2 t. dried
    mint leaves]
1 c. dry white wine

2 cloves garlic, crushed
1 t. salt
1/2 t. coarsely ground pepper
    [or lemon pepper]

Have butcher remove bone and flatten leg of lamb so that it is roughly the same thickness throughout and resembles a steak. Combine marinade ingredients in large shallow glass container. Put lamb in and turn to coat both sides. Cover with plastic wrap and refrigerate about 4 hours, turning once during marinating time. Remove lamb and grill about 4 inches from medium-hot coals for 20 minutes per side - or until medium done. Brush occasionally during grilling with marinade sauce. Place on cutting board and slice crosswise in 1/4 inch thick slices to serve. Serves 8.

Kenneth C. Lust

LAMB SHANK BORSCHT

6 lamb shanks, whole or
    cracked
1 can [47 oz.] chicken broth
    [about 6 c.]
1 1/2 c. water
1 bay leaf
6 whole black peppers
1 t. salt
1 small green pepper,
    seeded and diced

3 medium sized carrots,
    diced
1 medium sized onion,
    finely chopped
4 small beets, diced
4 c. finely shredded
    cabbage
1 small potato, diced
2 T. lemon juice

Put lamb shanks, chicken broth, water, bay leaf, black pepper and salt into a large Dutch oven. Cover and simmer until lamb is tender (about 2 hours). If desired, soup may be cooled and refrigerated at this point. Skim fat and discard. Strain broth and discard black pepper and bay leaf. Return meat to the stock; add green pepper, carrots, onion, beets, cabbage and potato and simmer 15 to 20 minutes, or until vegetables are tender. Remove from heat; stir in lemon juice. Ladle mixture into bowls and garnish with lemon wedges. Makes 6 servings.

Mrs. John Warner

Even non-lamb-eaters think this is delicious.

CHRISTMAS MORNING BREAKFAST

6 eggs
1 c. cubed bread
1 c. mild Cheddar cheese,
    grated

1 c. cubed ham
1 c. milk
1 t. dry mustard
1/2 t. salt

Beat eggs; add remaining ingredients. Pour into 8 x 8 inch greased pan. Bake at 350 degrees for 45 minutes. Cut into squares and serve 6 to 8.

Mrs. John Lenhart
Longview, Texas

HAM-ASPARAGUS ROLLS

32 stalks cooked asparagus
8 thin slices boiled ham
4 T. butter or margarine
2 T. flour

Salt and pepper to taste
2 c. milk
1 c. grated Swiss cheese

Wrap 4 or 5 stalks cooked asparagus in each thin ham slice. Secure with toothpick. Place in shallow baking dish, side by side. Do not stack. Make a cream sauce of butter or margarine, flour, salt, pepper and milk. When slightly thickened, add grated Swiss cheese and stir until cheese is melted. Pour over ham rolls. Bake in 350 degree oven for 25 minutes. Paprika sprinkled over top makes a more attractive dish. Serves 4 to 8.

Mrs. R. W. Eaton

HAM STRATA

12 slices bread [trim off
    edges]
Sliced Cheddar cheese
4 c. diced ham
2 pkgs. frozen chopped
    broccoli [cook as directed]

6 eggs
3 c. milk
1/2 t. salt
1/4 t. dry mustard
Onion flakes

Butter 3 quart pyrex dish generously. Layer bottom with bread slices; add sliced cheese, ham and cooked broccoli. Whip eggs in blender; add milk, salt and mustard to eggs; pour slowly over bread, etc. in pyrex dish and let soak in. Sprinkle lightly with onion flakes - don't forget the onion flakes as they are important.

IMPORTANT: Refrigerate 6 to 8 hours or overnight. Bake uncovered 1 hour 20 minutes at 325 degrees. Bake long enough to be able to cut into squares to serve. This will freeze well if covered with Saran wrap and foil. Serves 6 to 8.

Mrs. Robert Henry

Cheddar cheese must be used, as it will not "string".

CHEESE & HAM SOUFFLÉ

3 T. butter
3 T. flour
1/2 c. milk
1/2 t. salt
1/2 to 1 c. grated cheese

1 t. mustard
4 beaten egg yolks
1 c. chopped ham
4 egg whites, stiffly
   beaten

Melt butter. Add flour and milk and salt. Cook until thickened; then add cheese, mustard and egg yolks. Stir in ham and fold in beaten egg whites. Bake in buttered 1 1/2 quart deep casserole dish at 350 degrees for 20 to 30 minutes.

Mrs. Steve Nourse

HOT HAM SANDWICH

1 stick margarine
1 T. poppy seeds
1 T. onion flakes
1/4 c. mustard
12 buns, split [potato
   dinner rolls or 1 pkg.
   Pepperidge Farm small
   rolls for daintier ones]

Ham, very thinly sliced
   or "shaved"
Swiss cheese, thinly
   sliced

Melt margarine in saucepan and add poppy seeds, onion flakes and mustard. Spread split buns (or rolls) with this mixture and insert one portion of ham and cheese into each bun. Wrap in foil. (Freeze or refrigerate at this point if desired.) Bake 15 minutes at 350 degrees (or longer for chilled or frozen sandwiches).

Mrs. William C. Smyth

RUDI'S HAM LOAF

2 lbs. ground smoked ham
1 lb. ground veal [loin tips]
2 eggs
1 c. small broken pieces of
   day old Pepperidge Farm bread
1 1/2 c. milk
1 t. Worcestershire sauce

1/2 t. dry mustard
1/2 c. brown sugar
3 T. melted butter
1/4 c. apricot juice
   [from canned apricots]
Parsley

Mix first seven ingredients. Shape into loaf. Cover bottom of loaf pan with brown sugar, butter and apricot juice; add loaf. Bake at 350 degrees for about 2 hours. Turn loaf out upside down. Garnish with parsley and apricot halves. Can be served with horseradish sauce or mustard sauce if desired. Serves 8 or more. Will freeze in foil.

Mrs. Robert P. Lake

HAM LOAF

1 lb. ground center cut ham
1 1/2 lbs. ground lean pork
   shoulder
3 eggs
2/3 c. tomato juice

2/3 c. milk
1 c. fine bread crumbs
Salt and pepper
1/2 medium onion, chopped
   medium

Combine all ingredients and form into loaf 3 x 2 x 10 inches. Cook in 350 degree oven for about 1 hour and 15 minutes (1 hour and 30 minutes if fresh ham and pork are used). Baste during cooking with the following sauce:

Ham Loaf Sauce:

1 c. brown sugar
3/4 c. water
3/4 c. apple cider vinegar

1 t. dry mustard
1/2 medium onion, chopped
   fine

Combine all ingredients and boil together until blended. This ham loaf serves 6 and freezes beautifully before cooking.

Mrs. James L. Gulley

POTATO AND HAM CASSEROLE

3 medium potatoes
3 c. cooked diced ham
3 T. butter

Milk to cover
Pepper

Wash and pare potatoes and slice in thin slices. Place in alternate layers with ham and butter in a buttered 2 quart baking dish or casserole. Cover with milk and season with pepper. Bake covered at 350 degrees for 30 minutes. Remove cover and continue baking until potatoes are tender. Serves 4.

Mrs. William Finn

CASSEROLE PORK CHOPS

5 or 6 center cut pork chops
2 bouillon cubes
2 c. boiling water
1 c. raw rice
1 sliced onion

1 sliced tomato
1 sliced green bell
  pepper
Salt and pepper to taste

Brown pork chops in electric skillet and then remove from skillet. Add bouillon cubes dissolved in boiling water. Stir in rice and place pork chops back in skillet. Cover each chop with a slice of onion, slice of tomato and a slice of bell pepper and season. Cover and simmer until done, about 30 minutes. Serves 5 to 6.

Mrs. J. Donald Guinn

CREOLE PORK CHOPS

4 to 6 pork chops [nice size
  and medium thick]
1 c. uncooked rice
1 onion, chopped
1 c. diced celery

2 large cans tomatoes
1 t. salt
1/2 t. thyme
1/4 t. pepper

Trim excess fat from chops. Melt trimmings in an electric skillet to make 2 tablespoons of fat. Discard trimmings. Toast rice in fat and remove rice from pan. Brown chops in same pan and remove. Cook onion and celery in same fat until golden. Place the chops in pan, spoon rice between, add tomatoes, seasonings and cover. Cook over low heat for 1 hour. For softer rice, add 1/4 cup of water to tomatoes. Serves 4.

Mrs. Lynn F. Cobb

CZECH PORK CHOPS

6 pork chops, 3/4 in. thick
2 cloves garlic
1/2 c. chopped onion
2 T. shortening

1 t. caraway seed
Salt and pepper
1/2 c. water

Salt, pepper and flour chops. In heavy skillet, saute' pulverized garlic and chopped onion in shortening. Add chops and cook on medium heat until browned on both sides. Transfer chops and onion mixture to baking dish; sprinkle on caraway seed, salt and pepper and add water. Cover and bake until tender at 350 degrees. Turn every 30 minutes. Cook approximately 1 to 1 1/2 hours. Serves 6.

Mrs. Lonnie Holotik

Serve with Czech spinach and German potato salad.

BARBECUED SPARERIBS

2 rib sections of spareribs
1 can [8 oz.] tomato sauce
2 T. wine vinegar
2 T. minced onions
Salt and pepper
Red pepper

1/2 c. honey
1 clove garlic
1 t. Worcestershire sauce
1 t. celery seed
1/2 c. dry sherry

Cut ribs in serving size pieces and place in open roasting pan. Season with salt and pepper and cook them at 450 degrees for 30 minutes. Pour off excess grease. Coat with basting sauce made from other ingredients and cook over charcoal fire, basting frequently for 45 minutes to 1 hour. Serves 4.

Mrs. Harold Cameron

GERMAN PORK RIBS AND SAUERKRAUT

Lean pork spareribs
Sauerkraut, canned or in jar
Irish potatoes

Broil spareribs until slightly browned. Drain off grease. Place sauerkraut and liquid in deep casserole. Peel and slice potatoes and place on sauerkraut. Add ribs on top. Cover and cook in 350 degree oven for about 1 hour. Serves 6 to 8.

Mrs. J. Donald Guinn

OVEN BARBECUED RIBS I

5 or 6 lbs. pork ribs and
   blade pieces
2 cloves garlic, minced
2 T. butter or margarine
1 1/2 c. water
1 c. catsup
3/4 c. chili sauce

1/4 c. brown sugar
2 T. prepared mustard
2 T. Worcestershire sauce
1 T. celery seed
1/2 t. salt
1 or 2 dashes Tabasco

Cut ribs in serving size pieces (2 or 3 ribs per serving). Place on rack in large shallow baking pan. Bake, covered, in very hot oven (450 degrees for 45 minutes). In saucepan, cook minced garlic in butter over low heat for 4 to 5 minutes. Blend in remaining ingredients. Bring to boiling. Remove meat from pan. Drain off fat. Remove rack; return ribs to pan (foil may be placed in bottom). Pour on sauce. Reduce temperature to 350 degrees; bake uncovered for 1 1/2 hours (or a little less if foil is in bottom). Brush ribs occasionally with sauce. Makes 6 servings.

Mrs. Watson Simons

Beef ribs may be substituted.

OVEN BARBECUED RIBS II

3 or 4 lbs. spareribs [thin]   1 large onion, sliced
1 lemon, sliced

Basting Sauce:

1 c. catsup   1 t. chili powder
1/3 c. Worcestershire   1 t. salt
2 dashes Tabasco   1 1/2 c. water

Salt ribs. Place in shallow roasting pan, meaty side up. Roast at 450 degrees for 30 minutes. Drain fat. Top each rib with a slice of lemon and slice of onion. Make sauce and bring to a boil. Pour over ribs.

Lower temperature to 350 degrees, bake until well-done (about 1 1/2 hours), basting ribs with sauce every 20 to 30 minutes. Add water if sauce gets too thick. Serves 4.

Mrs. Julius L. Bergfeld, Jr.

SAUSAGE RING WITH SCRAMBLED EGGS AND SPANISH SAUCE

Sausage Ring and Eggs: **Spanish Sauce:**

2 eggs   3 T. vegetable oil
2 T. grated onion   1/3 c. chopped onion
1 c. fine dry bread crumbs   1/4 c. chopped green pepper
1/4 c. chopped parsley   3/4 c. sliced mushrooms
1 1/2 lbs. bulk pork sausage   1 T. cornstarch
                                     1 can [16 oz.] tomatoes
Eggs scrambled for 8   1 t. salt
                                     Dash of pepper
                                     2 t. sugar
                                     Dash of cayenne pepper

Sausage Ring - Beat 2 eggs in large bowl. Add onion, bread crumbs, parsley and sausage. Mix thoroughly. Pack mixture into a greased 8 1/2 inch ring mold. Bake 20 minutes at 350 degrees. Remove from oven and drain off fat. Bake 20 minutes longer. Drain; turn out onto heated platter and fill center with scrambled eggs for 8 people. Serve with Spanish Sauce on the side so guests can spoon over the eggs and sausage. Serves 8.

Spanish Sauce - Heat oil; add onion, pepper and mushrooms. Cook until lightly browned. Combine cornstarch with 2 tablespoons of juice from the tomatoes. Add to vegetable mixture with the tomatoes, salt, pepper, sugar and cayenne. Cook over low heat, stirring frequently about 15 minutes until thickened. Makes 3 cups.

The sausage ring may be molded ahead of time and cooked later. The Spanish Sauce may be cooked several days ahead.

Mrs. Lynn F. Cobb

This dish may be served with hot curried fruit and hot bread for a delicious brunch menu or late night supper.

SAUSAGE AND RICE CASSEROLE

1 lb. Owen's Hot Sausage
1/2 c. chopped celery
1/2 c. chopped onion
1 sm. can mushrooms, drained
1 c. uncooked rice

1 1/2 envelopes chicken
noodle soup mix
2 1/2 c. water
1 small pkg. slivered
almonds

Grease long pyrex pan. Brown sausage thoroughly; drain and set aside. Reserve 2 tablespoons grease to saute' celery, onion and mushrooms. Add remaining ingredients to sausage. (Freeze at this point, if desired.) Bake (tightly covered with foil) at 325 degrees for about 1 hour. (Check after 45 minutes.) Serves 6 to 8 or may easily be doubled or tripled.

Mrs. Dick Hightower

ITALIAN NOODLE CASSEROLE

8 oz. noodles
1 1/2 lbs. ground chuck
1 onion, minced
1 clove garlic, mashed
1/4 c. olive oil
2 c. tomato sauce
2 T. tomato paste

3 eggs, beaten
1 pkg. frozen chopped
spinach, defrosted
1 lb. cottage cheese
1/2 c. grated Parmesan
cheese

Cook the noodles in boiling salted water 8 minutes. Drain. Cook the meat, onion and garlic in the olive oil, stirring constantly, until the meat loses its red color. Mix meat and noodles with tomato sauce, tomato paste, eggs, spinach and cottage cheese in a 3 quart casserole. Top with grated Parmesan. Bake in 375 degree oven for 30 minutes, or until cheese is brown. Serves 6 to 8.

Mrs. F. Lee Lawrence

ITALERINE

3 lbs. hamburger
2 large onions, chopped
4 cloves garlic, chopped
1/2 lb. butter
1 large can tomato juice
3 pkgs. [medium size] noodles

1 sm. can whole kernel corn
1 can ripe olives, chopped
2 cans mushrooms and
juice
3 lbs. Velveeta, grated
2 T. chili powder

In large pan (electric skillet works well), brown ground meat, onions and garlic in butter. Add tomato juice and noodles. Cook slowly until noodles are done. Add corn, olives, mushrooms, grated cheese and chili powder. Cook slowly for 1 1/2 hours. Stir occasionally. Serves 10. Freezes well.

Mrs. R. B. Shelton

ITALIAN DELIGHT

2 lbs. ground chuck
1 large onion, chopped
1 T. chili powder [heaping]
1 1/2 t. salt
1/2 t. pepper
1 t. garlic salt

3 cans [8 oz.] tomato
  sauce
1/2 pkg. noodles
1 pkg. or can corn
  [cooked, if frozen]
1 c. grated Cheddar cheese

Brown ground meat with onion; add chili powder, salt, pepper, garlic salt. Add 3 cans tomato sauce and only enough water to rinse cans. Cook noodles; add to sauce. Add corn and mix well. Sprinkle with grated cheese. Bake at 350 degrees for 30 minutes. Serves 6 to 8.

Mrs. Edwin Simons

JOHNNY MAZUMI

4 T. butter
3 lbs. lean ground beef
2 T. salt
2 t. pepper
1/2 t. garlic salt
2 cans [8 oz.] tomato sauce
1 pkg. [10 oz.] medium egg
  noodles, cooked according
  to directions

2 c. creamed cottage
  cheese
2 c. sour cream
12 finely chopped green
  onions [plus about 3
  inches of tops]
1 1/2 c. grated sharp
  Cheddar cheese

Melt butter in skillet. Add meat. Cook and stir just until meat loses red color. (Should be slightly rare.) Add salt, pepper, garlic salt and tomato sauce. Simmer gently for 5 minutes. Remove from heat and set aside. Combine cooked noodles with cottage cheese, sour cream and onions. Mix with meat sauce. Pour into 1 large or 2 small casseroles. Top with grated cheese. Bake 30 minutes at 350 degrees. Serves 12.

Mrs. Thomas Swann

If preferred, prepare the day before serving, using 1 extra cup of sour cream and adding 15 minutes to baking time. Also freezes nicely.

LASAGNA I

1 to 1 1/2 lbs. ground chuck
1/4 c. olive oil
2 cloves garlic, chopped
1 onion, finely chopped
1 can [#2 1/2] Italian style
   or regular tomatoes
2 cans [6 oz.] tomato paste
1 t. salt
1 t. oregano

1/2 t. pepper
1 t. onion salt
1 pkg. lasagna noodles,
   cooked as directed on
   pkg.
3/4 c. Parmesan cheese
1/2 lb. Mozzarella cheese,
   sliced
1 lb. cottage cheese

Brown meat in olive oil with garlic and onion. Mix tomatoes and tomato paste in cooker (Dutch oven may be used) with a tight lid. Add seasonings and meat and cook slowly for 3 hours. Water may have to be added, but not much; mixture should be thick.

When sauce is done, place a layer of sauce on bottom of long baking pan, then layer of noodles, then sprinkle Parmesan, Mozzarella and cottage cheese. Repeat, ending with sauce. Bake 35 to 40 minutes until cheese melts and it is hot.

This freezes beautifully and serves at least 6.

Mrs. William C. Smyth

LASAGNA II

Sauce:

1 lb. ground meat
1 clove garlic, minced
1 T. whole basil
1 1/2 t. salt
1 can [1 lb.] tomatoes
2 cans [6 oz.] tomato paste

1 box lasagna noodles
3 c. cottage cheese
1/2 c. Parmesan cheese
2 T. parsley flakes
2 beaten eggs
2 t. salt
1/2 t. pepper
1 lb. Mozzarella cheese,
   sliced very thin

Brown meat, spoon off excess fat. Add rest of sauce ingredients and simmer uncovered 30 minutes. Cook noodles following directions on box. Combine remaining ingredients except Mozzarella cheese. Place one-half noodles in long baking dish. Spread with one-half cottage cheese mixture, one-half Mozzarella cheese and one-half meat sauce. Repeat layers, ending with meat sauce. Bake at 375 degrees for 30 minutes. Remove from oven and let cool 10 minutes before cutting into squares. Serves 12.

Mrs. J. L. Bergfeld, Jr.

PASTASCHUTA

1 large pepper, diced
2 large onions, diced
1 lb. ground beef
Salt and pepper
1 t. comino seed
1 t. chili powder

1/4 t. garlic salt
1 can creamed corn
1 can mushroom soup
1 lb. short spaghetti
Grated cheese

Brown pepper, onion and meat. Add salt, pepper, comino seed, chili powder, garlic salt and cook 15 minutes. Add creamed corn and soup. Cook 15 minutes more. Cook spaghetti; then add to meat mixture and place in casserole dish. Top with grated cheese. Bake at 350 degrees for 30 minutes. Serves 8.

Mrs. James E. Bass

PIZZA BURGERS

1 c. catsup
1/3 c. salad oil
2 T. wine vinegar
1/4 t. sweet basil
2 lbs. ground chuck

1 c. Mozzarella cheese,
  shredded
Pepperoni, thinly sliced
4 hamburger buns, split

Combine catsup, oil, vinegar and basil for sauce. Stir well and allow to simmer for about 5 minutes.

Form meat into 8 patties. Place meat on hot grill set 1 to 2 inches above gray coals. Barbecue about 4 minutes. Turn patties over. Cover each with sauce, shredded cheese and pepperoni. Cook an additional 4 minutes or until done. Toast buns on grill. Spread toasted sides with sauce; top with meat patty. Serve open-faced. Serves 8.

Mrs. L. Glenn Taylor

PIZZA MEAT LOAF

1 can tomato soup
1/4 c. water
1/2 t. oregano
1 small clove garlic, minced
1 c. small bread cubes
1/4 c. chopped onion

2 T. parsley
1 egg, beaten
1 t. salt
1/8 t. pepper
2 lbs. ground beef
2 slices Mozzarella cheese

Blend soup, water, oregano and garlic. In bowl, combine 1/4 cup soup mixture, bread, onion, parsley, egg, salt and pepper. Mix thoroughly with beef.

Shape firmly into loaf. Place in a shallow baking pan. Bake at 350 degrees for 1 hour, 15 minutes. Remove from oven and spoon off fat. Pour remaining soup mixture over loaf and heat thoroughly. Top with cheese; bake until cheese melts.

Mrs. Charles Clark

Variation: Add layer of Mozzarella in the middle of loaf.

PIZZA PIE

Dough:

1/2 yeast cake
2 c. flour
1/2 t. salt
3 T. olive oil

Filling:

1 can tomato paste
1 can tomato sauce
1 t. oregano
1/4 t. garlic powder
3/4 lb. Velveeta cheese, grated
Parmesan cheese
1 1/2 lbs. sausage [precooked]
1 green pepper, chopped

Dissolve yeast in 1/2 cup warm water. Sift dry ingredients into bowl and add dissolved yeast and olive oil. Knead well into soft dough; cover and let stand 5 to 6 hours until double in bulk. Divide into 3 parts and roll into 3 pizza pans.

Combine tomato paste and sauce with oregano and garlic powder. Spread equally on each crust. Next spread grated Velveeta. Sprinkle with Parmesan, crumbled sausage and green pepper. Bake at 450 degrees until bubbly and lightly browned (15 to 20 minutes). Makes 6 wedges to each pan and serves about 8. This may be made ahead or frozen, cooked or uncooked.

Mrs. Wade C. Ridley

Try adding favorite toppings of sausage, green pepper, mushrooms, hamburger, pepperoni or anchovy. All or a combination of several are great. Mozzarella cheese may be used in place of Velveeta.

TALLERINA

2 lbs. ground chuck
1 green pepper, chopped
1 large onion, chopped
2 T. chili powder
1 t. salt
Pepper

1 can [#1] tomatoes
1 can [#2] creamed corn
1 sm. can chopped mushrooms
1/2 c. stuffed olives
1 pkg. [5 1/2 oz.] noodles
1/2 lb. grated cheese

Brown meat, pepper and onion. Add all other ingredients except noodles and cheese. Cook noodles until tender. Drain and layer with meat mixture in two large casseroles. Top with cheese and bake 20 minutes at 400 degrees. Serves 16. Freezes well.

Mrs. James Coker
New Delhi, India
Mrs. Wayne Leake

Mrs. Jonathan E. Boyle prepares her Tallerina dish with the addition of garlic (crushed and stirred in with onion), 2 teaspoons of Worcestershire sauce and 2 teaspoons of soy sauce. She uses the whole kernel corn instead of creamed and 1 cup of sliced ripe olives instead of stuffed olives.

VEAL SCALLOPINI

1 lb. veal scallopini, cut
   very thin
1/3 c. flour seasoned with
   salt and pepper

6 T. butter
1/4 c. dry wine [white]

Coat scallopini with flour. Saute' in hot butter about 3 minutes on each side; add white wine, simmer 2 minutes longer. Serve at once. If desired, may be served over rice. Serves 4.

Mrs. Harry Hudson

BEEF AND PEPPERS ORIENTAL

1/4 c. vegetable oil
1 clove garlic, crushed
1 t. powdered ginger
2 1/2 lb. flank steak, cut in
   very thin diagonal slices
2 green peppers, cut in
   julienne strips

3/4 c. chopped onion
2 T. soy sauce
1 can [8 oz.] tomato sauce
1 t. sugar
Dash pepper
1 can [1 lb.] bean sprouts
Cooked rice

Heat oil, garlic and ginger in large skillet. Add steak slices; cook over high heat 5 minutes, stirring constantly; remove meat. Add peppers and onion to remaining oil in skillet; cook 2 minutes. Add soy sauce, tomato sauce, sugar and pepper; cook 3 minutes. Add meat and bean sprouts; cook 2 minutes longer, or until heated through. Serve on hot, cooked rice. Serves 6. Freezes well.

Mrs. Wade C. Ridley

CHINESE PEPPER STEAK

2 lb. boneless beef chuck
   or round steak
2 T. oil
1 bunch green onions,
   cut in 1 in. pieces,
   including tops
1 1/2 c. sliced celery
2 cloves garlic, minced

1 1/2 t. salt
1/8 t. pepper
1 c. full strength canned
   beef bouillon
2 large green peppers
2 T. cornstarch in 1/4 c.
   water
1 T. soy sauce

Trim fat off beef and cut in thin strips (about 1 x 2 inch). Put oil in Dutch oven and brown meat. Add a little water and cook covered until tender. Add onions, celery, garlic, seasonings and hot bouillon. Cook until vegetables are still crisp but partially cooked. Add the green pepper (cut into slices) and cook about 5 minutes longer. Add cornstarch blended with 1/4 cup cold water and cook until thickened. Add soy sauce. Serve on hot cooked rice topped with Chinese noodles. Serves 4.

Mrs. Edwin Simons

PEPPER STEAK

1 lb. round steak, cubed
2 T. shortening
1 T. flour
1/2 c. water
1/2 c. catsup
3 T. soy sauce
1/8 t. pepper
1 beef bouillon cube

1 garlic clove, minced
1/2 c. chopped onion
1 can mushrooms or fresh
   mushrooms
2 large peppers, cut in
   rings
2 medium onions, cut in
   rings

Brown meat in shortening, remove. Blend flour into the shortening from which the meat was removed. Add water, catsup, soy sauce, pepper, bouillon, garlic and chopped onion. Bring to boil, lower heat to simmer for 20 minutes. Drop meat into sauce and cook only until tender. This much can be done 2 or 3 days before serving and refrigerated. Ten minutes before serving, add chopped mushrooms, pepper and onion rings. Cook until crisply tender - about 10 minutes. Serve on fluffy rice. Do not add additional salt to meat. Serves 6.

Mrs. Ronald S. Smith

SUKIYAKI

3 lb. sirloin, cut in thin
   strips
1 large onion, coarsely
   chopped
3 T. cooking oil
1 bottle [5 oz.] soy sauce
4 cans [4 oz. each] sliced
   mushrooms, drained
1/2 t. black pepper

1/4 t. [scant] nutmeg
2 cans [8 oz. each] water
   chestnuts, drained
   and sliced
4 large tomatoes, cut
   in wedges
4 bell peppers, sliced
   in rings
1 can [16 oz.] bean sprouts

Saute' sirloin and onion in oil. Add soy sauce, mushrooms, pepper, nutmeg, and water chestnuts. Simmer, covered, until meat is tender and flavors are blended (about 40 minutes). Just before serving, place over high heat. Lay tomatoes, peppers and bean sprouts on top of meat mixture. Cover, and cook 5 to 7 minutes. (Japanese style vegetables should be cooked only a short time in order that they remain crisp.) Serve over white rice with extra soy sauce. Serves 8.

Mrs. Morris Gary

ISLAND TERIYAKI

1/2 c. soy sauce
1/4 c. brown sugar
2 T. olive oil
1 t. ginger

1/4 t. cracked pepper
2 cloves garlic, minced
1 1/2 lb. sirloin

Combine ingredients in deep bowl. (Sirloin should be cut into strips 1/2 inch thick and 1 inch wide). Marinate several hours at room temperature. Lace on skewers. Broil over coals until medium rare, basting with all of sauce. Serves 4 or 5.

Mrs. Francis Kay

JAVA'S NASI GORENG [FRIED RICE]

1/2 lb. ground chuck
2 T. packaged dried bread
 crumbs
1 egg, unbeaten
1 1/4 c. chopped onion
Salt
Pepper
Butter or margarine

1 c. diced celery
3 T. salad oil
1/2 lb. shelled, deveined
 fresh shrimp
2 T. curry powder
2 c. canned chicken broth
2 c. packaged precooked
 rice

Combine chuck, bread crumbs, egg, 1/4 cup chopped onion, 1/2 teaspoon salt and 1/8 teaspoon pepper. Form into tiny meat balls, using 1 tablespoon of mixture for each; set aside.

In large skillet, melt 2 tablespoons butter. Add 1 cup chopped onion and celery. Saute until golden; then remove from skillet. In same skillet, heat salad oil. Add shrimp and saute 3 to 5 minutes or until done. Remove from skillet. In same skillet, brown meat balls well, keeping them round by rotating skillet over heat as they cook.

In medium saucepan, melt 2 tablespoons butter. Add curry, 1 teaspoon salt, 1/8 teaspoon pepper and chicken broth; bring to boil. Add rice; cover; remove from heat and let stand as rice label directs.

Now add celery-onion mixture, shrimp and rice to meat balls in skillet. Cover and heat until piping hot. Serve heaped in a bowl or on a platter. Serves 4 to 6.

Mrs. C. Aubrey Smith, Jr.

CHOP SUEY

1 lb. pork, cut in small cubes
1 lb. beef [or veal], cut in
   small cubes
1 c. chopped onion
1 small bunch celery, sliced
   diagonally
3 T. soy sauce
1 T. brown sugar
1 t. molasses

Salt to taste
1 can fancy Chinese
   vegetables
1 can bean sprouts
1 small can mushrooms
1 can water chestnuts
   sliced in 1/3's
Cornstarch
Chinese noodles

Brown lightly the pork and beef (about 30 minutes). Add onion, celery, soy sauce, and juice from canned vegetables (except bean sprouts); then add brown sugar, molasses and salt. Add canned ingredients and heat thoroughly, but do not cook. Thicken juices with cornstarch and bean sprout juice. (1 T. Kitchen Bouquet may be added for color). Serve over rice. Sprinkle with Chinese noodles. Serves 6 to 8.

Mrs. William C. Lust

CANTONESE CASSEROLE

1 pkg. [10 oz.] French style
   green beans
1 T. butter
1 T. flour
3/4 c. milk
2 T. soy sauce
1 c. sour cream
2 3/4 c. diced ham

1 can [5 oz.] water
   chestnuts, drained and
   thinly sliced
1/2 c. sliced almonds,
   browned in 1 T. butter
1 c. buttered bread crumbs
Parmesan cheese

Pour boiling water over beans to thaw. Drain well. Melt butter; blend in flour. Gradually stir in milk and soy sauce. Cook and stir until sauce thickens. Add sour cream, ham, beans, chestnuts and almonds. Pour into greased casserole (10 x 6 x 1 1/2 inch). Sprinkle with bread crumbs and top with generous sprinkling of Parmesan cheese. Bake at 350 degrees 30 to 35 minutes until hot and bubbly. Serves 4 to 6.

Mrs. Arthur F. Cunningham

EGG FOO YUNG

1/3 c. bean sprouts, drained
1 stalk celery, chopped thin
3/4 c. diced onions
1/4 c. diced green onions

1/2 c. diced ham
   [or bacon bits]
3 eggs
Salt and pepper to taste

Combine all ingredients in mixing bowl. Mix very lightly. Ladle on hot greased grill forming patties. Cook each side 6 to 8 minutes or until vegetables are cooked. Serve with chicken gravy.

Chicken Gravy:

2 c. chicken broth [or bouillon]
1 T. cornstarch mixed with
   1 c. water

Salt and pepper
1 T. soy sauce

Bring the chicken broth to a boil; add the cornstarch mixed with water. Season with salt and pepper and add soy sauce. Boil 3 minutes.
Mrs. Mabel Thomson

CANTONESE PORK

1 1/2 lb. boneless pork roast
2 T. salad oil
2 envelopes instant chicken
   broth
1 1/2 c. water
2 medium green peppers
1 1/2 c. celery, sliced
   diagonally

1 can [1 lb. 4 oz.] pineapple
   chunks in juice
3 T. cornstarch
2 T. brown sugar
1/2 t. salt
1/3 c. white vinegar
3 T. catsup
4 c. hot cooked rice

Trim fat from pork; cut pork into thin strips. Brown in salad oil in a large skillet; pour off any excess fat. Stir chicken broth and water into skillet; heat to boiling; cover and simmer 20 minutes or until pork is almost tender.

Cut green peppers in half, seed, and cut into 1-inch squares. Stir into pork mixture with celery. Cook, stirring once or twice, 5 minutes, or until pork is tender and vegetables are crisp-tender.

Drain juice from pineapple into a cup. Mix cornstarch, brown sugar and salt in small bowl. Stir in pineapple juice and vinegar until mixture is smooth; stir into skillet. Cook, stirring constantly, until mixture thickens and boils (about 3 minutes). Stir in catsup and pineapple chunks; heat to boiling. Spoon into a deep serving platter; spoon rice around edge. Serves 6.
Mrs. Mabel Thomson

SWEET AND PUNGENT PORK WITH ALMONDS

1/4 c. oil
1 lb. lean pork
Cornstarch
1 green pepper
2 slices pineapple,
    plus 1/2 c. juice
1/2 c. chicken stock

1 t. soy sauce
1/2 c. blanched almonds
1/4 c. vinegar
1/4 c. sugar
1 to 2 T. cornstarch
1/4 c. water

Heat oil and add lean pork that has been cut in pieces and rolled in cornstarch. When nicely browned and well-cooked, add green pepper cut into small (1-inch) squares, pineapple cut into wedges, pineapple juice, chicken stock, soy sauce, blanched almonds, vinegar and sugar. Stir in cornstarch mixed with cold water. As soon as the sauce is thickened and clear, serve with hot fluffy rice. Serves 3 to 4.

Mrs. R. Don Cowan

 Remember that vegetables used in Chinese cooking should be crunchy, not limp, so don't cook them too long!

CHINESE SPARERIBS

2 lbs. pork ribs
1 T. Crisco
2 T. brown sugar
3 T. cornstarch
1/2 t. salt
1 T. meat extract [flavoring]
1/4 c. cider vinegar

1/4 c. cold water
1 c. pineapple juice
1 T. soy sauce
1/2 c. green pepper, chopped
1/2 c. onions, finely sliced
1 c. diced pineapple

Cook ribs until extra tender (either bake or broil). Mix other ingredients into sauce and cook until just thickened, about 5 minutes. Mix meat from spareribs or ribs themselves, as you prefer, and sauce. Serve with rice. Serves 2 to 3.

Mrs. Patrick Thomas

NEW MEXICAN CHILI

2 lbs. lean ground chuck
2 cans kidney beans
1 can chopped green chile
    peppers
1 onion, chopped
1 t. comino

1 to 2 t. salt
1/4 t. garlic powder
2 T. oregano
1 can tomatoes
1 can tomato sauce

Brown meat and add the rest of the ingredients. Simmer 2 hours. Serve over rice with grated cheese on top, or just plain. Serves 6. May be frozen.

Mrs. Ronald N. Schoenbrun

Very mild - good for children or anyone who doesn't care for very spicy foods.

CHILI

5 1/2 to 6 lbs. ground chuck
1 large onion, chopped
3 T. chili powder
3 t. ground cumin
2 t. salt
1/2 t. pepper
2 cans [6 oz.] tomato paste

2 cans [#303] tomatoes,
   mashed slightly,
   juice too
2 cans [15 oz.] chili beans
1 can [8 oz.] tomato sauce
3/4 bean can of water

In large pan (Dutch oven or like), brown chuck, using 2 tablespoons of oil, if desired. When browned, remove with slotted spoon from pan, draining carefully. Put aside. In grease in pan, saute' onion. Remove onion and pour out all grease. Return meat and onion to large pan and add ingredients listed above. Let mixture sort of bubble up and then reduce to low heat and let simmer for at least 3 hours. Serves 8 to 10 generously.

Mrs. R. Randall Cape

Mrs. William R. Clyde's quicker, smaller version calls for 2 lbs. ground beef, 4 medium chopped onions and 4 t. chopped garlic, browned and cooked slowly for 15 minutes in 1 t. shortening. Add 1 small (1 1/4 oz.) bottle chili powder, 2 t. ground cumin, 2 T. flour, 3 c. water, 1 T. salt and 1/4 t. pepper and simmer 35 minutes. Serves 6.

QUICK CHILE CON CARNE

1 c. finely chopped onion
4 T. diced green pepper
4 T. salad oil
1 lb. ground chuck
2 c. canned tomatoes
4 t. chili powder

4 T. water
1/2 t. salt
2 t. sugar
1/3 t. garlic powder
2 cans [#2] pinto beans
   and liquid

Saute' onion and green pepper in salad oil in skillet for 5 minutes; add chuck and cook 5 minutes. Add the other ingredients and simmer, covered, for 1 hour. Freezes well. Serves 4.

Mrs. James H. Rippy

CHILI VENISON OR BEEF

4 lbs. chili meat, floured
   lightly [3 lbs. venison
   and 1 lb. beef is a good
   combination]
4 med. onions, chopped
4 cloves garlic, chopped
1/2 can cumin seed

3/4 c. chili blend
1/4 c. chili powder
2 T. [heaping] sugar
4 cans [8 oz.] tomato sauce
Salt and pepper to taste
Red pepper, if desired
6 to 8 c. water

Brown meat, onions and garlic together. Add all other ingredients. Cook on low heat for several hours (4 to 5) until flavors are blended and all ingredients are well-done. If desired, pinto beans may be cooked separately and beans and cooking liquid added near end of chili cooking time. Serves 16 to 20.

Mrs. J. Donald Guinn

BEEF OLÉ

1 lb. ground beef
1 t. chili powder
1 pkg. spaghetti sauce mix
1 can [8 oz.] tomato sauce
   and 1 1/4 c. water OR
1 can [8 oz.] tomato paste
   and 1 1/2 c. water

Frito corn chips
Shredded lettuce
Chopped tomatoes
Grated cheese
Chopped onion
Sliced ripe olives

Brown ground beef and drain off fat. Add chili powder and spaghetti sauce mix to meat. Blend tomato sauce (or paste) and water together and add to meat mixture. Stir well. Bring to boil, reduce heat, and simmer 25 minutes. Serve over corn chips and top with lettuce, tomatoes, cheese, onion and olives.

This is a quickie and the children love it. Makes 3 cups of meat mixture and serves 4. A variation is possible by the use of taco sauce mix instead of spaghetti sauce mix.

Mrs. Jerry Bain

TORTILLA CASSEROLE

1 lb. ground beef
1 pkg. tortillas
1 lb. cheese, grated
1 onion, finely chopped
1 can cream of mushroom soup

1 can cream of chicken soup
1 small can taco sauce
1 small can green chiles
1/2 lg. can evaporated milk
1 c. water

Brown meat. Break tortillas in four pieces. Place in large baking dish. Layer the tortillas, meat, cheese and onion. Continue until all are used. Mix remaining ingredients and pour over all. Bake 30 minutes at 350 degrees. Serves 8 to 10.

Mrs. Brad Holmes

CHILES RELLENOS BAKE

1 lb. ground meat
1/4 c. chopped onion
1/2 t. salt
1/4 t. pepper
2 cans [4 oz.] green chiles,
cut in half and seeded
6 oz. sharp natural Cheddar
cheese, shredded [1 1/2 c.]

1 1/2 c. milk
1/4 c. all-purpose flour
4 beaten eggs
Several dashes hot
pepper sauce

Brown beef and onion; drain off fat. Sprinkle meat with 1/2 teaspoon salt and 1/4 teaspoon pepper. Place half the chiles in 10 x 6 x 1 1/2 inch baking dish; sprinkle with cheese; top with meat mixture. Arrange remaining chiles over meat. Combine remaining ingredients; beat until smooth. Pour over meat-chile mixture. Bake at 350 degrees for 45 to 50 minutes or until knife inserted just off center comes out clean. Let cool 5 minutes and serve. Serves 6.

Mrs. David K. Boice

MEXICAN ENCHILADAS

1 medium onion, chopped
1 lb. ground beef
1 can refried beans
1 small jalapeno pepper [or
more if you like it hot]
Salt to taste

1 pkg. tortillas [12]
1 can enchilada sauce [if too
thick, thin with water]
1/2 lb. Cheddar
cheese, grated

Saute' onion in small amount of cooking oil. Add meat and stir until done. Drain off all liquid and discard. Add refried beans and stir. Mash jalapeno pepper and add to mixture. Salt to taste.

In a round pie tin, as large as the tortilla, put the enchilada sauce. Dip each tortilla in the sauce. Do one at a time. Place it on wax paper and fill with a portion of mixture across the middle of the tortilla, leaving enough room on each side of the portion to roll. Sprinkle grated cheese on top of the mixture and roll. Immediately place in oblong pan. Place in 300 degree oven for 15 minutes. Remove from oven and sprinkle generously with grated cheese. Place back in oven only long enough to melt the cheese. This recipe may be doubled with the exception of top grated cheese and frozen for future use.

Mrs. George Grainger

In case of frozen enchiladas, place in oven to thaw and warm enchiladas, then remove and sprinkle cheese to be melted as above.

CHEESE ENCHILADAS

1 heaping T. Crisco
1 heaping T. chili powder
1 heaping T. flour
1 can tomato paste or purée
4 cans water

Salt to taste
1 large onion
1 lb. Cheddar cheese
1 pkg. corn tortillas
[preferably fresh]

Heat Crisco in skillet, add chili powder and flour and let thicken. Add tomato paste, water and salt, until it reaches consistency of cream soup. Grate onion and cheese. Dip tortillas in sauce until soft. Roll cheese and some onions in tortillas and put in flat pyrex pan. Cover with excess sauce, cheese and onions. Cook at 400 degrees about 10 minutes or until cheese is soft. Serves 6 to 8. Freezes well, covered.

Mrs. J. Donald Guinn

 Saute' onions before adding if you do not like as strong an onion flavor.

GREEN ENCHILADAS

1 medium onion, chopped
2 T. margarine
1 can [1 lb.] tomatoes
1 to 2 cans chopped green
   chile peppers or seeded,
   mild jalapenos

1 doz. tortillas
1 pt. sour cream
2 c. grated Cheddar cheese

Saute' onion in margarine. Add drained tomatoes and drained peppers. (Reserve juice to be added later if neeeded.)

Fry tortillas briefly to soften, then dip in above sauce.

Mix sour cream, grated cheese, salt and pepper to taste. Place heaping tablespoon of sour cream sauce in each dipped tortilla and roll. Place in greased baking dish; top with remaining sour cream sauce. Bake at 350 degrees for 30 minutes. Serves 6.

Mrs. Glen Dyer

 Make a day ahead, if desired; top with sour cream sauce just before baking.

TAMALE PIE

2 lbs. ground meat
2 medium onions, chopped
1 green pepper, chopped
1 can green chiles, chopped
5 T. chili powder
1 small can chopped ripe
    olives

2 cans tomatoes
1 1/2 c. corn meal mixed
    with 1 1/2 c. cold water
3 c. boiling salted water
2 c. grated sharp Cheddar
    cheese

Brown meat with onions. Add pepper, chiles, chili powder, olives and tomatoes, and simmer about 30 minutes.

Boil corn meal mix in water, stirring constantly until thick (about 5 minutes). Spread in bottom of 2 quart casserole dish (rectangle pyrex). Cover with meat mixture. Cover with cheese. Bake at 350 degrees for 30 minutes. Serves 8 to 10.

Mrs. Nelson Clyde

 Don't cook corn meal until meat mixture is ready. Spread quickly as it thickens very fast.

CORN AND TAMALE CASSEROLE

2 cans cream style corn
2 or 3 cans Wolf brand tamales
Margarine

Salt
Parmesan cheese

Put a layer of corn into a square pyrex baking dish. Next slice tamales 1/4 inch thick in a solid layer; slice 1/8 pound margarine over this and salt. Sprinkle Parmesan cheese over this; then repeat same procedure and bake 300 to 350 degrees for an hour. May be frozen. Serves 6 to 8.

Mrs. Will Mann Richardson

A very nice second meat dish for a party.

CHILI SAUCE I

12 large tomatoes
3 large onions
3 large peppers
1 c. brown sugar
1 c. vinegar |more if
    desired|

1 t. ground cloves
1 t. celery seed
1 t. nutmeg
1 t. cinnamon
1 t. ginger
Salt and pepper to taste

Combine tomatoes, onions, peppers, brown sugar and vinegar and cook, uncovered, slowly about 3 hours. Do not add spices until nearly done to avoid darkening. Yields approximately 3 1/2 pints.

Mrs. Walter Jones

CHILI SAUCE II

1 peck tomatoes [about 13 lb.]
1/2 doz. onions
3 bell peppers
1/3 c. salt

1/2 T. black pepper
2 T. cinnamon
1 c. sugar
1 pt. vinegar

Peel and cut up tomatoes and onions. Dice peppers. Place all ingredients except vinegar in large cooking kettle. Simmer for 2 hours stirring occasionally to prevent sticking. Add vinegar and cook about 1 hour longer. Relish should be thick and not watery when cooked sufficiently. Place in clean jars and seal while hot. Makes about 10 pints. This relish is good on peas and beans.

Mrs. C. Aubrey Smith, Jr.

RIPE TOMATO HOT SAUCE

2 gal. ripe tomatoes
3 qt. onions
1 qt. bell peppers
1 qt. red hot peppers

4 c. sugar
1/2 gal. vinegar
1/2 c. salt

Cut up vegetables, combine all ingredients and boil until mixture thickens. Place in hot jars and seal.

Mrs. James Godwin

BAR-B-QUE SAUCE

1 c. catsup
3/4 c. water
1/4 c. vinegar
3 T. sugar

2 t. Worcestershire
2 t. chili powder
1/4 t. salt
1/3 c. finely chopped onion

Combine ingredients; cook over medium heat to simmering, stirring often. Lower heat, cover and simmer gently 15 minutes. Yields 2 1/2 cups. Keeps indefinitely in refrigerator; warm and use as needed.

Mrs. Frank Budde

Use this when cooking or serve warm on table. Excellent for fondue.

HOT BARBECUE SAUCE

1 c. strong black coffee
2 c. Worcestershire sauce
1 c. tomato catsup
1/4 lb. butter

2 T. freshly ground black
  pepper [or less]
1 T. sugar
1 T. salt

Combine ingredients. Simmer over slow flame 30 minutes, stirring to mix thoroughly. This is hot to the taste and is good on most barbecued meats, such as hamburgers, chicken, briskets or beef tenders. Makes 3 cups.

Mrs. James Wynne

BETTY RAMSEY'S BARBECUE SAUCE

1/2 lb. margarine
2 cans tomato paste
1 t. chili powder
2 T. salt
1 large bottle catsup
1/2 bottle Worcestershire
1/2 c. brown sugar
1 T. black pepper
Juice of 2 lemons

Add following to taste:
Garlic
Paprika
Red pepper
Liquid smoke
Tabasco

Mix ingredients; simmer 10 minutes. Use for basting chicken, ribs, beef, etc. Makes lots!

Mrs. Nelson Clyde

HOT MUSTARD

1 c. light brown sugar
3 T. flour
1/2 can Campbell's beef
  consomme'

1 c. apple cider vinegar
2 cans [2 oz.] Coleman's
  hot dry mustard
3 eggs, well-beaten

Combine brown sugar, flour, consomme' and vinegar in a double boiler. Cook until it thickens. Dissolve mustard in small amount of water and add to above. Add eggs and beat. Chill. Great on sandwiches. Makes 1 1/2 pints.

Mrs. Wade C. Smith
Dallas, Texas

HOT SWEET MUSTARD

1 can Coleman's dry mustard
1 c. white vinegar

1 c. sugar
2 egg yolks, beaten

Soak mustard powder in vinegar overnight. Add vinegar slowly to prevent lumping. Next day, add sugar and egg yolks (well-beaten). Cook slowly in double boiler over hot water for one hour. Makes 1 pint. Will keep indefinitely in refrigerator.

Mrs. Robert Henry

CRANBERRY GLAZE
[for Ham]

1/2 c. brown sugar
2 T. cornstarch
Dash ground cloves
Dash salt

1/2 c. raisins
1 1/2 c. cranberry juice cocktail
1/2 c. orange juice

Mix brown sugar, cornstarch, cloves and salt. Add raisins and fruit juices. Cook and stir until mixture is thick and boiling. Spoon part of the sauce over ham the last 20 minutes of its baking time. Serve remaining sauce hot. Makes about 2 cups of sauce.

Mrs. Michael Hatchell

RAISIN SAUCE FOR HAM

1/2 pt. crabapple jelly
2 T. vinegar
1 t. dry mustard
1/4 t. allspice

1/2 t. cinnamon
1/4 t. cloves
1/2 c. raisins [softened
  in warm water]

Melt the crabapple jelly slowly. Add vinegar and dry ingredients and cook slowly until thickened. Add raisins and simmer at least 10 minutes. This will keep several days in the refrigerator.

Mrs. James Boring

STEAK MARINADE

1/2 c. pineapple juice
1/2 c. soy sauce
1/4 c. sherry
2 T. chopped ginger

1 T. olive oil
1 t. dry mustard
1/2 t. curry powder
Garlic salt

Combine and use to marinate steak, roast or other cut of beef for 3 hours. Broil or bake as usual.

Mrs. James E. Bass

TOMATO AND GINGER JAM

1 No. 2 1/2 can [28 oz.] tomatoes
1 1/4 c. sugar
1/2 lemon, quartered and
   sliced thin

1/3 c. chopped candied
   ginger

Combine ingredients and cook over low heat until thick, about 2 to 3 hours. Stir occasionally to prevent sticking. Pour in sterilized jar and seal. Makes 1 pint.

Mrs. C. Aubrey Smith, Jr.

WINE JELLY

2 c. sweet wine
   [port or sherry]
3 c. sugar

1/2 bottle liquid pectin
   [Certo]

Pour wine into a saucepan and mix in sugar. Cook over rapidly boiling water for 2 minutes or until heated thoroughly. Stir constantly, so that all the liquid reaches the right temperature at the same time.
   Stir the liquid pectin in at once. Pour immediately into five 6 ounce sterilized glasses or jars and seal each with paraffin.

Mrs. L. Glenn Taylor

Poultry and Game

ALMOND CHICKEN

1 lb. uncooked chicken meat, cut into cubes	1/2 t. Accent
3/4 t. salt	1 c. celery, diced
2 T. cornstarch	1 c. onion, chopped
1 t. sugar	1 c. bamboo shoots
2 T. sherry	3 T. soy sauce
3 T. peanut oil [or salad oil]	8 water chestnuts
1/4 c. chicken stock	1/2 lb. almonds, walnuts [blanched] or cashews

Dredge chicken meat in mixture of salt, cornstarch, sugar and sherry. Marinate for at least 1/2 hour. Boil chicken bones in small amount of water to obtain stock.

Heat oil in skillet and saute' chicken until tender. To the chicken, add stock and heat thoroughly. All vegetables should be sautéed slightly and added to the chicken mixture. Add remaining ingredients. Serve with rice or fried noodles. Serves 4 to 6.

Mrs. A. M. Limmer, Jr.

If walnuts are used, the bitter taste can be removed by covering shelled walnuts in cold water and bringing to a boil for 3 minutes. Drain immediately and blanch.

BAR-B-Q CHICKEN

2 t. paprika	1 t. Tabasco
2 t. chili powder	8 t. water
2 t. salt	2 t. lemon juice
1 t. red pepper	3 to 4 T. margarine
4 t. catsup	1 fryer [2 1/2 lb.]
4 t. Worcestershire	

Mix all ingredients, except fryer, in a saucepan. Bring to a boil, stirring constantly. Oil a paper sack completely with Wesson oil and pour out excess. Place chicken in the bag and pour in sauce. Put bag in baking dish and cover all with foil. Bake at 500 degrees for 15 minutes. Reduce heat to 350 degrees and continue baking for 1 hour and 15 minutes more.

Mrs. Charles Clark

For milder sauce, reduce amounts of chili powder, pepper and Tabasco.

CHICKEN WITH DRIED BEEF

6 chicken breasts	1 can cream of chicken soup
6 slices of dried beef	1 c. sour cream
1/2 c. sherry	
1 can cream of mushroom soup	

Wrap chicken breasts in slices of dried beef. Place in oblong baking dish. Mix sherry, soups and sour cream to make a sauce. Pour sauce over chicken and bake at 225 degrees for 2 hours.

Mrs. Robert Henry

CHICKEN LAS VEGAS

Per Person: 1/2 chicken breast, boned
1 oz. thinly sliced ham
1 slice bacon

Sauce:

1 c. chopped celery	1 qt. chicken stock
1 c. chopped onion	Dash Tabasco
2 T. butter	Dash Worcestershire
2 T. flour	1/3 to 1/2 c. sherry
1 t. salt	1 1/2 T. Parmesan
1/2 t. pepper	Paprika
1/4 t. Accent	

Salt and pepper breasts, roll around ham, wrap with bacon, secure with toothpicks, dip in flour and brown in shortening in skillet. Set aside.

Saute' celery and onion in butter; add 2 tablespoons flour, salt, pepper, Accent, chicken stock, Tabasco and Worcestershire. Stir as mixture thickens; then add sherry and Parmesan.

Arrange browned breasts in shallow baking pan; pour sauce over top. Sprinkle with paprika and bake at 400 degrees for 45 minutes to 1 hour (until browned). Serve hot over wild rice, noodles, white rice or potatoes. May be frozen.

Chef-De Cordova Club
Grandbury, Texas

CHICKEN PIE

1 large hen	1 small jar chopped
2 t. salt	pimiento
2 qts. boiling water	1 can English peas or
1 carrot	1 pkg. frozen peas
2 stalks celery	1 can sliced carrots or
1 onion	1 pkg. frozen carrots
3 c. broth	Pie crust dough [may use
3 T. flour	mix or favorite recipe]
Salt and pepper to taste	Paprika
1 can sliced mushrooms	

Boil chicken in salted water with carrot and celery and onion for about 2 1/2 hours or until meat begins to separate from bones. Let cool in broth. Remove from broth and debone. Make sauce by using about 3 cups of broth, strained and thickened with flour. Add seasoning to taste, mushrooms, pimiento, peas and carrots. Cook while preparing crust. Using large rectangular casserole dish, place a layer of chicken in dish, pour broth and vegetable mixture over this. Roll out pie crust and cut in strips. Make lattice top by laying strips diagonally over chicken and vegetable mixture. Sprinkle lightly with paprika. Bake at 350 degrees for about an hour or until crust is golden brown.

Mrs. Milburn Pool

CHICKEN EDEN ISLE

4 chicken breasts
1/2 t. white pepper
1 small jar dried beef
1 can cream of chicken soup

1 carton [8 oz.] sour
  cream
1 pkg. cream cheese
Hot cooked rice

Place breasts in single layer in baking pan. Sprinkle with pepper. Separate slices of dried beef and place over chicken. Spoon soup into pan. Cover. Bake at 325 degrees for 1 hour. Uncover and bake 20 minutes longer. Remove chicken from pan; keep warm. Let liquid in pan stand until fat rises to top; skim off and stir liquid into sour cream, in a small saucepan; slice cheese into pan. Heat slowly, stirring constantly, just until cheese melts and sauce is hot. Serve over rice which has been cooked according to package directions. Serves 4.

Red Apple Inn
Arkansas

SHERRIED GIBLETS

1 1/2 lbs. chicken hearts and
  gizzards
2 T. margarine
1/2 c. minced onion
1 can [4 oz.] mushroom stems
  and pieces

1 T. sherry
1 c. sour cream
1 pinch cayenne pepper
1 T. milk
1 t. salt

Cook hearts and gizzards in boiling water for 25 minutes. Chop coarsely. In skillet, melt margarine. Saute' onion until golden. Add mushrooms, sherry, sour cream, cayenne pepper, milk, salt and giblets.
Serve on warmed hamburger buns or rice. Sprinkle liberally with paprika.

Mrs. John D. Glass, Jr.

LEMON BARBECUED CHICKEN

1 fryer
1/4 t. salt
1/4 t. pepper
1/4 c. butter
1/2 clove garlic

2 T. salad oil
1/4 t. thyme
1/4 c. lemon juice
1 T. chopped onion

Cut chicken into serving pieces and season with salt and pepper. Brown in butter; combine other ingredients. Pour over chicken, cover. Cook slowly until tender, about 30 to 40 minutes. Serves 4 to 5.

Mrs. John F. Warren

As this splatters when being browned in butter, use a deep heavy pot. Prevents some of the mess. Good served over rice with drippings left from pot.

CUBAN CHICKEN AND RICE

1 fryer, cut up
4 T. white vinegar
Dash salt
1 t. oregano
1 t. cumin seed
1 t. chili powder
1 bay leaf
1 large onion, sliced
   very thin
1 green pepper, sliced
   very thin

2 T. safflower oil
2 T. olive oil
1 c. white wine
1 small can tomato paste
2 c. water
1 c. uncooked saffron
   rice
1 can Le Sueur English
   peas
1 jar chopped pimiento

Mix vinegar, salt, oregano, cumin seed, chili powder, bay leaf, onion and green pepper and pour over chicken and marinate for 1 hour.

Later, take chicken out of vegetables and brown in safflower oil and olive oil. Place vegetables that the chicken soaked in over the chicken in a shallow baking dish and add white wine and the tomato paste, which have been stirred together. Add water, uncooked rice, English peas and pimiento. Bake at 350 degrees until rice and chicken are tender, approximately 1 hour and 15 minutes. Serves 4 generously.

Mrs. Andrew R. Acosta

GRANDMA'S CHICKEN AND DUMPLINGS

1 hen [3 to 4 lbs.]
1 bay leaf
1 thick slice onion
1 stalk celery
Salt and pepper to taste
Dash salt

1 1/2 c. sifted self-rising
   flour, slightly shaken
   down
3 T. shortening
7 T. cold milk

Cook hen until tender in water to cover with bay leaf, onion, celery, salt and pepper. Bone chicken and set aside; cool broth and skim off fat.

Mix salt, flour, shortening and milk as for pie crust. Roll very thin and cut into 1 x 3 inch strips and drop, 1 at a time, into 1 1/2 quarts of vigorously boiling broth. After last strip is dropped into broth, allow to cook 6 minutes. Remove pot from heat, add boned chicken and stir gently. Let stand at least 1 hour before serving and warm gently to serving temperature. Serves 6 to 8.

Mrs. R. Randall Cape

Dumpling secret: roll very thin on lightly floured board; do no stir while cooking.

CHICKEN COUNTRY CAPTAIN

1 large bunch parsley,
   chopped fine
4 green peppers, chopped
2 large onions, chopped
Wesson oil
2 large cans tomatoes
1 t. mace

2 t. curry powder
Salt and pepper
1 clove garlic, chopped
16 pieces chicken,
   cut for frying
1/2 box currants
1/2 lb. slivered almonds

Saute' parsley, peppers and onions in Wesson oil. Put mixture in a roaster, pour in tomatoes and spices. Simmer 15 minutes on top of stove. Add chopped garlic. Dredge pieces of chicken in a mixture of salt, pepper, flour and paprika. Fry fast in deep fat until browned. Lay chicken pieces in the sauce and bake at 300 degrees for 1 1/2 hours. Half-hour before done, add currants. (Cut raisins can be substituted). Serve on a platter of rice and sprinkle with toasted almonds. Chutney is wonderful served with the main dish.

Mrs. Lynn F. Cobb

Serve with a green salad for dinner parties.

POLLO CON FUNGI

1 chicken [3 to 4 lb.]
Salt and pepper to taste
1 T. butter
2 cloves garlic, minced
6 T. olive oil

1 large onion, sliced
1 lb. fresh mushrooms,
   sliced
2 T. water
1/2 c. sherry

Cut chicken into pieces; salt and pepper to taste. Heat butter in skillet; add garlic and 4 tablespoons of oil. Brown chicken in skillet on both sides (about 10 minutes). Lower heat, cover and simmer 25 minutes.

In separate pan, saute' sliced onion in remaining 2 tablespoons of olive oil 5 minutes. Add sliced mushrooms and water and simmer 15 minutes.

Add mushrooms and onions to chicken; cover and simmer 15 minutes more; add sherry and boil up quickly for 1 minute. Serve very hot to 4.

Mrs. William R. Clyde

Great party dish with wild rice, green vegetable and salad!

GALLINA EN GUISADA [CHICKEN IN SAUCE]

1 chicken
1/2 c. shortening
1 onion, thinly sliced
1/2 green pepper, chopped
1 t. ground cumin seed
  [comino]
1 clove garlic, mashed

Salt and pepper to taste
1/2 can tomatoes
1 can tomato sauce, re-
  serve 3 T. for rice
Raw rice for 6
Water to cook rice
Green peppers as preferred

Cut up chicken and brown in shortening, remove. Saute' onion and bell pepper in same skillet until golden. Return chicken to pan; add comino, garlic, salt, pepper, tomatoes and tomato sauce. Simmer 45 minutes, or until thick. Serve over rice that has been cooked with water and 3 tablespoons tomato sauce and 2 small whole green peppers (or 1 medium, chopped) for color and flavor. If whole peppers are used, remove before serving. Serves 6.

Mrs. M. Earl Davis

SKILLET CHICKEN

1 stick butter
1 cut up fryer or chicken
  breasts
Red wine [port]
Salt, pepper and Accent
  to taste

1 clove garlic, chopped
Pinch marjoram, rosemary,
  thyme [optional]
1 c. blanched almonds
1 c. mushrooms

Melt butter in electric skillet; arrange chicken in melted butter and pour a generous tablespoon of red wine over each piece. Add salt, pepper, Accent and garlic to skillet and a pinch of spices mentioned above on each piece of chicken, if desired. Cover and cook 20 to 25 minutes. Turn and cook about 25 minutes more. Add blanched almonds and mushrooms (fresh if possible) and cook 10 minutes more. Serves 6 to 8.

Mrs. J. Donald Guinn

CHICKEN BREASTS AND RICE

1 pkg. Uncle Ben's long grain
  and wild rice
1 can cream of mushroom soup
1 can cream of celery soup

1/2 c. water
5 chicken breasts
1 pkg. Lipton's onion
  soup mix

Scatter rice in bottom of casserole and sprinkle packaged seasonings on top. Blend mushroom soup, celery soup and water, and pour over rice. Place chicken breasts on top of soup and rice. Sprinkle onion soup mix on top. Cover tightly with foil and bake for 2 hours at 350 degrees. Serves 5.

Mrs. Joe Huffstutler

CHICKEN BREASTS IN SOUR CREAM

4 chicken breasts
1 small can mushrooms
1 can cream of mushroom soup

1/2 soup can sherry
1 c. sour cream
Paprika

Arrange chicken in a shallow baking dish so that pieces do not overlap. Cover with mushrooms. Combine undiluted mushroom soup, sherry and sour cream; stir until blended. Pour over chicken, completely covering it. Dust with paprika. Bake, covered, at 350 degrees for 1 1/2 hours. Serves 4.

Mrs. Wilson Cozby

Easy and divine!

CHICKEN BREASTS SUPREME

6 to 8 chicken breasts,
  skin removed
Salt and pepper to taste
1 c. flour
1 stick butter
1 can cream of mushroom soup
1 can cream of celery soup
1 pkg. Lipton's dried
  onion soup mix

1 can sherry [about
  10 oz.]
1/2 can water [about
  5 oz.]
1 can [4 oz.] sliced
  mushrooms
Parlsey and paprika

Salt, pepper, flour chicken breasts and brown lightly on both sides in 3/4 stick of butter. Remove to pyrex baking dish. Mix soups, sherry and water. Pour over chicken. Saute' mushrooms in 1/4 stick butter and arrange over breasts. Sprinkle lightly with paprika and parsley. Bake at 350 degrees until done, approximately 1 hour to 1 hour 15 minutes.

Mrs. Arthur Cunningham

BREAST OF CHICKEN SMITANE

2/3 c. butter
2 c. chopped onion
4 to 6 chicken breasts,
  seasoned to taste

6 oz. dry white wine
2 c. sour cream

Melt butter and saute' onions until pale gold. Place seasoned chicken in baking dish and cover with onions and butter. Cover and bake at 350 degrees until done (about 1 hour). Remove and keep warm. Strain onions from butter with sieve and discard butter. Heat wine and onions until reduced by one-third. Lower heat and gradually stir in sour cream. Blend carefully, but do not cook. Pour over chicken and serve with wild rice. Serves 4 to 6.

Mrs. Robert L. Caton, III

CHICKEN DIVINE

2 pkgs. frozen broccoli
   spears
6 chicken breasts, cooked
   and boned
Garlic powder
2 cans cream of chicken
   soup
1 c. mayonnaise

3 t. lemon juice
3/4 t. curry powder
Generous dash cayenne
   pepper
Shredded sharp cheese
1/2 c. toasted bread
   crumbs
1 T. melted butter

Cook broccoli according to directions; drain and place in a greased 9 x 13 inch baking dish. Place chicken on top of broccoli. Sprinkle with garlic powder. Mix soup, mayonnaise, lemon juice, curry powder and cayenne together. Pour over chicken. Cover with shredded cheese and bread crumbs and sprinkle with melted butter. Bake at 350 degrees for 30 minutes or until bubbling. Serves 6 to 8. Freezes well.

Mrs. E. J. Mooney, Jr.
Chicago, Illinois

CHICKEN BREASTS WITH MUSHROOM SAUCE

6 chicken breasts, with
   skin removed
4 T. butter
1 small onion, chopped
1 T. chives
1 can beef broth

1 can water
1 can B & B mushrooms,
   sliced
1/4 c. sherry
Cornstarch

Quickly brown chicken breasts in butter. Remove. Add onion and cook until tender. Add rest of ingredients, except cornstarch, and bring to a boil. Mix cornstarch in cold water and add enough to thicken sauce slightly. Remove chicken breasts to sauce and simmer very slowly for 30 minutes, covered. Serves 6. May be frozen.

Mrs. Allen Pye

CURRIED CHICKEN BREASTS

4 chicken breasts
1 t. curry powder
1 can cream of chicken soup

1/4 c. chopped almonds
1 small carton [1 c.]
   sour cream

Lightly brown chicken breasts and place in baking dish. Mix cream of chicken soup with curry powder and pour over chicken breasts. Bake for 40 minutes at 350 degrees. Combine sour cream and almonds and pour over chicken breasts. Heat until bubbling. Serves 4.

Mrs. E. D. Fitzpatrick

Delicious served with brown rice and a peach half filled with chutney and topped with mayonnaise.

CHICKEN BREASTS

6 to 8 chicken breasts
Evaporated milk
6 to 8 T. butter

1 pt. sour cream
Fresh [or canned]
mushrooms

Dip chicken in canned milk; salt, pepper and sprinkle lightly with flour. Brown in butter (using about 4 tablespoons) and place in a flat baking dish. Dot generously with butter and cover pan with foil. Bake 30 to 40 minutes at 375 degrees. Place chicken on serving platter. Saute' mushrooms lightly in butter and combine with sour cream. Heat until just warm and pour over chicken breasts.

Mrs. William Smyth

CRAB-CHICKEN BREASTS

6 chicken breasts, boned
Salt and pepper to taste
2 T. flour
1/2 t. paprika
5 T. butter or margarine
3/4 c. chicken broth
1/2 c. chopped onion
1/2 c. chopped celery
5 T. dry white wine

1 can [7 1/2 oz.] crab-
meat, drained and flaked
1/2 c. herb-seasoned
stuffing mix
1 envelope hollandaise
sauce mix
3/4 c. milk
1/2 c. shredded Swiss
cheese

Pound chicken to flatten. Sprinkle with a little salt and pepper. Combine flour and paprika; coat chicken. Place in 11 x 7 x 1 3/4 inch baking dish; drizzle with 2 tablespoons melted butter and add 3/4 cup chicken broth to baking dish. Cook onion and celery in 3 tablespoons butter or margarine until tender. Remove from heat; add 3 tablespoons wine, crab and stuffing mix; toss. Divide mixture among breasts and form mixture into small ball on top of each breast. Bake, uncovered, in 375 degree oven for 1 hour. Transfer to platter. Blend sauce mix and milk; cook and stir until thick. Add remaining wine and cheese. Cook until well-blended and pour on chicken. Serve hot to 6. May be prepared and cooked ahead without sauce. Add sauce when reheated.

Mrs. R. B. Shelton

FOOLPROOF CHICKEN BREASTS

3 whole chicken breasts, boned,
skinned and split
1 can cream of celery soup
1 can cream of chicken soup

1 pkg. onion soup mix
1 soup can dry white wine
1 c. raw wild rice or
brown rice

Mix soups, wine and rice and let stand several hours. Arrange chicken on top of mixture. Cover. Bake at 350 degrees for 1 hour, then remove cover, stir gravy and cook another 20 to 30 minutes.

Mrs. Charles Clark

CHICKEN IN WINE

1 broiler [2 1/2 to 3 lbs.]
1/2 c. butter
1 small clove garlic
1/2 t. salt and pepper
1 T. flour
1 c. water [or stock made
  by boiling neck, wings
  and giblets]

1/2 c. red wine [sherry
  may be used]
Pinch of thyme
1/2 bay leaf
1 t. minced parsley
1/4 lb. fresh mushrooms,
  cooked

Cut up chicken and dust pieces with salt and pepper. Melt butter in skillet and saute' garlic for 5 minutes. Remove garlic from butter. Add chicken and fry to golden brown. Place chicken in a casserole dish. To the fat remaining in skillet add salt, pepper and flour. Stir until blended. Add stock; cook until sauce is smooth. Add wine, thyme, bay leaf, parsley and mushrooms. Pour sauce over chicken and bake covered at 350 degrees for 1 hour. Serves 4.

Mrs. L. Glenn Taylor

CORN BREAD-CHICKEN CASSEROLE

1/2 c. butter or margarine
1/4 c. chopped onion
1/2 c. chopped celery
1 c. chicken broth
1 can cream of chicken soup

1 can chicken and rice soup
1 qt. corn bread crumbs
Salt and pepper to taste
1 boiled chicken [or whole
  canned chicken]

Melt butter and saute' onion and celery.

Heat broth and soups and pour over corn bread crumbs and mix well. Add onions and celery to soup-corn bread mixture. Season with salt and pepper. If needed, add boiling water to moisten.

In greased casserole, alternte layers of chicken, which has been cut into bite-size pieces, and dressing (start and end with dressing). Bake at 350 degrees for 45 minutes. Serves 6. Freezes well.

Mrs. Robert Ungerecht

CHICKEN CASSEROLE

1 c. diced celery
1/2 c. salad olives
1 1/2 c. cooked, boned chicken
2 t. minced onion
1 can cream of chicken soup
1/2 t. salt

1/4 t. pepper
1 T. lemon juice
3/4 c. mayonnaise
1/2 c. slivered almonds
2 c. crushed potato chips

Mix all ingredients together, reserving about 1/2 cup potato chips. Pour into casserole dish and top with remaining potato chips. Bake at 450 degrees for 15 minutes. Serves 6.

Mrs. John B. White, III
Jacksonville, Texas

BUSY DAY CHICKEN CASSEROLE

1 chicken, cut in pieces
Melted butter
Salt and pepper to taste
1 can cream of celery soup

1 can cream of mushroom
  soup
2 cans water
1 1/3 c. raw rice

Coat chicken pieces with butter, salt and pepper. Mix together soups, water and rice. Pour soup and rice mixture into a greased casserole dish and top with chicken. Cover and bake 3 hours at 250 degrees. Serves 6.

Mrs. Billy Hall

CHICKEN SOPA CASSEROLE

1 fryer [3 lb.]
1 pkg. frozen corn tortillas
1/2 to 1 lb. yellow cheese

1 can green chiles,
  mashed
Stock from chicken

Boil or stew chicken, bone and cut into bite-sized pieces. Toast tortillas. In casserole, put a layer of cut up chicken, a layer of toasted tortillas, a layer of grated cheese, and a layer of green chiles. Repeat. Pour stock over layers, just enough to cover. Cook in oven about 30 minutes at 350 degrees. Serves 6 to 8. May be frozen.

Mrs. Joe S. Gentry

CHICKEN AND CHEESE RICE

5 lb. hen
1 onion, finely chopped
1 clove garlic, finely chopped
1 c. celery, finely chopped
3 T. margarine
2 pkg. [3 oz.] cream cheese
1 pkg. [8 oz.] Velveeta cheese

1 can ripe olives, chopped
1 small can sliced
  mushrooms
1 t. lemon juice
Dash red pepper
2 c. raw rice, cooked

Cook hen, bone and chop. Reserve broth. In a large pan, saute' onion, garlic and celery in margarine. Add 2 cups chicken broth and when hot, add cheeses and stir until melted. Add drained, chopped olives, drained mushrooms, chopped chicken, lemon juice, red pepper and cooked rice. Put in buttered casserole and bake at 325 degrees until hot. Serves 8.

Mrs. Ben Turner

This is better made the day before. Save extra stock in case this needs moistening.

CHICKEN SUPREME

1 fryer, cut-up, or 6 or 7
   chicken breasts
Shortening
1 can cream of chicken soup
1 can water

1/2 c. slivered almonds
1/4 c. chopped pimiento
Potato chips
Pinch of thyme
Salt and pepper

Brown chicken in shortening. Drain and place in casserole. Pour cream of chicken soup and water over chicken. Sprinkle slivered almonds and chopped pimiento over chicken and cover with crushed potato chips. Season with thyme, salt and pepper. Bake at 325 degrees for 45 minutes to an hour. Serves 4 to 6.

Mrs. Jud Adams

CHICKEN WITH MUSHROOMS

1 chicken, cut into
   quarters
1/4 c. flour
1/2 t. salt
1/4 t. pepper

1 t. paprika
1/4 c. butter or margarine
1 can cream of chicken soup
1 can [4 oz.] mushrooms
1 T. sherry

Combine flour, salt, pepper and paprika in paper bag and shake chicken until well-coated. Melt butter in shallow casserole. Lay chicken in casserole with skin side down. Bake in hot oven (400 degrees) about 30 minutes until golden brown on under side. While chicken bakes, combine cream of chicken soup, mushrooms (do not drain) and sherry and heat. When chicken is brown, turn and pour soup mixture over and bake 15 minutes more or until bubbly. Serves 6 to 8.

Mrs. Richard Harvey

CHICKEN AND SAFFRON CASSEROLE

1 1/2 c. saffron-tinted rice
   [or regular white]
3 chicken breasts
6 chicken thighs
1 t. salt
1/4 t. pepper
2 1/2 c. milk
1 can cream of celery soup

1 can cream of chicken
   soup
1 can cream of mushroom
   soup
1 1/2 c. crushed potato
   chips
1/2 c. melted butter
1/8 t. paprika

Put rice in bottom of 13 x 9 x 2 inch baking dish. Cut breasts in half. Arrange chicken in layer over rice. Sprinkle with salt and pepper. Blend milk and soups; pour over chicken. Sprinkle with chips; pour butter over all and top with paprika. Bake uncovered at 325 degrees for 2 hours, or until tender. Serves 8.

Mrs. Buddy Rogers

May be prepared with quail and wild rice or regular rice mixture.

ESCALLOPED CHICKEN OR SHRIMP

Rich Cream Sauce:

3/4 c. butter
3/4 c. flour

4 c. cream, half and half
or evaporated milk

For cream sauce, melt butter, stir in flour and cook until bubbly. Slowly add cream and cook over low heat until thickened.

4 T. butter or margarine
1 lb. fresh mushrooms, sliced
3 c. celery, diced
4 c. rich cream sauce [above]
1 large hen, cooked and cut
in bite sized pieces OR
1 1/2 lbs. shrimp, boiled, peeled
and deveined

1 t. grated onion
3 t. salt
Pinch red pepper
Ritz cracker crumbs
[about 40 crackers,
crushed]

Saute' mushrooms and celery in butter. Add cream sauce, chicken or shrimp, onion, salt and pepper. Place a layer of mixture in a 2 quart shallow baking dish. Sprinkle with a layer of crumbs and dot with butter. Repeat layers and bake at 350 degrees for about 30 minutes. Serves 10 to 12.

Mrs. Joe Huffstutler

For a gourmet touch, add 1/2 cup dry white wine to the cream sauce.

KING RANCH CHICKEN

1 doz. corn tortillas
Chicken stock
1 large hen, stewed, boned,
cut in bites
1 large green pepper, chopped
1 large onion, chopped
2 to 4 T. cooking oil
1 lb. Cheddar cheese, grated
1 t. chili powder

Garlic powder to taste
Salt to taste
1 can cream of chicken
soup
1 can cream of mushroom
soup
1 can Rotel tomatoes
with green chilies,
crushed

Soak tortillas in boiling chicken stock; place in bottom of 3 quart casserole. Top with chicken pieces.

Saute' green pepper and onion in oil until tender and layer over chicken. Add grated cheese to casserole, sprinkle chili powder, garlic powder and salt; spoon on undiluted soups and top with Rotel sauce.

Bake at 375 degrees for 30 minutes, or freeze, thaw and bake. Serves 6 to 8 generously.

Mrs. Richard Grainger

Mrs. J. L. Bergfeld, Jr. varies this by adding 1 beef bouillon cube and 1 cup of water to soups and Rotel sauce. She uses Longhorn cheese and layers as follows: tortilla pieces, chicken, soup mixture, onions, 1 can sliced mushrooms (instead of green pepper) and grated cheese.

CHICKEN AND WILD RICE CASSEROLE

1 hen [4 lb.] boiled
  and boned
1 pkg. wild rice [or Uncle
  Ben's long grain and wild rice]
1/2 lb. sausage
1 large onion, chopped

2 cans cream of mushroom
  soup
1 stick margarine
2 cans mushrooms
1 T. Worchestershire
1 c. bread crumbs

Cook rice according to directions. Cook sausage and onion in skillet until sausage is done and onion is clear. Heat condensed soup and margarine until margarine is melted; blend well, add mushrooms (with liquid) and blend again; add Worcestershire.

Place rice in large shallow baking dish. Cover with chicken chunks and 1/2 cup bread crumbs. Add sausage and onion to soup mixture and pour all over chicken and rice. Sprinkle rest of bread crumbs over top. Cover baking dish with foil and bake at 350 degrees for 30 to 40 minutes. Freezes well. Serves 12.

Mrs. Joe Clayton

CHICKEN AND DRESSING CASSEROLE

2 1/2 c. Pepperidge Farm herb
  stuffing [blue label]
1/2 c. melted margarine
3 c. cooked, boned chicken, cut-up
  [for speed, use a whole canned
  chicken]

1 T. grated onion
1/2 c. chicken broth
1 medium can English peas
1 can cream of celery soup

Mix stuffing with melted margarine. Mix 1 3/4 cup of stuffing with chicken, onion, broth and peas. Put in buttered baking dish. Cover with celery soup and top with remaining stuffing mix. Bake 15 to 20 minutes at 425 degrees. Serves 6.

Mrs. Hunter Brush

HUNTINGTON CHICKEN

1 pkg. [20 oz.] wide noodles
2 qts. chicken broth [may
  use canned]
3 c. chopped bell pepper
3 c. chopped celery
1 stick margarine
1 lb. sharp grated cheese

7 c. chopped cooked
  chicken
1 can chopped mushrooms
1 can undiluted mushroom
  soup
1 small jar chopped
  pimientos

Cook noodles in chicken broth until tender. There will be some chicken stock left, but leave it in with the noodles. To this add the bell pepper and celery which have been sautéed in margarine. Then stir in the cheese, chicken, mushrooms, soup and pimiento. Bake in large casserole dish for 30 minutes at 350 degrees. Serves 12 to 15.

Mrs. H. C. McCalman

HERB NOODLE-CHICKEN CASSEROLE

1 large hen [to make 4 c. cooked, chopped chicken]
1 stalk celery, whole
1 small onion, whole
Salt and pepper to taste
2 cans Campbell's cheese soup
1 can cream of mushroom soup
1 1/2 c. chicken broth [from cooking]
1/2 pkg. [6 oz.] herb noodles
1 c. chopped onions
1 c. chopped green pepper
1 c. chopped celery
1/2 c. cooking oil or butter
1 c. sliced stuffed green olives [7 oz. bottle]
Buttered bread crumbs
Slivered almonds [if desired]

Stew chicken until tender in water to cover with celery, onion, salt and pepper. Reserve chicken stock; bone and cut chicken into bite sized pieces, and set aside. In large mixing bowl, combine soups and 1 1/2 cups broth.

Cook noodles in remaining broth and saute' chopped onions, green pepper and celery in oil or butter.

Drain noodles and combine all ingredients in large bowl; adjust seasoning if necessary. Place in large buttered casserole; top, if desired, with crumbs or almonds, and bake at 350 degrees for 45 minutes or until bubbling. Freezes well; serves 15.

Mrs. Walter P. Jones, Sr.

CHICKEN AND HAM BAKE

1/4 c. chopped onion
1/4 c. butter
2 T. parsley flakes
1/2 t. poultry seasoning
1/4 t. pepper
1 c. cracker crumbs
1/4 c. water
1 egg
1 1/2 c. cooked chicken, chopped
1/4 lb. grated American cheese
6 slices boiled ham
1/4 lb. sliced American cheese

Saute' onion in butter. Add parsley, poultry seasoning, pepper, cracker crumbs, water, egg, chicken and the grated cheese. Mix well. Place an equal portion of the stuffing in the center of each ham slice. Fold the ham over it and secure with toothpicks. Place the ham in an 8 x 10 x 2 inch baking dish and cover with foil. Bake at 350 degrees for 25 minutes; then remove the foil and put the cheese slices on the ham. Bake for five more minutes or until cheese melts. Serves 4 to 6.

Mrs. George Echols
Lafayette, Louisiana

MORNAY CHICKEN CASSEROLE

2 to 3 c. baked or boiled
   white chicken meat
2 pkgs. frozen broccoli
   spears, cooked
1 pkg. Lipton's onion soup mix

1 pt. sour cream
1 c. whipping cream,
   whipped
1 T. Parmesan cheese

Cook broccoli and drain well. To make sauce, combine soup mix with sour cream and beat. Fold in whipped cream. Arrange broccoli in a flat casserole; cover with half the sauce; then the chicken and remaining sauce. Bake at 350 degrees for 20 minutes. Sprinkle with Parmesan cheese and slide under the broiler for a few minutes. Serves 4 to 6.

Mrs. John Ferguson

For variety, add 2 tablespoons dry white wine to the sauce.

PARTY CHICKEN BAKE

1 envelope [1 T.] Italian
   salad dressing mix
2 T. melted margarine
4 chicken breasts
1 can cream of mushroom soup

1/2 c. sauterne
1 container [4 oz.] whipped
   cream cheese with chives
1 c. Minute rice

In large skillet, combine 1/2 envelope dressing mix with margarine. Add the chicken and brown slowly until golden. Put in 1 1/2 quart casserole. Blend soup, sauterne and whipped cream cheese. Spoon over chicken. Bake, uncovered, at 325 degrees for 1 hour. Baste with sauce two or three times during baking. Prepare rice according to package directions, adding the remainder of the salad dressing mix to the water. Serve chicken and sauce over seasoned rice. Serves 4.

Mrs. Charles Clark

SURPRISE CASSEROLE

2 pkgs. Bird's Eye Spanish-
   Vegetable Medley
1 c. sour cream
2 T. mayonnaise
1/2 c. Parmesan cheese

2 c. diced white meat of
   chicken, cooked and boned
Bread crumbs
1/2 c. sharp cheese, grated

Prepare vegetables as directed on package in 2 tablespoons water except heat only until flavor cubes melt and vegetables break apart. Add sour cream mixed with mayonnaise, Parmesan cheese and chicken. Sprinkle with bread crumbs and sharp cheese or sprinkle with Parmesan cheese. Cook until bubbly at 350 degrees for 20 to 25 minutes. Bake in greased casserole dish. Serves 6.

Mrs. Arthur Cunningham

WILD RICE CHICKEN SUPREME

1 box [6 oz.] Uncle Ben's
   long grain and wild rice
1/3 c. chopped onion
1/4 c. melted butter
1/4 c. flour
1 t. salt
Pepper to taste

1 c. half and half cream
1 1/4 c. chicken broth
2 c. cooked cubed chicken
1/3 c. chopped pimiento
1/3 c. chopped parsley
3 T. chopped blanched
   almonds

Cook rice as directed on box. Saute' onion in butter. Blend in flour, salt and pepper. Gradually stir in half and half and chicken broth. Cook mixture until thickened. Mix sauce, chicken, pimiento, parsley and almonds into cooked rice. Bake in 2 quart casserole for 30 minutes at 425 degrees.

Mrs. Robert N. Bergfeld

CHICKEN CREPES I

Crepes:

1 1/4 c. all-purpose flour
3 eggs
1 c. milk
1/4 c. water

1/2 t. salt
3 T. butter, melted
   and cooled

Put all ingredients into blender and blend. Heat crepe pan, having greased for first crepe with a bit of butter and Wesson oil. When pan begins to smoke, lift off stove and pour in about 1/3 cup batter. Swish it around pan until bottom is coated, then pour off excess (back into batter). Cook about a minute or less on one side, then lift tab and turn over to other side for several seconds. Stack crepes on top of each other. (May be made in advance, covered with Saran and refrigerated or frozen, or filled and rolled with chicken mixture and frozen.)

Chicken Filling:

1 chicken, cooked and boned
1 1/4 lbs. Swiss cheese, grated
2 jalapeno peppers, chopped
1 t. salt

1 t. pepper
1 pt. heavy cream
Sherry

Chop chicken and mix with all but a cup of the Swiss cheese (reserve this for baking), peppers, salt and pepper. Put about 2 tablespoons mixture on each crepe and roll up. Place in a pyrex casserole. May be frozen at this point. To serve, mix cream with a little sherry and pour over crepes..Sprinkle 1 cup grated Swiss cheese over top and bake uncovered at 325 degrees for 20 minutes.

Mrs. J. Torrey Forman

CHICKEN CREPES II

Crepes:

1 c. flour
1 c. milk
2 eggs

1/2 t. sugar
5 T. butter

Combine flour and milk and stir until smooth. Add eggs, unbeaten, and beat until well-blended. Add sugar and melted butter. Lightly grease a crepe pan. Add 1 1/2 tablespoons batter to hot pan. Tilt pan until bottom is covered. Cook 1 minute, turn. Stack crepes between waxed paper.

Sauce:

1/4 c. butter
1/4 c. flour
1/2 T. salt
1/2 c. cream
1 1/2 c. milk
1 c. chicken stock

1 c. diced chicken
1/4 c. sliced mushrooms
1/4 c. slivered almonds
1/2 c. sliced water
    chestnuts

Melt butter in top of double boiler, add flour and salt and cook until bubbly; add cream, milk and chicken stock, stirring until smooth. Cook over hot water 30 minutes. Just before serving, add last 4 ingredients and fill crepes; roll and place securely in shallow baking dish. Top each with a whole sauteed mushroom and heat thoroughly in a moderate oven.
Yield: 8 to 10 crepes. Serves 4 or 5 for dinner or 8 to 10 for lunch. May be frozen.

Mrs. Francis Kay

For ladies' luncheon, serve sauce over cheese souffle'.

AUNT FRAPPIE'S CHICKEN SPAGHETTI

1 stewing hen [6 lb.]
2 pkgs. [7 oz.] spaghetti
1/4 c. butter
1 1/2 c. celery
1 large can mushrooms,
    chopped

2 large green peppers
1 c. pimientos
1 1/2 lbs. American cheese
2 cans cream of mushroom
    soup
Salt and pepper to taste

Boil hen in salted water until tender. Cool and debone, cutting into bite-sized pieces. Cook spaghetti in chicken broth, reserving 1 cup broth to dilute soup. Saute' celery, mushrooms, green pepper and pimientos lightly in butter. Grate cheese and add along with soup (diluted with chicken broth). Mix in chicken and continue cooking over low heat. Add cooked spaghetti. Season to taste. Pour into 3 quart casserole dish. Bake uncovered at 350 degrees for 30 minutes or until hot and bubbly.

Mrs. Glenn Collins

CHICKEN SPAGHETTI I

1 large onion, diced
1/2 c. diced celery
1 small can mushrooms, sliced
 [reserve liquid]
1/4 c. butter
1/4 c. chicken broth
2 cans cream of chicken soup
2 T. flour
1/4 c. mashed pimiento

3 to 4 c. cooked
 chicken, chopped
1 box spaghetti, cooked
1/2 c. sliced almonds
1 box [8 oz.] Kraft American
 cheese, grated
Sliced Spanish olives
 to garnish

Cook onion, celery and mushrooms in butter and broth in saucepan until golden. Add soup. Mix flour and juice drained from mushrooms and add to mixture. Heat this about 5 minutes; add pimiento and chicken. Pour the entire mixture over cooked spaghetti. Sprinkle almonds on top. Spread grated cheese on top and decorate with sliced olives. Bake at 325 degrees until bubbling. Serves 8 to 10.

Mrs. Steve Nourse

CHICKEN SPAGHETTI II

1 hen [4 lb.] cooked, boned
 and finely chopped
2 green peppers, chopped
1 large onion, chopped
1 clove garlic, chopped
3 T. salad oil
1 large can tomatoes
1 can tomato soup
1 c. drained mushrooms
1 lb. sharp Cheddar
 cheese, grated

Salt and pepper to taste
1 T. Lea & Perrins
1 lb. long spaghetti,
 cooked in chicken broth
1 small bottle stuffed
 olives, drained and
 sliced
Parmesan cheese

Saute' green peppers, onion and garlic in salad oil. Add tomatoes and soup and simmer in heavy pot until thick. Add mushrooms, cheese, salt, pepper and Lea & Perrins to sauce. Cook spaghetti in chicken broth; drain. Combine sauce, spaghetti, olives and chicken. Top with Parmesan and serve to 10 or 12.

Mrs. A. Y. Lewis

CHICKEN CACCIATORE

2 fryers [2 lb.] cut up
1/2 c. olive oil
1 c. green onion, chopped
1 c. celery, chopped
1 can [4 oz.] mushrooms
2 or 3 cans tomato paste
1 T. sugar

Salt and pepper to taste
3 c. water [1 1/2 c. to
  begin with - more
  if needed]
1 lb. spaghetti
1/2 c. dry sherry

Cut into serving pieces and brown chicken in olive oil. Remove from pan and saute' onions and celery in oil. Add all other ingredients except spaghetti and wine; add chicken and simmer, covered, until chicken is tender. Boil spaghetti according to directions and add to chicken sauce; add wine. Heat through and serve with Parmesan cheese. Serves 8.

Mrs. Allen C. Locklin

CHICKEN TETRAZZINI

1 large onion, chopped
1/2 c. green pepper, chopped
1 c. chopped celery
1/4 c. chicken fat or butter
3 T. flour
1 c. chicken broth
1 can mushroom soup
1/2 c. Parmesan cheese
2 or 3 pimientos, chopped
Salt and pepper to taste

1/4 t. paprika
1/2 t. celery salt
1 c. milk
4 1/2 c. chicken, cooked
  and cut up
1 pkg. [8 oz.] noodles,
  cooked
1/4 c. buttered crumbs
1/4 c. sharp Cheddar
  cheese, grated

Saute' onions, green pepper and celery in chicken fat or butter. Add flour, chicken broth, mushroom soup, Parmesan cheese, pimiento and other seasonings. Add milk last to make medium sauce. Add chicken and cooked noodles to sauce. Mix well. Put into 2 or 3 quart buttered pyrex dish. Sprinkle buttered crumbs on top. Bake at 400 degrees about 30 minutes, adding grated cheese the last 5 minutes of cooking or until melted. Freezes well (without crumbs or grated Cheddar). Serves 10 to 12.

Mrs. L. R. Rhine

BAKED GREEN ENCHILADAS

Soft tortillas
1 can cream of chicken soup
1 can cream of mushroom
  soup
1 can Heinz chicken
  consomme'

1 small can chopped
  green chiles
Grated cheese
1 onion, chopped fine

Place 6 tortillas in the bottom of casserole and cover with the soups and chiles. Sprinkle with grated sharp cheese and onions. Repeat and sprinkle top with grated cheese. Cook for 30 to 40 minutes at 350 to 375 degrees. Tortillas may also be filled with grated cheese and onion, rolled and placed in casserole. Mix soups and chiles together and pour over tortillas; then follow directions for baking. Serves 6 to 8.

Mrs. George B. Allen

CHICKEN ENCHILADAS I

1 medium onion, chopped
3 T. butter
1 can cream of chicken soup
1 can cream of mushroom soup
1 c. chicken broth
1 small can chopped green
  chiles

1 chicken [2 to 3 lb.],
  cooked and boned
1 pkg. corn tortillas
1 lb. Longhorn cheese,
  grated

Saute' onion in butter. Combine with soups, broth and green chiles. Add pieces of chicken and mix well. In large baking dish, place a layer of corn tortillas, layer of chicken sauce, and a layer of grated cheese. Repeat until casserole is filled. Bake at 350 degrees for 30 minutes. Serves 8.

Mrs. Sterling Moore

CHICKEN ENCHILADAS II

2 cans cream of chicken soup
1 soup can of milk
2 small cans of boned chicken
1 medium onion, chopped

1 or 2 cans chile peppers
1 doz. frozen tortillas
1 lb. cheese, grated

Mix soup, milk, chicken, onion and peppers in saucepan and cook over medium heat for about 30 minutes. Dip tortillas, one at a time, in boiling water until soft (this just takes a second). Place a handful of cheese in center of each soft tortilla, roll and place in baking dish. Pour liquid mixture over rolled tortillas. Sprinkle grated cheese on top and bake 25 to 30 minutes at 350 degrees. May be prepared ahead, but do not pour liquid over tortillas until ready to heat. Serves 4.

Mrs. David Russell

CHICKEN ENCHILADAS III

1 large fryer, baked or stewed,
   boned, cut into bite-size pieces
1 pkg. frozen corn tortillas
1 small can Rotel tomatoes
   with green chilies
1/2 lb. Velveeta, grated

1 t. garlic salt
1 t. chili powder
1 medium onion, chopped
2 cans cream of chicken
   soup

Grease large shallow baking dish. Dip thawed tortillas in boiling chicken broth to soften. Line casserole with tortillas. Mix chicken, tomatoes, cheese, seasonings and onion and spread over tortillas. Pour soup on top. Bake at 350 degrees for 40 to 50 minutes. Serves 6.

Mrs. R. Randall Cape

SOUR CREAM ENCHILADAS CON POLLO Y AGUACATE

Juice of 1/2 lime or lemon
1 large or 2 small avocados,
   sliced lengthwise
1 doz. corn tortillas
2 to 4 T. cooking oil
1 chicken [2 1/2 lb.] cooked,
   boned, cut in bites

1 lb. Monterey Jack
   cheese, grated
1 medium onion, finely
   chopped
1 pt. sour cream
Salt and pepper to taste

Preheat oven to 325 degrees. Sprinkle lime or lemon juice on avocado slices. Saute' tortillas, one at a time, in skillet until soft. Put a small amount of chicken, avocado pieces, cheese, onion and 1 teaspoon sour cream on each tortilla and roll. Continue this process until each tortilla has been filled, rolled and placed in a greased 9 x 13 inch casserole. Top with remaining sour cream and sprinkle with any remaining cheese. Salt and pepper to taste. Cover with aluminum foil and place in oven for 30 minutes at 325 degrees. Serves 4 to 6.

John D. Glass, Jr.

 Frozen avocado dip may be used instead of fresh avocado. Swiss cheese used instead of Monterey Jack makes Enchiladas Suisas.

MEXICAN CHICKEN CASSEROLE I

1 chicken [4 lb.] or 3 or 4
  chicken breasts
1 can cream of mushroom soup
1 can cream of chicken soup
2 t. salt
1 t. pepper

1/2 c. chicken stock
1 can Rotel tomatoes
  with green chilies
2 onions, chopped
1 medium pkg. Doritos
3 c. grated cheese [sharp]

Cook chicken and cut into bite-size pieces. Combine the soups, spices, stock, tomatoes and onions. Grease a 3 quart casserole and line it with Doritos. Arrange chicken on Doritos. Pour soup mixture over chicken and top with grated cheese. Bake at 350 degrees for 45 minutes. Serves 6 to 8.

Mrs. Glenn Collins

MEXICAN CHICKEN CASSEROLE II

1 large fryer, stewed, boned,
  cut in bites
1 large onion, chopped
1 stick butter
1 medium can sliced mushrooms
1 or 2 cans water chestnuts,
  sliced
1 can chopped pimiento

1 or 2 cans green chiles,
  mashed
3 cans cream of chicken
  soup
18 corn tortillas, cut
  in pieces
1 lb. grated Cheddar
  [sharp or mild to taste]

Prepare chicken; set aside. Saute' onion in butter; add mushrooms, water chestnuts, pimiento, chiles, soup (undiluted) and tortilla pieces. Alternate layers of tortilla mixture with layers of chicken pieces in 3 quart casserole. Top with cheese, bake at 350 degrees for 30 minutes. Serves 8 to 10. Freezes well.

Mrs. Ronald Schoenbrun

CHICKEN ENCHILADAS CASSEROLE

1 small onion, chopped
2 or 3 T. margarine
1 can cream of mushroom
  soup
1 can cream of chicken
  soup
1 c. sour cream
1 can green chiles, chopped

8 chicken breasts, stewed,
  boned and cut in large
  pieces
1 pkg. frozen tortillas
1 1/2 c. grated Longhorn
  cheese

Saute' onion in melted margarine. Add soups, sour cream, green chiles and chicken. Butter casserole. Layer broken tortillas, chicken, soup mixture and cheese. Bake at 350 degrees for 30 minutes. Serves 4 to 6.

Mrs. Dillard LaRue

CHICKEN AND RICE ORIENTAL

1 stewing chicken [4 lb.]
1 c. celery leaves
1 medium sized onion, halved
1 whole carrot
1 t. salt
2 boxes Uncle Ben's long
  grain and wild rice
1 large onion, chopped medium
  fine
4 T. peanut oil

1 large clove garlic, sliced
  in half
1 T. shredded fresh ginger
2 c. celery, cut diagonally
  in pieces 1/2 in. thick
1 1/2 c. green pepper, cut
  in 1/2 in. slices
1 lb. mushrooms, sliced
  medium thick
1/2 c. soy sauce

Put the chicken in a large pan, breast side down and cover with water. Add the celery leaves, onion, carrot and salt. Bring to a boil and simmer until the chicken leg pulls away tender. Remove the chicken from the broth and allow to cool. Bone and cut into bite-size pieces and put aside. Cook the rice according to directions on the box, using the chicken broth instead of the water called for. While the rice is cooking, heat 2 tablespoons of the oil in a Dutch oven and saute' the chopped onion until golden. Add the cooked rice and 3 cups of the chicken to the onion. All of this may be done ahead of time but the last step should be done not more than 30 minutes before serving. The crisp quality of the vegetables is important.

Heat the remaining 2 tablespoons oil in large skillet or wok pan. Add garlic and ginger and cook over high heat until browned. Remove from the oil and add celery and green pepper. Stir, frying these over high heat until done but still crisp--about 2 minutes. Toss with the rice along with sliced mushrooms. The heat from the rice cooks the mushrooms sufficiently. Add soy sauce and serve. Serves 10.

Mrs. William Rowe

CHICKEN AND RICE SALONIKI

1/2 c. raw rice
1/4 c. chopped onion
40 almonds [blanched]
4 T. butter
1 1/2 c. milk
3 T. chopped pimiento
1 t. salt

1 t. pepper
1/2 t. thyme
Pinch of sugar
3 lb. chicken, disjointed
2 T. flour
4 T. shortening or
  margarine

Saute' rice, onion and almonds in butter until golden. Place in greased casserole. Combine milk, pimiento, salt, pepper, thyme and sugar. Pour over rice mixture.

Dredge chicken in flour and brown in shortening or margarine. Lay on top of rice mixture. Cover casserole and place on a rack in a pan of warm water. Bake at 350 degrees about 2 hours or until rice is cooked and chicken is tender. Serves 4 to 6.

Mrs. L. R. Rhine

CHICKEN CASHEW

1 fryer [3 lb.], cut-up
2 c. water
2 t. salt
1 c. chopped celery
1 t. grated onion
1 T. butter
1 T. soy sauce

Dash Tabasco
1 can cream of mushroom
 soup, undiluted
1 c. chicken broth
1 can chow mein noodles
1/2 can chopped cashews

Place chicken, water and salt in pan. Cover and cook about an hour or more until chicken is tender. Cool. Remove skin and bones; leave meat in large pieces. Saute' celery and onion in butter for 5 minutes. Add soy sauce, Tabasco, mushroom soup and chicken broth. Heat to boiling. Add chicken, turn into casserole. Sprinkle noodles and nuts on top. Bake 45 minutes at 325 degrees. Serves 4.

Mrs. Patrick Thomas

CHICKEN CHOW MEIN

1 hen [4 to 5 lb.] cooked, boned,
 cut in small pieces
1 c. chicken broth [from
 cooking]
5 T. flour
1 or 2 T. soy sauce
1 c. chopped celery

1 can sliced mushrooms
1 can water chestnuts,
 sliced
1 can bean sprouts,
 drained
1 clove garlic, chopped

Cook hen; bone, cut up and reserve broth. Combine flour and broth to make sauce; add soy sauce and vegetables and simmer 10 minutes. Add chopped chicken and simmer 10 minutes more.

Serve with rice and/or chow mein noodles, Chinese egg rolls, hot mustard sauce and extra soy sauce. Serves 8 to 10.

Mrs. E. B. Yale

POLYNESIAN CHICKEN

1/4 c. butter
1 fryer, quartered
1 large onion, sliced
1 c. chopped celery

1 1/2 c. hot chicken
 bouillon
1 c. Minute rice
1/2 t. soy sauce
1/2 c. white seedless raisins

Melt butter and brown chicken pieces in skillet. Add onion and celery, toss for a minute, cover and simmer 30 minutes. Add hot bouillon and rice. Cover and cook on low heat for 30 minutes more. Add soy sauce and raisins. Blend and serve hot. Serves 4.

Mrs. Henry D. McCallum

TERIYAKI CHICKEN

4 or 5 chicken breasts,
  boned and skinned
1/4 c. pineapple juice
1/2 c. soy sauce
2 T. brown sugar
1 T. molasses

1/4 c. cooking oil
2 T. cider vinegar
1 small clove garlic
1/4 c. sauterne [or water]
1 can [1 lb. 4 1/2 oz.]
  pineapple slices

Combine juice, soy sauce, brown sugar, molasses, oil, vinegar, garlic and wine. Pour over chicken and marinate several hours; broil on the grill with pineapple slices until tender. Warm marinade to serve over rice. Serves 4.

Mrs. Mike Trant
Dallas, Texas

TRUE INDIA CHICKEN CURRY

2 large [or 3 small] onions,
  chopped
Butter or margarine
2 frying chickens, cut in
  pieces

1/2 c. water
4 T. curry powder
Juice of 1/2 lemon
Salt and pepper to
  taste

In heavy skillet, saute' onions in butter until golden and set aside. Brown chicken on all sides in butter in a large skillet. Add water, onions, curry, lemon juice, salt and pepper. Cover and cook on top of stove at low heat for 45 minutes to 1 hour or until chicken is tender. Serve with rice and condiments as desired. Suggested condiments might include salted peanuts, grated coconut, chutney, chopped hard cooked eggs, crumbled bacon, raisins, chopped tomato, green pepper, and onion in lemon juice.

Mrs. Bernard Wolf

DUCKS COOKED WITH ORANGE JUICE

4 ducks
4 c. orange juice
2 c. brown sugar
1 c. shredded orange rind

8 T. drippings
5 1/3 T. flour
4 T. cointreau

Roast ducks in 325 degree oven for approximately 3 hours, basting often. Pour off and reserve excess drippings. Heat orange juice, brown sugar, orange rind and drippings in saucepan. Add flour and cook slowly until sauce thickens. Pour sauce over ducks and return them to oven. Continue basting ducks while cooking, about 1 hour more. When done, add cointreau to sauce in pan and serve.

Mrs. Jack Woldert

ROAST DUCK WITH ORANGE AND PINEAPPLE

2 oven-ready ducks
  [5 lb. each]
2 oranges
4 slices canned pineapple
1 t. tarragon
3 garlic cloves
2 T. butter
1/2 c. brandy

1 c. dry Marsala wine
2 c. chicken bouillon
1 t. tomato paste
1/2 c. currant jelly
3 T. flour
1 t. salt
Freshly ground black
  pepper

Shred orange rinds and set aside. Quarter the oranges and mix with pineapple, tarragon and 2 chopped garlic cloves. Use mixture to stuff both ducks. Place ducks on rack in shallow baking pan and roast in slow oven (325 degrees) for 2 1/2 hours or until done. Saute' duck livers in butter in 10-inch skillet. Heat brandy; light it and pour over livers. When flame dies, remove livers, chop and keep warm. To sauce remaining in skillet, add orange rind and 1 minced garlic clove. Cook 5 minutes. Combine wine, bouillon, tomato paste, jelly, flour, salt and pepper. Add to sauce and cook, stirring until smooth. Add livers; simmer 15 minutes. Serve in sauceboat with duck. Serves 6.

Mrs. J. Harold Stringer

SAUSAGE STUFFED DUCK

1 duck or goose [2 to 3 lb.]

Stuffing:

1/2 lb. pork sausage
1/4 c. chopped onion
1/2 c. fine-cut celery
1 T. minced parsley
2 T. grated green pepper

1 1/2 c. cold water
1/2 t. pepper
1 t. salt
4 c. dry bread cubes

Mix well first 8 stuffing ingredients and cook 40 to 50 minutes. Remove from heat and cool until grease sets. Remove as much of the grease as possible. Add bread cubes. Toss to mix well, adding more moisture if necessary.

Rub inside of duck lightly with salt and pepper. Put stuffing lightly into cavity and skewer or lace opening. Brush outside with bacon drippings and dust with flour. Place in covered roasting pan, breast side up, and roast in 325 degree oven 3 1/2 to 4 hours, or until breast meat starts to fall off bone. Baste at 45 minute intervals. Serves 2.

Mrs. Nelson Clyde

PREPARATION AND COOKING OF WILD DUCK

Wild duck
1 onion, quartered
1 potato

2 chicken bouillon cubes
Bacon strips

Soak duck in cold water for 30 minutes or longer. Remove skin. Place quartered onion and unpeeled potato, cut in large pieces, inside duck. Simmer for 2 to 3 hours, covered. Drain off water. Bake duck using chicken bouillon cubes dissolved in hot water to baste. Lay solid strips of bacon on top of duck when baking as this prevents meat from drying out, adds salt flavoring, keeps stuffing moist and enhances the taste of the gravy. Baste bird frequently. Bake at 325 degrees 1 to 1 1/2 hours.

Mrs. Oscar West

Duck may be stuffed with your favorite dressing, but if stuffing is not desired, serve duck with wild rice and fresh mushrooms sauteed in butter.

VENISON CHUCK WAGON STEAK

Venison steaks [1 per person]
1/3 c. flour
1 t. salt
1/4 t. pepper
3 T. shortening
1 can undiluted beef broth

1/2 c. water
1/2 c. bottled barbecue
  sauce
1 t. chili powder
1 green pepper, diced
1/2 c. sliced stuffed olives

Soak venison steak in water all day, changing water as often as possible. Mix flour, salt and pepper together. Rub or pound mixture well into both sides of meat. Heat shortening in heavy skillet or Dutch oven; brown meat well on both sides. Blend beef broth, water, barbecue sauce and chili powder. Pour over meat and cover. Simmer 1 hour. Add green pepper and olives. Simmer 1 to 1 1/2 hours longer. Skim any fat from gravy at last simmering period. May be cooked or prepared the day before serving and reheated.

Mrs. Oscar West

BREADED VENISON STEAK

Venison chops or steaks
Salt and pepper
Flour

2 eggs
Cracker crumbs [fine]

Soak venison chops or steaks in water all day, changing water as often as possible. Salt and pepper meat, sprinkle with flour and pound meat well. Dip venison in well-beaten eggs, then cracker crumbs, working crumbs into meat. Brown in very little oil until tender.

Use your imagination on the crumbs - Club saltine crackers, herb seasoned crumbs or a mixture of both adds flavor.

Mrs. Oscar West

MARSHA'S TURKEY DRESSING

To make enough stock, add milk and water to turkey and giblet stock to make 8 cups of liquid.
Combine:

6 c. broken corn bread [2 10-inch pans]
4 c. broken white bread
4 c. stock

Cook in deep skillet until brown:

1 1/2 c. chopped onion
1 c. chopped celery
1/3 c. hot fat

Combine bread and onion mixtures with:

4 well-beaten eggs
2 t. salt
1 t. pepper
1 t. poultry seasoning,
  if desired
Sage, if desired

Thoroughly moisten with remaining 4 cups stock. Mix well. Bake in shallow uncovered pan at 350 degrees for 1 hour. Makes 12 cups.

Mrs. William E. Bertram

If very light fluffy dressing is desired, add 1 teaspoon of baking powder.

RICE AND CORN DRESSING

1/2 c. chopped celery
1/2 c. chopped green
  peppers
1/2 c. minced parsley
1 large onion, chopped
1/2 stick butter
2 c. raw rice

1 can Mexican corn with
  peppers
1 c. chopped pecans
2 cans chicken or beef broth
  [depending on what meat
  this is to be served with]
Salt and pepper

Saute' all vegetables until soft. Add rice and cook until grains are slightly brown. Add corn and nuts. Mix well. Add broth and seasonings. Cover and cook slowly over low heat until liquid is absorbed and rice is dry. Serves 8 to 10.

Mrs. Frank Fite

Try serving this with all kinds of barbecue.

HOLIDAY DRESSING

1 green pepper
1 bunch green onions
1 small white onion
1 red apple
3 stalks celery
  [plus a few celery leaves]
1 clove garlic
2 c. rice

5 or 6 corn bread patties
Turkey giblets
  [liver, gizzard and neck]
2 T. Worcestershire sauce
1 t. salt
1/2 t. pepper
3 eggs
1 pt. oysters

Day before serving, cook turkey half done and save fat and juices. Chop the green pepper, onions, apple, celery, and garlic, and store in refrigerator. Cook the rice and prepare the corn bread (Jiffy corn bread mix may be used. Fry as directed on package). Boil the turkey giblets in salt water until tender and cut into small pieces. Refrigerate.

On the day of serving, while turkey finishes baking, combine chopped vegetables and apple with the corn bread(crumbled) and the cooked rice. Add Worcestershire sauce, seasonings and beaten eggs. Drain oysters and add along with turkey giblets. For moisture, add the turkey juices from the baking turkey (that was reserved from the day before). Bake dressing in large casserole at same temperature as baking turkey.

Mrs. Floyd Murphy

SAUSAGE DRESSING

4 medium onions, chopped
1 1/2 stalks celery, chopped
2 T. butter
2 pans corn bread
7 or 8 biscuits

2 cans mushroom soup
1 1/2 c. water
2 lbs. seasoned sausage
Salt and pepper to taste
1 T. sugar

Saute' onions and celery in butter until they are transparent, but not brown.

Crumble corn bread and biscuits into large mixing bowl. Mix together mushroom soup and water, and add to above mixture. Add sausage, onions, celery, salt and pepper, and sugar. If your brand of sausage does not have enough sage, add more. Be sure it is well seasoned before cooking. Different brands of sausage cause seasonings to be different.

Steam 3 hours or bake, covered at 325 degrees for 1 hour. Serves 8.

Mrs. Jack M. King

Seafoods

CRABMEAT-ARTICHOKE CASSEROLE

3 T. butter
3 T. flour
1 t. salt
1/8 t. black pepper
1/8 t. powdered mustard
1 1/2 c. milk
1/2 t. Worcestershire sauce
Dash of Tabasco sauce

1/4 c. Parmesan cheese
1 lb. crabmeat
1 can [1 lb.] artichoke hearts,
   drained
4 hard-cooked eggs, sliced
1/2 c. buttered bread crumbs
1/4 c. Parmesan cheese

Melt butter, stir in flour, salt, pepper and mustard until smooth. Gradually add milk and cook until thickened, stirring constantly. Add Worcestershire sauce, Tabasco, 1/4 cup Parmesan cheese and crabmeat; mix well.

Arrange artichoke hearts in bottom of a 1 1/2 quart casserole and cover with sliced eggs. Spoon in crab mixture. Top with buttered bread crumbs which have been mixed with 1/4 cup Parmesan cheese. Bake at 350 degrees for 30 to 40 minutes. Serves 6 to 8.

Mrs. E. N. Kittrell, Jr.

CRAB CASSEROLE

3 beaten eggs
1/2 c. butter
1/2 t. Worcestershire sauce
1 t. salt
1/2 t. prepared mustard

1 1/2 c. evaporated milk
1 T. minced green pepper
1 T. parsley
1 lb. fresh lump crabmeat
1/2 c. buttered crumbs

Combine all ingredients except crabmeat and crumbs. Pour this mixture over crabmeat and mix lightly. Pour into casserole (9 x 12 inch) and spread crumbs over the top. Bake at 325 degrees for 30 to 45 minutes or until well set. Serves 6.

Mrs. E. B. Yale

 Fresh or frozen lump crabmeat is the secret. Canned crabmeat can be used but is not as good.

QUICK CRABMEAT AU GRATIN

1 egg, well-beaten
Juice of 1/2 lemon
Dash Tabasco sauce

1 can [6 1/2 oz.] crabmeat
1/4 c. sharp Cheddar cheese, grated

Beat egg thoroughly. Add lemon juice and Tabasco sauce. Wash crabmeat with cold water, drain and remove any shells or membrane. Add crabmeat to egg mixture and stir. Place in individual ramekins or sea shells. Top with grated cheese and bake in 350 degree oven until cheese is melted and serve immediately. Serves two. This may be prepared early in the day and refrigerated until it is baked.

Mrs. William Finn

CRABMEAT AU GRATIN

4 T. butter
4 T. flour
2 c. milk
1/2 c. grated cheese
2 egg yolks
1 t. onion juice
1/4 t. paprika

1/2 t. salt
1 t. Worcestershire sauce
1 lb. crabmeat
1 can mushrooms
Chopped parsley
2 T. sherry

Melt butter in double boiler. Blend in flour and add milk slowly. Cook until thick. Fold in cheese, egg yolks (beaten with onion juice, paprika, salt and Worcestershire sauce), crabmeat, mushrooms, parsley and sherry. Add more seasonings if necessary. Cover and cook 20 minutes over medium heat. Serve on avocado slices or pastry shells.

Mrs. E. J. Mooney, Jr.

CRABMEAT MORNAY

1 stick butter
1 small bunch green onions, chopped
[use part of green tops]
1/2 c. finely chopped fresh parsley
2 T. flour
1 pt. cream [half-and-half]
1/2 lb. grated Swiss cheese

Red pepper to taste
1 T. sherry [or more, to taste]
Salt to taste
1 lb. white crabmeat [canned or fresh]

Melt butter in heavy skillet and saute' onions and parsley. Blend in flour, cream, and cheese until cheese is melted. Add other ingredients and gently fold in crabmeat. Let simmer several minutes, stirring constantly. Serve in chafing dish as a dip--or serve over Melba toast, toast cups, or pastry shells.

Mrs. A. M. Limmer, Jr.

CRAB MOUSSE

2 pkgs. plain gelatin
1/2 c. water
1 can tomato soup
2 pkgs. [3 oz.] cream cheese
1 T. lemon juice

1/4 c. chopped onion
1/2 c. diced green pepper
1 c. diced celery
1 c. mayonnaise
1 can [6 1/2 oz.] crabmeat

Soften gelatin in water. Heat soup to boiling, add gelatin and stir. Remove from heat; add cubed cream cheese and beat until smooth. Cool. Add lemon juice and fold in chopped ingredients, mayonnaise and crabmeat. Pour into mold and chill. This may be made the day before and refrigerated. Serves 8.

Mrs. A. B. Wilson, Jr.

CRAB MELBA

1 can [4 oz.] mushrooms
2 T. butter
2 T. flour
1 c. milk
1 c. medium sharp cheese,
   grated

2 T. sherry
1 t. Worcestershire sauce
1/4 t. seasoning salt
2 cans [6 1/2 oz.] crabmeat
   [or fresh or frozen crab]
Bread crumbs

Drain mushrooms and saute' in butter until lightly browned. Remove from pan and blend flour into butter. Add milk and cook until thick. Add 3/4 cup of cheese and stir until melted. Remove from heat; add remaining ingredients except bread crumbs, and combine well. Pour into greased casserole; sprinkle remainder of cheese on top and add bread crumbs. Bake at 350 degrees for 20 minutes. Serve in pastry shells or over English muffins or toast. Serves 4 to 6.

Mrs. Joe O'Conner
Ft. Worth, Texas

CRAB-SHRIMP MELBA

6 T. flour
1 stick butter
2 c. milk
2 c. cream [half and half]
1 c. Cheddar cheese, grated
1 t. salt
1 t. paprika
1 t. MSG
1 can [4 oz.] buttered mushrooms [including liquid]

1 lb. tin crabmeat or
   2 cans [7 oz.]
1 1/2 lbs. cooked shrimp
2 T. catsup
Dash of red pepper
1 T. lemon juice
3 T. sherry

Blend flour with melted butter. Add milk and cream and cook until thickened. Add cheese, salt, paprika, MSG, and mushrooms; then add crab and shrimp. Add catsup, red pepper, lemon juice and sherry. Serve over Melba rounds, toast points or in pastry cups. Will freeze.

Mrs. Edwin Simons

CRAB QUICHE

Pastry:

1 1/2 c. flour
1/4 t. salt
6 T. butter

2 T. shortening
3 to 6 T. ice water

Sift dry ingredients together. With a pastry blender, cut in butter and shortening until size of small peas. Gradually sprinkle with water and toss with a fork. Cover tightly and chill for 3 hours. Shape into ball and roll out. Bake 9-inch crust at 400 degrees for 10 minutes. Cool. Lower oven to 375 degrees.

Filling:

3 eggs
3/4 c. sour cream
1/2 c. milk
1/2 t. salt
1/4 t. dry mustard
Dash cayenne

1 c. fine grated Swiss cheese
1 can [7 1/2 oz.] Geisha
    crabmeat
2 T. lemon juice
1 T. chopped chives, [optional]

Beat eggs just until well-blended. Add sour cream, milk, salt, mustard and cayenne; beat to blend. Stir in cheese, crab, lemon juice and chives. Turn into pie shell, distributing crab evenly. Bake until knife inserted into center comes out clean, 30 to 40 minutes.

Mrs. Mage Honeycutt
Little Rock, Arkansas

CURRIED CRAB QUICHE

Unbaked 10-inch pastry shell
2 cans or 1 lb. Alaskan
    King Crab
2 T. lemon juice
2 T. sherry

1 T. finely chopped onion
1 t. curry powder
1 t. parsley, chopped
    fine
1 c. cubed Swiss cheese

Sour Cream Custard:

3 eggs, well-beaten
3/4 c. milk

1/2 c. sour cream
1/4 t. salt

Bake pie shell in 400 degree oven for 10 minutes to set. Remove from oven.

Drain crab and slice. Combine crab with lemon juice, sherry, onion, curry powder and parsley. Refrigerate 1 to 2 hours to blend flavors. Cover bottom of pastry shell with cubed Swiss cheese. Add crabmeat mixture. Combine ingredients for Sour Cream Custard and pour over all. Bake at 350 degrees for 45 minutes or until custard is slightly browned and set. Cool slightly and cut in wedges. Serves 6.

Mrs. George Oge

CRAB RAREBIT

4 T. butter or margarine	2 T. catsup
4 T. sifted flour	1 1/2 t. lemon juice
2 c. milk	1 t. salt
1/2 t. salt	Coarse ground pepper to taste
1/8 t. coarse ground pepper	Dash of cayenne pepper
1/8 t. paprika	1 c. coarse-grated sharp
1 T. minced onion	cheese
1 t. Worcestershire sauce	2 cans crabmeat, flaked

Prepare white sauce by combining butter, flour, milk, salt, pepper and paprika in double boiler and stir constantly until thick. Add onion, Worcestershire sauce, catsup, lemon juice and seasonings. Add cheese and stir until melted. Add crabmeat and blend together.

Mrs. Jonathan E. Boyle

Try this as a dip or in pastry shells for a ladies' luncheon.

CRAB SUPREME

5 or 6 T. butter or margarine	2 T. chopped parsley
3 T. flour	1 c. milk
3/4 t. salt	1/2 c. sauterne
1/4 t. garlic salt	2 slices Swiss cheese
1/2 t. pepper	1 small can crabmeat

In top of double boiler, melt butter; add all dry ingredients and seasonings, and stir until thoroughly mixed. Stirring constantly, slowly add milk, then sauterne. Add Swiss cheese, broken into pieces, and stir until cheese melts. Add crabmeat that has been rinsed in cold water and drained. Serve over toast triangles, corn bread squares or in crepes. Serves 6.

Mrs. Thomas R. Garvin

CRABMEAT SOUFFLÉ

2 cans crabmeat [Geisha]	2 t. grated onion
Juice of 1 lemon	1 1/2 c. mayonnaise
4 slices bread, soaked in	Salt and pepper to taste
1 c. milk	Ritz cracker crumbs
6 hard-cooked eggs, chopped	

Remove all small bones from crabmeat. Add lemon juice. Soak bread in milk until all milk is absorbed in bread; mix with fork. Add to crab. Mix in eggs, onion and mayonnaise. (Add salt and pepper if desired.) Spread in buttered 9 x 13 inch pan. Cover with Ritz cracker crumbs. Bake in a 350 degree oven for 1 hour. May be mixed the day before and refrigerated before baking. Serves 6.

Mrs. Don Fisher
Richardson, Texas

A lovely luncheon dish

CRAB SOUFFLÉ

8 slices bread
2 c. crab or shrimp
1/2 c. mayonnaise
1 onion, chopped
1 green pepper, chopped
1 c. chopped celery
4 eggs, beaten

3 c. milk
1 can cream of mush-
 room soup
1 c. grated Cheddar
 cheese
Paprika

Dice half of bread into baking dish. Mix crab, mayonnaise, onion, green pepper and celery. Spread over diced bread. Trim crusts from remaining 4 slices of bread, and place trimmed slices over crab mixture. Combine eggs and milk and pour over all. Cover and refrigerate over night.

Bake at 325 degrees for 15 minutes. Take from oven and spoon soup over the top. Top with cheese and paprika. Bake 1 hour at 325 degrees. Serves 6 to 8.

Mrs. J. B. Belue

CLAM SPAGHETTI I

2 cans minced clams and juice
1/2 stick butter
1 t. salt
1 t. black pepper
Dash of cayenne pepper

1 t. grated onion
2 cloves garlic, crushed
1/2 t. oregano
6 T. dry white vermouth
1 pkg. thin spaghetti

Combine ingredients, except spaghetti, and heat to boiling. Cook spaghetti; drain. Toss the sauce into spaghetti. Place in greased casserole and heat in oven. Serves 4.

Mrs. E. N. Kittrell, Jr.

CLAM SPAGHETTI II

2 onions, chopped
2 oz. bottle olive oil
3 cans minced clams and juice
1 t. Italian Herb Seasoning
 [Spice Islands]
Salt and pepper to taste

1 T. minced parsley,
 [dried or fresh]
Garlic powder
1 pkg. spaghetti, cooked
Parmesan cheese

Brown onions in olive oil; add clams and juice. Add 1 teaspoon Italian Seasoning (more may be added if desired), salt, pepper, parsley and generously sprinkle with garlic powder. Simmer 30 minutes over low heat. Serve over cooked spaghetti. Sprinkle with cheese.

Mrs. Bernard Wolf

BAKED FISH FILLETS, SHRIMP AND MUSHROOMS

8 small or 4 large fish fillets
Lemon slices
1/2 lb. fresh mushrooms or 1
    can [8 oz.] button mushrooms
20 shrimp, uncooked
4 T. butter or margarine

4 T. flour
1 t. salt
1 c. milk
1 T. lemon juice
Chopped parsley
Paprika

Cut 4 pieces of aluminum foil in 12-inch squares. Wash and dry fish and arrange 1 large or 2 small pieces on each piece of foil. Lay one or two slices of lemon on each. Chop stems off mushrooms, and lightly saute' stems and buttons (or use straight from can). Peel and devein shrimp. Make a cream sauce of butter, flour, salt and milk. When thick, add lemon juice. Cover fish with shrimp, mushrooms and sauce. Sprinkle with chopped parsley. Gather 2 edges of the foil together over fish and make a double fold to seal tight. Double fold the ends. Place squares on cookie sheet and bake in hot oven (425 degrees) for 40 minutes. Place on platter, cutting slit in top and folding back foil to make a silver bag. Sprinkle with paprika. May also be removed from bags for serving.

Mrs. Wade Ridley

May also be prepared in a casserole dish.

FISH 'N CHIPS

2 lbs. fish fillets
1/4 c. milk
1 c. crushed potato chips
1/4 c. grated Parmesan cheese

1/4 t. thyme
1/4 c. butter or margarine,
    melted

Dip fillets in milk and then in mixture of crushed potato chips, Parmesan cheese and thyme. Place in baking dish greased with butter or margarine. Sprinkle with extra potato chip mixture. Drizzle melted butter over top. Bake in extremely hot oven (500 degrees) for 12 to 15 minutes. Serves 6.

Mrs. Jack Harper

Flounder fillets are good to use.

FRESH FRIED FISH

Salt and pepper fresh fish fillets, such as crappie or bass. Dip in buttermilk; then coat with Waverly Wafer crumbs. Fry in hot peanut oil, as peanut oil can maintain a high temperature without burning or smoking up the kitchen. Cook fish until golden brown.

Mrs. Ronald Smith

SNAPPER AMANDINE

4 fillets of snapper or
 1 whole snapper
Flour
Salt
1/2 c. butter

1/2 t. onion juice
1/4 c. sliced blanched
 almonds
1 T. lemon juice

Wash and dry the fish. Dust lightly with flour and salt. Heat 1/4 cup butter and onion juice in a heavy skillet. Cook fish until light brown. Remove and place on hot serving dish. Pour off grease left in pan and add remaining butter to same pan. Add almonds and brown slowly. Add lemon juice and when the mixture foams, pour over fish and serve. Serves 4.

Mrs. Terry J. Cooper

BROILED LOBSTER

4 lobster tails [8 to 12 oz.],
 frozen
2 sticks of butter or margarine

Juice of 2 lemons

Drop frozen lobster tails into large pot of boiling salted water. Return to a boil and cook, uncovered, 17 minutes. Drain and cool. With kitchen shears, cut and remove the inside covering. Gently scoop out the lobster from the shell and remove the vein from the back. Place lobster back in the shell and make a slit down the center with a sharp knife. Prepare lemon butter by melting 2 sticks of butter or margarine and adding the juice of 2 lemons. Drizzle small amount of lemon butter over each lobster tail; place in a shallow pan and broil 3 minutes. Serve with individual cup of lemon butter for dunking. Serves 4.

Mrs. Allen Pye

 May be prepared ahead and broiled just before serving. Return to room temperature before broiling.

SEAFOOD NEWBURG

2 pkgs. [6 oz.] frozen crabmeat [or 2 cans]
2 pkgs. [10 1/2 oz.] frozen
  lobster tails
2 pkgs. [10 oz.] frozen
  shrimp
3 cans cream of shrimp soup

2 cans cream of mushroom
  soup
1 c. heavy cream
1/4 c. sherry [more if
  desired]
Pepper

Cook seafood according to package instructions. Cut into bite sized pieces. Combine all other ingredients and heat; then add seafood pieces. Can be served in Cheese Toast Cups.

Cheese Toast Cups:

Cut crusts from slices of cheese bread. Melt butter and brush lavishly on slices. Press into muffin pan cups and brown in oven at 375 degrees for 10 to 15 minutes. Can be made ahead and reheated.

Makes 12 servings and can be served from a chafing dish.

Mrs. A. M. Limmer, Jr.

ESCALLOPED OYSTERS

1/2 c. butter or margarine
3/4 c. flour
3 t. paprika
1 t. salt
1/2 t. pepper
4 T. finely chopped onion
4 T. finely chopped green
  pepper

1/2 t. finely chopped garlic
2 t. lemon juice
1 T. Worcestershire sauce
1 qt. oysters and liquid
2 T. cracker crumbs

Melt butter or margarine. Add flour and cook for 5 minutes, or until dark brown, stirring constantly. Add paprika, salt, pepper and cook 3 minutes. Add onion, green pepper and garlic and cook slowly for 5 minutes more. Remove from heat and add lemon juice and Worcestershire sauce. Pick shell pieces from oysters and heat oyster liquid to just below boiling. Stir into vegetable mixture. Pour into large baking dish and sprinkle with cracker crumbs. Bake in hot oven, about 400 degrees, for 30 minutes. Yields 6 servings.

Mrs. C. R. Hurst

This is a good side dish or a light meal with a lettuce salad.

SCALLOPED OYSTERS

1 pt. oysters
1/2 t. pepper
1 1/4 t. salt
1 1/2 c. soft bread crumbs [or
   1 c. cracker crumbs and
   1/2 c. bread crumbs]

4 T. butter
1/2 c. light cream

Drain oysters and add salt and pepper. Place half the oysters in a well-greased 2 quart casserole. Cover with half the bread crumbs and dot with half the butter. Repeat; pour cream over the top. Bake at 350 degrees for 30 minutes.

Mrs. Dan Calihan
Trinity, Texas

 A "must" for Christmas dinner.

SALMON CROQUETTES

1 can [16 oz.] red salmon, drained
1/2 c. buttermilk
1/2 c. flour
2 beaten eggs

1/4 t. soda
1 small onion, chopped fine
Salt and pepper
1 c. cracker crumbs

Remove large bones and skin from salmon. Place in a bowl and flake well. Add the rest of the above ingredients. Shape into small croquettes, roll in additional cracker crumbs, and fry in hot grease.

Mrs. Don Crysup
Rusk, Texas

 The buttermilk makes this very fluffy.

SALMON LOAF

1 can [#303] salmon, drained
1 c. bread or cracker crumbs
1/4 c. chopped parsley
   or drained pickle relish

4 T. melted butter
Salt and pepper to taste
4 eggs, beaten

Mix all ingredients together, place in greased pan and bake at 350 degrees for 45 minutes. Serve with white sauce and peas, or if desired, pour a can of mushroom soup over the loaf before baking.

Mrs. William Marsh

SALMON LOG

2 pkgs. gelatin, dissolved
   in 1 1/2 c. water
1 large can salmon [deboned]

1 1/2 c. mayonnaise
3 T. pickle relish
1 large onion, chopped

Mix all ingredients together and place in loaf pan that has been lightly greased. Congeal in refrigerator. To serve, invert on serving plate. Serves 6.

Mrs. E. B. Yale

BAKED SHRIMP AND CHEESE

1/4 lb. sliced fresh mushrooms
2 T. butter
1 lb. cooked shrimp
1 1/2 c. cooked rice
1 1/2 c. grated cheese

1/2 c. evaporated milk
3 T. catsup
1/2 t. Worcestershire sauce
1/4 t. salt
1/8 t. pepper

Saute' mushrooms in butter for 10 minutes. Lightly mix in shrimp and all other ingredients. Bake in casserole in a 350 degree oven for 20 to 30 minutes until bubbly and lightly browned.

Condensed mushroom soup may be substituted for the evaporated milk and fresh mushrooms. Mix with 1/4 cup milk until smooth before adding remaining ingredients.

Mrs. Albert Morriss

BLACK SHRIMP

3 sticks margarine, melted
8 T. black pepper
1 large bottle Wishbone
   Italian dressing

1 t. salt
5 lbs. shrimp in shell

Combine margarine, pepper, dressing and salt in long, shallow baking dish, or bottom of roasting pan. Add shrimp and bake at 350 degrees for 45 minutes, stirring once or twice. Serves 8.

Serve with a tossed green salad and French bread to dip up the sauce. Let each peel his own--messy, but fun!

Mrs. Jack Crow
Longview, Texas

Mrs. Fred Haberle varies her New Orleans Barbecued Shrimp by using only 4 tablespoons of pepper, and adding an additional stick of margarine and the juice of 4 lemons.

SHRIMP CREOLE

1 T. cooking oil
1 clove crushed garlic
3 large onions, diced
2 large bell peppers, diced
1 t. chili powder
2 or 3 T. flour
1 large can chopped mush-
  rooms, drained
3 cans [1 lb.] stewed
  tomatoes, chopped

1 small can tomato paste
1 can [16 oz.] tomato sauce
2 c. water
2 t. Worcestershire sauce
1 bay leaf
3 lbs. cooked, cleaned shrimp
  [medium size preferred]
1 large box white rice

In a large pot, place cooking oil and crushed garlic clove. Saute' with finely chopped onions and bell peppers. Cook these until they become translucent (not brown). Sprinkle with chili powder and flour. Mix this, forming a paste-like mixture. Add mushrooms, stewed tomatoes and their juice, tomato paste, tomato sauce and water. Mix; then add Worcestershire sauce and bay leaf. Simmer 30 minutes; then let stand for an hour or so. Just before serving, add shrimp and heat. Do not overcook the shrimp or they will be tough. Serve a large ladle of the creole over steaming rice. Serves 8 to 10.

The shrimp can be cooked ahead and refrigerated. The creole sauce may be made 2 or 3 days ahead which enhances its flavor. To cook shrimp, boil in salted water for 12 to 15 minutes. It is easier to peel shrimp after cooking.

Carole Brockington

QUICK SHRIMP CREOLE

1 onion, chopped
4 stalks celery, chopped
2 T. Crisco
1 T. flour
1 t. salt

2 T. chili powder
1 c. water
2 c. canned tomatoes
1 T. vinegar
2 c. cooked shrimp

Saute' onion and celery in fat until brown; add flour and seasonings. Slowly add 1 cup water. Cook 15 minutes. Add tomatoes, vinegar and shrimp. Cook 10 minutes more. Serve over hot boiled rice. About 3 cups of cooked rice is sufficient for the recipe of creole. Serves 4 to 6.

Mrs. Gene Caldwell

SHRIMP AND ARTICHOKE CASSEROLE

1 pkg. frozen artichoke hearts
  or 1 can
1 lb. shelled cooked shrimp
1/2 lb. fresh or 1 can sliced
  mushrooms
4 T. butter
2 1/2 T. flour
1/2 t. salt
1/4 t. pepper

Dash of cayenne pepper
1 c. cream
1 T. Worcestershire
  sauce
1/4 c. dry sherry
1/4 c. grated Parmesan
  cheese
Paprika
Parsley

Cook artichoke hearts according to directions on package (or remove from can). Drain and arrange them in a buttered shallow baking dish. Spread the shrimp over them. Saute' coarsely sliced mushrooms in 2 tablespoons of butter for 6 to 7 minutes; add to contents of the baking dish.

Make a medium cream sauce by melting 2 tablespoons of butter in saucepan and stirring in flour. Add salt, pepper, cayenne and cream. Stir until smooth and add Worcestershire sauce and sherry. Blend in well and pour over ingredients in baking dish. Sprinkle top with grated Parmesan cheese and dust top with paprika. Garnish with finely chopped parsley. Bake 20 minutes in 375 degree oven. Serves 6.

Mrs. Raymond Hedge, Jr.

SHRIMP AND WILD RICE CASSEROLE

2 T. butter
2 T. flour
1/2 t. salt
1 1/2 c. chicken stock
1/2 c. milk
2 T. sherry
1 T. Worcestershire sauce
3 or 4 drops Tabasco
1/4 c. butter

1/4 c. diced onion
1/4 c. diced green pepper
1 can [4 oz.] button mushrooms
1 pkg. Uncle Ben's long
  grain and wild rice
1 1/2 lbs. shrimp, cooked
  and deveined
Parmesan cheese

Prepare a thin cream sauce by melting 2 tablespoons butter in pan and adding flour to make a paste. Add salt, chicken stock, milk, sherry, Worcestershire and Tabasco.

Melt 1/4 cup butter and saute' onions, pepper and mushrooms lightly. In buttered 9 x 13 inch casserole dish, combine wild rice mixture (which has been prepared according to directions on the box), onions, peppers, mushrooms and cream sauce. Add shrimp which have been coated with melted butter and lightly sprinkled with salt. After mixing all ingredients in casserole, sprinkle top freely with Parmesan cheese. Pake at 350 degrees until bubbly (about 20 to 25 minutes). Serves 6. May be prepared several hours before needed.

Mrs. Arthur Cunningham

SHRIMP CASSEROLE I

1/2 c. chopped green pepper
1/2 c. chopped onion
2 large pkgs. cooked shrimp
1 T. lemon juice
2 c. cooked long-grain rice
1 can tomato soup

1/2 c. cream [half and half]
1/2 c. sherry
3/4 t. salt
1/4 t. nutmeg
1/4 to 1/2 c. toasted slivered
  almonds

Saute' pepper and onion in butter until tender but not brown. Stir in remaining ingredients except almonds. Pour into 2 quart casserole. Bake at 350 degrees for 30 minutes or until bubbly. Top with almonds. Serves 8 to 10. This can be made early in the day to be used that night or frozen for 2 weeks or more.

Mrs. Glenn Collins

A favorite for dinner parties!

SHRIMP CASSEROLE II

1/2 large onion, chopped
1 T. butter
1 c. mushroom soup
1/2 T. lemon juice
Dash garlic salt
Salt and pepper to taste
3/4 c. rice, cooked

1 1/4 lbs. shrimp, cooked
  and cleaned
1/2 c. sour cream
3/4 c. grated sharp cheese
1/2 bell pepper, cut into
  rings

Saute' onions in butter until tender. Make a sauce by adding the soup, lemon juice and seasonings. Fold rice and shrimp into sauce and add the sour cream. Pour into a buttered baking dish. Sprinkle grated cheese on top and decorate with pepper rings, which have been parboiled for 2 minutes. Bake in 325 degree oven for 30 minutes.

Mrs. Robert E. Knox, Jr.

SHRIMP ASPIC

4 c. tomato juice
2 T. onion juice
4 T. vinegar
Salt and pepper to taste
1 large pkg. lemon Jello

2 c. finely cut celery
1 c. finely cut green olives
  [or bell peppers]
1 pkg. [10 oz.] frozen shrimp
  [or 2 cans]

Bring to boil tomato juice, onion juice, vinegar, salt and pepper and pour over Jello. Allow to set for a short time. Fold in celery, olives and shrimp. Pour into ring mold or individual molds. Chill overnight. May be prepared several days in advance. Serves 16.

Mrs. Bernard Jones

SHRIMP CURRY

2 t. curry powder
3/4 c. cream

1 can cream of chicken soup
2 lbs. fresh shrimp, cooked

Mix curry with a little cream; add to chicken soup with rest of cream. Heat to boiling point and add cooked shrimp. Keep hot until ready to serve.

Cook enough rice for a ring mold. Pour shrimp mixture in the center and over rice. Serves 4 to 6. The following condiments are good with this, though not essential:

Chopped hard-boiled eggs
Chopped peanuts
Coconut
Chutney
Crumbled crisp bacon
Finely chopped green onions
Seedless raisins

Mrs. C. Avery Mason

INDIAN CURRY-SHRIMP ALOHA

2 T. chopped onion
1 small apple
2 T. butter or bacon drippings
4 t. curry powder
1/16 t. powdered cloves
1 t. lemon juice
2 lbs. frozen raw shrimp

White Sauce:

8 T. butter
8 T. flour
4 c. milk

Chop onion and apple together and slowly saute' in drippings until soft. Mash together, add seasonings, and simmer for 10 minutes. Prepare white sauce and add to mixture.

Boil shrimp 7-10 minutes. Drain, cool, devein. Cook 5 minutes with curry mixture. Serve to 6 over rice and top with any of the following suggested condiments:

Chopped peanuts
Coconut
Mango chutney
Chopped boiled eggs
Bacon
Onions
Raisins

Mrs. Ford King, Jr.
Honolulu, Hawaii

CANTONESE FRIED RICE

2 c. chopped onion
3 T. salad oil
4 eggs, slightly beaten
1 lb. fresh shrimp
2 c. cooked chicken or pork,
  diced fine

6 T. soy sauce
Salt and pepper to taste
1 T. chopped chives
4 c. cold cooked rice

Brown onions in 1 tablespoon salad oil. Add eggs and stir until slightly set. Remove from pan and set aside. Reheat pan with 2 tablespoons oil and saute' shrimp and pork or chicken. Add soy sauce, salt, pepper and chives. Add rice and when ingredients are thoroughly heated, add egg mixture and stir until mixed. Add more soy sauce, salt or pepper to taste (if desired). Serves 4 to 6.

Mrs. A. M. Limmer, Jr.

SHRIMP FOO YONG

3/4 c. cooked shrimp, diced
1 T. chopped green onions
1 T. chopped water chestnuts
1 t. MSG
1 c. bean sprouts

1 T. bamboo shoots
3 large mushrooms, chopped
Salt to taste
4 eggs

Combine all ingredients adding beaten eggs last. Form small cakes from a large spoonful of mixture and fry in hot fat until brown, turning once during cooking. Serve with the following sauce.

Egg Foo Yong Sauce:

1 c. chicken broth
2 T. soy sauce
1/4 t. sugar

2 t. MSG
1 T. cornstarch
1/4 c. cold water

Heat broth and add soy sauce, sugar and MSG. Combine cornstarch and water. Add to broth and cook, stirring constantly until thickened. Salt to taste. Serves 4.

Mrs. A. M. Limmer, Jr.

SHRIMP MARINIERE

1/2 c. butter
1 c. shallots, finely chopped
3 T. flour
2 c. milk
1/2 t. salt

1/4 t. cayenne pepper
1/3 c. white wine
1 lb. boiled shrimp, peeled
   and deveined
1 egg yolk, beaten

In a 9-inch skillet, melt butter and saute' shallots until tender. Blend in flour and cook slowly 3 to 5 minutes more, stirring constantly. Stir in milk until smooth. Add salt, pepper and wine. Cook about 10 minutes more. Remove from heat, add shrimp and quickly stir in egg yolk. Return to heat and slowly cook until heated through. Place in ramekins and sprinkle tops with paprika. Heat under broiler until piping hot. Serves 3 or 4.

Mrs. Roy Tidwell

 This is also delicious served over cheese souffle.

SHRIMP MOUSSE

2 T. gelatin
1/2 c. water
1 can tomato soup
1 pkg. [8 oz.] cream cheese
1 c. Hellmann's mayonnaise
1 T. Durkee's dressing
1 lb. shrimp, cooked and
   cleaned

1/4 c. chopped green
   pepper
1/2 c. chopped celery
1 T. grated onion with
   juice
1 t. Worcestershire
1/4 t. salt

Soak gelatin in cold water. Heat undiluted soup; add gelatin; stir until dissolved. Mash cream cheese; add to soup; continue heating until dissolved; cool. Fold in mayonnaise, and Durkee's dressing; add chopped shrimp, vegetables and seasonings. Mix thoroughly. Pour into oiled fish mold; chill. Serves 8.

Mrs. Alice White

SHRIMP IN SOUR CREAM

1 c. green onions, chopped
4 T. butter
2 T. flour
1 can cream of mushroom soup
1 can cream of shrimp soup

1 c. sour cream
1/2 t. white pepper
2 lbs. cooked, shelled, deveined
   shrimp
Dash of sherry

Chop onions and tops very fine and saute' in butter until tender. Mix flour into soups until smooth and add to onions. Add sour cream and pepper and heat very slowly. Add shrimp and small dash of sherry. Serve over rice or Melba toast.

Mrs. James B. Owen

For variation, try serving this in pastry shells.

Page 237

SHRIMP SCAMPI I

1 lb. large raw shrimp	2 T. chopped parsley
1/2 c. butter	1 t. grated lemon peel
1/2 t. salt	1 T. lemon juice
6 cloves garlic, peeled and crushed	

Wash, peel and devein shrimp. Melt butter in a 13 x 9 inch baking dish. Add salt, garlic, 1 tablespoon of the parsley and mix together well. Arrange shrimp in a single layer and bake uncovered for 5 minutes at 400 degrees.

Turn shrimp and sprinkle with lemon peel, lemon juice and remaining tablespoon of parsley. Bake 8 to 10 minutes more, or just until shrimp are tender.

To serve, arrange shrimp on heated platter and pour garlic butter drippings over all. Garnish with lemon or lime wedges. Serves 4.

Mrs. Rolf Schroeder

SHRIMP SCAMPI II

12 large raw shrimp	1/2 to 3/4 c. flour
Milk to cover shrimp	Salt and pepper to
Cooking oil	taste

Sauce:

2 c. white wine [sauterne is good]	4 T. softened butter
1 T. chopped shallots or	Lemon wedges
1/2 t. minced garlic	Parsley

Shell, clean and devein shrimp. (If large enough, make 3 cuts from tail to head, giving the shrimp 4 inch "tails." If smaller shrimp are used, make one cut from tail almost to head). Place cleaned shrimp in a large bowl and cover with milk. Soak for 15 to 30 minutes.

In a deep skillet, heat cooking oil (about 1 1/2 inches deep) to 350 degrees. Drain shrimp on absorbent paper and dredge in flour seasoned with salt and pepper. Fry shrimp in deep fat for about 2 minutes or until lightly browned. Drain and keep warm.

For the sauce, combine the wine and chopped shallots (or garlic) in a 12-inch skillet and bring to a boil. Cook until wine is reduced to 1 cup. Add shrimp and boil briskly for 1 minute. Add butter and stir all together until the sauce is creamy and smooth. Remove from heat immediately as butter is melted and serve garnished with lemon and parsley. Serves 3 or 4.

Mrs. Jack M. King

TUNA-CHICKEN BAKE

1 pkg. [7 oz.] cut spaghetti
1/2 c. chopped onion
1/4 c. chopped green pepper
6 T. butter
1/4 c. flour

2 1/2 c. milk
2 cans cream of chicken soup
1/2 c. chopped pimiento
2 cans [6 1/2 oz.] tuna
Slivered almonds

Cook spaghetti by directions on package. Saute' onion and pepper in butter until tender. Blend in flour. Slowly add milk and cook over low heat until sauce thickens. Stir in soup, pimiento and tuna. Garnish with almonds and pimiento. Bake at 350 degrees for 35 minutes. Serves 8.

Mrs. William F. Turner

TUNA CASHEW CASSEROLE

1 can chow mein noodles
1 can cream of mushroom soup,
   undiluted
1/4 c. water
1 c. tuna

1/4 lb. cashew nuts
1 c. finely diced celery
1/4 c. minced onion
Dash of salt and pepper

Heat oven to 325 degrees. Reserve 1/2 cup noodles for top of casserole. In 1 1/2 quart casserole, combine the rest of the noodles with the other ingredients. Sprinkle reserved noodles on top and bake for 40 minutes at 325 degrees. If baked in individual casseroles or scallop shells, the baking time is 25 minutes.

Mrs. J. Torrey Forman

 A delightful ladies' luncheon dish.

TUNA-SPINACH CASSEROLE

2 pkgs. frozen spinach,
   cooked and drained
2 hard cooked eggs
2 cans [6 1/2 oz.] tuna

1 can cream of celery soup
1/2 c. cream
1/2 c. grated Cheddar cheese

Butter a 1 1/2 quart casserole dish. Place drained, chopped spinach in dish and mix with chopped egg whites. Arrange tuna on top. Combine remaining ingredients and pour on. After baking, garnish with sieved egg yolks. Bake at 325 degrees for 15 minutes. Serves 6.

Mrs. William C. Lust

TANGY TUNA MOUSSE

2 envelopes unflavored gelatin
1/2 c. cold water
1 c. mayonnaise
2 cans [6 1/2-7oz.] tuna
1 c. diced celery
1/4 c. chopped stuffed green olives

2 T. finely chopped onion
2 T. lemon juice
1 1/2 t. horseradish
1/4 t. salt
1/4 t. paprika
1 c. heavy cream, whipped

Soften gelatin in cold water; dissolve over boiling water. Stir into mayonnaise. Add remaining ingredients except cream. Mix well. Fold in whipped cream. Pour into 10 x 6 x 1 1/2 inch pan. Chill until firm. Cut in squares and serve on lettuce leaves. Serves 8 to 10.

Mrs. Dale Turner

Tasty for ladies' luncheon with fresh fruit salad and crisp crackers.

TUNA PINWHEELS

2 c. sifted flour
2 t. baking powder
1/2 t. salt
1/4 c. shortening
3/4 c. milk
1/2 c. chopped celery

2 T. butter
1 c. flaked tuna, drained
1 c. cooked English peas
2 T. chopped pimiento
1 egg, slightly beaten

Sift flour, add baking powder and salt. Cut in shortening until mixture resembles coarse meal. Add milk. Mix only until all flour is dampened. Turn out on floured board; knead lightly to smooth dough. Roll into rectangle about 3/8 inches thick. Saute' celery in butter. Remove from heat and add tuna, peas, pimiento and egg, combining thoroughly. Spread over dough; roll up as a jellyroll. Seal edges. Cut into 8 slices. Flatten out and shape each slice to about 3 1/2 inches in diameter. Place on greased cookie sheet. Bake at 400 degrees for about 15 to 20 minutes. Serve with the following Cheese Sauce.

Cheese Sauce:

2 T. butter, melted
4 T. flour
1/2 t. salt
1/4 t. paprika

2 c. milk
1/2 lb. American cheese,
   grated

Combine butter, flour, salt and paprika. Add milk gradually. Place over boiling water and cook, stirring constantly until thickened. Add cheese and stir until melted. Pour over pinwheels. Serves 8.

Mrs. Ted Chilcote

GUMBO I

6 slices bacon
2 T. butter
2 large onions, chopped
2 cloves garlic, crushed
6 T. flour
1 qt. tomatoes
1 1/2 qts. consomme'
1 carrot, chopped
1 1/2 lbs. shrimp

1 1/2 lbs. crabmeat
Salt and pepper to taste
Tabasco to taste
1/2 t. thyme
1 t. Accent
2 lbs. okra
3 T. parsley
2 T. gumbo file'

Fry bacon in skillet until brown. Remove. Add butter, onions, garlic and saute' until brown. Add flour and brown. Transfer to a large kettle and add tomatoes and consomme'. Bring to a boil and add chopped carrot. Boil 30 minutes and add raw, peeled and deveined shrimp and crabmeat. Season with salt, pepper, Tabasco, thyme and Accent. Add okra and cook 30 minutes more. Add parsley and gumbo file'. Serves 4 to 5. Freezes.

Mrs. Harold B. Cameron

GUMBO II

3 lb. fryer, cut up
1 c. Wesson oil
3/4 c. flour
1/3 c. green onion tops,
  chopped
1 c. celery, chopped
1 medium onion, chopped
1/3 c. bell pepper, chopped
3 qts. water
1 bay leaf
3 t. McCormick seafood
  seasoning

4 t. salt
1 t. pepper
Dash red pepper
2 c. okra, sliced
1 clove garlic, crushed
1 can [#2] tomato wedges,
  chopped
2 shakes Tabasco
2 lbs. shrimp, peeled
  and deveined
6 small crabs and claws
1 c. rice

Salt, pepper and flour chicken. In skillet, fry pieces in Wesson oil until lightly browned. Remove from skillet and set aside. Pour off oil and return 3/4 cup to skillet along with chicken dregs. Add flour to make a roux. Stir constantly over medium heat until dark brown. Add onion tops and stir until they are browned. Add celery, onion, bell pepper and stir for 3 minutes. Transfer roux-vegetable mixture to large kettle (5 quart). Stir in water and add bay leaf, seasonings, okra, garlic, tomatoes and Tabasco, and bring to a boil. Debone chicken. Cut in small pieces and add to gumbo. Cook for 45 minutes at medium-low temperature. As this cooks, clean shrimp. Add shrimp, crabs and rice to gumbo, and simmer about 2 hours. Cool and refrigerate overnight. Next day return to heat and simmer another hour.

Mrs. M. Earl Davis

JOHNNY CACE'S GUMBO

1 c. onion, chopped
3 T. cooking oil
3 cloves garlic, crushed
4 T. flour
1/2 can tomato paste
1 can [#2] tomatoes
2 qts. water
2 bay leaves
Pinch of thyme

1 c. celery, chopped
2 T. parsley
Salt and pepper to taste
Dash Accent
1 c. crabmeat
2 lbs. small shrimp,
    peeled and deveined
1 T. gumbo file'

Saute' onion in oil and add garlic. Stir in flour to make a roux. Stir constantly as it browns. Add tomato paste, tomatoes, water, bay leaves, thyme, celery, parsley, salt, pepper, Accent and crab. Bring to a boil and simmer for 1 hour. Add shrimp and cook 20 minutes more. Remove from heat and take out 1 cup of the broth. To this, add gumbo file' and stir until dissolved. Return to soup. Serve over cooked rice.

Mrs. William Marsh

GUMBO FILÉ

1 turkey or chicken
    carcass [smoked turkey
    can be used, gumbo will
    be richer]
2 T. grease
2 T. flour
3 or 4 slices bacon, cut up
1 large onion, chopped
1/2 lb. okra, cut up

2 tomatoes, cut up
3 or 4 stalks celery, chopped
1 bay leaf
1 pt. oysters [with liquid]*
1 lb. shrimp, cleaned*
1 T. file'

*Other seafood may be added
 or substituted

On the day before, boil turkey or chicken bones at least 5 or 6 hours. Cool. Remove bones from stock. Refrigerate stock until gumbo making day. Make a roux as follows: in a large pan (at least 4 quart size) cook, stirring constantly, grease, flour and bacon until very brown. Add onion and continue cooking until onion is slightly browned. Add stock to the roux. Add okra, tomatoes, celery and bay leaf. Cook several hours. Add water as needed to make about 4 quarts gumbo. About 1/2 hour before serving, add shrimp and oysters. Season to taste. Just before serving, add file'. Do not use iron spoon and do not cook any more after adding file'. Serve over steamed rice.

Mrs. Bert Creel

CREAMY CREOLE GUMBO

3 T. butter
2 med. onions, sliced
   into rings
1/4 c. chopped green pepper
2 T. flour
2 t. salt
1/2 t. black pepper
1/2 t. thyme, powdered or
   pulverized

5 drops Tabasco sauce
1 lb. fresh crabmeat or 2
   cans [7 1/2 oz.] crabmeat
4 c. okra with liquid or
   2 cans [#303]
3 1/2 c. [#2 1/2 can]
   tomatoes with juice
1 c. milk
1/2 t. gumbo file'

In saucepan, melt butter and saute' onion and green pepper until tender. Blend in flour, salt, pepper, thyme and Tabasco sauce to form a smooth paste. Stir in crabmeat, okra and tomatoes and heat to boiling point. Reduce heat; cover and simmer for 25 to 30 minutes. Gradually stir in milk and cook a few minutes more over medium heat, stirring occasionally until heated through. Add the gumbo file' powder which you have liquified with a little of the hot gumbo. Stir in thoroughly. This recipe will serve 6 generously. Gumbo should always be served in individual bowls, with a scoop or spoonful of hot fluffy rice in the middle of the bowl.

Mrs. Henry M. Bell, Jr.

Try adding shrimp for a variation.

SEAFOOD GUMBO

1/4 c. butter
1 onion, chopped
1 clove garlic, chopped
1 c. chopped celery
1 green pepper, chopped
4 c. bouillon
1/2 t. salt
1/2 t. pepper

1/4 c. crabmeat
1 lb. raw shrimp
1 jar [6-8 oz.] oysters
1 1/4 c. canned tomatoes
2 T. butter
2 T. flour
1 t. gumbo file'
1/2 c. water

Melt butter and saute' onion, garlic, celery and green pepper. While vegetables cook, combine bouillon, salt and pepper in a large saucepan and bring to a boil. Add seafood and boil for 5 minutes. Remove seafood and store in refrigerator. Add sauteed vegetables and tomatoes to bouillon mixture and bring to a boil. Make a roux by melting 2 tablespoons butter in small skillet, stirring in flour. Cook until dark brown, stirring constantly, about 15 minutes. Add roux to soup mixture and simmer 1 hour. Combine file' with water and add near end of cooking period. Add seafood. Serve with rice.

Mrs. Steven B. Roberts

SHRIMP GUMBO

1/4 c. margarine or butter
2 T. flour
2 minced garlic cloves
2 sliced onions
1/2 thinly sliced green
   pepper
1 can [6 oz.] tomato
   paste [2/3 c.]
1 can[#2] okra,
   drained or 1 pkg.
   frozen whole okra
3 beef bouillon cubes or 1 T.
   meat extract paste

4 t. Worcestershire
1/8 t. ground cloves
1/2 t. chili powder
Pinch dried basil
1 bay leaf
1 1/2 T. salt
1/4 t. pepper
3 c. water
1 1/2 lbs. shelled deveined raw
   shrimp
3 c. hot cooked rice
1/4 c. snipped parsley

Several hours before time to serve, melt butter in Dutch oven or heavy kettle. Stir in flour and cook over low heat until browned. Add garlic, onions, green pepper and cook slowly until tender. Add tomato paste, okra, bouillon cubes, seasonings and water. Simmer uncovered 45 minutes. Cool and refrigerate. To serve, heat soup mixture over medium heat until just boiling. Add shrimp and simmer, covered, for 5 minutes or until shrimp are pink and tender. Serve gumbo in shallow bowls, adding a dash of Spice Islands gumbo file' seasoning. Toss hot rice with parsley and serve at side of each serving. Serves 8.

Mrs. Frank Agar

REMOULADE SAUCE

2 hard cooked sieved egg
   yolks
2 cloves garlic, pressed
1 1/2 T. mustard
1 1/2 c. mayonnaise
1 T. Worcestershire

1 T. paprika
1 1/2 T. horseradish
2 T. cider vinegar
1/4 c. chopped parsley
Dash Tabasco

Combine all ingredients. Chill 12 hours before serving.

Mrs. Joe Herrington

TARTAR SAUCE
[for fish]

1 c. mayonnaise
1 T. chopped parsley
   [or dried parsley flakes]
1 T. chopped pickles

1 T. chopped capers
1 T. chopped stuffed olives
1 T. onion juice
   [or dried onion flakes]

Mix all ingredients. Return to refrigerator for an hour or more to "season".

Mrs. John F. Warren

Cakes

CAKES

ANGEL BAVARIAN CAKE

Duncan Hines angel food
  cake mix
1 pt. milk
4 eggs, separated
1 c. sugar
2 T. flour

Pinch of salt
1 1/2 pkgs. gelatin
1/4 c. bourbon
1/4 t. vanilla
1 pt. cream, whipped
Small can coconut

Prepare angel food cake according to directions on box. Let cool. Scald 2 cups milk. In top of double boiler, mix egg yolks, sugar, flour and salt. Add milk slowly. Cook until slightly thick over hot, not boiling, water. While hot, add gelatin soaked in bourbon. When cool, fold in whipped egg whites, vanilla and whipped cream. Break up angel food cake.

In angel food pan, alternate layers of cake and custard. Cover and refrigerate overnight. Unmold. Serve with sprinkled coconut.

Mrs. Ronald N. Schoenbrun

ANGEL CAKE WITH LEMON BUTTER

1 10-inch angel food cake

Filling:

3 eggs
1 c. sugar
1 T. butter

Grated rind and juice
  of 2 lemons

Frosting:

1 pt. heavy cream, whipped

1/4 c. powdered sugar

Beat eggs and sugar together until thick and very light colored. Add butter, lemon juice and rind. Cook in top of double boiler, stirring constantly, until mixture is consistency of mayonnaise (about 10 minutes). Cool. Slice cake crosswise making 2 layers. Spread lemon filling on bottom half, then set top half on and frost entire cake with the whipped cream frosting. More lemon rind may be grated and sprinkled on cake. Chill in refrigerator.

Mrs. Milburn Pool

This is easy to make but elegant - especially good for Easter or any spring party.

LEMON ANGEL CAKE

6 eggs, separated
1 1/2 c. sugar
3/4 c. lemon juice
Grated rind of 2 lemons

1 envelope plain gelatin
1/4 c. cold water
1 angel food cake

Combine egg yolks with 3/4 cup of the sugar and beat well. Add lemon juice and grated rind. Cook in double boiler until mixture begins to thicken. Dissolve gelatin in water and add to egg yolk mixture while mixture is still hot. Beat egg whites and slowly add 3/4 cup sugar. Fold into lemon mixture. Break cake into small pieces and pour lemon mixture over it. Mix well and spoon into pan lined with waxed paper. When congealed, spread with the following icing:

Icing:

2 c. heavy whipping cream
1 T. powdered sugar

1 t. vanilla

Whip cream, add sugar and vanilla. Serves 16.

Mrs. Allen Locklin

STRAWBERRY ANGEL FOOD CAKE

1 large angel food cake
1 pkg. [10 oz.] frozen strawberries
1 envelope unflavored
gelatin

2 c. heavy cream,
whipped
1/4 c. sugar

Cut angel food cake crosswise to make 2 layers. Prepare frosting by draining strawberry syrup into top of double boiler and sprinkling on gelatin to soften. Place over boiling water and stir until gelatin is dissolved. Add to berries and chill 5 minutes, until mixture thickens. Fold into whipped cream which has been sweetened with sugar. Frost each layer, top and sides of cake. Chill several hours before serving.

Mrs. Milburn Pool

CAKE AND BERRIES

1 large angel food cake
2 c. strawberries or peaches,
sweetened [may use frozen]

1 to 2 c. heavy cream,
whipped

Split cake crosswise and cover bottom layer with berries or peaches and about 2/3 carton sweetened whipped cream. Place on top layer and ice entire cake with sweetened whipped cream. Serve at the table and pass more berries or peaches to add.

Mrs. Elam Swann

ANGEL FOOD CAKE

1 c. granulated sugar
1 c. cake flour
1 1/2 c. powdered sugar
1 1/2 c. egg whites
1/3 t. salt

1 1/2 t. cream of tartar
1 t. vanilla
1/2 t. almond flavoring
1/2 t. lemon flavoring

Sift granulated sugar once. Sift cake flour and powdered sugar together 4 times. Have eggs 3 or 4 days old (after chilling 24 hours, set out one-half hour before using). Beat egg whites and salt until foamy. Add cream of tartar and beat until moist. Gradually add granulated sugar, 1 tablespoon at a time, and beat until mixture holds a peak. Add vanilla, almond flavoring and lemon flavoring. Fold in sifted flour and powdered sugar in amounts of 2 tablespoons at a time. Pour into ungreased tube pan and put in cold oven. Set oven for 375 degrees and bake for 35 minutes. Cool in pan 1 hour upside down on rack, then run knife around edges of cake and remove. May be frozen.

Mrs. Will Mann Richardson

This is a very old recipe and once you try it, you will never bake a mix again.

IDE'S FRESH APPLE CAKE

2 c. sugar
1 c. shortening
3 eggs
3 c. flour
1 t. soda
1/2 c. warm water

1 t. vanilla
1/2 t. cinnamon
1/2 t. allspice
1/2 t. nutmeg
1/8 t. salt
3 apples, peeled and grated

Cream sugar and shortening. Add other ingredients. Bake in greased and floured bundt or tube pan for one hour at 350 degrees. Test for doneness.

Icing:

1 stick margarine, melted
3 T. flour
1/2 c. milk
1/2 c. brown sugar

1 t. vanilla
1 box powdered sugar
1 c. pecans

Combine all ingredients except pecans. Cook and stir until yellow streaks appear. Add pecans. Spread or pour on cooled cake.

Mrs. Glen Dyer

One and one-half cups honey may be used instead of the two cups of sugar in cake.

RAW APPLE CAKE

2 c. sugar	1 1/2 t. soda
1 1/2 c. Wesson oil	1/2 t. nutmeg
2 eggs	1/2 t. cinnamon
3 c. chopped apples, peeled	1/2 t. salt
3 c. flour	1 c. chopped pecans

Mix sugar, oil and eggs. Add apples. Chop 1 cup at a time and add to batter so they do not turn dark. Sift flour with soda, spices and salt. Add gradually to batter. Mix well and add chopped pecans. Bake in a greased and floured bundt pan at 350 degrees for 1 hour.

Ice when cool with 1 cup powdered sugar mixed with juice of 1 lemon. Drizzle over top of cake.

Mrs. Glenn Bracken
Mrs. A. C. Smart
Mrs. Horace Smith

Edna Gail Walls, Atlanta, Texas, combines 1 1/4 c. oil, 2 t. vanilla and 3 eggs. In another bowl, she mixes 3 c. flour, 2 c. sugar, 1 t. salt, 2 t. cinnamon and 1 1/2 t. soda. After combining the two mixtures, she folds in 3 c. chopped apples and 3/4 c. chopped nuts and bakes in bundt pan 1 hour at 350 degrees. This cake freezes well.

Mrs. Francis Kay calls hers "Apple Blossom Cake." Her ingredients differ in that she prefers 3 eggs, 1 t. salt, 1 t. cinnamon, 1 t. nutmeg and she includes 1 t. baking powder and 1 t. vanilla. She bakes in tube pan 1 1/2 hours at 325 degrees.

APPLESAUCE CAKE I

1/2 c. shortening [or oil]	1 3/4 c. flour
1 c. sugar	1 t. cinnamon
1 egg	1/2 t. ground cloves
1 c. raisins, chopped	1 t. soda
1 box [8 oz.] dates, chopped	1/4 t. salt
1 c. nuts, chopped	1 c. applesauce

Cream together shortening (or oil) and sugar. Add egg. Mix raisins, dates and nuts with 3/4 cup of flour. Add to sugar-shortening mixture. Sift 1 cup flour and spices together and add. (Mixture is very thick - cannot use a mixer.) Heat applesauce and add. Bake in greased, floured pan for 1 hour at 350 degrees. (If using a glass pan, bake at 325 degrees.) Delicious served warm with whipped cream. This cake freezes well.

Mrs. G. N. Taylor
Nashville, Tennessee

APPLESAUCE CAKE II

1 c. sugar
1 c. brown sugar
1 c. shortening
2 eggs
3 c. flour
2 t. soda
1/2 t. salt
1 t. cinnamon

1/2 t. cloves
1/2 t. nutmeg
2 c. warm applesauce
1 t. vanilla
1 c. nuts
1 c. golden raisins
1 c. dates, chopped

Cream sugars and shortening. Beat in eggs. Add flour, soda, salt, spices, applesauce and vanilla. Add nuts and fruit. (If desired, sprinkle with part of the flour.) Pour into a greased and floured tube pan. Bake at 325 degrees for 1 1/2 hours. This cake freezes well.

Mrs. William T. Read

BANANA CAKE

2/3 c. butter
[1 1/3 sticks]
2 c. sugar
2 eggs
2 1/4 c. flour
1 t. soda
1/4 t. salt

1/2 t. baking powder
1/2 c. light cream
1 t. vanilla
3 medium bananas
3/4 c. pecans, chopped and floured

Cream butter and sugar. Add whole eggs, one at a time. Sift dry ingredients together and add alternately with cream. Add vanilla. Then add bananas (mashed) and nuts. Bake 45 minutes in 325 degree oven.

Icing:

1/2 c. butter
2 T. cream
1 1/2 to 2 c. powdered sugar
1 t. vanilla

1 pkg. [3 oz.] Philadelphia cream cheese
Chopped nuts

Melt butter with cream. Add powdered sugar, then vanilla and cream cheese. Spread on cake and sprinkle with chopped nuts. (If cake is baked in layers, double recipe for icing.)

Mrs. William Murphy

BANANA NUT CAKE

1/2 c. butter
1 1/2 c. sugar
2 eggs
1 t. vanilla
1 c. mashed bananas

1 1/2 c. flour
1 t. soda
1 t. baking powder
2 T. buttermilk
1 c. pecans, chopped

Cream butter and sugar. Add eggs and vanilla. Add mashed bananas. Sift together flour, soda, and baking powder and add to mixture. Add buttermilk, and stir in nuts. To prepare pan for baking, line angel food cake pan with foil after lightly greasing. Grease the foil lightly. Bake at 325 degrees about one hour. This cake is best cooked in the type of angel food pan in which the center part pulls out.

When cake tests done, remove from oven and cool cake in pan for 20 minutes. Spread topping (recipe below) and put back in oven at 400 degrees until top is brown--few minutes. Then remove foil as soon as cake comes from oven.

Topping:

6 T. butter, softened
1 c. brown sugar
4 T. milk

1 c. coconut
1/2 c. pecans, chopped

Combine all ingredients and spread on cake as described above.

Mrs. H. L. Gist

BANANA SPLIT CAKE

2 c. crushed vanilla wafers
1 1/2 sticks margarine
2 c. powdered sugar
2 sticks margarine
2 eggs
5 or 6 bananas, sliced
lengthwise

2 cans [6 oz.] crushed
pineapple, well-drained
1 large carton Cool Whip
Finely chopped pecans
Maraschino cherries

Combine crushed vanilla wafers and 1 1/2 sticks softened margarine. Press mixture into 9 x 13 inch pan. Mix powdered sugar, 2 sticks margarine and eggs and beat for 10 minutes. Pour over crumb mixture and then layer with bananas. Cover bananas with drained crushed pineapple. Top with Cool Whip and garnish with chopped pecans and cherries. Refrigerate.

Mrs. Hullen J. Cook, Jr.
Wichita Falls, Texas

BARBARA JOHNSON'S CHEESECAKE

1 1/2 T. butter
1/2 c. graham cracker crumbs
12 oz. soft cream cheese
3/4 c. sugar
4 eggs, separated

2 T. flour
1 1/2 t. vanilla
1/4 t. salt
2 c. light cream

Grease spring-form pan with butter and cover with graham cracker crumbs. Freeze for 30 minutes. Preheat oven to 325 degrees. Place cheese, sugar, yolks, flour, vanilla and salt in bowl and beat with mixer until smooth. Turn to lowest speed and gradually add scalded light cream. Beat egg whites stiff, but not dry. Add to cheese mixture, folding in lightly. Pour into spring-form pan and set in another shallow pan containing one inch hot water and bake 1 1/2 hours. Refrigerate 6 hours before serving. Cover top with layer of fresh strawberries, or with red currant glaze.

Glaze:

2/3 c. red currant jelly   2 T. sherry

Heat currant jelly and sherry. Cook, stirring with wooden spoon, until melted and bubbling. When mixture coats spoon lightly, pour over cheesecake.

This dessert can be prepared several days in advance and refrigerated. Serves 8 to 10.

Mrs. Robert L. Caton III

CHEESECAKE

Crust:

1 pkg. Zwieback, crushed
2 T. sugar
1/4 lb. margarine, melted

Topping:

1/2 pt. sour cream
2 T. sugar
1 1/2 t. lemon juice

Filling:

1 1/2 lbs. [3 pkgs. 8 oz.
    each] cream cheese
4 eggs
1 c. sugar
1 T. vanilla

Mix Zwieback, sugar and margarine and press in bottom of buttered spring-form pan. Chill.

Mix cream cheese, well-beaten eggs, sugar and vanilla in electric mixer. Pour over Zwieback mixture and bake 25 to 30 minutes in 350 degree oven. Cool 10 minutes. Spoon sour cream, sugar and lemon juice (well-mixed) over cake and cook at 470 degrees for 5 minutes more. Cool and chill. Serve either plain or with strawberries over it.

This may be baked in two large pie pans (instead of spring-form pan). If so, double sour cream topping mixture. This will freeze well, or may be prepared in advance, as it keeps well for several days in the refrigerator. Makes 16 servings.

Mrs. Allen Locklin

BROWN SUGAR SHEATH CAKE

3 c. sifted flour
1 lb. box light brown sugar
1 t. soda
1/2 t. salt
2 sticks margarine

1 egg
1 c. buttermilk
2 t. vanilla
1 c. chopped pecans

Mix flour, brown sugar, soda and salt. Cut in margarine. Measure 1 cup of the mixture and set aside. Add egg and buttermilk to remaining mix. Add vanilla. Pour into greased and floured 9 x 13 inch pan (or may use two 8 x 8 inch pans). Add 1 cup nuts to the cup of reserved mix and sprinkle on top of batter. Press in lightly. Bake at 350 degrees for 30 minutes. Serves 12.

Mrs. W. D. Lovelady

CHOCOLATE CAKE

2 squares unsweetened
  chocolate
2 c. sugar
1 stick margarine or butter
2 eggs

2 c. flour
1/2 c. buttermilk
1 c. hot water
1 t. soda
1 T. vanilla

Melt chocolate in the top of double boiler with 1/2 cup hot water. Cream sugar and margarine. Add beaten eggs, flour and buttermilk. Bring 1/2 cup water to a boil; add the soda and stir this into the melted chocolate. Pour this chocolate mixture into the batter and add vanilla. Pour into a greased 2 quart pyrex loaf pan and bake at 325 degrees until the cake pulls away from sides of pan. Time varies from 45 minutes to 1 1/2 hours. This cake need not be iced. Freezes well.

Mrs. L. Glenn Taylor

CHOCOLATE CHIP-DATE CAKE

1 1/2 c. boiling water
1 c. chopped dates
1 3/4 t. baking soda
1/2 c. margarine
1 1/2 c. sugar

2 eggs
1 3/4 c. flour
1 pkg. [6 oz.] chocolate
  chips
1/2 c. chopped nuts

Pour boiling water over dates and 1 teaspoon baking soda; cool.
Cream margarine and 1 cup sugar. Add eggs, beat well, and add to date mixture. Sift together flour and 3/4 teaspoon soda; add to above mixture and pour into 9 x 13 inch pan, greased and floured.
Combine chocolate chips, 1/2 cup sugar, and nuts and sprinkle over batter in pan. Bake at 350 degrees for 35 minutes or just until done.

Mrs. C. W. Geue
Ft. Worth, Texas

CHOCOLATE ICEBOX CAKE

24 ladyfingers
2 squares bitter chocolate
1/2 c. cold water
1/2 c. granulated sugar
4 eggs, separated
1 t. vanilla
2 c. powdered sugar
1 c. butter

Topping:

1/2 pt. whipping cream
2 T. powdered sugar
Maraschino cherries
[for garnish]

Line bottom and sides of tube pan with split ladyfingers, round side out. Heat chocolate, water and sugar in double boiler until chocolate melts. Cook about 5 minutes and remove from heat. Add beaten egg yolks gradually. Put back over hot water and cook 5 minutes longer, stirring constantly. Take off, add vanilla and cool. Sift 2 cups powdered sugar. Add to butter which has been creamed. Cream by hand or mixer until smooth. Add to chocolate mixture. Fold in stiffly beaten egg whites. Pour into the tube pan. Refrigerate for 24 hours.

Remove from tube pan. Cover with whipped cream (add 2 tablespoons powdered sugar when whipping) and decorate with cherries.

Use 1 1/2 quart size tube pan. (Needs to be tall enough on the sides for a ladyfinger to stand up along the side). Serves 10 to 12.

Mrs. A. S. McBride

CHOCOLATE CINNAMON CAKE

1 stick butter
1/2 c. Crisco
1/2 c. water
2 squares chocolate
[unsweetened]
2 c. sugar

2 c. flour
1 t. cinnamon
1 c. buttermilk
1 t. soda
2 eggs
1 t. vanilla

Combine the butter, Crisco, water and chocolate in a saucepan and heat until butter and shortening are melted. Pour this mixture over the sugar, flour and cinnamon which have been sifted together in a large bowl. Then add buttermilk (in which soda is dissolved), eggs and vanilla. Bake in a greased 9 x 13 inch pan at 375 degrees for 30 minutes. While cake is still hot, ice with the following icing.

Icing:

1 stick margarine
6 T. milk
2 squares chocolate
[unsweetened]

1 box powdered sugar
1 t. vanilla
1 c. pecans

Bring the margarine, milk and chocolate to a boil. Then combine with powdered sugar, vanilla and pecans, and spread over the warm cake. Serves 20 to 24.

Mrs. Maxie Wilson

Page 253

HEAVENLY HASH CAKE

1 stick butter	1 c. flour
1 c. sugar	1 t. baking powder
4 eggs	1 small pkg. Kraft's
1 large can Hershey's syrup	miniature marshmallows

Blend together butter, sugar and eggs. Add Hershey's syrup. Mix well. Add flour and baking powder. Bake 30 minutes at 350 degrees in 13 x 9 x 2 inch pan. Remove from oven and cover top with small marshmallows.

Topping:

1 stick butter	2 c. powdered sugar
2 T. cocoa	1 t. vanilla
1 egg	1 c. chopped nuts

Melt butter with cocoa over direct heat. Remove from heat and beat in egg. Add powdered sugar and vanilla. Stir in nuts and spread over top of the cake.

Mrs. Ronald N. Schoenbrun

MAMA "B" 'S CHOCOLATE CAKE

Cake:

Filling:

2 sticks butter or	1 stick butter
1 c. Crisco	1 c. pecans, toasted
2 c. sugar	slowly until brown
2 eggs, beaten	1/3 c. milk
3 1/2 c. flour	2 c. powdered sugar
1 1/2 t. soda	
3 T. + 1 t. cocoa	
2 c. buttermilk	
2 t. vanilla	

Cream butter or Crisco with sugar. Add beaten eggs. Sift flour with soda and cocoa. Add alternately with buttermilk, beginning and ending with flour mixture. Add vanilla. Pour into 4 layer (8-inch) cake pans (greased and floured). Bake at 350 degrees for 20 to 30 minutes.

For filling, melt butter, add toasted pecans and milk. Sift powdered sugar into mixture. Spread between layers and frost with Chocolate Icing.

Chocolate Icing:

1 stick butter	3 T. cocoa
2 c. powdered sugar	Milk

Melt butter and sift in powdered sugar. Add cocoa and small amount of milk (if needed) to make mixture of spreading consistency.

Mrs. George Grainger

RED EARTH CAKE

4 T. cocoa
4 T. strong coffee
1 t. red cake coloring
1 t. vanilla
1/2 c. shortening
1 1/2 c. sugar

2 eggs, well-beaten
2 c. less 2 T. flour
1/4 t. salt
1 t. soda
1 c. buttermilk

Make paste of cocoa, coffee, red cake coloring and vanilla. Cream shortening and sugar; add eggs. Add dry ingredients and buttermilk, followed by the cocoa paste. Beat well. Place in 2 round greased and floured cake pans; bake at 350 degrees for 30 to 45 minutes. Cool and frost.

Icing:

1 box powdered sugar
1 stick butter [room
   temperature]
4 T. cocoa

4 T. strong coffee
1 t. vanilla
1 t. red cake coloring

Blend well with mixer and spread on cake.

Mrs. Jerry Bain

MISSISSIPPI MUD CAKE

2 sticks butter or margarine
1/2 c. cocoa
1 1/2 c. all-purpose flour
Pinch of salt
2 c. sugar

4 eggs, slightly beaten
1 1/2 c. chopped nuts
1 t. vanilla
Miniature marshmallows

Melt butter and cocoa together. Remove from heat and stir in flour, salt, sugar, and beaten eggs; mix well. Add nuts and vanilla. Spoon batter into a greased 13 x 9 x 2 inch cake pan. Bake at 350 degrees for 35 to 45 minutes. Sprinkle marshmallows on top of warm cake and return to oven just to melt, not to brown. Cover with chocolate frosting.

Frosting:

1 box powdered sugar
1/2 c. whole milk
1/3 c. cocoa

1/2 stick softened butter
   or margarine

Combine sugar, milk, cocoa, and softened butter. Mix until smooth and spread on hot cake. Serves 12.

Evelyn Feldman
Bryan, Texas

SIREN'S CHOCOLATE CAKE

2 eggs
2 c. buttermilk
2 t. vanilla
2 1/2 c. cake flour
1/2 t. salt

2 c. sugar
2 t. soda
1 stick butter or margarine
4 squares bitter chocolate

Beat eggs with buttermilk and add vanilla. Sift dry ingredients and add to egg mixture. Then add butter and chocolate which have been melted together in a double boiler. Beat thoroughly. Pour into 2 greased 8-inch cake pans and bake about 30 minutes at 350 degrees.

Frosting:

1 small can evaporated milk
2 t. vanilla
1 lb. powdered sugar

4 squares bitter chocolate
1 stick butter

Add milk and vanilla to sifted sugar. Melt chocolate and butter together and add to first mixture. If icing is not thick enough to spread nicely, add more sifted powdered sugar.

Mrs. Jack M. King

RUTH ANN'S CHOCOLATE CAKE

1/2 c. cocoa
2 c. sugar
1/2 c. shortening
2 eggs
2 c. flour
1 t. baking powder

1/2 t. salt
1/2 c. buttermilk
1 t. baking soda
1 t. vanilla
1 c. boiling water

Cream cocoa, sugar, shortening. Add eggs, one at a time. In separate bowl, sift together flour, baking powder and salt. Add to creamed mixture, alternately with buttermilk, in which baking soda has been dissolved. Mix in vanilla and hot water and pour into two 9-inch greased and floured cake pans. Bake in 350 degree oven until cake springs back when touched in center, about 20 to 30 minutes. Frost with the following frosting when cooled.

Icing:

7 T. margarine
2 c. sugar
1 T. white corn syrup

2 T. cocoa
1/2 c. milk
1 t. vanilla

Combine margarine, sugar, corn syrup, cocoa and milk. Boil rapidly for 2 minutes. Then remove from heat. Place pan in larger pan of cold water (or sink). Add vanilla and beat about 5 minutes until spreading consistency.

Mrs. R. Wilson Cozby

DEVIL'S FOOD CAKE

1 t. soda
1 c. strong coffee
3/4 c. butter or margarine
2 c. sugar
2 t. vanilla

4 eggs, separated
2 c. cake flour, sifted
3 heaping T. cocoa
1/2 t. salt

Dissolve soda in warm coffee. Cream butter and sugar. Add vanilla and well-beaten egg yolks. Sift flour, cocoa and salt together. Add flour and coffee alternately beginning and ending with flour. Beat well (about 2 minutes on medium speed of electric mixer). Beat egg whites until stiff but not dry, and fold into chocolate batter. Bake in two 9-inch greased and floured cake pans for 30 to 35 minutes at 325 degrees.

Frosting:

5 T. butter or margarine
1/2 c. cocoa
4 T. strong coffee

1 lb. powdered sugar
1 t. vanilla

Cream butter and cocoa. Add coffee and sugar alternately. Add vanilla. Spread on cooled layers.

Mrs. C. Aubrey Smith, Jr.

MOTHER'S FILLED COFFEE CAKE

1 c. sugar
2 eggs
1/4 c. melted butter
   [1/2 stick]
1 1/2 c. flour, sifted

1 1/2 t. baking powder,
   sifted
1/2 c. sweet milk
1 t. vanilla

Filling:

1 c. brown sugar
2 T. flour
1 T. cinnamon

2 T. melted butter
1 c. chopped nuts

Cream sugar, eggs and melted butter. Sift flour and baking powder together and add alternately with milk. Add vanilla. Combine filling ingredients separately. Spread half the cake batter in a shallow pan, 12 x 7 1/2 inches. Sprinkle with half the filling and add remainder of cake batter. Cover with remaining filling mixture. Bake 30 to 40 minutes starting in 300 degree oven. When cake begins to rise, increase heat to 350 degrees. Cook until cake tests done. Cut in squares and serve with coffee. For a dessert, omit cinnamon and serve with whipped cream.

Mrs. Watson Simons

SPANISH COFFEE CAKE

1/2 t. salt
2 1/2 c. flour
1 c. brown sugar
1 t. cinnamon
3/4 c. sugar
3/4 c. Wesson oil

1 egg
1 c. buttermilk
1 t. soda
1 t. baking powder
1 t. vanilla

Combine salt, flour, brown sugar, cinnamon, sugar and Wesson oil. Set aside 1 cup mixture. Blend mixture with remaining ingredients, pour into two 9-inch foil pie tins; top with reserved mixture and bake at 300 degrees for 45 minutes.

Mrs. B. F. Shieldes

May be frozen. Let thaw for 30 minutes and heat slowly for 20 minutes.

CRUMB CAKE I

2 sticks margarine
2 c. sugar
6 eggs
1 box [7 oz.] flaked
coconut

1 c. broken pecans
1/2 c. milk
1 box [12 oz.] crushed
vanilla wafers

Cream margarine and sugar well. Add eggs one at a time, beating after each. Add coconut and pecans. Mix. Add milk alternately with vanilla wafer crumbs. Pour mixture into greased 13 x 9 inch cake pan and bake one hour and 30 minutes to one hour and 45 minutes at 275 degrees. Do not overcook. (Cake is done when a toothpick inserted into the center of the cake comes out clean.) This cake freezes well.

Mrs. J. Robert Dobbs, Jr.

The vanilla wafers can be crushed quickly by putting them in a paper sack and rolling over them with a rolling pin.

CRUMB CAKE II

2 c. flour
1 c. sugar
1 t. cinnamon
1/4 t. salt
1/2 c. margarine

1/2 c. chopped pecans
1/2 c. raisins
1 t. soda
1 c. sour milk
1 t. vanilla

Sift flour, sugar, cinnamon and salt together. Add margarine and blend as for biscuits. Set aside 1/3 cup of this mixture for topping. Add nuts and raisins and mix. Add soda in sour milk to mixture. Add vanilla, stir, and pour into a greased 7 x 11 inch pan. Sprinkle with reserved crumbs. Bake for 35 minutes at 350 degrees. Serves 6. Can be frozen.

Mrs. H. Don Smith

WHITE FRUIT CAKE

1/2 lb. butter
2 c. sugar
5 c. flour
2 t. baking powder
1 lb. pecans
1 lb. almonds
1 lb. candied red and
  green cherries

1 lb. candied pineapple,
  cut up
1/2 lb. white raisins
1 1/2 c. milk
1 t. vanilla
1 t. almond extract
8 egg whites, stiffly
  beaten

Grease a large tube pan and line bottom with heavy brown paper. Grease paper.

Cream butter and sugar. Sift 4 cups flour and baking powder together. Roll nuts and fruit in remaining 1 cup of flour. Add flour and baking powder mixture alternately with milk. Add vanilla and almond extract. Fold in stiffly beaten egg whites. Add nuts and fruits that have been rolled in flour. Pour in prepared tube pan and bake at 275 degrees for 2 1/2 to 3 hours or until a toothpick stuck in middle comes out clean.

Mrs. Frank Fite

JAPANESE FRUIT CAKE

1 c. butter
2 c. sugar
4 eggs
3 c. flour
2 t. baking powder

1/4 c. milk
1 c. seedless raisins
1 c. nuts, chopped
Spices as preferred
  [1/2 t. each]

Cream butter and sugar. Add eggs. Sift flour and baking powder together and add alternately with the milk. Divide batter in 2 portions and add raisins, nuts and spices to half, leaving the other portion plain. Pour batter into 4 greased and floured layer cake pans. This will make 2 light layers and 2 dark layers, which should be alternated in stacking the cake. Bake at 300 degrees until tests done, about 30 to 45 minutes.

Filling:

1 T. flour
2 c. sugar
Juice of 1 orange and 1 lemon
Grated rind of 1/2 orange
  and 1/2 lemon

1 can [med. or lg.] crushed
  pineapple
1 can shredded coconut
1 c. boiling milk

Combine flour, sugar, juice, rind, pineapple and coconut and pour boiling milk over mixture. Then spread this filling on top and between the cake layers. This filling recipe may be doubled to make filling thicker between layers of cake. Top with English walnut halves. This cake should be made a week or two before serving.

Mrs. William E. Bertram

AUNT RUBY'S FRUIT CAKE

2 oz. bottle lemon extract
1 lb. candied cherries
1 lb. candied pineapple
1 lb. sugar [white or
   brown as preferred]
1 lb. butter

6 large eggs, well-beaten
3 1/2 c. flour
1 t. baking powder
1 1/2 qts. pecans [coated
   with 1/4 c. flour]

Pour lemon extract over chopped fruit and let stand for 1 hour. Cream sugar, butter and eggs. Sift flour with baking powder and add along with fruit and nuts. Bake in large stemmed pan for 2 hours at 275 degrees.

Ruby Wood Boone
Marshall, Texas

Unlike most fruit cakes, this is better eaten within 3 or 4 days after baking.

LEMON NUT CAKE

2 c. sugar
2 c. margarine or butter
6 eggs
1 oz. orange juice
1 oz. pure lemon extract

4 c. sifted flour
2 c. pecans
1 lb. white raisins
1/2 c. candied cherries [red or
   green], cut up

Cream sugar and margarine or butter. Beat in eggs. Add orange juice and lemon extract. Beat in flour (reserve 1 cup to dredge nuts, raisins and cherries). Add remaining flour and pecans, raisins and cherries. Bake at 300 degrees for two hours in ungreased tube pan. Line bottom of pan with waxed paper. This can be baked in four small loaf pans for about 45 minutes to 1 hour. Serves 15 to 20 and freezes well.

Mrs. Bill F. Bales

LEMON-PECAN FRUIT CAKE

1 lb. butter
1 lb. brown sugar
6 egg yolks
2 c. flour
1 t. baking powder
1 1/2 oz. lemon extract

4 c. pecans, chopped
1/2 lb. cherries
1/2 lb. pineapple
2 c. flour
6 egg whites

Cream butter and sugar. Add egg yolks one at a time, beating well after each addition. Sift 2 cups flour with baking powder and add alternately with lemon extract. Chop nuts and fruits and dredge with remaining 2 cups flour. Add to batter and mix well. Beat egg whites until stiff but not dry. Fold in and pour into 2 greased loaf pans (6 x 10 x 3 inches) lined with brown paper. Place uncooked batter in refrigerator overnight. Cook for 3 hours at 250 degrees.

Mrs. Louie Cobb, Jr.

LEMON FRUIT CAKE

1 lb. white raisins
4 slices candied pineapple
8 oz. green cherries
8 oz. red cherries
1 lb. chopped pecans
1 lb. butter

2 c. sugar
6 eggs
2 oz. lemon flavoring
Pinch of salt
1 t. baking powder
4 c. flour

Cut up fruit and pecans in small pieces and set aside. Cream butter and sugar. Add eggs and mix thoroughly. Add lemon flavoring. Add salt and baking powder to the sifted flour. Coat nuts and fruits with the sifted flour, then add to first mixture. Bake at 275 to 300 degrees for 1 1/2 hours. Makes 1 large or 2 small cakes.

Mrs. Mickey Pfaff

ORANGE FRUIT CAKE

1 c. butter
2 c. sugar
4 eggs
2 T. orange peel, grated
1 t. soda

1/2 c. buttermilk
3 1/2 c. cake flour
1 c. pecans, chopped
and toasted [not salted]
1 lb. dates, chopped

Glaze:

2 c. powdered sugar
1 c. orange juice

2 T. orange peel, grated

Cream butter and sugar; add eggs one at a time; then add orange peel. Dissolve soda in buttermilk. Add flour and milk alternately. Mix well. Add pecans and dates last. Pour into greased and floured tube or bundt cake pan. Bake at 250 degrees for approximately 1 hour and 45 minutes. Combine glaze ingredients and pour over the hot cake.

Mrs. Joe Huffstutler

FUDGE CUP CAKES

2 sticks margarine or butter
4 squares semi-sweet chocolate
4 eggs
1 3/4 c. sugar

1 c. sifted flour
1 t. vanilla
2 c. finely chopped nuts

Melt the margarine and chocolate in a double boiler. Drop eggs into a large bowl and stir just enough to break the yolks. Add sugar and flour and blend to wet the dry ingredients. Add chocolate and butter mixture, vanilla and nuts. Stir all together. Put in paper baking cups (fill about 2/3 full). Bake at 325 degrees for about 30 to 35 minutes. Makes about two dozen. These freeze beautifully.

Mrs. S. W. Brookshire

FUDGE UPSIDE-DOWN PUDDING CAKE

1/2 c. brown sugar
1/2 c. granulated sugar
1/4 c. cocoa
1 T. butter
3/4 c. sugar
1/2 c. milk

1 c. flour
1 t. baking powder
1/2 t. salt
1 1/2 T. cocoa
1/2 c. chopped nuts
1 1/4 c. boiling water

Sift brown sugar, granulated sugar and 1/4 cup cocoa together and set aside. Mix butter and 3/4 cup sugar. Add milk. Sift flour, baking powder, salt and 1 1/2 tablespoons cocoa together and add to batter. Beat thoroughly. Pour into a greased 11-inch cake or pie pan. Cover the batter with the chopped nuts. Spread the sugar and cocoa mixture over the nuts. Pour the boiling water over the top of the sugar and cocoa mixture. Bake at 350 degrees for 30 to 40 minutes. Test with toothpick for doneness. There will be a thick chocolate sauce at the bottom and the top will have a rough, uneven appearance. Cut in squares or wedges taking up the sauce with each serving. Top each serving with whipped cream or a scoop of ice cream. This makes eight generous servings and should be eaten the same day.

Mrs. H. L. Gist

OATMEAL CAKE I

1 1/2 c. boiling water
1 c. quick-cooking oatmeal
1 1/2 c. butter
1 c. brown sugar, packed
1 c. white sugar
2 eggs

1 1/2 c. flour
1 t. cinnamon
1 t. nutmeg
1 t. soda
1/2 t. salt
1 t. vanilla

Pour boiling water over oatmeal and let stand for 20 minutes. Cream butter and sugars together and add eggs. Sift dry ingredients together and stir in. Add vanilla, then oatmeal mixture. Mix well and pour into a greased 9 x 13 inch pan. Bake at 350 degrees for 30 to 35 minutes. When cake has cooled, frost with the following icing.

Icing:

1/2 c. butter
1 c. brown sugar
1/2 c. evaporated milk

1 t. vanilla
1 c. coconut
1/2 c. chopped nuts

Combine butter, sugar, milk and vanilla in saucepan and boil about 10 minutes. Add coconut and nuts.

Mrs. Rolf Schroeder

OATMEAL CAKE II

1 c. quick-cooking [not
    instant] oatmeal
1 1/4 c. boiling water
1 c. sugar
1 c. brown sugar
1/2 c. shortening

2 eggs
1 1/3 c. flour
1/3 t. salt
1 t. soda
1/2 t. nutmeg

Pour boiling water over uncooked oatmeal and set aside for 20 minutes. Cream sugars and shortening. Add eggs and mix well. Add flour, salt, soda and nutmeg. Add oatmeal and mix in well. Bake in a greased 9 x 13 inch pan at 375 degrees for 35 to 40 minutes. When cake is done, remove from oven; add topping and replace in oven. Broil until lightly browned.

Topping:

6 T. melted butter or
    margarine
2/3 c. brown sugar
1/2 c. nuts, chopped

6 T. cream
1 c. coconut
1/2 t. vanilla

Combine all ingredients and spread on hot cake before returning to oven to broil lightly.

Mrs. Bill C. Ross

ORANGE CAKE

1 c. Crisco
2 c. sugar
4 eggs
1 t. soda

1 1/4 c. buttermilk
3 c. flour
1 T. grated orange peel

Cream Crisco and sugar. Add eggs, one at a time, blending well after each. Dissolve soda in buttermilk and add alternately with flour. Add orange peel. Pour into greased and floured tube or bundt pan. Bake at 350 degrees for 45 minutes to 1 hour. While cake bakes, prepare the glaze.

Glaze:

1 c. orange juice
2 c. sugar

2 T. grated orange peel

Combine ingredients; bring to a boil; then simmer until cake is done. Pour over the cake while it is still warm.

Mrs. Gene Caldwell

ORANGE NUT CAKE

2 c. sugar
2 T. grated orange rind
1 c. shortening
Pinch of salt
4 eggs
4 c. flour

1 1/3 c. buttermilk
1 t. soda
1 t. vanilla
1 c. chopped nuts
1 pkg. dates, chopped and
   floured

Glaze:

2 c. sugar
1 c. orange juice

2 T. grated orange rind

Cream sugar, orange rind and shortening until creamy. Add salt and eggs. Beat well. Add flour alternately with buttermilk in which soda has been dissolved. Add vanilla, nuts and dates. Pour into large tube pan, greased and floured. Bake 1 hour (or until cake tests done) at 375 degrees. Mix glaze ingredients and spoon over cake while still in pan. Allow cake to cool in pan.

Mrs. Homer Clapp

CREAM CHEESE POUND CAKE

3 sticks margarine
8 oz. pkg. cream cheese
3 c. sugar
Dash of salt

1 1/2 t. vanilla
6 large eggs
3 c. cake flour

Cream margarine, cream cheese, and sugar. Add salt, vanilla and eggs. Sift cake flour and add. Bake in a greased and floured tube pan at 325 degrees for 1 1/2 hours.

Mrs. Watson Simons

HERSHEY BAR CHOCOLATE POUND CAKE

6 to 8 small plain Hershey bars
2 sticks butter or margarine
2 c. sugar
4 eggs
2 1/2 c. sifted cake flour
1 t. baking powder

1/4 t. salt
1 c. buttermilk
Dash soda
1 c. broken pecans [optional]
2 t. vanilla

Melt chocolate bars and butter in a double boiler. Add sugar and cream well. Add eggs, one at a time and mix well after each. Sift together flour, baking powder, and salt. Add to mixture. Add buttermilk with soda dissolved in it. Add nuts and vanilla and mix well. Bake at 325 degrees in greased and floured tube or bundt pan. Bake 1 hour and 15 minutes or until cake tests done. Cool in pan for 10 to 15 minutes, then turn out on rack.

Mrs. Hunter Brush
Mrs. James H. Rippy

SOUR CREAM POUND CAKE

3 c. flour
1/4 t. soda
3 c. sugar
2 sticks butter
6 eggs

1 c. sour cream
1 t. vanilla extract
1 t. almond extract
1 t. lemon extract

Sift flour twice with soda. Cream sugar and butter. Add eggs, one at a time. Add flour, a little at a time. Add sour cream and flavorings. Put in a greased tube pan. Bake at 350 degrees for 1 1/2 hours. Cool in pan on rack for 5 minutes.

Mrs. Nelson Clyde

OLD-FASHIONED POUND CAKE

2 sticks butter
2 c. sugar
5 eggs
2 c. cake flour

2 t. vanilla
1 T. lemon juice
1/4 t. salt

Cream butter and sugar until light and fluffy. Add whole eggs, one at a time. Sift flour before measuring 2 cups. Sift again and add to mixture. Add vanilla, lemon juice and salt. Pour into greased and floured bundt or tube pan. Bake at 325 degrees for one hour. This cake can be frozen. Serves 12 to 15.

Mrs. William B. Hilliard

PINEAPPLE POUND CAKE

1 c. shortening
2 sticks butter
2 3/4 c. sugar
6 eggs
3 c. flour

1 t. baking powder
1/4 c. milk
1 t. vanilla
3/4 c. crushed pineapple,
 drained

Cream shortening, butter and sugar. Add eggs, one at a time, and beat well after each. Sift flour with baking powder; add to mixture with milk. Add vanilla and pineapple. Pour into a greased 10-inch tube pan. Place in cold oven and set oven at 325 degrees. Bake for 1 1/2 hours. Let stand a few minutes and turn out. Use the following glaze.

Glaze:

1/4 c. softened butter
1 c. crushed pineapple,
 drained

1 1/2 c. powdered sugar

Combine ingredients and pour over hot cake.

Miss Lorene Ellerd

POTATO CAKE

1 c. butter
2 c. sugar
4 egg yolks, beaten
2 1/2 sqs. unsweetened
  chocolate
1 c. warm mashed potatoes
2 c. flour
1 t. cinnamon
1 t. cloves

1 t. nutmeg
2 t. baking powder
1 c. finely chopped
  English walnuts
1/2 c. milk
4 egg whites, stiffly
  beaten
1 t. vanilla

Cream butter and sugar; add well-beaten egg yolks. Add cooled melted chocolate; add warm mashed potatoes and mix thoroughly. Add combined dry ingredients and walnuts alternately with milk. Fold in egg whites and vanilla. Bake in greased and floured tube or bundt pan in slow oven at 325 degrees for 1 hour and 15 minutes. Freezes well.

Mrs. George B. Allen

Add pinch of salt to chopped potatoes before cooking and mashing to make 1 cup or use instant mashed potatoes.

PRUNE CAKE I

3 eggs
1 1/2 c. sugar
1 c. cooked chopped prunes
1 c. buttermilk
1 t. soda
1 t. cinnamon

1 t. cloves
1 t. vanilla
2 c. flour
1/8 t. salt
2 c. chopped pecans
1 c. Wesson oil

Mix ingredients in order given. Pour into three 8-inch or two 9-inch pans and bake 30 minutes at 350 degrees.

Frosting:

2 c. sugar
2 sticks butter

2 small cans evaporated milk
1 t. vanilla

Melt sugar and butter in a 3 quart saucepan and brown slowly. Add milk slowly and continue cooking to soft ball stage. Add vanilla and beat until smooth. Frost layers and sides of cake.

Mrs. George Grainger

Mrs. Will A. Knight makes the same cake without the frosting and bakes her cake in a greased and floured tube or bundt pan. She uses the same ingredients above except for 2 c. sugar, 1 t. salt, 1 c. pecans, and 1 t. nutmeg. Mix sugar and oil; add beaten eggs. Blend in buttermilk and prunes that were cooked the day before. Sift dry ingredients together and stir into mixture. Add vanilla and pecans. Bake 55 to 60 minutes at 325 degrees.

PRUNE CAKE II

1 c. sugar
1/3 c. shortening [part butter]
3 beaten eggs
1 c. flour

1 t. soda
Pinch of salt
1 c. mashed cooked prunes
4 T. sour cream

Cream sugar and shortening. Add well-beaten eggs. Sift flour, soda and salt together and add. Then add prunes and sour cream. Cook in two 8-inch layer cake pans that have been well-greased and dusted with flour. Bake at 300 degrees for 20 to 25 minutes. Do not overcook. This is a very tender cake.

Icing:

2 beaten eggs
1 c. sugar
2 generous T. cornstarch
1 c. sour cream

1 c. chopped pecans
2 t. butter
1/2 c. cooked mashed prunes
Pinch of salt

Beat eggs well. Add mixture of sugar and cornstarch. Add sour cream. Cook over low heat until mixture thickens. Remove from heat and add the nuts, butter, prunes and salt. Spread on layers and sides of cake.

Mrs. H. L. Gist

PRUNE CAKE AND BUTTERMILK ICING

2 c. flour
1 t. soda
1 t. allspice
1 t. nutmeg
1/2 t. salt
1 c. Wesson oil

1 1/2 c. sugar
3 eggs, beaten
1 c. buttermilk
1 t. vanilla
1 c. cooked prunes, drained and chopped

Sift dry ingredients together. Add oil, sugar and beaten eggs slowly. Then add buttermilk, vanilla and prunes. Beat at medium speed until well-blended.

Pour into greased and floured long (9 x 14 inch) baking pan. Bake at 350 degrees approximately 40 minutes. Remove from oven, cool, top with:

Glaze:

1 c. sugar
1/2 c. buttermilk

1/2 stick butter
1 t. vanilla

Combine ingredients and boil 3 minutes. Let cool, then beat a few minutes with mixer until thickened. Pour over cooled cake. Serves 10 to 12.

Mrs. Dick Hightower

BUTTER RUM CAKE

1/2 lb. margarine or butter
1 3/4 c. sugar
5 eggs
1 t. vanilla

1 t. butter flavoring
1 t. rum flavoring
2 c. sifted flour

Cream margarine thoroughly; add sugar gradually. Add eggs one at a time; mix well. Add extracts. Add sifted flour a little at a time and blend well. Pour batter into greased and dusted 10-inch tube pan and bake at 325 degrees for about 1 hour, or until toothpick inserted into center comes out clean. While warm, brush with:

Butter Rum Glaze:

1 c. sugar
1/2 c. water

1 t. rum flavoring

Bring sugar and water to boil. Cool and add rum flavoring. Use pastry brush and apply to warm cake.

Mrs. C. R. Hurst

RUM CAKE

1 c. shortening
2 c. sugar
4 eggs
3 c. flour

1/2 t. soda
1/2 t. baking powder
1/4 t. salt
1 c. buttermilk

Cream shortening and sugar. Add eggs one at a time. Sift dry ingredients together. Add to egg mixture along with buttermilk. Pour into greased tube pan and bake at 325 degrees for 1 hour and 15 minutes.

Icing:

1 c. sugar
1/2 c. water

1/2 stick butter
1 1/2 t. rum extract

Mix all ingredients and bring to a boil for 2 minutes. Spoon onto warm cake.

Mrs. Martha Hubbard

COCONUT CAKE SUPREME

3 1/4 c. sifted flour
4 1/2 t. baking powder
1/2 t. salt
3/4 c. butter
1 1/2 t. grated orange peel
1 1/2 c. sugar

2 egg yolks, well-beaten
3/4 c. water
1/2 c. orange juice
1/2 c. flaked coconut
4 egg whites
1/2 c. sugar

Sift flour, baking powder and salt together. Cream butter and orange peel. Add 1 1/2 cups sugar. Add beaten egg yolks and mix well. Combine water and orange juice. Add to mixture, alternating with dry ingredients. Add coconut. Beat egg whites, adding 1/2 cup sugar gradually. Fold into other ingredients. Bake in two 9-inch greased and floured pans at 350 degrees for 30 minutes, or until cake tester comes out clean. Frost and fill with icing and sprinkle top with coconut.

Frosting:

1 1/2 c. sugar
3/4 c. boiling water

1/2 t. white vinegar
3 egg whites

Combine sugar, boiling water and white vinegar and cook over low heat. Stir until dissolved. Cover pan and bring to boil. Boil five minutes. Uncover pan and put in candy thermometer. Cook without stirring, about 30 minutes, to 244 degrees. Beat the egg whites until stiff. Pour syrup slowly over egg whites and continue beating for 2 to 3 minutes until melted and frosting holds shape.

Mrs. Homer Clapp

CREME SUPREME CAKE

1 box Duncan Hines butter
    cake mix
1/2 c. sugar
3/4 c. Wesson oil

1 small carton sour cream
4 eggs
1 t. cinnamon
3 T. brown sugar

Combine cake mix, sugar, oil and sour cream and mix well. Add eggs, one at a time, beating well. Pour three-fourths of batter in greased and floured bundt pan. Then mix the cinnamon and brown sugar and sprinkle over batter. Add remaining batter and bake at 350 degrees for 50 to 60 minutes. When cool, the cake may be glazed with the following:

Glaze:

1 c. powdered sugar
2 T. half-and-half

1 t. vanilla
2 T. melted butter

Mix all ingredients and pour over cooled cake.

Mrs. Alice White

COCA-COLA CAKE

2 c. sugar
2 1/2 c. flour
1/2 c. margarine
1/2 c. Crisco
3 T. cocoa
1 c. Coca-Cola

1/2 c. buttermilk
1 t. soda
2 whole eggs, beaten
1 t. vanilla
1 1/2 c. miniature marshmallows

Sift together sugar and flour. Bring to a boil the margarine, Crisco, cocoa, and Coke. Pour over flour and sugar mixture. Mix well. Add buttermilk with soda dissolved in it, beaten eggs, vanilla, and marshmallows. Pour into greased and floured 9 x 13 inch pan. Bake at 350 degrees 30 to 45 minutes or until center tests done. Ice while warm.

Frosting:

1/2 c. margarine
3 T. cocoa
6 T. Coca-Cola

1 box sifted powdered sugar
1 t. vanilla
1 c. pecans, chopped

Combine margarine, cocoa, and Coke and bring to a boil. Beat in powdered sugar and add vanilla and pecans. Spread on warm cake. Serves approximately 20.

Mrs. Walter L. Johnson

CARROT CAKE

4 eggs
2 c. sugar
1 1/4 c. Wesson oil
2 c. plain flour
2 t. cinnamon

1 1/2 t. soda
1 t. salt
3 c. grated carrots
[loosely packed]

Beat eggs; add sugar, oil and dry ingredients and mix well. Add grated carrots until well-mixed.

Bake in 3 or 4 layers at 375 degrees for about 20 minutes. (Three 9-inch greased cake pans work nicely.) Cool; then put together with the following:

Filling and Icing:

1 stick butter or margarine
1 pkg. [8 oz.] cream cheese
1 box powdered sugar

2 t. vanilla
1 c. chopped pecans
1 c. chopped raisins

Soften margarine and cream cheese to room temperature. Cream margarine, cheese and powdered sugar. Add vanilla, pecans and raisins.

Mrs. L. Glenn Taylor

This may be baked in a large greased rectangular pan (13 1/2 x 9 x 3 inch) at 350 degrees for 30 minutes. Filling is then placed on top.

Page 270

COLONIAL HOLIDAY RING

1 c. butter
2 c. sugar
4 eggs
4 c. sifted flour
1 t. soda

1/2 t. salt
1 1/2 c. buttermilk
1 c. chopped pecans
1 pkg. [8 oz.] chopped dates
1 T. grated orange rind

Cream butter and sugar together. Beat eggs and add to butter and sugar. Beat well. Sift together flour, soda, and salt. Add to creamed mixture, alternating with buttermilk. Add pecans, dates, and orange rind. Pour into greased and floured tube pan. Bake at 325 degrees for 1 1/2 hours or until it tests done. While cake is still hot and before removing from pan, punch many holes in cake all the way to the bottom. Use ice pick or skewer. Then pour the following glaze over cake.

Glaze:

2 c. sugar
1 c. orange juice

2 T. grated orange rind

Combine sugar and orange juice in small saucepan over heat. Dissolve sugar, but do not boil. Add orange rind. Pour hot glaze over cake. Let glaze drip into holes in cake. If cake has not pulled away from sides of pan and the tube of pan, loosen with a knife, so that some of the glaze runs down sides and center of cake. Let cake stand in pan for several hours (or overnight). Decorate top of cake with pecans.

Mrs. R. Wilson Cozby, Jr.

MEXICAN WEDDING CAKE

1 c. boiling water
1 c. chopped dates
1 t. soda
1/2 stick margarine
1 c. sugar
1 beaten egg

1/3 t. salt
1 1/2 c. flour
1 t. baking powder
1 t. vanilla
1/3 c. chopped nuts

Frosting:

5 T. evaporated milk
5 T. brown sugar
2 T. margarine

Coconut
Chopped nuts

Pour boiling water over chopped dates and soda. Let stand until cool. Combine margarine, sugar, egg, salt, flour, baking powder, vanilla and nuts. Add date mixture. Mix well. Bake in 7 x 11 x 1 1/2 inch greased and floured pan. Bake at 325 degrees for 25 to 30 minutes. Frost immediately and cut in squares.

For frosting, boil evaporated milk, brown sugar and margarine for 3 minutes. Pour over the hot cake. Sprinkle with chopped nuts and coconut.

Mrs. Watson Simons

ITALIAN CREAM CAKE

1 stick margarine
1/2 c. shortening
2 c. sugar
5 egg yolks
2 c. flour
1 t. soda

1 c. buttermilk
1 t. vanilla
1 small can flaked coconut
1 c. chopped nuts
5 egg whites, stiffly beaten

Cream margarine and shortening. Add sugar and beat until mixture is smooth. Add egg yolks and beat well. Combine flour and soda and add to creamed mixture alternately with buttermilk. Stir in vanilla. Add coconut and chopped nuts. Fold in stiffly beaten egg whites. Pour batter into three greased and floured 8-inch cake pans. Bake at 350 degrees for 25 minutes or until cake tests done. Cool and frost with Cream Cheese Frosting.

Cream Cheese Frosting:

1 pkg. [8 oz.] cream cheese,
  softened
1/2 stick margarine

1 box powdered sugar
1 t. vanilla
Chopped pecans

Beat cream cheese and margarine until smooth. Add sugar and mix well. Add vanilla and beat until smooth. Spread between layers and on top and sides of cake. Sprinkle top with pecans.

Mrs. Ralph Hendrix
Mrs. Bob L. Herd
Mrs. R. R. Ivy (Waco, Texas)
Mrs. Worth Johnson
Mrs. A. E. McCain
Mrs. E. J. Mooney, Jr.

HAZEL'S POPPY SEED QUICKIE

1/4 c. poppy seed
2/3 c. salad oil
1 box yellow cake mix
1 pkg. instant coconut
  cream pudding

2/3 c. water
4 eggs
1 t. almond extract

Mix poppy seed in salad oil. Blend cake mix, pudding, water and salad oil (with poppy seed) together in mixer at medium speed. Add eggs, one at a time, blending thoroughly after each. Add extract. Pour batter into a greased and floured tube pan and bake one hour at 350 degrees. Serve plain or with sauce.

Sauce:

1 c. powdered sugar
Juice of 1 lemon

1 t. almond extract

Mix and pour over cake while still hot.

Mrs. William H. Starling

OLD-FASHIONED JAM CAKE

1 c. butter, softened	1 t. nutmeg
2 c. sugar	1 t. cinnamon
4 eggs	1 1/2 c. jam [strawberry or
2 t. soda	blackberry]
1 c. buttermilk	1 1/2 c. dates
3 c. sifted flour	1 1/2 c. nuts [pecans]
1 t. allspice	

Cream softened butter and sugar. Add eggs one at a time and beat after each. Mix soda with buttermilk and add alternately with flour to creamed mixture. Add spices, jam, dates and nuts. Bake at 350 degrees for about 25 to 30 minutes in 3 or 4 greased and floured cake pans, depending on size of pan. This cake is very tender.

Filling:

1 1/2 c. milk	2 T. butter
1 1/2 c. sugar	1/2 t. vanilla

Boil the milk and sugar together a few minutes. Then add butter and vanilla. (This is not thick like icing.) With fork stick holes in each layer of cake as it is stacked, pouring filling generously over each.

This cake improves with age like fruit cake. It can be made several days ahead so it will have time to soak up filling. This was always baked at Christmas at grandmother's.

Mrs. H. L. Gist

PLUM CAKE "BABS"

2 c. self-rising flour	1 c. Wesson oil
2 c. sugar	3 eggs
1 t. cinnamon	2 small jars plum baby food
1 t. cloves	1 c. chopped pecans

Combine all ingredients in a large bowl and mix well. Bake in a greased and floured bundt pan for 1 hour and 15 minutes at 350 degrees. Can be cut into about 24 slices. This is a moist cake and can be made several days before serving, or it freezes well.

Mrs. T. Carlton Billips
Mrs. Norman Bishop
Longview, Texas

LADY BALTIMORE CAKE

1 c. butter	1 c. milk
2 c. sugar	1 t. vanilla
3 c. flour	6 egg whites
3 t. baking powder	

Cream butter and sugar well. Sift flour and baking powder 3 times. Add to the creamed butter and sugar alternately with the milk. Add vanilla. Add the egg whites (beaten stiffly). Bake at 350 degrees in 3 greased and floured 8 or 9-inch pans until layers are lightly browned and test done.

Filling:

3 c. sugar	1 c. nuts [pecans or
1 c. boiling water	walnuts]
3 egg whites	1 c. raisins

Stir the sugar and water together until sugar dissolves. Then boil without stirring until the mixture "spins a thread" off the spoon. While cooking, beat the egg whites until stiff but not dry; then pour syrup into egg whites. Add nuts and raisins which have been ground together. Spread between each layer as cake is stacked and then frost sides and top.

Mrs. Joe Sheehy

PINEAPPLE PRESERVE CAKE

2 sticks margarine	1 c. buttermilk
2 c. white sugar	3 c. flour
1 c. pineapple preserves	1 t. cinnamon
1 t. vanilla	1/4 t. cloves
4 eggs	1 c. nuts, chopped fine
1 t. soda	

Cream margarine and sugar. Add pineapple preserves and vanilla. Add eggs one at a time. Dissolve soda in buttermilk and add with flour and remaining ingredients. Pour into greased stem pan and bake at 300 degrees for 1 hour and 15 minutes. Cool completely. Glaze if desired. Makes a moist holiday cake.

Glaze:

1 T. soft butter	1/2 t. lemon juice
1/2 small can crushed	2 c. sifted powdered sugar
pineapple, drained	

Blend butter, pineapple and lemon juice. Add sugar and 2 to 3 tablespoons hot water until spreading consistency. Pour over cake and allow to drip down sides.

Mrs. J. H. Brogan
Mrs. Robert Peters

STRAWBERRY CAKE

1 box Duncan Hines cherry
   cake mix
1 box [3 oz.] strawberry
   Jello
3 T. sifted flour
1/2 c. water

1 c. cooking oil
4 eggs
1 small pkg. frozen
   strawberries, well-
   thawed

Combine cake mix, Jello, flour and mix well. Add water and cooking oil. Add eggs 1 at a time and beat well after each addition. Add strawberries. Bake at 350 degrees until tests done with cake tester. This may be cooked in 2 cake pans (greased and floured) or one 9 x 13 inch pan. It may be iced or eaten hot or served in squares with whipped cream and fresh strawberries. Cake may be baked in round aspic mold pans and served with center filled with strawberries or ice cream.

Mrs. William C. Smyth

Mrs. Ted C. Chilcote of Newburgh, New York, varies this by using either white or yellow cake mix and adding 1 can coconut and 1 cup chopped pecans. She reserves half the strawberries, half the coconut and half the pecans for use in the frosting of 1 box powdered sugar and 1 stick margarine.

PEAR CAKE

3 T. margarine
1 c. sugar
1 egg, beaten
1 c. sifted flour
1 t. soda
1/2 t. nutmeg

1/2 t. salt
1/2 t. cinnamon
1 1/2 c. fresh diced pears
1/4 c. chopped nuts
1 t. vanilla

Cream margarine and sugar. Add egg, then dry ingredients, sifted together. Add pears, nuts and vanilla. Bake in 350 degree oven for 40 to 45 minutes in a greased 8 x 8 inch pan.

Mrs. James O. Clark

VANILLA WAFER CAKE

6 eggs
2 sticks butter
1/2 c. milk
2 c. sugar

1 can [7 oz.] flaked coconut
1 pkg. [12 oz.] vanilla
   wafers, crushed
1 c. chopped pecans

Blend eggs, butter, milk and sugar. Add coconut, crushed vanilla wafers and chopped nuts. Bake in greased bundt pan for 1 1/2 hours at 350 degrees. Cool in pan before removing.

Mrs. Robert Henry

MIMI'S FUDGE ICING

1 c. milk
2 c. sugar
2 T. cocoa
1 T. white Karo

Dash of salt
1 t. vanilla
1 T. butter

Mix milk, sugar, cocoa, Karo and salt in large saucepan and cook over medium heat until it reaches the soft ball stage. Remove from heat and add vanilla and butter. Beat until icing begins to hold its shape and begins to lose its gloss. Spread on cake. Do not stir while cooking, as this makes the icing sugary.

Mrs. Allen Locklin

RUM SAUCE

1 can [12 oz.] apricot nectar
1 c. sugar [or adjust to
   taste]
1 1/2 T. cornstarch [use more
   if a thicker sauce is
   desired]
2 T. cold water [more if more
   cornstarch is used]

1/2 c. light or dark rum
   [rum flavoring may be used]
2 cans [11 oz.] mandarin
   oranges, drained
2 T. [or more] lemon juice
   [optional]

Combine apricot nectar and sugar. Bring to boil, stirring often. Simmer 8 minutes. Blend cornstarch and water into smooth paste. Stir into hot sauce. Cook, stirring constantly, until sauce thickens and clears. Cool slightly. Add rum or rum flavoring, orange sections and lemon juice.

This may be used to glaze whole cake or served hot or cold over cake slices or ice cream. Makes about 1 pint of sauce.

Mrs. Ralph R. Hanson

WHIPPED CREAM ORANGE ICING

1 T. cornstarch
1 T. flour
1 t. grated orange rind
1/2 c. sugar
1/4 t. salt

1/2 c. orange juice
2 t. lemon juice
1 t. butter
1/2 c. heavy cream, whipped

Mix cornstarch, flour, orange rind, sugar and salt. Stir in orange juice and lemon juice gradually, working to a smooth paste. Cook in top of double boiler, stirring constantly, until mixture begins to thicken. Add butter and cook until thick (15 to 20 minutes). Let cool and fold in whipped cream. This is good on yellow cake. Recipe should be doubled to frost top and sides of three-layer cake.

Mrs. Watson Simons

Pies

BANANA-CARAMEL PIE

10 candy caramels
2 c. milk
1/3 c. flour
1/3 c. sugar
1/4 t. salt

3 slightly beaten egg yolks
1 t. vanilla
2 bananas
1 baked pie shell
1 c. heavy cream, whipped

Melt caramels in milk over low heat. Combine flour, sugar and salt in double boiler. Add caramel-milk mixture and cook over water until thick, stirring constantly. Add beaten egg yolks to which a little hot mixture has been added. Cook 5 minutes longer, stirring. Remove from heat. Add vanilla, cover and chill.

Arrange 2 sliced bananas on baked pie shell. Cover with filling. Top with whipped cream.

Mrs. Donald E. Payne

BLACK GOLD PIE

4 Hershey bars [small size]
1/2 c. milk
20 marshmallows [2 c. miniature marshmallows]

1/2 pt. heavy cream, whipped
9-inch baked pie shell

Melt broken Hershey bars in 1/4 cup of milk over low flame. Add 1/4 cup milk and blend. Add marshmallows and blend. Let mixture cool. Fold in stiffly beaten heavy cream. Pour into shell. Chill. Serves 6 to 8.

Mrs. Hunter Brush
Mrs. John Noble

BLUEBERRY PIE

1 can Eagle Brand condensed milk
Juice of 2 lemons
1/2 pt. whipping cream

1 c. pecans
1 can blueberries
1 baked pie shell

Mix Eagle Brand milk with lemon juice and 1/2 cup of whipping cream (not whipped). Stir in pecan halves and drained blueberries. Pour in baked pie shell. Top with remainder of cream, whipped. Store in refrigerator until served. Serves 8. This may be made the day before or several hours before serving.

Mrs. Richard Harvey

BOSTON CREAM PIE

4 eggs, separated
1 c. sugar
1 c. flour

2 t. baking powder
1/4 c. cold water

Beat whites until stiff. Add yolks one at a time beating after each one. Gradually add sugar. Sift flour and baking powder together. Add alternately with water. Place in two 8-inch greased and wax paper lined pans. Bake 30 to 35 minutes at 375 degrees.

Filling:

1 pt. milk
1 c. sugar

2 eggs, beaten
1/2 c. flour

Heat milk and sugar together until just warm. Mix beaten eggs and flour together. Add some of warm milk mixture to eggs and flour; then add all to milk and sugar. Heat until thickened. Cool.

Slice cakes in half and place filling between layers. Frost top with chocolate icing or dust with confectioner's sugar.

This makes two double-layer cakes or one four-layer cake.

Mrs. Robert Skoglund

BUTTERMILK PIE

1/2 c. buttermilk
1 2/3 c. sugar
1/2 stick butter or
   margarine, melted

3 eggs, beaten slightly
1 t. vanilla
1/4 t. cinnamon
1 unbaked pie shell, 9-inch

Blend buttermilk, sugar and butter. Add eggs and mix well. Blend in vanilla and cinnamon thoroughly. Pour into unbaked pie shell. Bake at 350 degrees for 45 minutes or until golden brown.

Mrs. Raymond Whitney, Jr.

CHERRY BURGUNDY PIE

1 can [16 oz.] dark pitted
   sweet cherries
1 pkg. [3 oz.] cherry flavored
   gelatin

1 pt. vanilla ice cream
3 T. Burgundy
1 t. lemon juice
1 8-inch baked pie shell

Drain cherries. Reserve syrup. Add enough water to syrup to make 1 cup liquid. Heat to boiling. Dissolve gelatin in boiling liquid. Add ice cream by spoonfuls. Stir until melted. Blend in wine and lemon juice. Chill until partially congealed. Halve the cherries. Fold into gelatin mixture. Chill again if necessary. Spoon into baked pie shell and chill until firm. Top with whipped cream and extra cherries if desired. Serves 6 to 8.

Mrs. Rolf Schroeder

CHERRY PECAN CRISP

1/2 c. flour	1/4 c. margarine
1/2 c. quick rolled oats	1 can cherry pie filling
1/2 c. brown sugar,	1/4 c. pecans
firmly packed	

Combine flour, oats and brown sugar. Cut in margarine until the mixture is the size of coarse meal. Pat one half of the mixture into bottom and sides of a 9-inch pie plate. Spread cherry pie filling in crust. Add nuts to remaining crumb mixture and sprinkle over top, covering completely. Bake at 375 degrees for 30 minutes. Serve with whipped cream or ice cream.

Mrs. Frank Agar

CHOCOLATE MOCHA ICEBOX PIE

1 graham cracker pie shell	1/2 jigger Kahlua
1 pkg. instant chocolate	Topping of your choice
pudding	Slivered almonds
1 c. milk	
1 1/3 c. coffee ice cream,	
softened	

Bake crust until a little golden; let cool. Mix pudding with milk, ice cream and Kahlua until thick. (Amount of ice cream may vary according to thickness.) Pour mixture into cooled pie shell. Top with any type whipped topping. Sprinkle with almonds and chill. Serves 8.

Mrs. G. M. Lehnertz

MOCHA ANGEL PIE

Meringue Shell:

Filling:

2 egg whites	4 oz. milk chocolate |Hershey|
1/8 t. salt	3 T. hot strong coffee
1/8 t. cream of tartar	1 t. vanilla
1/2 c. sugar	1/2 pt. heavy cream, whipped
1/2 c. chopped nuts	
1/2 t. vanilla	

For meringue shell, beat egg whites until foamy. Add salt and cream of tartar. Beat until soft peaks are formed. Add sugar slowly. Continue to beat until very stiff. Fold in nuts and vanilla. Put in well-greased pyrex pie pan and bake at 300 degrees for 55 minutes. Cool.

For filling, melt chocolate in double boiler. Cool. Add coffee, vanilla, and fold in whipped cream. Fill meringue shell and chill several hours or overnight. Garnish with shaved dark chocolate. Serves 6 to 8. May be prepared several days ahead.

Mrs. Lynn F. Cobb

CHOCOLATE PIE

Filling:

2 c. sugar [scant]
4 T. flour
4 T. cocoa
Pinch of salt
4 egg yolks

1 whole egg
1 1/2 c. milk
2 T. butter
1 t. vanilla
1 9-inch baked pie shell

Mix sugar, flour, cocoa and salt thoroughly. Add beaten egg yolks and whole egg. Then add milk and stir well. Cook in a double boiler, stirring frequently, until mixture thickens. Add butter and vanilla and pour into baked pie shell.

Meringue:

4 egg whites

8 T. sugar

For meringue, beat the egg whites until soft peaks form. Gradually add the 8 tablespoons of sugar. Beat until stiff peaks form. Pile lightly on filling. Bake at 350 degrees for 10 to 15 minutes.

Mrs. Don Crysup
Rusk, Texas

GERMAN CHOCOLATE PIE

3 sticks margarine
1 pkg. German's chocolate
3 c. sugar
2/3 c. flour

1 t. salt
9 eggs
3 t. vanilla
3 c. pecans [or less]

Grease and flour three 9-inch pie pans. Melt margarine and German's chocolate together. Add sugar, flour and salt. Slowly add beaten eggs, then vanilla and chopped pecans. Bake at 325 degrees for 45 minutes. Will be very crusty on top. Cool and top with whipped cream or ice cream. Makes three pies and will serve 24. Pies may be frozen after baking.

Mrs. Dick Hightower

EASY FUDGE PIE

1 stick margarine	1/2 c. flour
2 T. cocoa	2 eggs
1 c. sugar	1 t. vanilla

Melt margarine and mix in cocoa, sugar and flour. Stir in unbeaten eggs and vanilla. Pour in greased pie pan and bake at 350 degrees for 30 minutes. Serves 6 to 8.

Mrs. Ronald Schoenbrun

 Serve with vanilla ice cream

LIZZIE'S FUDGE PIE

1/2 c. butter	1/3 c. flour
1 c. sugar	1/8 t. salt
2 egg yolks	1 t. vanilla
2 squares Baker's bitter chocolate	2 egg whites

Cream butter and sugar thoroughly. Add beaten egg yolks. Melt and cool chocolate. Add to mixture. Add flour, salt, and vanilla. Fold in beaten egg whites. Pour into greased pie pan. Bake 30 minutes at 325 degrees. Cut into wedges like pie. May be served with vanilla ice cream and slivered almonds.

Mrs. Will Mann Richardson
Mrs. L. Glenn Taylor

 This pie has been a favorite at Willowbrook Country Club for years!

MARIE'S FUDGE PIE

3 eggs, beaten	3 oz. dark unsweetened
1 1/4 c. sugar	chocolate, melted
1/4 c. flour	1 stick margarine, melted
1 t. vanilla	

Combine ingredients. Pour into ungreased pie pan and bake at 350 degrees for 20 to 25 minutes. Cool (for a firmer pie) and cut pie-like wedges. Top with whipping cream or serve hot in small bowl, topped with vanilla or peppermint ice cream. Serves 6 to 8.

Mrs. Bill Ross

Mrs. W. F. Bridewell makes the same pie but uses only 2 squares of chocolate. She also suggests that the recipe may be doubled and baked in shallow sheet cake pan. This may be cut in squares and dusted with powdered sugar for a delicious "fudgey" brownie.

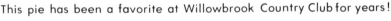

CHEESECAKE PIE

Crust:

1 1/4 c. graham cracker crumbs
1/4 c. butter, melted
2 T. sugar

Topping:

1 c. sour cream
2 T. sugar
1/2 t. vanilla

Filling:

1 pkg. [8 oz.] cream
  cheese
1/2 c. sugar
1 T. lemon juice
1/2 t. vanilla
Dash salt
2 eggs

Make graham cracker crust and set aside. Beat cream cheese until fluffy. Blend in sugar, lemon juice, vanilla and salt. Add eggs one at a time, beating well with mixer after each. Pour filling into crust. Bake at 320 degrees 25 to 30 minutes or until just set. Combine sour cream, sugar and vanilla. Spoon over top of pie. Bake 10 minutes longer. Chill before serving. May be served with strawberries. (Frozen are fine). Serves 6 to 8.

Mrs. Edwin Simons

COCONUT ICEBOX PIE

1 c. sugar
1/2 c. cornstarch
1/4 t. salt
3 c. scalded milk
3 eggs, separated

1 t. vanilla
1/8 to 1/4 t. almond extract
2 c. coconut
1 baked pie shell
1/2 c. heavy cream, whipped

Mix sugar, cornstarch and salt. Pour in warm milk slowly. Add beaten egg yolks. Cook until thickened and fold in beaten egg whites. Add flavorings and 1 1/2 cups coconut. Put in cooled baked pie crust. When cool, top with whipped cream and 1/2 cup coconut.

Mrs. E. N. Holland

MAMA'S JEFF DAVIS PIE

1 1/2 c. sugar
1 c. sweet cream
1 T. butter
3 eggs, well-beaten
2 t. flour

1 t. cinnamon
1/4 t. salt
1 unbaked pie shell
  [9-inch]

Combine all ingredients and beat well. Pour into unbaked pie shell and place in a slow oven - 300 degrees. The cinnamon comes to the top forming a crust. Bake about 50 to 60 minutes or until knife inserted in center comes out clean.

Mrs. Rowland Baldwin, Sr.

FRUIT COCKTAIL PIE I

Filling:

1/2 c. lemon juice
1 can [#202] fruit cocktail,
  drained
1 can Eagle Brand milk
1 c. nuts, chopped

1 graham cracker pie crust
1 or 2 bananas
1 small container Cool Whip

Mix filling ingredients and pour into crust. Top with sliced bananas. Cover with Cool Whip. Chill and serve. Serves 6 to 8.

Mrs. George Allen Barker

For variety, add a small can of drained crushed pineapple.

FRUIT COCKTAIL PIE II

1 graham cracker crust
2 c. tiny marshmallows
  [or 20 large ones]
2 T. milk
1 pkg. [3 oz.] cream cheese,
  softened

1 c. sour cream
1 t. vanilla
1 t. salt
1 can [1 lb.] fruit
  cocktail, drained

Melt marshmallows with milk over low heat. Cool for 10 minutes. Combine cream cheese, sour cream, vanilla, salt and beat until smooth. Stir in marshmallow mixture and drained fruit cocktail. Pour into crust and chill or freeze. May be served either chilled or frozen. Keeps well in the freezer.

Mrs. Gene Caldwell

HAWAIIAN LEMON PIE

7 T. cornstarch
1 c. sugar
1/4 t. salt
2 c. unsweetened pine-
  apple juice
3 eggs, separated

1 T. butter
1 t. grated lemon rind
2 T. lemon juice
1 baked pie shell
6 T. sugar
8 large marshmallows

Mix cornstarch, sugar and salt in saucepan. Add pineapple juice slowly and stir until smooth. Cook until thickened, stirring constantly. Stir small amount of hot mixture into 3 slightly beaten egg yolks and then add to hot mixture. Continue to cook 3 to 5 minutes longer. Remove from heat and add butter, lemon rind, and lemon juice. Cool to room temperature and pour into pie shell. Beat egg whites until stiff; then slowly add sugar. Spoon on top of filling and seal to crust. Take marshmallows, cut in half, and press into meringue, cut side up, and bake at 325 degrees for 25 minutes.

Mrs. Homer Clapp

FROZEN LEMON PIE

3 egg yolks
1/2 c. sugar
1/4 c. lemon juice
2 t. grated lemon peel
1/4 t. salt

1 c. heavy cream, whipped
3 egg whites, stiffly
  beaten
1/2 c. graham cracker crumbs

Beat yolks until thick and lemon-colored. Gradually beat in sugar; add lemon juice, grated lemon peel and salt. Cook until thickened, stirring constantly. Remove from heat and cool. Fold in whipped cream and stiffly beaten egg whites. Cover bottom of buttered pie plate with graham cracker crumbs and pour in mixture, topping with more graham cracker crumbs. Freeze.

Mrs. Tom B. Ramey, Jr.

LEMON CHESS PIE

4 eggs
2 c. sugar
1 T. flour
1 T. corn meal
1/4 c. melted butter

1/3 c. evaporated milk
1/3 c. lemon juice
Grated rind of 1 lemon
9-inch unbaked pastry shell

Beat eggs. Mix dry ingredients and add to eggs. Beat thoroughly. Add butter, milk, lemon juice and grated rind. Pour into 9-inch unbaked pastry shell. Bake in preheated 350 degree oven for 10 minutes. Reduce heat to 300 degrees and bake for 35 to 40 minutes or until set.

Miss Lorene Ellerd
Mrs. Jack Harper

SPRING LEMON PIE

1 baked pastry shell or graham
  cracker shell [9-inch]
1 carton [9 oz.] Cool Whip
1 can [6 oz.] frozen pink
  lemonade concentrate

1 can [14 oz.] sweetened
  condensed milk
  [Eagle Brand]

Blend Cool Whip with lemonade concentrate, stir in condensed milk and pour into shell. Decorate top with thin lemon slices and chill for 3 hours.

Mrs. A. S. Bryan
Mrs. John W. Turner
Kilgore, Texas

Super quick and wonderful!

LIME PIE

Crust:

1 1/2 c. crushed graham crackers
2 T. sugar
3/4 stick margarine

Filling:

2 egg yolks
1 can Eagle Brand milk
Juice of 3 small or 2 large
    limes [about 1/3 c. juice]
1 T. grated lime rind
2 egg whites
1/3 c. sugar

Prepare graham cracker crust. Beat egg yolks. Add milk, juice and grated rind. Beat egg whites with sugar. Fold lime mixture into whites. Pour into crust and bake at 350 degrees for 15 minutes. Cool. Garnish with whipped cream if desired. Serves 6.

Mrs. Robert Hood

Very light and yummy.

MINCEMEAT-APPLE PIE

Dough for a 2 crust pie
1 jar mincemeat
1 can pie apples
1/2 c. granulated sugar
1/2 c. brown sugar
1/3 c. flour

OR:

1 can apple pie filling
    instead of apples,
    sugars & flour

Line a 10-inch pie pan with crust. Combine mincemeat, apples, sugars, and flour. Pour into crust. Cover with top crust and bake at 400 degrees for 30 to 45 minutes until golden brown. Serve warm with vanilla ice cream on top.

Mrs. Malcolm Hammett

ORANGE PIE

1 c. cold water
3/4 c. sugar
Pinch of salt
1 envelope unflavored gelatin

3 eggs, separated
1 can [6 oz.] frozen
    orange juice
Baked pastry shell

Place water, 1/2 cup sugar, salt and gelatin in top of double boiler. Cook about 5 minutes until gelatin and sugar dissolve. Add beaten egg yolks to mixture and put back on double boiler. Cook until mixture coats a metal spoon (about 10 to 15 minutes). Remove from heat and add orange juice, undiluted. Place in refrigerator until it chills and jells slightly. Whip egg whites and remainder of sugar until stiff. Fold in chilled mixture and pour in baked pastry shell. Serve with whipped cream and toasted almonds. Can be made a day ahead. Add whipped cream and almonds just before serving. Serves 8.

Mrs. L. Glenn Taylor

OSGOOD PIE

1/4 lb. margarine
1 c. sugar
2 eggs, separated
1/2 c. chopped pecans
1/2 c. raisins

1/2 t. allspice
1/2 t. cinnamon
2 t. cocoa
1 t. vinegar
9-inch unbaked pie shell

Cream margarine, sugar and beaten egg yolks. Add pecans, raisins, spices, cocoa and vinegar. Mix well, then stir in stiffly beaten egg whites. Pour into 9-inch unbaked pie shell. Bake at 375 degrees for 10 minutes, reduce heat to 325 degrees and bake for 30 minutes. Serves 6 to 8. Freezes well.

Mrs. Bill F. Bales

FRESH PEACH PIE

5 to 6 medium sized
  peaches
1 9-inch unbaked pie shell
1 c. sugar

2 T. melted butter
2 beaten eggs
1/2 t. vanilla
Cinnamon

Peel peaches and slice in quarters. Place in pastry shell, cut side up. Mix sugar, melted butter, eggs and vanilla and pour over the peaches. Sprinkle with cinnamon. Bake at 450 degrees for 30 minutes. Serves 6 to 8.

Mrs. William B. Hilliard

PECAN-PEACH PIE

3 egg whites
1 c. sugar
16 crushed soda crackers
1/4 t. baking powder

1/2 c. chopped pecans
1 t. vanilla
1 large can sliced peaches
1/2 pt. whipping cream

Beat egg whites very stiff. By hand (do not use mixer), fold sugar in gradually. Then fold in crackers to which baking powder has been added. Fold in pecans and vanilla and bake in greased pie tin or square pan for 30 minutes at 325 degrees. Cool. Drain sliced peaches and arrange over crust. Top with whipped cream flavored with a small amount of sugar and vanilla. (Save a few peach slices to garnish). Chill at least 2 hours before serving. The crust may be made ahead and wrapped in foil or Saran Wrap.

Peggy Unfried
Dallas, Texas

PETITE PEACH PIES

1 t. unflavored gelatin
2 T. cold water
1 12 oz. jar [1 cup] apricot
   preserves
1/2 c. sherry
Dash salt

1 can [#2 1/2] peach halves,
   well-drained
8 baked 3 1/2 in. pastry tart
   shells [can be bought or
   made at home]
1/2 c. whipping cream, whipped

Soften gelatin in cold water. Heat the preserves to boiling; add softened gelatin and stir to dissolve. Add sherry and salt. Cool mixture until it begins to thicken. Place a peach half, cut side down, in each tart shell. Spoon the cooled preserve mixture over peach. Chill until set. Serve with whipped cream.

Maraschino cherries may be added to top for color.

Pastry Shells:

1 c. sifted all-purpose
   flour
1/2 t. salt

1/2 c. shortening
3 T. cold water

Blend flour and salt in a mixing bowl. Cut shortening into dry ingredients with 2 knives or a pastry blender. Sprinkle water evenly over dry mixture at the same time tossing it with a fork until all portions are evenly dampened. Press mixture into a ball. Tear off portion and roll out on lightly floured board using just enough dough to make one shell. Place dough in tiny pie tins or pastry shells. If these are not available, a glass custard cup may be used by baking the dough on the outside of the inverted cup. To avoid shrinking during baking, pastry must not be stretched. Prick bottom and sides of pastry with fork tines. Bake at 450 degrees 12 to 15 minutes or until lightly browned. Makes 4 or 5 pastry shells, depending on size.

Mrs. Lynn F. Cobb

MAPLE PECAN PIE

1 can Eagle Brand milk
2/3 c. pure maple syrup
1/4 t. salt
1 c. pecans

1 baked pie shell
1/2 pt. whipping cream
1/2 c. toasted coconut

Cook milk, syrup and salt in iron skillet. Boil three minutes. Cool. Add pecans. Pour into a baked pie shell and top with whipped cream and toasted coconut.

Mrs. T. Carlton Billups

PECAN PIE

1/2 c. sugar
Dash salt
1 heaping T. flour
3 eggs, beaten

1 c. Karo [white]
1 t. vanilla
3/4 c. pecans
Unbaked pie shell

Mix sugar, salt and flour. Pour into the beaten eggs and blend by hand until well-mixed. Add Karo, vanilla and pecans. Pour mixture into unbaked pie shell, dot with butter on top, and bake very slowly in preheated oven (300 to 325 degrees) until it just slightly shakes in the center, 1 hour to 1 hour ane 10 minutes.

Mrs. Wilson Cozby

 Very easy and good!

RITZ PECAN PIE

Pinch of cream of tartar
3 egg whites
1 c. sugar
1 1/2 t. baking powder

1 t. vanilla
16 Ritz crackers, crushed
fine
1 c. chopped nuts

Add cream of tartar to egg whites and beat until stiff. Slowly add sugar and baking powder. Add vanilla. Fold in crackers and pecans. Bake in buttered pie plate 30 minutes or less at 350 degrees. Chill but do not freeze. To serve, top with whipped cream. Serves 6 to 8.

Mrs. Hunter Brush
Mrs. Bob Buford
Mrs. E. D. Wilcox

PINEAPPLE CHESS PIE

3 T. flour
2 c. sugar
3 eggs
2 T. vanilla

1 1/2 sticks melted margarine
1 med. can crushed pineapple
2 unbaked pie shells

Mix all ingredients except pineapple in blender. Drain pineapple and add. Pour into unbaked pie shells. Bake at 350 degrees for about 25 minutes.

This makes two pies and is so simple because a blender is used. Coconut, pecans or lemon extract may be substituted for the pineapple, if desired.

Mrs. E. T. Holly
Austin, Texas

PINEAPPLE PIE

2 c. sugar	2 T. flour
1 stick margarine, softened	1 can [#2] crushed pineapple
4 eggs	2 t. vanilla
4 T. corn meal	2 unbaked pie shells

Mix all ingredients and pour into 2 unbaked pie shells. Bake at 350 degrees for 45 minutes.

Mrs. Glenn Collins

PUMPKIN PIE

3/4 c. milk	5 egg yolks
2 c. canned pumpkin	2 envelopes gelatin
1 1/2 c. brown sugar	1/3 c. cold water
1/8 t. salt	5 egg whites
3/4 t. ginger	1 1/2 c. whipping cream
3/4 t. cinnamon	1/3 c. sugar
1/3 t. nutmeg	10-inch baked pie shell

Heat milk with pumpkin, brown sugar, salt, and spices. Beat egg yolks slightly and add hot mixture gradually to yolks. Mix well and cook in double boiler until thick, stirring constantly. Soften gelatin in cold water and add to hot custard. Stir until dissolved. Cool until it begins to thicken. Beat egg whites until stiff but not dry. Fold in custard. Cool a little while, but not until set. Whip cream. Fold sugar into whipped cream, then fold cream into pumpkin mixture. Chill until very thick and pour into baked pie shell. (Add toasted sesame seeds to pie dough before baking). Chill until set. Before serving, sprinkle each piece with caramelized almonds, dribble with butterscotch sauce, and top with whipped cream.

Caramelized Almonds:

1/2 c. sugar
1 c. slivered blanched almonds

Stir constantly in heavy skillet until light caramel color. Spread on greased cookie sheet. Break apart when crisp. These will keep indefinitely in an airtight container. (They are also delicious on coffee ice cream).

Use your favorite butterscotch syrup for dribbling. This pie is not complete without the almonds, sauce, and whipped cream.

Mrs. H. L. Gist

 This is so outstanding even non-pumpkin eaters love it. It takes time from start to finish, but is worth every minute!

COFFEE SUNDAE PIE

18 cream-filled chocolate
  cookies
1/3 c. melted butter
2 squares [2 oz.]
  unsweetened chocolate
1/2 c. sugar
1 T. butter

2/3 c. evaporated milk
1 qt. coffee ice cream
1 c. whipping cream
1 oz. creme de cocoa
  [optional]
1/2 c. chopped walnuts

Crush chocolate cookies to fine crumbs with a rolling pin, and add melted butter. Mix well; then press around sides and bottom of a 9-inch pie pan and chill. Melt chocolate over hot water and stir in sugar and butter. Slowly add evaporated milk. Cook over hot water, stirring occasionally, until thickened. Chill. Fill pie shell with coffee ice cream and spread chocolate mixture over top. Whip cream to which creme de cocoa has been added, and spoon over surface of pie. Sprinkle top with chopped walnuts. Serve at once or store in freezer. Serves 6.

Mrs. William Turner

PRALINE ICE CREAM PIE

1/2 c. crunchy peanut butter
1/2 c. white Karo
2 c. Rice Krispies

1 qt. Baskin-Robbins
  Pralines n' Cream
  ice cream

Mix peanut butter and Karo, add the Rice Krispies, and mix well. Shape as a crust in a buttered 9-inch pie pan. Put in freezer for at least 15 minutes. Remove from freezer and fill with ice cream, then return to freezer. Serve with caramel sauce dribbled over it. Serves 6.

Mrs. Frank Fite

Take the basic crust and use your imagination. Your favorite ice cream will be wonderful!

FRESH STRAWBERRY PIE

2 boxes fresh strawberries
2 c. milk
1 stick butter or margarine
3 T. flour

1 c. sugar
1 baked pie shell
1/2 pt. whipping cream

Wash and hull strawberries. Do not sweeten. Heat milk with butter until butter melts. Mix flour with the sugar and add to milk mixture. Cook until thick. Cool. Put strawberries in cooled pie crust. Pour filling over berries and top with whipped cream. Chill until firm. Serves 6 to 8.

Mrs. Mickey Pfaff

Simple and delicious -- a favorite of children!

STRAWBERRY FLUFF PIE

Crust:

1 c. flour
1/4 c. brown sugar
1/2 c. nuts, chopped
1/2 c. butter

Filling:

1/2 c. sugar
1 envelope unflavored gelatin
1/2 c. water
1 pkg. [10 oz.] frozen
    strawberries
Juice of half a lemon
1/8 t. almond extract
1 c. heavy cream, whipped

For crust, crumble together and bake for 20 minutes at 350 degrees, stirring occasionally. Use crumb mixture to line bottom of 10-inch pie pan, pressing firmly. Retain some of the mixture to sprinkle on top.

For filling, stir sugar with gelatin in saucepan. Stir in water; then cook over low heat, stirring, until just below boiling point. Remove and add strawberries (frozen), lemon juice, and almond extract. Stir, breaking up strawberries with fork until berries thaw and mixture thickens. Fold in whipped cream. Pour over chilled crumb mixture in pan and refrigerate for 6 to 8 hours or overnight. May be served with whipped cream. Serves 8. This will freeze well.

Mrs. Arthur Cunningham

TWO-TIERED STRAWBERRY PIE

1/2 c. sifted powdered sugar
1/2 t. vanilla
1/2 t. almond extract

1 pkg. [3 oz.] cream cheese
1 c. whipping cream, whipped
Graham cracker crust

Add sugar and flavorings to cream cheese and beat until smooth and fluffy. Fold in whipped cream and spread evenly over bottom of crust. Chill thoroughly.

Glazed Strawberry Filling:

1 qt. fresh strawberries
Sugar
1 t. lemon juice

1 T. cornstarch
Red food coloring
1 t. butter

Slice and sweeten strawberries. Let stand and drain thoroughly. Save liquid. Combine liquid and lemon juice and add enough water to make 1 cup. Blend small amount of liquid with cornstarch in saucepan. Gradually add remaining liquid. Cook over medium heat 3 to 5 minutes or until thick and clear. Remove from heat and add 3 or 4 drops of red food coloring and butter. Cool. Arrange drained strawberries over chilled cheese layer. Spoon glaze over strawberries. Chill until served. This makes 1 large or 2 small pies.

Mrs. Mickey Pfaff

STRAWBERRY PIE I

18 marshmallows
1 pkg. [small] frozen
strawberries

1/2 pt. whipping cream
1 baked pie shell

Melt marshmallows in double boiler with frozen strawberries. Put aside and allow to cool and thicken slightly. Fold in whipped cream. Pour in a baked pie shell and refrigerate.

Mrs. Ben Turner
Cleburne, Texas

On a busy day try 3/4 to a scant cup of marshmallow cream as a substitute. This is also great in small tart shells.

Mrs. Edwin Simons uses the same filling recipe but makes her own graham cracker crust by combining 1 1/4 cups graham cracker crumbs, 1/4 cup melted butter, and 2 T. sugar. She presses this into a 9-inch pie pan and bakes it for 10 minutes at 350 degrees.

STRAWBERRY PIE II

1 pkg. [8 oz.] cream cheese
1 c. sugar
1 pkg. [small] frozen
strawberries

1 large container
Cool Whip
2 graham cracker pie
shells

Combine softened cream cheese, sugar and strawberries. Fold in Cool Whip and pour into 2 graham cracker crumb pie shells. Refrigerate.

Mrs. Hollis Pinyan

EASY PIE CRUST

1/2 c. boiling water
1 c. Crisco
3 c. sifted cake flour

1 t. salt
3/4 t. baking powder

Pour boiling water over Crisco. Beat until creamy. Set bowl in a pan of cold water while you sift flour. Sift, measure three cups cake flour, and sift again with salt and baking powder. Stir shortening mixture into flour until blended. Wrap dough in heavy waxed paper and put in refrigerator until firm enough to roll. This can be made several batches at a time and frozen. Recipe makes 3 pie crusts or 8 or 9 individual crusts.

Mrs. Jack King

Desserts

DESSERTS

BRANDY DELIGHT

1/2 gal. vanilla ice cream   1 c. kahlua
1 c. brandy

Place ice cream, a little at a time, in a large bowl; beat with an electric mixer. When it becomes soft, add brandy and kahlua; mix well and pour into tulip wine glasses and freeze. When ready to serve, remove from freezer at beginning of meal. Stir lightly with a teaspoon just before serving. May be drunk from the glass or eaten with spoon. Serves 12.

Mrs. Frank Fite

APRICOT SQUARES

1 lb. apricots [moist pack dried]   2 c. flour
3/4 c. sugar   1 t. salt
1 3/4 c. water   1/2 t. soda
1 c. butter   1 c. coconut
1 c. sugar   1 c. nuts

Combine apricots, 3/4 cup sugar and water. Cook until water is absorbed. Stir and make paste. Cool.

Combine butter, 1 cup sugar, flour, salt, soda, coconut and half the nuts. Press into bottom of 9 x 13 inch pan. Bake at 400 degrees for 15 minutes or until lightly browned. Spread apricot mixture and remaining 1/2 cup nuts onto pastry. Bake 15 minutes. Cool. Cut into squares and top with cream or ice cream.

Mrs. Joe Huffstutler

 These improve with age.

COFFEE CHARLOTTE SQUARES

2 T. instant coffee   1 c. cream, whipped
1 c. hot water   18 double ladyfingers
32 large marshmallows,
     cut in half

Dissolve instant coffee in hot water. Add cut marshmallows. Place over low heat and stir until marshallows are completely melted. Then chill until slightly thickened. Fold in whipped cream. Separate ladyfingers, line bottom of shallow oblong serving dish. Cover with layers of coffee mixture and ladyfingers Top with remaining coffee mixture. Chill 8 hours or overnight. Cut in squares. Serves 8 to 10.

Mrs. William D. Lawrence, Jr.

ORANGE COCONUT SQUARES

1/2 c. butter
1/2 c. brown sugar

1 c. flour

Combine and spread over bottom of buttered 8 x 14 inch pyrex pan; bake at 350 degrees for 15 minutes.

1 c. brown sugar
2 T. flour
1/4 t. baking powder
1/2 t. salt
2 eggs, beaten

1 c. coconut
1 c. chopped pecans
[if desired]
1 t. vanilla

Combine brown sugar, flour, baking powder and salt; add to beaten eggs, coconut, nuts and vanilla. Spread over hot first layer; return to oven and bake 15 minutes more at same temperature.

1 1/2 c. powdered sugar
2 T. orange juice

1 T. lemon juice
Grated rind of 1 lemon

Combine and use as icing for hot baked mixture. Cool; cut into squares. Makes about 2 dozen squares.

Mrs. Bruce Brookshire

ANGEL CAKE FILLING

6 egg yolks
1 t. salt
2 T. flour
2 T. sugar
2 heaping T. butter
2 T. vinegar

1 c. milk, warmed
1 lb. marshmallows
1 large can pineapple
[chunk or tidbits]
1 pt. heavy cream,
whipped

Beat egg yolks until pale lemon-colored. Add (at low speed) salt, flour, sugar, softened or melted butter, vinegar and warmed milk. Pour into large saucepan. Cook over medium heat, stirring constantly, until thickened. Add marshmallows and stir until they melt. Add well-drained pineapple, cut into small pieces. Cool, then fold in whipped cream. This quantity makes enough to fill 4 large layers of angel cake. May be frozen if desired.

Mrs. Joe Huffstutler

CHOCOLATE CAKE ROLL

5 eggs, separated	3 T. cocoa
1/2 t. cream of tartar	1/4 t. salt
1 c. sugar	1 t. vanilla
1/4 c. flour	Powdered sugar

Beat egg whites and cream of tartar until stiff, but not dry. Gradually add 1/2 cup of sugar. In a large bowl, beat yolks well. In another bowl, sift remaining 1/2 cup sugar, flour, cocoa and salt twice. Fold cocoa mixture into egg yolks and add vanilla (use mixer). By hand, fold egg whites into cocoa and yolk mixture.

Line a jellyroll pan (or sheetcake pan, 15 1/2 x 10 1/4 x 5/8 inch) with waxed paper, then grease lightly on top of paper and sides of pan. Spread batter and bake 25 minutes at 325 degrees. Cool exactly 5 minutes. Turn out on clean cup towel sprinkled with powdered sugar. Then sprinkle top of cake with powdered sugar after waxed paper is pulled off. Roll cake with towel and cool (45 minutes to 1 hour is usually long enough). Unroll, spread with topping (below), reroll and refrigerate at least 6 hours before serving. Trim edges before serving. Serves 8 or 9.

Topping:

1/2 pt. cream, whipped stiff
1/4 c. sugar
1/2 t. vanilla

Mrs. Joe Max Green
Nacogdoches, Texas

FUDGE PUDDING CAKE AND SAUCE

1 c. flour	1 t. vanilla
2 t. baking powder	1 c. chopped nuts
1/4 t. salt	1 c. brown sugar
3/4 c. sugar	1 3/4 c. hot water
6 T. cocoa	Whipped cream, [optional]
1/2 c. milk	
2 T. melted shortening	
[or 1 T. butter and	
1 T. shortening]	

Sift flour, baking powder, salt, sugar and 2 tablespoons cocoa together into bowl. Stir in milk, melted shortening and vanilla. Blend in chopped nuts. Spread in buttered 9-inch square pan. Sprinkle with mixture of brown sugar and 4 tablespoons cocoa. Pour hot water gently over batter. Bake at 350 degrees for 45 minutes. Serve hot or cold with whipped cream, if desired. Either cut in squares and serve or turn upside down and cut and serve. This cake is like an upside down cake and makes a sauce of its own as it bakes. Serves 6 to 8.

Mrs. Milburn Pool

FABULOUS BROWNIE DESSERT

Betty Crocker Brownie Mix
 [family size]
1/2 c. chopped nuts

2 c. whipping cream
1/2 c. sifted powdered sugar
1 t. vanilla

Line 15 1/2 x 10 1/2 x 1 inch jellyroll pan with heavy aluminum foil, extending foil 2 inches on both ends of pan; grease foil.

Prepare brownie mix as directed on package, adding chopped nuts. Spread batter in pan. Bake 15 to 20 minutes at 350 degrees. Cool in pan. Cut into 4 strips (crosswise). Whip cream with sifted powdered sugar and vanilla. Spread 1/2 cup whipped cream on each brownie layer. Stack strips, cream sides up. Frost with rest of cream. Chill at least 6 hours (preferably overnight). Garnish with nuts. Serves 12. Very good and very rich.

Mrs. L. Glenn Taylor

ICE CREAM CAKE

First Layer:

2 pkgs. ladyfingers
1 qt. vanilla ice cream
1 can [6 oz.] frozen orange
 juice

Second Layer:

2 pkgs. [10 oz.] frozen
 raspberries
2 cans [9 oz.] crushed
 pineapple
1 T. frozen lemonade
 concentrate

Third Layer:

1 qt. vanilla ice cream
1 t. almond flavoring
1 t. rum flavoring
 [optional]
6 maraschino cherries,
 chopped
3 T. chopped nuts

Line bottom and sides of a 9-inch spring-form pan with ladyfingers, split in half. Mix 1 quart vanilla ice cream with the frozen orange juice, undiluted. Pour this into mold over the ladyfingers. Freeze firm.

Crush (or use an electric blender) two packages frozen raspberries; strain to remove the seeds. Add crushed pineapple, and the lemonade concentrate. Freeze until partially frozen, then beat slightly and spoon over orange layer. Freeze firm.

To one quart vanilla ice cream, add almond and rum flavorings, chopped cherries and chopped nuts. Pour over raspberry layer and freeze overnight.

Remove from pan and garnish with sweetened whipped cream, fresh strawberries and mint. Serves 12.

Mrs. Hascall H. Muntz

CELY'S PORTUGUESE QUINDIN

4 whole eggs
3 egg yolks
3 heaping c. sugar
1 fresh coconut, grated

3 T. grated Parmesan cheese
3 T. melted butter
3 egg whites
9 T. sugar

Beat four eggs and three egg yolks until very thick. Add sugar, mix in coconut, Parmesan cheese and melted butter. Put mixture into 3 quart mold which has been buttered and sprinkled with sugar. Place in pan of water and bake at 325 degrees until brown (45 to 50 minutes). Beat egg whites until stiff, gradually adding the remaining sugar. Spread this meringue on top of baked pudding and return to oven until meringue is brown (30 to 35 minutes). Cool slightly and refrigerate until time to serve. Remove from mold and slice as desired. Serves about 16.

Mrs. Joe Huffstutler

Cracking a coconut: Puncture eyes of coconut and drain milk. Put coconut in oven at 200 degrees for one hour. The shell of the coconut will crack and a slight tap with a hammer will get you to the meat. The brown skin on the coconut can be peeled off with a potato peeler.

CHERRY DESSERT

1 can Eagle Brand milk
Juice of 2 lemons
1/2 pt. whipping cream,
  beaten stiff

1 can tart pie cherries,
  well-drained
1 c. nut meats [pecans]
Vanilla wafers

Combine milk and lemon juice. (Milk will thicken.) Fold whipped cream into milk mixture. Fold in cherries and nuts. Line an 8 x 8 inch square dish with vanilla wafer crumbs. Pour mixture into dish and top with more crumbs. Let stand in refrigerator for 24 hours.

Mrs. Bert Creel

S AND D CHERRIES

1 can Eagle Brand milk
1 small pkg. cream cheese
1 pkg. [6 oz.] small
  marshmallows

1 can cherry pie filling
2 pkgs. Dream Whip

Melt condensed milk, cream cheese and marshmallows in top of double boiler. Stir in cherry pie filling. Cool. Fold in two packages Dream Whip prepared according to directions on box. Freeze in 8 x 12 inch pyrex dish. Serves 12.

Mrs. John D. Glass, Jr.

QUICK CHERRY CREAM TART

1 c. milk
1 c. sour cream
1/4 t. almond extract
1 pkg. [3 5/8 oz.] instant
   vanilla pudding mix
Tart shells

1 can [21 oz.] cherry
   pie filling
Cool Whip
2 T. slivered almonds,
   toasted

In mixing bowl, mix milk, sour cream and almond extract. Add pudding mix and beat until creamy (about 2 minutes). Spoon into tart shells. Top with cherry pie filling. Add a dollop of Cool Whip and sprinkle with almonds. Chill. This amount will fill eight regular sized tart shells or thirty-six miniatures.

Mrs. Don Smith

NEVER-FAIL PEACH COBBLER

3/4 stick butter or margarine
*1 qt. sweetened fruit
   with juice
1 c. sugar

1 c. flour
1 T. baking powder
1/2 t. salt
3/4 c. milk

*For peach cobbler, use 2 large cans Elberta freestone peaches; draining off enough juice to make 1 quart. Sweeten to taste. Fresh fruit may be used.

Melt butter in large casserole; pour in fruit over butter. Sift together sugar, flour, baking powder and salt; add milk and mix. Pour batter over fruit in casserole and bake at 375 degrees for 30 minutes. Serves 12.

Mrs. James Boring

PINEAPPLE-PEACH COBBLER

3/4 c. flour
Dash of salt
2 t. baking powder
3/4 c. sugar
3/4 c. milk
1/2 c. butter
1 can [#303] peaches, cut
   in bite-size pieces

1/2 the syrup from peaches
1 small can crushed pineapple,
   packed without sugar
Syrup from pineapple
1/4 t. cinnamon
1/4 t. nutmeg
1/2 c. sugar

Sift flour, salt, baking powder and sugar. Stir in milk. Melt butter in 8 x 8 x 2 inch baking dish. Pour batter over melted butter without stirring. Spoon on the peach-pineapple mixture (thoroughly mixed with syrups, spices and sugar). Bake at 350 degrees for 1 hour. Delicious served hot or cold and can be reheated. Good served with ice cream or cream. Serves 6 to 8.

Mrs. T. Carlton Billups

QUICK COBBLER

1 large can sliced peaches
1 regular size can sliced
  peaches
1 c. brown sugar

Cinnamon
1 box yellow cake mix
1 1/2 sticks margarine

Use large rectangular pyrex dish (7 x 11 x 3 inch). Grease casserole lightly with butter. Place ingredients in casserole in the following order: layer peaches, half of brown sugar, sprinkle of cinnamon, cake mix, rest of brown sugar, sprinkle of cinnamon. Top with margarine, cut in squares.

Bake at 350 degrees for 50 to 60 minutes.

Mrs. H. Kelly Ireland

CREAM PUFFS

1/4 lb. butter
1 c. boiling water
1 c. flour

1/4 t. salt
4 eggs

Stir butter into boiling water until butter is melted. Add flour and salt all at once, stirring vigorously until mixture is smooth and forms a soft ball that doesn't separate. Cool slightly.

Add eggs, beating vigorously after each addition until mixture is smooth. Drop 2 inches apart on greased cookie sheet. Bake 15 minutes at 450 degrees, then 25 minutes more at 325 degrees.

Cool before filling with Blancmange; glaze with chocolate, if desired. Makes 1 dozen large puffs (or more smaller puffs).

Blancmange:

3 T. cornstarch
1/3 c. sugar
Dash salt

1/2 c. cold milk
1 1/2 c. milk, scalded
1 t. vanilla

Combine cornstarch, sugar, salt and cold milk; gradually add to hot milk in top of double boiler. Cook, stirring until thick; cover and cook 15 to 20 minutes. Add vanilla and chill. Fills 1 dozen large puffs.

Mrs. Francis Kay

For coffee or brunch, fill tiny puffs with chicken salad.

BAKED CUSTARD

3 eggs
2 1/2 c. milk
1/3 c. sugar

Pinch of salt
1/2 t. vanilla

Gently beat eggs in mixing bowl with fork until well-mixed. Add milk, sugar, salt and vanilla. Pour into 6 individual custard cups or ramekins. Sprinkle ground nutmeg on top if desired. Place ramekins into a pan of warm water to bake. Bake at 250 degrees for approximately 1 1/2 hours or until knife comes out clean. Custard will not be firm at this time. It will thicken as it cools.

Mrs. W. Dewey Lawrence

POPIE'S BOILED CUSTARD

1/2 gal. sweet milk
1 tall can evaporated milk
1 thick orange rind
2/3 c. sugar
8 or 9 egg yolks

2 rounded T. flour
Vanilla
Whipped cream
Nutmeg

Pour sweet milk and evaporated milk together in large vessel and heat slowly until it comes to steaming point. Take peel from one thick-skinned orange, bruise with cleaver so flavor will get into milk; add to milk and steam but do not boil. Stir constantly.

Cream together sugar, egg yolks and flour. Slowly add small quantities of steaming milk into egg mixture until all mixture has been blended with milk. Pour through collander and put back in a double boiler and stir until it thickens. Remove from heat but leave orange peel in until cool. Flavor with vanilla. Serve in small cup, dessert dish or glass. Top with whipped cream and dash of nutmeg, if desired. Serves 12 to 14.

Mrs. J. E. Alexander, Sr.

DATE ICEBOX DESSERT

1 c. graham crackers,
   rolled fine
1 c. coarsely chopped dates
1/2 c. chopped nuts
1/8 t. salt

1 c. cream, whipped
1/4 c. orange juice
1 c. marshmallows, cut
   in small pieces
1 t. grated orange rind

Combine all ingredients, saving enough crumbs to roll mixture in at the end (about 1/4 cup). Form into roll. Roll in graham cracker crumbs. Wrap in waxed paper or clear plastic paper. Place in refrigerator 4 hours or overnight.

Slice to serve. Top with additional whipped cream, if desired.

Mrs. Tom Ramey, Jr.

CHINESE FRUIT DESSERT

2 c. sugar
2/3 c. butter
2 whole eggs
1 1/2 c. sour milk
Dash of salt
3 c. flour
2 t. soda [1 t. in milk and 1 t. in flour]

1 t. baking powder
1 c. ground raisins
1/2 c. ground dates
1 c. nuts, toasted and chopped
Rind of 1 lemon and 1 orange

Blend sugar and butter. Add beaten eggs one at a time. Add dry ingredients and liquid alternately, then fruits and nuts. Add the grated rind of the lemon and orange. Bake at 350 degrees for 45 minutes in a buttered and floured bundt pan. Serves 24.

Icing:

Squeeze into a cup the juice of 1 lemon and 1 orange. Fill the cup with sugar. Spoon over the cake while still warm. This dessert is best served slightly warm, with a hard sauce or whipped cream.

Mrs. Will Mann Richardson

ENGLISH TRIFLE

1 med. sized sponge cake loaf
1 c. cream sherry
1 small box raspberry Jello
1 large can frozen raspberries
1 1/2 c. hot water
1/2 c. raspberry juice

1 small box vanilla pudding [made according to directions on box]
Sliced bananas
Sweetened whipped cream

Break sponge cake into chunks and place in decorative serving bowl. Add cream sherry to cake. Cover and let stand overnight in refrigerator.

Combine Jello, raspberries, water and juice and pour over cake. Mix lightly together. Pour the vanilla pudding mixture over cake. Return to refrigerator.

Before serving, add heavy layer of sliced bananas and top with a layer of whipped cream. Serve at table or from a dessert cart in sherbet glasses or dessert bowls. Serves 8.

Mrs. William E. Bertram

FLAN [FLAHN]

1/3 c. sugar
6 eggs
6 T. sugar

2 c. milk
2 t. vanilla
1/4 t. cinnamon

Take 9-inch pan and melt 1/3 cup of sugar over low heat, stirring constantly until sugar caramelizes. Beat the remaining ingredients together and immediately pour over the caramelized sugar. Place in a pan of hot water and bake at 350 degrees until firm, about 40 minutes. When custard is firm, remove from pan of water, and invert on round plate or tray. Take knife and edge rim of custard to help release it from pan. Refrigerate for two hours before serving. Slice like pie and serve, adding caramelized sauce remaining in pan.

Mrs. E. B. Yale

FLOATING ISLAND

For full recipe:

6 egg yolks
3/4 c. sugar
1/2 t. salt
3 3/4 c. milk
1 1/2 t. vanilla

For small recipe:

2 egg yolks
1/4 c. sugar
1/4 t. salt
1 1/4 c. milk
1/2 t. vanilla

Heat milk in top of double boiler. Beat yolks until light yellow. Slowly add sugar, salt, and hot milk. Return mixture to top of double boiler and cook, stirring constantly, over boiling water, watching to see when spoon is coated. Stir one minute more; then remove from heat and pour into cold bowl. Continue to stir until cooled. Add vanilla and stir again. Chill. Serve topped with a dab of tart jelly, or meringue, or grated bittersweet chocolate. Full recipe serves 6 to 8; smaller one, 2 to 3.

Mrs. H. D. McCallum

FROZEN BUTTERMILK DESSERT

1 egg white
1/4 c. sugar
1/2 c. heavy whipping cream

1 c. buttermilk
1/2 t. vanilla
1/8 t. baking soda

In small bowl with mixer at high speed, beat egg white until foamy. Gradually sprinkle in sugar, beating at high speed until sugar is dissolved and egg white is stiff.

In another bowl beat cream until soft peaks form. Reduce speed to low and add buttermilk, vanilla, soda and beaten egg white mixture. Put in muffin papers (in the muffin tins so they will hold their shape) and freeze. Top with whipped cream and a cherry or strawberries. Use bonbon papers when making these for pick-up food. Makes 10 to 12 of the large size.

Mrs. William C. Smyth

GLORIFIED RICE

1 c. cooked rice [cold]
1 small can crushed
  pineapple
1 c. sugar

1/2 lb. miniature marsh-
  mallows
1/2 pt. cream, whipped

Cook rice until tender; rinse in cold water. Drain syrup from pineapple. Mix rice, sugar, pineapple and marshmallows. Gently fold whipped cream into first mixture. Refrigerate for several hours. Serves 6 to 8.

Mrs. Jerry Bain

 The children will love this one.

ICEBOX GINGERBREAD

1 c. butter or margarine
1 c. sugar
4 eggs
4 c. flour
2 t. soda

1/2 t. cinnamon
1/2 t. allspice
4 t. ginger
1 c. sour cream
1 c. molasses

Cream butter and sugar. Add eggs one at a time, beating well after each addition. Sift flour, soda and spices. Add alternately with sour cream. Beat in molasses. Bake in paper muffin cups in 350 degree oven for about 15 to 20 minutes. Batter can be refrigerated for about two weeks.

Mrs. Glenn Collins
Mrs. Clifford Swift
Houston, Texas

GINGERBREAD I

1 c. sugar
3 eggs, beaten
1 c. oil
1 c. molasses
1/4 t. salt
1 t. cinnamon

1 t. ginger
1 t. cloves
2 t. soda, dissolved
  in 1/8 c. water
2 c. flour
1 t. vanilla

Mix all well. Add 1 cup boiling water. Mix. Pour in greased 9 x 13 inch pan. Bake at 350 degrees about 30 to 40 minutes.

Mrs. Joe Herrington

GINGERBREAD II

1/2 c. Crisco
1/2 t. salt
1 t. cinnamon
1 t. ginger
1/4 t. nutmeg
1/8 t. cloves
1/2 c. sugar

1 egg, unbeaten
1 c. molasses
2 1/2 c. sifted flour
1/2 t. baking powder
1 t. soda
1 c. boiling water

Combine Crisco, salt and spices. Add sugar gradually and cream until light and fluffy. Add egg and beat thoroughly. Add molasses and blend. Sift flour with baking powder and soda three times. Add to creamed mixture, blending well. Add boiling water and beat until smooth. Pour batter into a 10 x 10 x 2 inch greased pan. Bake in moderate oven, 350 degrees, 50 to 60 minutes. Serve in squares with whipped cream.

Evelyn Odom
Rusk, Texas

For date gingerbread, add one cup dates (pitted and cut into small pieces) to sifted flour mixture.

HUNGARIAN BUTTER HORNS

Pastry:

1 1/2 c. shortening or
   margarine
4 c. flour
1/2 t. salt
1 yeast cake
3 egg yolks, beaten
1/2 c. sour cream
1 t. vanilla

Filling:

1 c. sugar
3 egg whites, beaten
   stiff
3/4 c. chopped pecans
1 t. vanilla

For pastry, cut shortening into flour and salt with pastry blender. Crumble yeast into this mixture. Stir in egg yolks, sour cream and vanilla. Refrigerate this dough while preparing filling.

For filling, add sugar gradually as egg whites are beaten. Stir in pecans and vanilla.

Divide dough in 8 parts, working with 1 at a time leaving remaining portions in refrigerator. Roll out each part (on a board dusted with powdered sugar) into circle. Cut each circle into 8 wedge-shaped pieces. Put filling on large end of each wedge and roll up. Bake on ungreased cookie sheet at 400 degrees for 15 to 18 minutes.

Mrs. Milburn Pool

HORNS OF PLENTY

2/3 c. semi-sweet chocolate
  pieces
1/2 c. margarine
1/2 c. sugar

1/8 t. salt
1/4 t. ginger
1/3 c. light corn syrup
1 c. plus 2 T. flour

Melt chocolate, margarine, sugar, salt and ginger in top of double boiler. Remove from heat and stir in syrup and flour. Drop by teaspoon on greased cookie sheet, about 4 to sheet or by 1/2 teaspoon, 6 to the sheet. Bake 10 minutes at 350 degrees. Shape into cones while still warm. When cones have hardened, fill with flavored whipped cream, peppermint or coffee ice cream, lime sherbet, etc. to make attractive dessert.

Mrs. Doyle Simmons

Tricky, but worth the effort!

ICE CREAM I

5 eggs, beaten separately
2 1/2 c. sugar
2 T. flour [scant]
1 qt. milk

1 t. vanilla
Any fruit [optional]
3 to 4 sq. bitter chocolate
  [optional]

Beat egg yolks and whites separately and thoroughly; then fold together. Mix sugar and flour together and fold in. Add to milk which has been scalded in a double boiler and cook, stirring, until it thickens. Remove from heat and add 1 teaspoon vanilla when cool.

Pour into 1/2 gallon freezer and add peaches, strawberries, or any other fruit for desired flavor (about 1 to 1 1/2 pints, crushed). Finish filling freezer with milk, half and half or whipping cream, according to richness desired.

To make chocolate from this recipe, scald chocolate with the milk and follow above proportions and directions.

Mrs. George Allen

ICE CREAM II

5 eggs
2 c. sugar
1/4 t. salt

2 cans Carnation milk
1 1/2 t. vanilla
2 to 3 qts. whole milk

Beat eggs, sugar and salt until creamy. Add Carnation and vanilla. Mix thoroughly. Pour into can of one gallon electric freezer. Fill can with milk 2 inches from the top. After freezer stops, remove dasher and place container in freezer until ready to serve.

Mrs. James E. Bass

CONNIE'S CHOCOLATE ICE CREAM

7 to 12 c. homogenized milk
3 1/2 c. sugar
7 T. cocoa
1/2 c. flour
Dash salt
3 whole eggs

3 egg yolks
2 c. cream
1 large can evaporated
   milk
1 1/2 T. vanilla

Scald 1 quart milk in large saucepan (may use a Dutch oven). Combine sugar, cocoa, flour, salt, 1 cup milk; add to scalded milk. Combine eggs, yolks, 1 cup milk and add to chocolate mixture, stirring rapidly. Return to heat; stir constantly until quite thick (this requires at least 10 minutes). Cool. Add cream, can of milk, and vanilla to thickened mixture. Strain (if necessary) into freezer can; add homogenized milk to 2 inches from top of can. Freeze in ice cream freezer.

Mrs. Max W. Minton
Ft. Worth, Texas

CHOCOLATE ICE CREAM

3 t. gelatin
6 T. cold water
3 c. milk
1 1/4 c. sugar
Dash salt

Vanilla
1 c. cream [whipped
   not too stiff]
1/2 small can chocolate
   syrup [or more]

Soak gelatin in cold water about 5 minutes. Heat milk and mix with gelatin to dissolve. Add sugar and salt. Cool and add flavoring. Turn into freezing tray. When it begins to thicken, turn into bowl and beat until frothy. Fold in cream and syrup. Return to tray and freeze.

Mrs. W. Dewey Lawrence

LEMON ICE CREAM

6 lemons, juiced
4 c. sugar

2 qts. milk
1/2 pt. whipping cream

Pour lemon juice over sugar and let set until sugar melts.
Mix all other ingredients in can of electric freezer. Add sugar and lemon juice mixture. If not full, add enough milk to fill until 2 inches from top. Freeze; remove dasher and store in freezer.

Mrs. James E. Bass

MANGO ICE CREAM

3 T. flour
2 1/2 c. sugar
1/2 t. salt
5 egg yolks, slightly beaten
5 c. milk
1 T. vanilla

5 c. thin cream [or half
  milk and half heavy
  cream]
1 can [#2] mangos [1 c.
  fresh peaches is good
  added to this]

Mix flour, sugar and salt. Gradually add slightly beaten egg yolks and milk; cook over medium heat, stirring constantly until mixture coats a spoon. (Should custard have curdled appearance, it will disappear in freezing.) When cool, add flavoring and cream. Strain, if necessary, and freeze in 4 quart freezer. When ice cream is partly frozen, add the mangos, which have been chopped or blended in electric blender. Serves 6 to 8.

Mrs. Brad Holmes

MOM'S HOMEMADE ICE CREAM

1/2 gallon milk [approx.]
1 pt. whipping cream
7 egg yolks
2 T. cornstarch

1 T. flour
1 1/2 c. sugar
2 t. vanilla
1 can [13 oz.] evaporated milk

Cook milk and one half of whipping cream slowly until a light scale covers top. Beat egg yolks until light, add cornstarch and flour to sugar and blend in with egg yolks. Add to milk/cream cooking over low flame until thickened. Add vanilla, canned milk and remainder of whipping cream. Set aside until cool. Fresh peaches, strawberries (sugared to taste) and juice may be added to above. Both ice cream and fruit may be prepared the day before, allowing plenty of time for juice to thicken from sugar added to fruit. Freeze (in advance, if desired) in ice cream freezer. Then put ice cream in parfait glasses in freezing compartment of refrigerator. Remove from freezing compartment before serving or allow an hour in the refrigerator for this to soften.

Mrs. Oscar West

EASY STRAWBERRY ICE CREAM

2 pkgs. frozen strawberries
1 1/2 c. marshmallow topping

1 2/3 c. evaporated milk
1/4 c. lemon juice

Mix berries and topping in bowl and let stand. Chill evaporated milk in freezer until crystals form (25 to 30 minutes) and whip until stiff. Add lemon juice and whip very stiff. Blend with berries and freeze. Makes 3 to 4 pints.

Mrs. Malcolm Hammett

LEMON CRISP

Filling:

1 whole egg
2 egg yolks
1/2 c. sugar
Pinch of salt
1/4 c. lemon juice
2 egg whites
1 c. whipping cream

Crust:

16 graham crackers
1/4 c. melted butter

Beat together egg and egg yolks. Add sugar slowly. Add salt and lemon juice. Cook in double boiler over hot (not boiling) water until mixture thickens. Cool.

Whip egg whites until peaks form. Whip cream. Fold whipped cream into custard. Lightly fold in beaten whites.

Crush graham crackers. Blend butter and crumbs. Press into 9 or 10-inch pie plate. Pour in custard mixture. Sprinkle crumbs lightly on top. Freeze. Can be stored in freezer for several weeks.

Mrs. Julius Bergfeld

LEMON SNOW

1 pkg. unflavored gelatin
1/2 c. sugar
1/4 t. salt
1 1/4 c. hot water
1 can frozen lemonade
   concentrate, thawed
2 egg whites, unbeaten

Sauce:

3 egg yolks
2 T. sugar
Pinch of salt
1 c. scalded milk
1/4 t. vanilla

Combine gelatin, sugar, and salt. Stir and mix thoroughly. Add hot water and stir until gelatin is dissolved. Add lemonade and blend well. Chill until slightly thickened. Place bowl in ice, add unbeaten egg whites and beat with mixer until mixture forms soft peaks..Pour into 1 1/4 quart mold or individual molds. Chill until firm. Serve with soft custard sauce. Other concentrates may be substituted.

For sauce, beat egg yolks, add sugar, salt and mix well. Add scalded milk. Cook and stir constantly over hot water until mixture is thickened or coats a dry spoon. Pour into bowl and add vanilla. Pour over Lemon Snow when serving.

Mrs. R. K. Peters

LEMON CUSTARD MUFFINS

1 c. sugar
1/4 c. flour
1/8 t. salt
2 T. melted butter

Juice from 2 lemons
3 eggs, separated
1 1/2 c. milk
Sweetened whipped cream

Mix sugar, flour, salt; stir in melted butter, lemon juice, well beaten egg yolks and milk. Beat at medium speed until smooth and creamy; fold in stiffly beaten egg whites. Turn mixture into 8 greased custard cups; set in pan of hot water and bake at 325 degrees for 40 to 50 minutes. Cool; turn out and the custard will be on top. Serve with whipped cream. Serves 8.

Clementine Warren

LEMON SQUARES

1 c. butter
2 c. flour
1/2 c. powdered sugar
4 eggs
4 to 5 T. lemon juice

2 c. sugar
1 t. baking powder
4 T. flour
1/2 t. salt

Melt butter. Add flour and powdered sugar; mix and press down firmly in a 13 x 9 inch pan. Bake 20 minutes at 350 degrees. Meanwhile, beat together eggs and lemon juice. Sift together sugar, baking powder, flour, and salt. Add to egg mixture. Pour mixture on top of hot baked crust. Bake 25 minutes at 350 degrees. Powdered sugar may be sifted over top while hot. Cut in squares.

Mrs. W. H. Merrell, Jr.
Irving, Texas
Mrs. Kelly W. Walker

LEMON MOUSSE

1 c. whipping cream
1 envelope unflavored gelatin
2 T. water

1/3 c. lemon juice
4 eggs
1 c. sugar

Whip cream and refrigerate. Soften gelatin in water in a small saucepan. Heat slowly until gelatin is dissolved. Cool. Add lemon juice. Beat the eggs with the sugar until thick and lemon-colored. Beat in gelatin mixture. Fold in the whipped cream and pour into glasses. When set, garnish with whipped cream. Makes 8 servings.

Mrs. J. Torrey Forman

A very lovely, fancy dessert that's easy to make.

GRASSHOPPER MOUSSE

2 pkgs. unflavored gelatin
1 c. cold water
1 c. sugar
1/4 t. salt
6 eggs, separated

1/2 c. green creme de menthe
1/2 c. white creme de cacao
2 c. heavy cream, whipped
Chocolate cookie crumbs

Sprinkle gelatin over water in medium saucepan. Add 1/2 cup of the sugar, salt, and egg yolks; stir until thoroughly blended. Place over low heat; stir constantly until gelatin dissolves and mixture thickens slightly, about 5 to 10 minutes. Remove from heat; stir in creme de menthe and creme de cacao. Chill, stirring occasionally, until mixture mounds slightly when dropped from spoon. Beat egg whites in large bowl until stiff but not dry. Gradually add remaining 1/2 cup sugar and beat until very stiff. Fold in gelatin mixture. Fold in whipped cream. Turn into 12-cup buttered mold. Chill until firm. Unmold; garnish with additional whipped cream and sprinkle with chocolate cookie crumbs. Serves 20 to 24.

Mrs. C. R. Hurst

PUMPKIN MOUSSE

2 envelopes unflavored gelatin
1/2 c. cold water
1 c. sugar
4 egg yolks
1 can [16 oz.] pumpkin
1/2 t. salt
1/2 t. cinnamon
1/2 t. ginger

1/4 t. nutmeg
1/4 t. ground cloves
1 1/2 T. brown sugar
1/2 c. evaporated milk
1/4 c. rum
4 egg whites
1/4 t. cream of tartar
6 T. sugar

Sprinkle gelatin in water over low heat, stirring until dissolved, about 3 minutes. Set aside to cool. In saucepan, combine 1 cup sugar, egg yolks, pumpkin, salt, spices, brown sugar and milk and cook over medium heat, stirring constantly, until mixture simmers about 2 minutes. Cool; add gelatin mixture, then rum. Beat egg whites and cream of tartar until fluffy. Gradually add 6 tablespoons sugar and continue beating until whites are stiff but not dry. Fold egg whites into custard mixture and pour into a 1 quart mold which has been lightly greased with mayonnaise. Chill 12 hours or more. Serve with Rum-Orange Topping and sprinkle with toasted slivered almonds.

Rum-Orange Topping:

2 T. butter
1/4 c. powdered sugar
1 t. grated orange rind

1/2 c. heavy cream, whipped
2 T. rum

Combine butter, powdered sugar and orange rind. Fold into whipped cream and gently stir in rum.

Mrs. Arthur Cunningham

CHOCOLATE MOUSSE

3 eggs, separated
4 oz. German's Sweet chocolate
1 1/2 t. butter
1 1/2 T. hot water

1/4 c. heavy cream,
  whipped
2 1/2 T. sugar

Separate eggs. Beat yolks until light and fluffy. Melt chocolate and butter with water in a saucepan over low heat; cool to room temperature. Whip cream; fold in sugar. Beat egg whites until stiff. Fold all ingredients together until smooth. Turn into pie plate and chill, or place individual servings in demitasse cups. Top with more whipped cream. Serves 5 to 6.

Mrs. Joe Huffstuttler

MAPLE PARFAIT

6 egg yolks
3/4 c. pure maple syrup

2 egg whites
1 pt. cream

Beat egg yolks and add syrup to them. Cook in top of double boiler until thick, stirring constantly. Cool. Add whites to whipping cream and beat until stiff. Fold syrup mixture into cream. Pour into parfait glasses. Freeze. Serves 8.

Mrs. Wilbert Lasater

A traditional Christmas dessert. Delicious with fresh coconut cake or bourbon-soaked fruit cake.

PEACH MELBA PARFAITS

1 pkg. thawed frozen raspberries
1/2 c. currant jelly
1 1/2 t. cornstarch
1 T. cold water
Vanilla ice cream [2 pints or more]
Peach slices [canned; or frozen, slightly thawed;
  or fresh, lightly sugared]

Mash thawed raspberries with juice in saucepan; add currant jelly and bring to boil. Mix cornstarch with water; add to jelly mixture. Simmer, stirring until clear. Strain to remove berry seeds. Cool.

Make parfaits by layering sauce, peaches, ice cream, peaches, sauce, ice cream, peaches, sauce. Top with whipped cream if desired. Freeze. To serve, thaw 15 to 20 minutes. Makes eight 8 oz. parfaits, although recipe can easily be expanded by using more ice cream and less sauce and peaches.

Mrs. Michael Hatchell

This is really delicious, pretty and easy!!

ALMOND MACAROON PUDDING

1 qt. whole milk
1 small can evaporated milk
1/2 pt. whipping cream
5 eggs, separated
1 c. sugar

1 1/2 pkg. Knox gelatin
1 c. cold water
2 t. vanilla
1 1/2 doz. almond macaroon
   cookies

Heat milk and cream. Do not boil. Add well-beaten egg yolks and sugar, stirring constantly until custard begins to thicken. Remove from heat and add gelatin that has been dissolved in cold water. When cool, add stiffly beaten egg whites and vanilla. Line mold with almond macaroon cookies. Fill with custard and chill. Serve with whipped cream. You may garnish with fresh strawberries or peaches. Serves 12.

Mrs. Evans Estabrook

CHERRY ICEBOX PUDDING

1 c. sugar
1 small pkg. cherry Jello
4 eggs, separated
2 c. liquid [add water to
   cherry juice]

48 vanilla wafers,
   broken small
1 c. chopped pecans
1 can pitted cherries
1 pt. whipping cream

Mix sugar, Jello and beaten egg yolks with liquid and boil 2 or 3 minutes. Cool. Add broken wafers, nuts and cherries and stir lightly, but thoroughly. Fold in beaten egg whites. Place in refrigerator overnight. Top each serving with heaping teaspoon whipped cream.

Mrs. Billy Hall

DATE-NUT PUDDING

1 pkg. Dromedary dates,
   chopped fine
1/2 stick margarine
1 t. baking soda

1 c. sugar
1 c. flour
1 egg
1 c. chopped nuts

Pour 1 cup boiling water over first three ingredients and let stand until margarine melts. Add next four ingredients and bake 45 minutes at 300 degrees in a greased 2 quart oblong pyrex pan.

Mrs. Robert E. Henry

CHRISTMAS PUDDING

2 T. unflavored gelatin
1 c. cold milk
2 c. milk
2/3 c. sugar
5 egg yolks
3 T. ground almonds
1/4 lb. macaroons or vanilla
    wafers, broken

2/3 c. maraschino cherries
    [red and green are
    prettier]
2 t. vanilla
1 T. brandy or rum
5 egg whites
1/8 t. salt

Soak the gelatin in 1 cup cold milk. Scald 2 cups milk in double boiler. Add sugar; beat and stir in the egg yolks. Cook and stir these ingredients for a minute or two - just enough to let the egg yolks thicken slightly. Stir in the gelatin mixture until it is dissolved. Add almonds, cookies and cherries. Allow the mixture to cool, then add vanilla and rum or brandy. Whip the egg whites until firm and fold lightly into other mixture and place the pudding in a wet mold. Chill well. Unmold onto plate; garnish with maraschino cherries and surround with holly sprigs. Serve with whipped cream. Serves 10 to 12.

Mrs. Russell B. Watson, Jr.

STEAMED CRANBERRY PUDDING

2 c. raw cranberries, halved
1/4 c. white corn syrup
1/4 c. black molasses
1/3 c. hot water

2 t. baking soda
1 1/2 c. flour
1 egg, beaten

Mix ingredients in order. Place in greased mold with tight cover or in greased loaf pan, covering with foil and holding foil in place with rubber band. Steam for 1 1/2 to 2 hours. May use a trivet in a Dutch oven and partially cover. Place hot water in Dutch oven, the level to be about half way up the loaf pan while bubbling gently.

Sauce:

1 c. sugar
1/2 c. butter

1/2 c. cream

Mix sauce ingredients and simmer until well-blended. Serve pudding warm with hot sauce. Serves 12.

Mrs. Madison J. Lee

May be prepared several days in advance and frozen. To freeze, turn out of pan and wrap in foil. Reheat before serving by resteaming, or dampen and heat in top of double boiler.

ENGLISH TOFFEE PUDDING

2 c. powdered sugar
2 T. cocoa
1/4 t. salt [omit if
  margarine is used]
1/2 c. butter or margarine

2 eggs, separated
1 c. chopped pecans
1 t. vanilla
1 pkg. vanilla wafers

Sift sugar, cocoa and salt together, then cream with butter. Add egg yolks, nuts and vanilla. Fold in beaten egg whites. Line pan (8 x 8 x 2 inches) with waxed paper and then with crushed vanilla wafer crumbs. Pour mixture on top of crumbs and top with more crumbs. Chill 4 to 6 hours or overnight. Makes 16 two inch squares.

Mrs. John Minton

FUDGE PUDDING

2 eggs
1 c. sugar
1/2 c. melted butter
1 heaping T. cocoa

1 c. nuts
2 scant T. flour
Pinch salt

Beat eggs and sugar. Add melted butter and cocoa. Add nuts, then other ingredients. Pour into a greased 9-inch square pan. Bake in a pan of hot water for 30 minutes at 350 degrees. Serve in squares topped with whipped cream. The bottom will be creamy and top crusty. Can be easily doubled and made in larger pan (approximately 9 x 13 inches). Serves 6.

Mrs. Jack M. King
Mrs. Bud Price

AUNTY'S LEMON PUDDING

1 lg. can evaporated milk
3 eggs
1/3 c. lemon juice
3/4 c. sugar

Medium pkg. vanilla
  wafers, crushed
Whipped cream for
  topping

Place milk in freezer for 30 minutes to chill. Separate eggs. Combine yolks, lemon juice and sugar and beat well. Beat whites until stiff and combine with first mixture in top of double boiler; cook 7 minutes, stirring constantly. Remove from heat.

Whip chilled milk until rather stiff and fold into cooked mixture. Pour into pyrex dish (1 1/2 to 2 quart) lined with wafer crumbs and top with wafer crumbs. Chill; cut into squares and serve topped with whipped cream.

Mrs. Watson Simons

LEMON SPONGE PUDDING

3 eggs, separated
Grated rind of 1 lemon
Juice of 1 1/2 lemons

1 c. sugar
2 T. flour
1 c. milk

Beat egg yolks until thick. Add rind and juice of lemons. Add sugar, flour and milk slowly. Beat egg whites until they form soft peaks and fold into mixture. Pour into 6 individual dishes or into a shallow baking dish. Set in pan of cold water and bake at 325 degrees for 45 minutes. This will have sponge top and custard base. Serves 6.

Mrs. W. F. Bridewell, Jr.

MONTEGO BAY COCONUT PUDDING

Pudding:

3/4 c. soft butter or
   margarine
1/2 t. ground mace
3/4 c. sugar
1 egg, beaten

3 egg yolks
3 c. finely grated fresh
   coconut
1 1/4 c. light cream
1 t. vanilla

Cream butter, mace and sugar together until fluffy. Add egg, yolks, coconut, cream and vanilla; mix well and pour into 8 buttered individual baking dishes (fill 3/4 full). Bake in pan of hot water in 350 degree preheated oven for 45 minutes or until firm. Remove from oven and cool. Top with Lime Meringue and return to 325 degree oven for 15 minutes. Serve with Cream and Brandy Sauce below.

Lime Meringue:

3 egg whites
9 T. sugar

1 1/2 T. lime juice
1/2 t. vanilla

Beat egg whites and add sugar gradually. Add lime juice and vanilla and continue beating until sugar is dissolved and the mixture holds stiff peaks. Spoon onto desserts and bake.

Cream and Brandy Sauce:

1/2 pt. whipping cream
1/4 c. brandy

Whip cream until stiff; fold in brandy. Total recipe serves 8.

Mrs. Fred Bosworth

MOTHER'S ICEBOX PUDDING

Layer I:
3/4 lb. vanilla wafers
1/2 c. butter
1 c. powdered sugar

3 eggs, separated
1 c. [or more] chopped
   pecans

Crush vanilla wafers and cover the bottom of a buttered 2 quart casserole with a thick layer of crumbs. Cream butter and powdered sugar; add well-beaten egg yolks and pecans and mix well. Beat egg whites to stiff peaks and fold into mixture. Spread over crumbs, top with more crumbs and Layer II.

Layer II:
1 c. powdered sugar
1/2 c. cocoa

4 T. boiling water
3 eggs, separated

Combine powdered sugar, cocoa, and boiling water. Add well-beaten egg yolks and fold in stiffly beaten egg whites. Spread over crumbs on Layer I and top with thin layer of wafer crumbs. Cover with Saran or foil and refrigerate at least 12 hours before serving. Cut in squares to serve 12.

Mrs. Woodson Nash
Kaufman, Texas

PLUM PUDDING

6 c. flour
5 t. baking powder
1 t. cinnamon
1 t. nutmeg
1 t. allspice
1 t. ground cloves
1 1/2 lbs. currants
1/2 lb. cut raisins
1 c. chopped pecans
1 c. chopped dates
1 lb. candied fruits

1/2 c. candied citron,
   cut small
1 lb. ground suet
10 eggs, beaten
3/4 c. milk
Juice and grated rind of
   1 lemon
3/4 c. brown sugar
Brandy, rum, apricot liqueur
   [whatever preferred]

Combine flour, baking powder and spices and sift together. Chop nuts and fruits (may be ground in food grinder if desired) and toss all with the dry ingredients. Combine all other ingredients and mix together well, then stir in fruits-flour mixture. Grease and line with paper (parchment is best, but waxed paper may be used) 6 coffee cans (1 pound size) or pudding molds. Fill 1/2 to 3/4 full, cover with paper and tie with string. Steam about 5 hours over medium heat in large covered roaster with cans on rack over simmering water. Cool and remove from cans. Wrap in brandy or rum soaked cheese cloth and return to cans. Store in refrigerator for at least 3 weeks. To serve, steam for one hour (or heat in top of double boiler after sprinkling with water). At the table, brandy may be poured over the pudding and lighted. Cut into small servings and top with hard sauce.

Mrs. L. G. Skillman
Kalamazoo, Michigan

PINEAPPLE CREAM PUDDING

1 can [1 lb. 4 1/2 oz.] crushed
  pineapple
1 pkg. [3 oz.] orange-
  pineapple gelatin

1 c. sour cream

Drain pineapple; place syrup in saucepan; reserve pineapple. Bring syrup to boiling point; add gelatin; stir until it dissolves. Combine pineapple and cream in blender and whirl until completely blended. Add gelatin mixture, blend well. Pour in individual molds and serve with whipped cream.

Mrs. Joe Huffstutler

HOT CHOCOLATE SOUFFLÉ

2 sq. unsweetened chocolate
2 c. milk
1/2 c. sugar
1/2 c. flour
1/2 t. salt

2 T. butter
1 t. vanilla
4 egg yolks, beaten thick
4 egg whites, beaten stiff

Add chocolate to milk and heat in double boiler. When chocolate is melted, beat with rotary beater until well-blended. Combine sugar, flour and salt. Add small amount chocolate mixture to dry ingredients, stirring until smooth. Return to double boiler with remaining chocolate mixture and cook, stirring constantly, until thickened. Continue cooking 5 minutes, add butter, vanilla and cool. Add egg yolks and mix well. Carefully stir in egg whites, and turn into greased baking dish. Place dish in pan of hot water and bake 1 hour and 10 minutes in preheated oven, 350 degrees. Serve with hot chocolate sauce. Serves 8 to 10.

Mrs. Dan C. Woldert

RASPBERRY DESSERT

1 can Eagle Brand milk
1/2 c. lemon juice
1/2 pt. cream, whipped
4 T. raspberry jam [Smucker's
  Seedless Black Raspberry
  Preserves]

1 c. nuts, coarsely
  chopped
1 box graham cracker
  crumbs

Combine Eagle Brand milk and lemon juice. Fold in whipped cream, raspberry jam and nuts. Put a layer of graham cracker crumbs on bottom of oblong pyrex dish (12 x 7 1/2 inch size). Pour in pudding. Sprinkle a generous layer of crumbs on top and refrigerate. Cut in squares. Top with a spoonful of whipped cream. Serves 9.

Mrs. Watson Simons

For a special touch, top with crushed candied violets.

RED HOT APPLES

2 c. sugar
2 c. water

1 pkg. [8 oz.] red hots
4 lbs. apples

Boil sugar, water and red hots, until red hots are melted. Peel and quarter apples. Cook in red hot mixture until soft but not falling apart. Serve hot or cold.

Mrs. Jack M. King

SWEDISH FRUIT SOUP

1 lb. mixed dried fruit
8 oz. dried apricots
2 c. red wine
8 c. water
1 can sour red cherries
1 lemon, sliced thin
1 c. sugar
Dash of salt
1/8 t. mace
1/3 c. Kirsch

3 sticks cinnamon
4 whole cloves
1/8 t. allspice
1/4 t. nutmeg
1 whole cardamom seed
1/4 t. ground coriander
    seeds [optional]
1 1/4 T. cornstarch mixed
    with 3 T. cold water

Place all ingredients except cornstarch in a soup kettle, cover tightly, and let simmer until fruit is done. (If fruits are soaked overnight or a few hours, they will cook in 1/2 hour; otherwise cooking time will be about 1 hour.) Taste for seasonings, adding more sugar or spices if desired. Thicken by adding cornstarch the last 2 minutes of cooking. Serves 16. Freezes well.

Mrs. George Echols
Lafayette, Louisiana

 Strawberries or any favorite fruit could be added. This is a great light finish to a heavy meal. Men like it because it isn't too sweet.

STRAWBERRY ALASKA

Bag of frozen strawberries or
    2 pts. fresh strawberries
1 pt. vanilla ice cream

5 egg whites
10 T. sugar
Powdered sugar

Thaw strawberries; if using fresh berries, wash and hull. Place in the bottom of a deep 2 quart baking dish. Just before ready to serve, spoon ice cream over berries. Whip egg whites until stiff; slowly add sugar, continuing to beat. Lightly spoon meringue on top of ice cream and berries. Sprinkle with a little powdered sugar. Bake in very hot oven, 525 degrees, until browned, about 5 minutes. Serve immediately. Serves 8 to 10.

Leave any that is left over in baking dish and freeze, but partially thaw before serving. This can be varied with any fruit and size changed easily.

Mrs. John F. Warren

 For added elegance, try serving in champagne glasses.

STRAWBERRY DELIGHT FREEZE

1 c. strawberries, sliced
Sugar to taste
1 pkg. gelatin
1/2 c. water

6 ice cubes, crushed
2 t. lemon juice
1 egg white

Add sugar to sliced strawberries and set aside. Dissolve gelatin in water. Place all ingredients, except egg white, in blender. Blend a few seconds. Pour in sherbet glasses. Top with stiffly beaten egg white and garnish with sprig of mint.

Mrs. Gordon Brelsford

 A good diet dessert.

STRAWBERRY ANGEL FOOD DESSERT

1 pkg. Duncan Hines angel
food cake mix [made and
cooled] or 1 prepared
angel food cake
2 pkg. [10 oz.] frozen sliced
strawberries
1 pkg. [3 oz.] strawberry
Jello

1/2 c. sugar
1 c. hot water
1 c. whipping cream,
whipped
Whole fresh strawberries
for garnish

Thaw and drain strawberries (save juice). Dissolve Jello and sugar in hot water. Add 1 cup of reserved juice from strawberries. Chill until slightly thickened.

Cut cake in 1-inch slices. Arrange one-half in a 13 x 9 x 2 inch dish. Fold berries into Jello mixture. Pour half of mixture over cake in dish. Add rest of cake, then rest of Jello. Chill until set.

Spread whipped cream on top and garnish with fresh strawberries. Serves 12 to 15.

Mrs. Joe Max Green
Nacogdoches, Texas

STRAWBERRIES ROMANOFF

2 boxes [1 pt.] fresh
strawberries
1 c. powdered sugar

1 c. heavy cream
1 t. almond or vanilla extract
2 T. cointreau or orange juice

Wash, drain and hull berries. Place in medium size bowl, sprinkle sugar over berries and toss gently. Chill for 1 hour, stirring occasionally. Whip cream until stiff, fold in extract and cointreau. Fold cream mixture into berries. Serve at once.

Mrs. Albert Morriss

BLACK FOREST TORTE

Cake Layers:

1 3/4 c. unsifted flour
1 3/4 c. sugar
1 1/4 t. soda
1 t. salt
1/4 t. baking powder
2/3 c. soft-type margarine,
  containing liquid
  safflower oil
1 1/4 c. water
1 t. vanilla
4 squares [1 oz. each]
  unsweetened chocolate,
  melted and cooled
3 eggs

Filling and Topping:

2 pkgs. [4 oz.] German's
  Sweet Chocolate
1/2 c. soft-type margarine
1/2 c. toasted sliced almonds
2 c. heavy cream
1 T. sugar
1 t. vanilla
Flaked coconut, candied
  cherries and angelica

Measure flour, sugar, soda, salt, baking powder, margarine, water and vanilla into large mixer bowl. Add melted chocolate. Beat at low speed to blend, then beat two minutes at medium speed, scraping sides and bottom of bowl frequently. Add eggs; beat two minutes longer. Brush sides and bottom of four 9-inch layer cake pans with soft-type margarine. (Two layers may be baked while the remaining batter stands.) Pour one-fourth batter (little over one cup) into each pan. Layer will be thin. Bake in 350 degree oven 17 to 20 minutes until wooden pick comes out clean. Cool slightly and remove from pan. Cool completely.

Melt chocolate over hot water. Cool. Blend in soft-type margarine and almonds. Whip cream with sugar and vanilla until stiff. Place bottom layer on serving plate. Spread half chocolate mixture over it. Add second layer and half whipped cream. Repeat layers, having whipped cream on top. Do not frost sides. Sprinkle coconut over top. Garnish with cherries and angelica. Cover with plastic food wrap and refrigerate until ready to serve. Serves 16.

Mrs. Allen Locklin

BLUEBERRY TORTE

16 graham crackers
1/3 c. butter
1 c. sugar
1 pkg. [8 oz.] cream cheese

2 eggs
1 can [1 lb. 6 oz.] blue-
  berry pie filling

Preheat oven to 350 degrees. Crush graham crackers with rolling pin and mix crumbs with melted butter and 1/2 cup sugar. Pat firmly onto bottom of 8-inch square baking pan.

Blend cream cheese and 1/2 cup sugar together until soft. Add eggs one at a time, beating well after each. Pour over crumbs and bake 25 to 30 minutes. Cool and then spoon blueberry pie filling over top.

Chill overnight. Top with whipped cream. Cut into 2-inch squares. Serves 8.

Mrs. William E. Bertram

FRENCH STRAWBERRY TORTE

Torte:

1 1/3 c. all-purpose
  biscuit mix
3/4 c. sugar
3 T. shortening
1 egg
3/4 c. milk
1 t. vanilla

1 1/2 c. strawberries
1 c. whipping cream

Glaze:

1/2 c. strawberries
1/4 c. water
1/4 c. sugar
1 T. cornstarch
1 T. water

Heat oven to 350 degrees. Grease and flour a 9-inch round layer pan. Mix biscuit mix and sugar. Add shortening, egg and 1/4 cup of the milk. Beat 1 minute at medium speed on electric mixer. Add remaining milk and vanilla. Beat 1/2 minute longer. Pour into pan and bake 35 to 40 minutes. Allow to cool 5 minutes, then remove from pan. Cool.

To prepare glaze, simmer 1/2 cup strawberries with 1/4 cup water for 3 minutes or until berries start to break up. Blend sugar, cornstarch and 1 tablespoon water; add to boiling mixture. Cook, stirring constantly, until mixture thickens and boils. Boil and stir 1 minute. Cool.

Invert cake on serving plate; arrange 1 1/2 cups strawberries on top of cake; pour glaze over strawberries and put whipped cream on top. Refrigerate. Serves 6 to 8.

Mrs. C. R. Hurst

May be made with blueberries, blackberries or peaches.

SUNDAY SPECIAL TORTE

1 c. butter or margarine
1 1/2 c. sugar
5 eggs, separated
2 T. milk
2 t. vanilla
3/4 t. salt

1/2 t. baking powder
2 c. sifted flour
1 c. raspberry preserves
1 can [3 1/2 oz.] flaked
  coconut
2 c. sour cream

Cream butter or margarine. Add 1/2 cup sugar. Cream well and blend in yolks, milk, 1 teaspoon vanilla, 1/2 teaspoon salt and the baking powder. Beat well; stir in flour. Spread in three 9-inch round pans, greased on the bottom. Spread 1/3 cup of preserves on each layer to within one inch of edge.

Beat egg whites and 1/4 teaspoon salt until slight mounds form. Gradually add one cup sugar and beat well after each addition. Continue beating until stiff peaks form. Fold in coconut and 1 teaspoon vanilla. Spread over preserves. Bake at 350 degrees for 35 to 40 minutes. Cool 15 minutes, remove from pans, and cool completely.

Spread sour cream between layers. Garnish on top with cream and preserves. Chill several hours.

Mrs. E. Davis Wilcox

HEAVENLY HOT FUDGE SAUCE

4 squares Baker's unsweetened
   chocolate
1/4 lb. margarine or butter

3 c. sugar
Pinch of salt
1 large can evaporated milk

Melt chocolate and margarine in the top of a double boiler. Add sugar a little at a time, blending thoroughly after each addition. Add salt and evaporated milk in the same manner.

Mrs. R. Don Cowan

LEMON CREAM SAUCE

3/4 c. sugar
Juice of 1 orange
2 T. flour, mixed with enough
   water to make a paste
2 eggs

Juice and grated
   rind of 1 lemon
1/2 pt. whipping cream,
   whipped

Mix thoroughly all ingredients except cream. Cook in double boiler until thickened. Cool. Add whipped cream. Delicious over angel food cake.

Mrs. Gene Caldwell

Fun for the children to make.

MOTHER WARREN'S BRANDY SAUCE

1 c. sugar
1 c. butter
2 egg yolks, beaten

1 c. boiling water
Brandy or whiskey to
   taste

Cream the sugar and butter; add the beaten egg yolks and boiling water. Stir together in top of double boiler. Cook until thickened, stirring constantly. Add brandy or whiskey to taste. Pour over pound cake, custard, angel food cake, or whatever dessert preferred.

Mrs. H. L. Goodson
Gladewater, Texas

Candies
and
Cookies

CANDIED GRAPEFRUIT PEEL

3 c. cut grapefruit peel
   [rinds from about 3 grapefruit]
2 c. sugar
1 c. water
1/8 t. salt

1 t. or more red food coloring
   [other color if desired]
1/2 T. gelatin dissolved in
   1 T. cold water
Granulated sugar for rolling

To prepare peel: After fruit has been discarded, remove membrane from halves of grapefruit. Grate outside of peel slightly to open pores and release bitter oils. Starting with cold water each time, bring peel to boil 3 different times. After third boiling, scrape out excess white and cut peel into strips approximately 3/8 inch by 2 1/2 inches.

To candy peel: Cook peel, sugar, water, salt and coloring until it spins a thread (most of the liquid is consumed and the peel is evenly colored - about 15 minutes). Remove from heat. Add gelatin dissolved in 1 tablespoon water. Cool slightly, drain in slotted spoon, roll in granulated sugar and place on waxed paper or cake rack to cool completely. Store in tightly covered containers. If peel absorbs sugar, reroll before serving.

Yield: Tons of candied peel; probably would be adequate for 40 to 50 party-goers.

Mrs. C. Aubrey Smith, Jr.

Prior to preparation, preserve rinds in refrigerator.

CANDIED STRAWBERRIES

2 boxes [6 oz.] strawberry
   Jello
1 c. sweetened condensed milk
2 t. vanilla
2 c. finely chopped nuts
1 c. grated coconut

2 t. red food coloring
Slivered almonds [soaked
   in 3 drops green coloring
   and 1/2 t. water]
Red granulated sugar

Mix first 6 ingredients thoroughly; chill in refrigerator. Color almonds and drain. Shape Jello mixture into strawberries; roll in red sugar and insert almond "stems". Dry on waxed paper; store in airtight container.

Variations: Orange or lemon Jello, using appropriate food colorings and shapes; slivers of green candied cherries may be substituted for almonds. May be frozen.

Mrs. Hoyt Berryman, Jr.

Fun and easy enough for children!

DATE LOAF CANDY

2 c. sugar
2/3 c. milk [evaporated for
  extra richness]
1 T. margarine or butter

1 pkg. [8 oz.] chopped dates
1 c. chopped pecans
Powdered sugar [to roll]

In heavy saucepan, combine sugar, milk and butter. Cook over moderate heat until firm ball stage. Add chopped dates and stir thoroughly. Remove from heat; beat until creamy; stir in pecans.

Pour candy out on slightly dampened tea towel; knead like bread 5 minutes. Form into roll; roll in powdered sugar; wrap in waxed paper and aluminum foil. Chill. Slice in 1/4 inch slices and serve. May be kept refrigerated several days.

Mrs. Bill C. Ross

For ease in handling, when forming roll, dust hands with powdered sugar.

APRICOT BALLS

2 oranges
1 lb. dried apricots

2 c. sugar
1 c. chopped pecans

Peel oranges, being careful not to peel off white membrane. Grind apricots and orange peel together. Place in saucepan and add juice from oranges and sugar. Cook together for about 10 minutes, stirring constantly. Remove from heat and add nuts, then pour onto platter to cool. Form into balls and roll in granulated sugar. Makes about 8 dozen 1-inch balls.

Mrs. Carl Greer

DATE BALLS "AUNT RUBY"

1 stick margarine
3/4 c. sugar
1/2 lb. pitted dates, chopped
1 T. white Karo syrup
1 egg
1 T. milk

1 t. vanilla
1/2 t. salt
2 1/2 c. Rice Krispies
1 c. chopped nuts
Coconut

Melt the margarine and sugar in large saucepan and mix well. Then add pitted dates and Karo syrup. Bring to boil, stirring constantly. Remove from heat and set aside. Combine the well-beaten egg, milk, vanilla and salt in mixing bowl. Mix with first mixture and boil 2 minutes, stirring constantly. Cool slightly and add Rice Krispies and nuts. Mix well and shape in balls the size of walnuts. Roll in coconut. Place on wax paper and refrigerate until ready to use.

Ruby Wood Boone
Marshall, Texas

ORANGE BALLS

1 can [6 oz.] frozen
   orange juice
1 box [1 lb.] vanilla
   wafers, crushed

1 box powdered sugar
1 stick melted margarine
1 can coconut

Mix the orange juice, vanilla wafers, powdered sugar and melted margarine. Form into balls. Roll in coconut.

Mrs. Charles Clark

Try these for brunch.

ORANGE CREAM CANDY

1 c. sugar
1/4 c. boiling water
2 c. sugar
1 c. evaporated milk
Few grains salt
Grated rind of 1 1/2 oranges
   [Spice Islands can be used]

Grated rind of 1/2 lemon
   [Spice Islands can be used]
2 T. butter
1 c. nuts

To caramelize sugar, place 1 cup sugar in heavy skillet and cook over low heat, stirring constantly. When sugar has completely melted and has turned light brown in color, add the boiling water and cook until heavy syrup is formed, about 4 to 5 minutes. Add the 2 cups sugar, evaporated milk and salt. Cook until it forms a firm ball in cold water or reaches a temperature of 242 degrees on candy thermometer. (May curdle here, but will come out creamy and smooth when beaten.) Just before candy is done, add orange and lemon rind. Remove from heat. Add butter and let stand until cool. Beat until creamy. Add chopped nuts, and continue beating until candy holds its shape. Turn into a buttered 8-inch square pan. When completely cooled, cut into squares. Let stand in pan several hours before removing. Makes 30 to 40 pieces of candy.

Mrs. Ralph R. Hanson

MINTS

4 T. butter or margarine
1/8 t. salt
1 lb. powdered sugar

3 T. cream
5 drops oil of peppermint
Food coloring as desired

Cream butter. Work salt and sugar into butter, adding the cream as needed. Put in oil of peppermint and coloring. Dough should be workable but fairly stiff. Add sugar to thicken or cream to thin. Roll on surface dusted with powdered sugar and cut with tiny aspic cutter or run through pastry tube. Store in fruit cake tin between layers of waxed paper. Makes about 200 mints the size of a quarter.

Mrs. C. Aubrey Smith, Jr.

TURKISH DELIGHT

3/4 c. fresh orange juice
3 T. gelatin
2 c. sugar
1/2 c. water
Rind of 2 oranges, grated
2 T. lemon juice

1 c. green candied pineapple, cut small
1 c. red candied cherries, quartered
1 c. pecans, chopped

Mix orange juice and gelatin. Soak for 5 minutes. Stir sugar in water. Boil until clear. Add the sugar and water mixture to orange juice-gelatin mixture and boil slowly for 20 minutes. Slowly add orange rind, lemon juice, pineapple, cherries and pecans. Pour into a 9 x 9 inch pan. Place in refrigerator until set (overnight). Cut in squares and roll in granulated sugar.

Mrs. Frank Fite

This will keep for months in an airtight container in refrigerator.

CRYSTAL CUT CANDIES

2 c. sugar
1/2 c. light corn syrup
1/2 c. water
Dash salt
Few drops red or green
food coloring

4 to 6 drops oil of cinnamon or oil of wintergreen [may be purchased at drug store]

Combine sugar, syrup, water and salt. Bring to boiling in heavy saucepan. Cook, without stirring, to hard crack stage (290 degrees). Add food coloring and flavoring - gently swirl to blend (use red with cinnamon or green with winter-green). Pour into 8 x 8 x 2 inch metal pan, lightly greased. Let stand a few minutes till a film forms over the top.

Using a metal spatula, mark candy into little puffs about 3/4 inch square - being careful not to break through film. Work from pan edge to center; candy cools at edges first. As candy cools, retrace lines, pressing deeper each time, but not breaking film. Continue until spatula can touch bottom in all lines. Let cool completely; turn out on wax paper and break into pieces. Makes 100 puffs.

Mrs. Joe D. Clayton

Tips: Candy thermometer is a MUST. If lines will not hold marks at first, candy is not cool enough, but once it starts cooling, it cools fast, so retrace lines quickly.

CHOCOLATE CANDY

3 pkgs. German's chocolate
1 pkg. [16 oz.] marshmallows
1 T. water
1 T. butter

1 1/2 t. vanilla
3 to 4 c. salted,
toasted pecans

Melt chocolate in top of double boiler. Add marshmallows, water, butter, vanilla and pecans. Drop from a teaspoon. Chill in refrigerator. Makes 4 to 5 dozen pieces.

Mrs. Clarence T. Melton
Troup, Texas

TEXAS MILLIONAIRES

1 pkg. Kraft caramels
2 T. water
2 c. chopped pecans

8 [1.26 oz.] Hershey bars
1/3 bar paraffin

Melt caramels with water in top of double boiler. Add pecans and drop by teaspoons on waxed paper or cookie sheet. Place in freezer until firm and candy will peel off paper.

Melt Hershey bars and paraffin in double boiler. Working with a few at a time, remove candy from freezer, dip into chocolate and place on buttered waxed paper.

Mrs. Hoyt Berryman, Jr.

TOFFEE CRUNCH

2 sticks margarine [1/2 lb.]
1 c. sugar
2 T. water
1 T. light corn syrup

1/2 c. semi-sweet
chocolate pieces
2/3 c. chopped pecans

In 2 quart heavy saucepan, over low heat, melt margarine. Add sugar and stir until melted. Stir in water and syrup. Continue cooking over low heat without stirring, until 1 teaspoon of mixture is brittle when dropped into cup of cold water (290 degrees on candy thermometer). Pour at once into shallow buttered pan. Cool. Place chocolate over hot, not boiling, water until soft. Stir to blend, spread over cool candy. Sprinkle with nuts, patting them down. To serve, chip candy into irregular pieces.

Mrs. Moliere Scarborough, Jr.

Mrs. John B. White, III, of Jacksonville, prepares her English Toffee by spreading the pecans into an unbuttered 10 x 15 inch pan and pouring the cooked candy mixture over them. She uses a large (8 oz.) milk chocolate bar, finely grated, to sprinkle over the warm candy mixture (instead of melted semi-sweet chocolate).

OLD-FASHIONED BUTTER CRUNCH

2 c. finely chopped almonds
1 c. butter
1 1/4 c. sugar
2 T. light corn syrup

2 T. water
1 pkg. [12 oz.] semi-sweet
   chocolate chips, melted

Spread almonds in a shallow pan; toast in a moderate oven (350 degrees) until golden. Melt butter in a large heavy saucepan; add sugar, corn syrup and water. Stir often while cooking to hard crack stage, 300 degrees on candy thermometer. Remove from heat and add 1 cup toasted almonds. Pour quickly into 13 x 9 x 2 inch pan. Cool completely. When set, turn out on waxed paper. Spread half of melted chocolate over top. Sprinkle with 1/2 cup almonds and let set. Turn candy over, spread with remaining chocolate and sprinkle with remaining almonds. Let stand until chocolate sets. Break into pieces.

Mrs. Robert E. Knox, Jr.

ROCKY ROAD

2 [10 oz.] Hershey bars
1 1/2 c. miniature marshmallows

1/2 c. chopped pecans

Melt chocolate in covered top of double boiler over hot (not boiling) water. Pour half of chocolate into buttered pan (8 x 10 inch). Top with marshmallows. Mix nuts into remaining chocolate and pour over marshmallows. Refrigerate until firm. Cut into squares. Makes 15 large squares.

Mrs. Joe D. Clayton

GOOF BALL CANDY

1 can Eagle Brand milk
1 stick butter or margarine
2 boxes powdered sugar
3 c. pecans or walnuts,
   finely chopped

2 cans Angel Flake coconut
2 pkgs. [12 oz.] chocolate
   chips
1/4 lb. paraffin

Mix milk, butter, sugar, nuts and coconut together until smooth. (May have to mix with hands.) Form into balls and set aside. Melt chocolate chips and paraffin in top of double boiler. Dip balls with a toothpick into this mixture and place on waxed paper. These will keep very nicely for about 2 weeks without refrigeration. For longer storage, refrigerate.

Mrs. Buddy Rogers

Mrs. Charles Clark varies by using 1 (11 oz.) jar cherries, finely chopped, only 1 can coconut, 2 cups pecans and 1 large and 1 small package chocolate chips, and places in freezer before dipping in chocolate.

FUDGE

3 c. sugar
3/4 c. margarine
2/3 c. evaporated milk
1 pkg. [12 oz.] chocolate chips

1 jar [7 oz.] Kraft Marshmallow
  Cream
1 c. chopped pecans
1 t. vanilla

Combine sugar, margarine and milk. Bring to boil. Stir. Boil 5 minutes. Scorches easily, so watch out! Remove from heat, stir in chocolates until melted. Add marshmallow cream, nuts and vanilla. Beat until blended. Pour into greased 13 x 9 inch pan. Cool. Cut in squares.

Mrs. James E. Bass

Mrs. Joe D. Clayton's larger recipe, cooked in a 6 to 8 quart saucepan, includes 4 1/2 c. sugar, 1 T. butter, 13 oz. can evaporated milk, 12 oz. chocolate pieces, 3 (4 1/2 oz.) plain Hershey bars, 2 jars marshmallow cream, 2 c. pecans and 1 t. vanilla. Prepare as above, drop spoonfuls of mixture on waxed paper; let stand 4 hours. Makes 6 pounds.

FUDGE NUT CRUNCH

1/2 c. [or more] chopped nuts
2/3 c. firmly packed brown
  sugar

1/2 c. butter
1 pkg. [6 oz.] chocolate chips

Sprinkle nuts over bottom of lightly greased 8-inch square pan. Combine sugar and butter in medium saucepan; bring to rolling boil, stirring constantly. Boil 4 to 5 minutes (or to 270 degrees). Pour over nuts in pan. Sprinkle with chips. Cover for 2 minutes; then evenly spread "fudge". Chill until firm. Remove from pan and break or cut into pieces. Yields about 1 pound.

Mrs. D. P. Harris
Austin, Texas

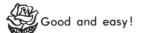Good and easy!

PEANUT BUTTER FUDGE

1 box powdered sugar
1/2 c. milk
1/2 c. margarine

10 oz. jar peanut butter
10 oz. jar marshmallow whip

Combine sugar, milk and margarine and boil 5 minutes. Remove from heat and stir in peanut butter and marshmallow whip. Pour into baking pan and cool.

Mrs. Joe Bill Belue

Fun and easy enough for children!

PEANUT BRITTLE

1 c. white corn syrup
2 c. sugar
1/2 c. water
2 c. raw Spanish peanuts

1 1/2 t. butter
1 1/2 t. vanilla
2 t. soda

Place the syrup, sugar, and water in a deep heavy pan and cook to 240 degrees on a candy thermometer. Add the peanuts, stir, and cook these ingredients to the crack stage - 301 degrees. Remove from heat and stir in butter, vanilla and soda. Stir until blended and pour onto greased surface - either marble or a couple of large cookie sheets. Sprinkle with salt.

As candy begins to cool a little, pull and stretch quickly to make as thin as possible. (Don't wait very long before beginning to pull and stretch). When cool, break into pieces and put in covered tin. This will keep a long time if contained in a closed tin.

Mrs. Bruce Brookshire

BUTTERMILK PRALINES

1 c. buttermilk
3 c. sugar [white]
1 t. soda

3 T. butter or margarine
1 c. broken pecans
1 t. vanilla

Combine buttermilk, sugar and soda in a large pot and cook to soft ball stage. Mixture will foam and turn a light brown color. Add butter and allow to cool for 3 minutes; then beat until creamy. Add pecans and vanilla. Drop by spoonfuls on waxed paper.

Mrs. John F. Warren

NEW ORLEANS PRALINES

1 c. brown sugar
1 c. white sugar
5 T. boiling water

1/2 stick butter
1 c. pecans
1 t. vanilla

Place sugars, water and butter in pan over high heat. Boil 2 minutes or to soft ball stage. Remove from heat and add pecans and vanilla. Beat until mixture becomes creamy and begins to sugar on the side of the pan. Then drop from spoon onto waxed paper.

Mrs. Frank Budde

Mrs. Glen Dyer suggests using a can (6 ounce) of evaporated milk instead of the water and adding 2 tablespoons of light corn syrup. She cooks sugar, syrup and milk to soft ball stage; then adds 1/2 teaspoon soda, 2 tablespoons butter (instead of 1/2 stick), vanilla and pecans, and beats as described above.

QUICK PRALINES

1 pkg. butterscotch
   instant pudding
1/2 c. evaporated milk
1 c. white sugar
1/2 c. brown sugar

1 T. butter
1 1/2 c. pecan halves [or
   1 1/2 c. toasted chopped
pecans]

Combine the pudding mix, milk, sugars and butter and cook over low heat to soft ball stage (235 degrees on candy thermometer). Remove from heat; add pecans and beat until mixture thickens and becomes creamy. Drop by spoonfuls on waxed paper.

Mrs. James E. Bass
Mrs. Joe Huffstutler

EASY ORANGE FLAVORED PECANS

1 1/2 c. sugar
1 1/2 c. orange juice

1 T. grated orange peel
2 1/2 c. pecan halves

Combine sugar and orange juice; cook to 240 degrees or soft ball stage. Remove from heat and add orange peel and pecan halves. Stir until syrup begins to look cloudy. Put on wax paper in small clusters or individual halves and allow to cool.

Ruby Wood Boone
Marshall, Texas

SUGARED NUTS

1 c. sugar
1/4 c. cream or half-and-half
3/4 t. salt
1 T. brown sugar

1 T. butter or margarine
2 T. whiskey, brandy or rum
   [or 1/4 c. orange juice]
1/2 lb. whole nuts

Boil sugar, cream, salt and brown sugar to soft ball stage. Remove from heat and add butter and whiskey. Return to heat and boil to soft ball stage. Add nuts. Mix until well-coated. Lift nuts from mixture in slotted spoon and drain syrup well. Drop on waxed paper and separate with two forks. If orange juice is used as flavoring, it should be boiled with sugar, cream, and salt instead of added later. Makes about 2 cups of nuts. ·

Mrs. C. Aubrey Smith, Jr.

SWEDISH NUTS

3 1/2 to 4 c. pecans
1 c. sugar
Dash salt

2 egg whites, beaten stiff
1/2 c. butter

Toast nuts in 325 degree oven until lightly browned. Fold sugar and salt into egg whites and beat until stiff. Fold nuts into this mixture. Melt butter in a jellyroll pan. Spread nut mixture over butter. Bake in a 350 degree oven, stirring every 10 minutes until coated with brown covering and no butter remains in pan. Cook about 30 minutes. Makes about 4 cups. Store in a tightly sealed container, and freeze if not to be used for a few weeks.

Mrs. Charles Primer

WHITE DIVINITY

2 c. sugar
1 c. water
1 egg white, beaten stiff

1 t. vanilla
1 c. chopped pecans

Bring sugar and water to boil and cook until candy thermometer registers 238 degrees (soft ball stage). Beat egg white. Gradually pour hot syrup over egg white and continue to beat. Add vanilla. When firm enough, quickly stir in pecans and drop from spoon onto waxed paper. (It will lose its gloss when ready).

Mrs. James E. Bass

ALMOND BARS

1 c. margarine
2 c. sugar
1 t. vanilla
1 egg yolk

2 1/4 c. sifted flour
1 egg white
1 T. sugar
1/2 c. sliced almonds

Cream margarine and sugar. Add vanilla and egg yolk. Stir in flour. Pour into ungreased 10 x 6 x 2 inch pan. Spread top with slightly beaten egg white. Sprinkle with sugar and almonds, (or colored sugar and coconut and almonds). Bake 40 minutes at 350 degrees. Cut into bars while warm. Makes 1 1/2 dozen.

Mrs. Henry D. McCallum

Mrs. Patrick Thomas makes her Dutch Cookies using butter instead of margarine, 1 cup sugar and pecans instead of almonds. She varies by spreading the batter very thin in a larger pan and baking until golden brown.

BROWN SUGAR COOKIES

1 box brown sugar
2 sticks soft margarine
2 c. flour
2 eggs
2 t. baking powder

Pinch of salt
1 or 2 t. vanilla
1 1/2 c. pecans, coarsely
chopped

Combine all ingredients and pour into greased and floured 3 quart pyrex dish. Bake at 350 degrees for 30 to 45 minutes. Sides will be browner than middle and somewhat chewy. Cut into 24 to 30 squares.

Mrs. Ted C. Chilcote
Newburgh, New York

BLOND BROWNIES

4 eggs, well-beaten
1 lb. brown sugar
2 c. Bisquick

1 t. vanilla
2 c. pecans

Combine all ingredients and pour into a greased 9 x 13 inch pan. Bake at 325 degrees for 30 minutes. Cut into squares after cooled.

Mrs. Francis Kay

BROWNIES

1 c. butter
2 squares bitter chocolate
4 eggs
2 c. sugar

Pinch of salt
2 T. vanilla
1 c. flour, sifted
1 c. chopped nuts

Melt butter and chocolate over hot water in double boiler and set aside to cool. Beat eggs and add sugar, salt and vanilla. Add cooled chocolate mixture. Fold in flour and chopped nuts. Pour into greased and floured 9 x 13 inch pan. Bake at 350 degrees for 45 minutes over pan of hot water.

Icing:

1/4 c. cocoa
1/4 c. butter
1/4 c. milk

1 c. sugar
1 t. vanilla

Combine all ingredients except vanilla and boil one minute. Add vanilla and beat a few minutes. Pour over brownies.

Mrs. R. J. McMurrey, Jr.

Double this - the first pan will go too fast.

MARSHMALLOW FUDGE BROWNIES

1 c. sugar
1/2 c. melted butter
1 c. sifted flour
Dash of salt
2 eggs, beaten

2 squares melted chocolate
2 t. vanilla
1 c. pecans
20 large marshmallows

Mix sugar, butter, flour, salt, eggs, chocolate, vanilla and pecans. Spread in 12 x 7 1/2 inch pyrex dish. Bake for 25 to 30 minutes at 350 degrees. (Do not overcook). After removing from oven, place large marshmallows evenly over baked brownies. Put under broiler and allow marshmallows to toast until soft enough to spread with a knife over top of brownies. Then spread with the following uncooked icing:

1 lb. powdered sugar
1/2 c. cocoa
1/8 t. salt

1/4 lb. soft butter
1 t. vanilla
5 to 7 T. milk

Mix all ingredients until spreading consistency.
These freeze well and are even better if served frozen.

Mrs. E. B. Yale

FUDGE SQUARES

1 c. sugar
1/2 c. butter or margarine
3/4 c. flour
1/2 c. pecans, chopped

4 T. cocoa
2 eggs
1 t. vanilla
Dash salt

Grease cookie sheet. Mix all ingredients together, bake at 300 degrees for 20 minutes. (Use cookie sheet with sides, approximately 15 x 10 inches.) While baking, prepare icing as follows:

2 t. cocoa
2 T. butter, melted
1 t. vanilla

1 3/4 c. powdered sugar
Enough milk to mix

Ice while brownies are warm. Makes 3 to 4 dozen. Freezes well. Store in covered container.

Mrs. Cruger Ragland
Dallas, Texas

BLACK WALNUT CHOCOLATE SQUARES

3 squares bitter chocolate
1 c. butter
4 beaten eggs
2 c. sugar
1 c. cake flour

1/4 t. salt
2 t. vanilla
1 1/2 c. chopped
   black walnuts
Powdered sugar

Melt chocolate over hot water in double boiler. Set aside to cool. Cream butter. Add eggs and sugar alternately; then flour, sifted with salt. Stir in vanilla and walnuts. Spread into greased and floured 11 x 13 inch pan. Bake for 35 minutes at 350 degrees. Turn out on board immediately and cut into squares. Roll in powdered sugar while warm and again when thoroughly cooled.

Mrs. A. K. Baker
McAllen, Texas

JANYCE'S COOKIES

1st Layer:

1/2 c. sifted flour
1/4 t. baking soda
1/4 t. salt
1/2 c. brown sugar
1 c. oats
6 T. butter, melted

3rd Layer:

1 square unsweetened
   chocolate
2 T. butter
1 1/2 c. sifted powdered sugar
1 t. vanilla
2 to 3 T. boiling water
1/2 c. chopped nuts

2nd Layer:

1 square unsweetened
   chocolate
4 T. butter
3/4 c. sugar
1 egg
2/3 c. flour
1/4 t. baking powder
1/4 t. salt
1/4 c. milk
1/2 t. vanilla
1 c. Angel Flake coconut

For first layer, sift together flour, baking soda, and salt and mix with brown sugar and oats. Stir in melted butter and pat mixture into 11 x 7 x 1 1/2 inch pan. Bake at 350 degrees for 7 minutes.

While this bakes, prepare second layer by melting chocolate and butter together. To this add sugar and egg and beat well. Sift flour, baking powder and salt together and add alternately with milk. Add vanilla and coconut. Spread over baked layer, return to oven and bake at 350 degrees for 25 minutes more. Then add top layer.

For third layer, melt chocolate and butter together. Add powdered sugar, vanilla, water and nuts. Stir vigorously, adding more water if needed to make spreading consistency. Spread over cookies in the baking pan. Cut into small squares as these are very rich.

Mrs. H. L. Gist

This is an original - and really outstanding!

CHOCOLATE CHIP ANGEL KISSES

2 egg whites
1/8 t. cream of tartar
Pinch of salt
3/4 c. sugar

1/2 t. almond extract
1 t. vanilla extract
1 c. chocolate chips
1 c. chopped pecans

Beat egg whites, cream of tartar and salt until stiff but not dry. Gradually add sugar and flavorings. Stir in chips and pecans. Line cookie sheet with foil and drop by teaspoonfuls. Heat oven to 350 degrees. Place cookies into the oven and turn off heat. Leave cookies in cooling oven for several hours (6 to 8) or overnight. Makes 3 dozen.

Mrs. Carlton Billups
Mrs. Gene Caldwell
Mrs. Elise Gallaher
Mrs. David Russell

This is a popular recipe and has several variations - and several descriptive names, such as "Overnight" Cookies, "Sleepy" Cookies, or "Cookies-While-You-Sleep". Flavorings are optional and some use more or less (or omit) vanilla and almond extracts. For less sweetness, use only 2/3 cup sugar.

CHOCOLATE CHOW MEIN

1 pkg. [6 oz.] semi-sweet chocolate morsels
1 pkg. [6 oz.] butterscotch morsels
1 can chow mein noodles

Melt chocolate and butterscotch morsels in double boiler. Add noodles. Mix well and drop by teaspoons on waxed paper. Chill until hard.

Mrs. Hoyt N. Berryman, Jr.

CHOCOLATE MACAROONS

1 pkg. [6 oz.] semi-sweet
   chocolate bits
2 egg whites
1/4 t. salt

1/4 c. sugar
1 pkg. coconut
2 t. vanilla

Melt chocolate bits and let cool. Beat egg whites until stiff. Add salt and sugar to egg whites, adding sugar gradually. Pour chocolate into meringue and fold in coconut and vanilla. Drop by spoonfuls on brown wrapping paper. Bake at 325 degrees for 13 minutes.

Mrs. E. D. Fitzpatrick

CHOCOLATE DROP COOKIES

1 c. sugar [may use 1/2 c.
   brown, 1/2 c. white]
1/2 c. butter or shortening
1 egg
2 squares chocolate, melted
1 1/2 c. flour

1/4 t. salt
1 t. baking powder
1/2 t. soda
1 t. cinnamon
1/2 c. buttermilk
1 c. chopped nuts

Cream sugar and butter well. Add egg and melted chocolate. Sift dry ingredients together and add alternately with milk. Stir in nuts. Drop by teaspoonfuls on greased cookie sheet. Bake at 350 degrees for about 15 minutes. Makes about 4 dozen. When cool, ice with following:

2 c. powdered sugar [sifted]
1/4 t. salt
1 square chocolate, melted
Warm milk [very little] to make consistency to spread
1 t. vanilla

Mrs. Francis Penn

Add tiny decorations and turn this into a beautiful Christmas cookie.

CHOCOLATE WAFERS

1/2 c. butter
2 oz. bitter chocolate
1/2 c. flour
1 c. sugar

1/4 t. salt
2 eggs, well-beaten
1 t. vanilla
1 c. chopped nuts

Melt butter and chocolate over gently boiling water in a double boiler and blend together. Sift flour with sugar and salt and add to the chocolate mixture. Beat, using wire whisk. Stir in beaten eggs and vanilla; mix in thoroughly. Spread the mixture on a well-buttered cookie sheet and sprinkle the nuts on top. Bake at 400 degrees for 10 minutes. Remove from oven and cut into squares while still warm. Makes 2 dozen.

Mrs. Milburn Pool

CINNAMON PUFFS

2 c. flour
1/2 c. sugar
3 t. baking powder
1 t. nutmeg

1 egg, well-beaten
3/4 c. milk
1/3 c. Wesson oil

Sift flour, sugar, baking powder and nutmeg together. Add egg, milk and Wesson oil. Drop dough by spoonfuls into deep hot salad oil and fry. Drain on absorbent paper and roll in cinnamon-sugar (confectioner's sugar).

Mrs. Shirley Simons, Jr.

COOKIES WITH ICING

1 c. shortening	1 t. vanilla
2 c. sugar	3 1/2 c. flour
3 eggs, beaten	1/2 t. salt

Cream shortening and sugar. Add beaten eggs and vanilla. Stir in flour and salt, sifted together. Chill dough. Roll out and cut with cookie cutter. Bake at 350 degrees from 8 to 10 minutes. Cool and spread with the following icing:

1/2 box powdered sugar, sifted	2 t. vanilla
3 T. butter, melted	Cream or canned milk

Combine powdered sugar, melted butter and vanilla. Slowly add cream until icing is spreading consistency. Icing may be divided into separate containers and colored with different food colors for decorating cookies.

Mrs. Moliere Scarborough

CREAM JUMBLES

1/2 c. shortening or butter	1/2 t. salt
1 c. sugar	1/2 c. buttermilk
1 egg	1 t. vanilla
2 c. sifted flour	Sugar and cinnamon
1/2 t. soda	

Cream shortening and sugar. Beat egg in thoroughly. Sift dry ingredients together and stir into butter and sugar mixture alternately with buttermilk. Add vanilla. Drop by teaspoonfuls about 2 inches apart on lightly greased cookie sheet. Sprinkle with sugar and cinnamon. Bake at 400 degrees for 12 to 15 minutes. Makes 3 dozen cookies.

Mrs. Harvey Wallender, Jr.

DATE KISSES

2 egg whites	1 c. pecans, chopped
1 c. powdered sugar	1 c. dates, chopped

Beat egg whites stiff. Add sugar, pecans and dates. Drop from teaspoon onto buttered pans and bake until delicately brown, (approximately 10 to 12 minutes), in a slow oven, 300 degrees. Makes about 2 1/2 dozen. Store in tightly covered container.

Mrs. Gene Caldwell

Excellent for a snack with coffee.

DATE NUT PINWHEELS

1 1/2 c. shortening
1 c. brown sugar, firmly
  packed
1 egg
1 T. sweet or sour cream

1/2 t. vanilla
1 3/4 c. sifted flour
1/2 t. soda
1/2 t. cream of tartar
1/8 t. salt

Cream shortening, brown sugar and egg thoroughly. Stir in cream and vanilla. Sift flour, soda, cream of tartar and salt and stir in until mixture is smooth. Divide dough into 2 parts. On waxed paper over a pastry board or cloth, roll each section of dough into a rectangle about 11 x 17 inches. Spread each half with half the date-nut mixture (recipe below). Roll up the rectangles tightly, beginning at wide side by lifting the wax paper. When rolled, seal the edges and ends by pinching dough together. Wrap each roll in waxed paper and chill until firm, several hours or overnight. Slice 1/4 inch thick and bake on lightly greased cookie sheet about 10 minutes at 400 degrees.

Date Nut Filling:

3/4 lb. moist pitted dates,
  cut up
1/3 c. sugar

1/3 c. water
1/2 c. nuts, finely chopped

Combine dates, sugar and water in a saucepan and cook over moderate heat until slightly thickened, stirring constantly. Remove from heat, cool and stir in nuts. Cookie roll can be frozen if desired.

Mrs. Rowland Baldwin, Sr.

DUZEN KONFECT

4 c. flour
1 lb. butter
  [not margarine]
1 c. sugar
1/2 lb. ground almonds
  [not blanched]

1 T. vanilla
1/2 t. almond extract
Currant jelly
Sugar

Mix dough with hands like pie crust. Chill at least 1 hour. Roll thin and cut in small rounds. Bake at 375 degrees until golden brown, about 7 minutes, watching closely. While hot, spread with tart red current jelly and stack another cookie on top. Then dip in granulated sugar while still hot.

Mrs. A. K. Baker
McAllen, Texas

It's easier to make this with a friend as two hands can't operate fast enough when the cookies come from the oven! These store in a tin in a cool place for ages. They freeze beautifully, too.

FRUIT CAKE COOKIES I

1/2 c. butter
1/2 c. sugar
2 eggs
1 1/2 c. flour
1/2 t. soda
1/2 t. cinnamon

1 T. hot water
1/2 pkg. [7 oz.] dates
3/4 lb. candied cherries
   and pineapple
3 c. chopped nuts

Cream butter and sugar. Add eggs and beat well. Sift dry ingredients together and add to egg mixture. Add hot water and mix well. Coat nuts and fruit with flour and add to dough. Place rounded teaspoonfuls on lightly greased cookie sheet. Bake at 300 degrees until lightly browned. Makes about 4 dozen.

Mrs. Bart Moore

FRUIT CAKE COOKIES II

1/2 c. butter [or 1 stick
   margarine]
3/4 c. sugar
2 eggs
1 t. vanilla
1/2 t. soda
Pinch of salt
1/4 t. nutmeg

1/2 t. cinnamon
1 1/2 c. flour
2 c. fruit mix [fruit for
   fruit cakes]
1 c. raisins
1 c. dates
2 c. pecans

Blend butter, sugar, eggs and vanilla. Add soda, salt, nutmeg and cinnamon to 1 cup of flour. Add to mixture. Coat chopped fruit and nuts with 1/2 cup flour and blend with first mixture. Drop by teaspoons on a lightly greased cookie sheet. Bake at 325 degrees for 20 to 25 minutes. Freezes well or will keep in tins.

Mrs. F. E. Starling

OLD-FASHIONED GINGERSNAPS

3/4 c. shortening
1 c. sugar
1/4 c. light molasses
1 egg, beaten
2 c. flour

1/4 t. salt
2 t. soda
1 t. cinnamon
1 t. cloves
1 t. ginger

Cream shortening and sugar; add molasses and egg and beat well. Sift together dry ingredients and mix in thoroughly. Roll in small balls. Dip into sugar and place 2 inches apart on greased cookie sheet. Bake at 375 degrees about 10 minutes. Makes 5 dozen.

Mrs. Raymond Whitney, Jr.

Mrs. Jack Warren makes her Molasses Sugar Cookies from a similar recipe, decreasing amounts of cloves and ginger to 1/2 teaspoon each and adding 1/2 cup of broken pecans and 1/2 teaspoon vanilla.

GHOORABEE [LEBANESE HOLIDAY COOKIE]

1 c. clarified butter
1 c. sugar
3 c. sifted flour
1 t. orange flower water
  [optional]

Pecan halves or
  almonds [blanched]

Cream butter until light and fluffy. Add sugar gradually and continue beating until very well-creamed. Add flour slowly, mixing until all is added. Add flavoring, if desired. Shape into rolls with hands (as refrigerator cookie dough) on bread board. Smooth surface with patting motion making the roll flat on bottom and top, about 1 1/2 inches wide on top and 1 inch deep. With sharp knife slice diagonally to form diamond-shaped cookies. Place on ungreased cookie sheet and press pecan or almond in center of each cookie. Bake in 300 degree oven for 15 to 20 minutes. Watch closely while baking. Bakes light. Allow to cool before removing from cookie sheet. Makes about 6 dozen.

Mrs. Joy Massad

To prepare clarified butter, heat butter in a heavy saucepan until foam and tiny particles have settled completely to bottom of pan. Strain into a jar and store in refrigerator. Keep heat very low in order to prevent scorching or browning. This process takes approximately 30 minutes to an hour, depending on amount of butter being clarified.

GRAHAM CRACKER COOKIES

1 1/2 sticks margarine
1 c. sugar
1 egg, beaten
1/2 c. milk
1 t. vanilla

1 1/2 c. crushed graham
  crackers
1 c. coconut
1 c. chopped nuts
Whole graham crackers

Combine margarine, sugar, egg and milk in saucepan and boil for 2 minutes. Add vanilla, crushed graham crackers, coconut and nuts and mix all together well. Cover bottom of 9 x 12 inch pan (or larger) with whole graham crackers. Break to fill in all spaces. Cover with half the filling mixture and a layer of crackers. Spread with remainder of filling and cover with another layer of crackers. With palm of hand, press down on top layer until crackers break. Ice with the following:

1/2 stick margarine
2 T. canned evaporated milk

1/2 box powdered sugar
1/2 t. maple flavoring

Combine all ingredients and spread over cookies. Cover with foil and refrigerate overnight. Cut into tiny squares. Makes 3 dozen.

Mrs. Patrick Thomas

GOOD COOKIES

1/2 c. margarine
1/2 c. plus 2 T. shortening
1 c. powdered sugar
1 1/2 c. sifted flour

2 t. vanilla
1 c. pecans, chopped
    coarsely

Preheat oven to 350 degrees. Cream margarine and shortening together until smooth. Beat in powdered sugar gradually. Stir in flour and blend thoroughly. Add vanilla and pecans. Form into small balls and place on ungreased baking sheet. Flatten balls with bottom of a glass dipped in flour. Bake 15 to 20 minutes or until light brown. Yields about 5 dozen.

Mrs. Paul Wick

ICEBOX COOKIES

1 lb. margarine or
    shortening
1 c. brown sugar [packed
    down]
1 c. granulated white sugar
2 eggs, beaten

1/8 t. salt
1 t. baking soda
1 t. vanilla
1/2 to 1 cup chopped nuts
4 to 5 c. flour
1/2 t. cream of tartar

Mix all ingredients and divide into 4 portions. Form each portion into a roll and wrap in waxed paper. Refrigerate and bake when needed. Unbaked rolls of dough may be frozen, if desired. Slice cookies from roll and bake at 350 degrees for 10 to 15 minutes until edges are brown.

Mrs. William Marsh

For a sweeter cookie, sprinkle tops of unbaked cookies with sugar.

KING FAMILY ICEBOX COOKIES

1 c. brown sugar
1 c. white sugar
1 1/2 c. shortening
4 1/2 c. flour
3 eggs

1 1/2 t. soda
1 t. salt
3 t. cinnamon
1 c. nuts

Mix all ingredients thoroughly and shape dough into rolls. Makes 5 rolls, 10 inches long. Wrap each roll in waxed paper and store in refrigerator or freeze. Slice and bake at 350 degrees for 10 to 12 minutes. Makes about 2 dozen cookies per roll of dough.

Mrs. Tom Ramey, Jr.

MARIE'S ICEBOX COOKIES

2 sticks butter
1 c. dark brown sugar
1 c. white sugar
2 eggs

1 t. vanilla
2 1/4 c. flour
1/2 t. soda
1 c. chopped pecans

Cream butter with sugars (which have been mixed together). Add lightly beaten eggs, vanilla and flour to which soda has been added. Stir in nuts. Chill dough a few minutes for easier handling. Divide in two or three parts and roll each in plastic wrap to form a long roll. Twist ends of wrap and store in refrigerator or freezer. Slice and bake 10 to 15 minutes in slow oven, 300 to 325 degrees.

Mrs. Thomas Swann

So chewy and good!

LEMON BARS

1 c. margarine
1/2 c. powdered sugar
2 c. flour
Pinch of salt
4 eggs, beaten

2 c. sugar
6 T. lemon juice
6 T. flour
Rind of 1 lemon, grated

Blend margarine, sugar, flour and salt with pastry blender and pat into a greased 13 x 9 inch pan. Bake at 350 degrees for 20 minutes.

Beat eggs and gradually add the sugar. Then mix in lemon juice, flour, lemon rind and pour over crust. Bake 25 minutes at 350 degrees. Sprinkle with powdered sugar. Cut into squares and serve.

Mrs. Neil Velvin

LEMON SOURS

1/2 c. plus 2 T. flour
1/2 stick margarine
2 eggs
1 c. brown sugar
1/2 c. chopped nuts
3/4 c. coconut

1/8 t. baking powder
1/2 t. vanilla
1 1/2 T. lemon juice
1/2 t. lemon rind
3/4 c. powdered sugar

Mix flour and margarine until crumbly. Sprinkle evenly in 11 x 7 inch pan and bake at 350 degrees for 10 minutes. Beat eggs; add brown sugar, nuts, coconut, baking powder and vanilla. Spread over first mixture as it comes from oven. Return to oven and bake 20 minutes longer. Mix lemon juice, rind, powdered sugar, and spread on top while still hot. Cool; cut into squares. Makes 2 dozen.

Mrs. Bill C. Ross

"JOE FROGGERS"

1 c. shortening	1 t. nutmeg
2 c. sugar	1/2 t. allspice
7 c. flour, sifted	1/2 c. water
1 T. salt	1/2 c. rum
1 T. ginger	2 t. baking soda
1 t. cloves	2 c. dark molasses

Cream shortening and sugar. Sift flour, salt and spices together and add. Combine water and rum. Add soda to molasses. Add water mixture and molasses mixture alternately in 2 additions each to creamed mixture, blending well after each addition. Chill dough overnight. Roll to 1/4 inch thickness on floured board. Cut with 4-inch or 5-inch cutter (may use coffee can). Place on greased cookie sheet (use a spatula to place on pan to prevent tearing). Bake at 375 degrees for 9 to 10 minutes. Let stand on cookie sheet for several minutes before removing to prevent breaking. Store in covered container.

Mrs. A. M. Limmer, Jr.

 This is a teenage favorite!

MEXICAN COOKIES

1 lb. butter	1 t. cinnamon
1 c. sugar	1/2 c. sugar
5 c. flour, sifted	

Cream butter and sugar until well-mixed. Add flour gradually to make stiff dough. Pinch off small amount and place in palm of hand. Squeeze gently forming an irregular ball about the size of a pecan. Bake at 375 degrees for 10 minutes. While still warm sprinkle with the cinnamon and sugar mixed.

Mrs. Moliere Scarborough

NUT CRUMB MERINGUES

3 egg whites	1 c. finely ground almonds
1/2 t. baking powder	[blanched]
1 c. sugar	3/4 c. Kellogg's crumbs
1 t. almond extract	

Beat egg whites until they form soft peaks; add baking powder. Gradually add sugar and continue to beat until meringue forms fairly stiff peaks. Fold in almond extract, ground almonds and crumbs. Line cookie sheets with foil; drop mixture by small teaspoons onto foil. Bake in a preheated 325 degree oven until slightly browned, 25 to 30 minutes. Watch closely. Gently lift off foil and cool on wire rack. Makes about 3 1/2 dozen cookies.

Mrs. John M. Burke, Jr.

LACE COOKIES

1/2 c. margarine
1/2 c. butter
1 c. sugar
1 c. brown sugar
2 eggs

2 1/2 c. oats
1 t. baking powder
1 t. vanilla
1 c. pecans, chopped

Cream margarine, butter and sugars; add eggs, oats, baking powder, vanilla and pecans. Line pan with foil. Drop by teaspoonfuls allowing 4 inches between cookies. Bake at 350 degrees for 8 minutes or until foil can be pulled from cookies. Makes 5 dozen cookies.

Mrs. H. L. Gist

OATMEAL COOKIES

1/2 c. Wesson oil
1/2 c. milk
1 egg
2 t. vanilla
1 1/2 c. flour
1 1/2 c. oatmeal

1 c. brown sugar
1/2 t. soda
1 t. salt
1 t. cinnamon
1 c. pecans
1 c. raisins

Mix Wesson oil, milk, egg and vanilla and combine with flour, oatmeal, brown sugar, soda, salt and cinnamon. Stir in pecans and raisins. Add more oatmeal if stiffer dough is needed to keep cookies from running together. Drop by teaspoons onto cookie sheet. Bake at 350 degrees about 10 minutes or until very lightly browned.

Mrs. F. Lee Lawrence

OATMEAL MACAROONS

1 c. shortening
1 c. brown sugar
1 c. granulated sugar
1/2 t. vanilla
2 eggs, unbeaten
1 1/4 c. flour
1 t. soda

1/2 t. salt
1/2 t. cinnamon
3 c. Quick Quaker oats
[uncooked]
1/2 c. chopped nuts
[optional]

Cream shortening, sugars, vanilla and eggs thoroughly. Sift flour, soda, salt and cinnamon together. Add flour mixture to sugar mixture gradually and blend thoroughly. Stir in oats and nuts. Drop by spoonfuls on greased cookie sheet. Bake at 350 degrees for 12 to 15 minutes. Cool on pan 2 minutes before removing. Makes 6 dozen or more cookies.

Mrs. Jerry Bain

OATMEAL MOLASSES COOKIES

1 1/2 c. flour
1 t. soda
1/2 t. salt
1/2 t. ground cloves
1/2 t. ginger
1 c. sugar

3/4 c. butter or
margarine [soft]
1 egg
1/4 c. dark molasses
[or pancake syrup]
3/4 c. quick-cooking oats

Sift together flour, soda, salt, cloves, ginger and sugar. Add butter, egg and molasses; beat until smooth - about 2 minutes. Stir in oats. Drop by level tablespoonfuls, 2 inches apart, on ungreased cookie sheets. Bake in preheated 375 degree oven until browned, approximately 8 to 10 minutes. Let stand a minute or so before removing to wire racks to cool.

Mrs. Jack Harper

KOKONUT KRISP KOOKIES

2 c. flour
1 t. soda
1 t. baking powder
1/2 t. salt
1 c. butter
1 c. sugar
2 eggs, well-beaten

1 c. brown sugar
2 c. Rice Krispies
2 c. oatmeal
1 c. shredded coconut
1 t. vanilla
1/2 c. chopped dates
1/2 c. nuts

Sift flour, soda, baking powder and salt together. Cream butter and granulated sugar. Beat eggs and brown sugar together and add to creamed mixture. Add dry ingredients, then stir in Rice Krispies, oatmeal, coconut, vanilla, dates and nuts. Drop by teaspoonfuls onto greased cookie sheet. Bake at 350 degrees for 12 to 15 minutes, until lightly browned.

Mrs. Noble Hood
Tucson, Arizona

RICE KRISPIE COOKIES

1 c. Crisco
1 c. butter [not margarine]
3 c. powdered sugar

1 T. vanilla
3 c. flour
3 c. Rice Krispies

Cream Crisco, butter, sugar and vanilla until consistency of thick whipping cream. Add flour and stir in Rice Krispies. Dough will be soft. Chill. Form into 4 rolls about the diameter of a 50c piece. Wrap and refrigerate. Cut slices 3/8 to 1/2 inch thick. Bake at 350 degrees on ungreased cookie sheet until bottom of cookie begins to brown (10 to 12 minutes). Cool on wire rack. Makes approximately 4 dozen.

Mrs. Joe Max Green
Nacogdoches, Texas

RANGER COOKIES

1 c. shortening
1 c. brown sugar
1 c. white sugar
2 eggs
1 t. vanilla
2 c. flour
1/4 t. baking powder
1 t. soda

1/4 t. salt
2 c. uncooked oats
2 c. dry cereal [Rice
   Krispies, Frosted Flakes,
   or other]
1 pkg. [6 oz.] chocolate chips
Nuts [optional]

Cream shortening and sugars. Add eggs and vanilla. Sift flour, baking powder, soda and salt together and add. Add oats, cereal, chocolate chips and nuts, if desired. Drop by spoonfuls on greased cookie sheet and bake at 375 degrees for 10 to 12 minutes. Makes 8 to 10 dozen.

Mrs. Robert L. Edge

ORANGE COOKIES

1 3/4 c. brown sugar [packed]
3/4 c. Crisco [or butter]
2 whole eggs
2 t. grated orange rind
Juice of 1 orange
3 c. sifted flour

1 t. soda
1 1/2 t. baking powder
1/2 t. salt
1/2 c. buttermilk
1 t. vanilla
2 c. chopped nuts

Cream sugar and Crisco. Add eggs one at a time. Add orange rind and juice. Add flour (sifted with soda, baking powder and salt) alternately with milk. Mix well. Add vanilla and nuts. Place in refrigerator at least 2 hours and then drop by teaspoons on greased cookie sheet. Bake at 350 degrees about 10 minutes. When cool, frost with the following icing:

3/4 stick butter, melted
1 box powdered sugar, sifted
Grated rind of 1 lemon and 1 orange
Enough orange and lemon juice [combined]
   to make spreading consistency.

Combine all together and spread on cookies. Makes about 4 dozen.

Mrs. Francis Penn

PEANUT BUTTER BLOSSOMS

1 3/4 c. flour
1 t. soda
1/2 t. salt
1/2 c. shortening
1/2 c. sugar
1/2 c. brown sugar

1/2 c. smooth peanut butter
1 egg
2 T. milk
1 t. vanilla
Hershey's Kisses

Sift dry ingredients together. Cream shortening, sugars and peanut butter. Add the egg, milk and vanilla. Beat well and add dry ingredients. Shape into teaspoon-sized balls. Roll in white granulated sugar. Place on ungreased cookie sheet. Bake 8 minutes at 350 degrees, then remove from oven. Press Hershey Kiss into center until cookie cracks around edge. Bake 2 to 5 minutes longer.

Mrs. Don Carroll

PEANUT BUTTER COOKIES

1/2 c. shortening
1/2 c. peanut butter
1 c. sugar
1 1/4 c. flour
1 egg

4 T. milk
1/4 t. salt
3/4 t. soda
1/2 t. baking powder
1 t. vanilla extract

Cream together shortening, peanut butter and sugar. Sift in flour. Add egg, milk, salt, soda and baking powder. Knead dough with hands for thorough mixing. Add vanilla. Dough will be sticky and moist. Drop by teaspoonfuls on lightly greased cookie sheet. Place in preheated 350 degree oven and bake until light brown. Remove with spatula. Makes 4 dozen cookies.

Mrs. Alice White

Satisfying and filling as a dessert cookie or on any occasion.

PECAN PUFFS

2 sticks butter
4 T. sugar
2 t. vanilla

2 c. pecans,
    finely ground
2 c. sifted flour

Cream butter; blend in sugar, vanilla and pecans. Add flour. Roll into small balls and place on ungreased cookie sheet. Bake in slow oven, 300 degrees, for 30 minutes. These should not be browned. Roll in powdered sugar while hot and again when cool.

Mrs. Jim Gray

PECAN TASSES

Crust:

1 pkg. [3 oz.] cream cheese, softened
1/4 lb. margarine, softened
1 c. flour

Filling:

3/4 c. brown sugar
1 T. butter, softened
1 egg
Pinch of salt
1 t. vanilla
3/4 c. chopped pecans

For crust, blend all ingredients together and refrigerate one hour. Pat out in 1-inch balls and shape into miniature muffin pan (1 1/2 inch cups, greased).

For filling, blend sugar and butter; add egg, salt and vanilla.

In uncooked formed crusts, put 1/2 teaspoon chopped pecans. Add filling and top with pecans. Bake 20 minutes at 325 degrees.

Mrs. John Minton

SOUTHERN PECAN BARS

Crust:

1 c. flour
1/4 t. baking powder
1/4 c. butter
1/3 c. brown sugar
1/4 c. pecans, chopped finely

Pecan Topping:

2 eggs
3/4 c. dark corn syrup
1/4 c. brown sugar
2 T. flour
1/2 t. salt
1 t. vanilla
3/4 c. pecans

For crust, sift together flour and baking powder. Cream butter and brown sugar well. Add the dry ingredients and mix until mixture resembles coarse meal. Stir in pecans. Pat firmly into bottom of well-greased 12 x 8 x 2 inch pan. Bake at 350 degrees for 10 minutes.

For pecan topping, beat eggs until foamy. Add corn syrup, brown sugar, flour, salt and vanilla. Mix well. Pour over partially baked crust. Sprinkle with pecans, chopped if desired. Bake at 350 degrees for 25 to 30 minutes. Cool in pan, then cut into bars. Makes 2 1/2 dozen.

Mrs. Sam Adams
Henderson, Texas

POTATO CHIP COOKIES

1 c. shortening
1 c. sugar
1 c. brown sugar
1 t. salt
1 t. soda
2 eggs

2 c. sifted flour
2 c. crushed potato chips
1 t. vanilla
1 c. chopped pecans,
    [optional]

Cream shortening, sugars, salt, soda and eggs thoroughly. Add flour, potato chips and vanilla and nuts. Drop by spoonfuls on cookie sheet and bake at 350 degrees for 10 minutes. Makes about 7 dozen. Cookies can be frozen.

Mrs. Brad Holmes, Jr.

SAND TARTS

1/2 lb. butter
1/2 c. powdered sugar, sifted
2 c. sifted cake flour

1 c. chopped pecans
1 t. vanilla

Cream butter; add sugar. Add flour, nuts and vanilla. Shape into balls or crescents and bake on ungreased cookie sheet at 325 degrees for 20 minutes or until light brown. Roll in powdered sugar immediately. Makes 4 dozen.

Mrs. Jack King

VARIATION OF SAND TART

1/4 c. butter or margarine
1 c. sugar
1 egg
1 t. vanilla
1 3/4 c. flour

1/4 t. salt
2 t. baking powder
1/4 c. chopped pecans
    [or more if needed]
1/4 c. powdered sugar

Cream butter and sugar. Beat in egg and vanilla. Sift together flour, salt and baking powder. Sift again, and blend with butter, sugar and egg mixture. Roll dough in wax paper and chill for 3 or 4 hours. Slice 1/4 inch thick. Press into pecans firmly enough for pecans to stick. Place on ungreased cookie sheet and bake at 400 degrees for 10 minutes. Cool for a few minutes before removing from cookie sheet. Drop into sack of powdered sugar to coat. Makes approximately 6 dozen.

Mrs. Jack Woldert

SNICKERDOODLES

1 c. shortening
1 1/2 c. sugar
2 eggs
2 3/4 c. flour, sifted
2 t. cream of tartar

1 t. soda
1/2 t. salt
2 T. sugar
2 T. cinnamon

Cream shortening and sugar. Add eggs and beat well. Sift flour, cream of tartar, soda and salt and mix in thoroughly. Roll into balls about 1-inch in diameter. Roll balls in a mixture of sugar and cinnamon. Place on ungreased cookie sheet 2 inches apart. Bake 8 to 10 minutes at 400 degrees until lightly browned but still soft. Makes 5 dozen cookies.

Mrs. Joe Clayton

SNOW DROPS

1 c. butter [no substitute]
4 T. powdered sugar
2 c. cake flour

1 t. water
2 t. vanilla
1 c. chopped pecans

Beat butter and sugar until creamy. Stir in flour, add water and blend well. Add vanilla and pecans. Chill until firm enough to shape with fingers. Form into small crescent-shaped pieces and bake at 400 degrees for 10 to 12 minutes. Roll in sifted powdered sugar while still warm. Makes 5 dozen.

Mrs. Charles Helliwell

BUTTER SUGAR COOKIES

1 lb. butter, slightly
    softened
2 eggs
5 c. flour
2 c. sugar
1/8 t. salt

1 T. vanilla
1 t. soda, dissolved in
    milk
3 T. milk
Nuts and fruit [if desired]

Combine all ingredients in a large bowl. Using hands, mix thoroughly. Form dough into a ball, sprinkle lightly with flour and chill. (This dough keeps well in refrigerator and parts of it may be used as needed). On lightly floured surface roll dough thin. You may sprinkle sugar and/or nuts on dough. Cut into desired shapes. Fruits may be added to dough or used to decorate the cookies. Bake at 350 degrees for about 12 minutes. Makes about 6 dozen.

Mrs. Milburn Pool

 For a special touch, decorate before cookies are baked or ice after they are cool.

SUGAR COOKIES

1 c. butter	1 t. vanilla
1 c. powdered sugar	4 c. flour
1 c. granulated sugar	1 t. soda
1 c. vegetable oil	1 t. cream of tartar
2 eggs	1 t. salt

Cream butter and sugars. Add oil, eggs and vanilla and beat. Add dry ingredients and mix. Refrigerate several hours until dough is firm. Form into balls; then roll balls in granulated sugar. Put balls on greased cookie sheet and press thin with a fork. Bake at 375 degrees for 10 to 12 minutes. Makes approximately 6 dozen cookies.

Mrs. Fred C. McCoun

SUGAR COOKIES AND "PAINT"

2 c. sifted flour	1 c. sugar
1 1/2 t. baking powder	1 egg
1/4 t. salt	1 t. vanilla
1/2 c. butter [no substitute]	

Mix and sift 1 1/2 cups flour, baking powder and salt. Cream butter until soft. Beat in sugar, egg and vanilla. Stir in flour mixture, then gradually add enough of the remaining 1/2 cup flour to make the dough stiff. Chill at least one hour. Roll out 1/8 inch thick on surface dusted with powdered sugar (rather than flour). Cut with cookie cutters and place on ungreased cookie sheet. "Paint" (see below) cookies. Bake at 375 degrees for 8 to 10 minutes. Makes 3 to 4 dozen, depending on size of cookie cutter.

"Paint" for decorating cookies:

1 egg
1/4 t. water

Blend in small bowl. Divide mixture among three or four small custard cups. Add a different food coloring to each cup to make bright colors. If "paint" thickens, add a few drops of water.

Mrs. Jack Harper

Great fun for children on a rainy day!

ANNIE'S SUGAR COOKIES

1 c. butter [2 sticks]
2 c. sugar
2 eggs, beaten

3 1/2 c. flour
1 t. soda
1/2 t. salt

Cream butter and sugar. Add eggs and dry ingredients, sifted together. After well-blended, form dough into 2 long rolls. Wrap in foil or waxed paper and refrigerate overnight. For a crisp cookie, slice thin for baking. Bake on a greased cookie sheet for approximately 6 minutes at 350 degrees.

Mrs. J. L. Patton

STRAWBERRY COOKIES

2 sticks butter
1 c. sugar
2 c. flour
2 egg yolks

1 c. nuts
1/2 t. salt
1 c. strawberry preserves

Cream butter and add sugar, flour, egg yolks, nuts and salt. Spread half of dough in a 6 x 9 inch pan. Place strawberry preserves on top of dough and cover with other half of dough, spreading evenly on top (may need to use hands). Bake at 325 degrees for 30 minutes until light brown. Serves 12.

Mrs. Upton Beall

GRANDMOTHER'S POPCORN BALLS

8 qts. cooked salted popcorn
1 c. ribbon cane or Brer Rabbit
    syrup [do not use Karo -
    ribbon cane is best!]

1 1/2 c. sugar
1/2 c. butter
2 t. vinegar
Dash salt

Cook all (except popcorn) until soft ball stage is reached. Divide corn into 2 large shallow pans. Pour half of syrup mixture over each pan of corn. With damp hands, shape into balls when corn and syrup have cooled slightly.

Mrs. Watson Simons

A traditional Halloween treat!

NOTES AND EXTRA RECIPES

Men's
Potpourri

MEN'S
POTPOURRI

GUACAMOLE

1 lg. [or 2 small] avocado
   [about 1/2 c. mashed pulp]
1/4 t. lemon juice
1/4 t. garlic salt
1/4 t. chili powder
1/4 t. salt
1/4 t. Tabasco sauce

1 1/2 T. mayonnaise [not
   salad dressing]
1 T. grated onion
Generous dash of cayenne
1 fresh tomato, diced
   and drained [optional]

Peel and mash avocado. Add other ingredients except tomato and mix well. If desired, dice tomato and drain excess juice on paper towel. Then add to avocado mixture. Serve as a dip with tostados or as a salad over shredded lettuce.

C. Aubrey Smith, Jr.

This does not keep well. If prepared early, place avocado seeds in mixture to retard discoloration.

CEVICHE

1 lb. flounder fillets, cut
   in 1 1/2 x 1 in. strips
Juice of 2 limes
Juice of 2 lemons
2 t. dried chives

1 green pepper, cut in
   thin strips
1 t. salt
1/4 t. black pepper
1/4 t. cayenne pepper

Combine all ingredients. Toss mixture lightly. Cover and refrigerate overnight (preferably 2 or 3 days, if possible). Serves 6 to 8.

John D. Glass, Jr.

GLENN'S PIMIENTO CHEESE

1 lb. Velveeta cheese
1/2 lb. Longhorn cheese
2 hard boiled eggs
2 medium size Kosher dill
   pickles [or garlic dill]
1 can [7 oz.] pimientos

1 pt. Miracle Whip
2 heaping T. mustard
1 t. sugar
Salt and pepper to taste
1 oz. pickle juice

Grind the cheese, eggs, pickles and pimientos together. Add salad dressing, mustard, sugar, salt, pepper and pickle juice, and mix well. Makes approximately 2 quarts of sandwich filling.

L. Glenn Taylor

BLOODY MARY COCKTAILS

46 oz. tomato juice
1/2 c. lemon juice
1/4 c. Worcestershire sauce

1 T. Red Devil
1 t. salt
1 1/4 c. vodka

Mix all the ingredients in a half gallon container. Serve over ice. The vodka may be added later if you wish to make these ahead.

Dr. L. D. Cobb

ICE CREAM CAFÉ

1 1/2 scoops of ice cream
[vanilla or coffee]

1 1/2 jiggers Kahlua

Blend and serve with a straw or a spoon. Serves 1.

John White

MOCHA FLOAT

1 1/2 sq. unsweetened chocolate,
cut into pieces
1/4 c. boiling water
2 t. instant coffee
3 T. sugar

Dash of salt
1 1/2 c. cold milk
Vanilla ice cream

Place chocolate pieces into blender and cover. Blend on high for about 6 seconds. Add boiling water. Cover. Blend on high about 6 seconds. Add instant coffee, sugar, salt and milk. Cover. Blend on high for 15 seconds. Pour into 2 tall glasses. Top with scoops of vanilla ice cream. Serves 2.

Stuart M. Scarborough

For a party, make this in quantity and serve as Mocha Punch.

SATIN DOLL

1 oz. vodka
1/2 oz. Cointreau

1/2 oz. Creme de Banana
1 oz. fresh lemon juice

Mix and serve over ice in an Old-Fashioned glass. This is the notorious "yellow drink". It can be dangerous.

Dean H. Perry
Cisco, Texas

FRENCH ONION SOUP

2 or 3 soup bones with some
    meat on them or 1 1/2 c. diced
    leftover roast
4 qts. water
1 or 2 boullion cubes
1 carrot, chopped
Dash Worcestershire sauce
2 sprigs marjoram
1/2 c. celery, including
    leaves, chopped

1 bay leaf
1 T. [or less] salt
1 t. pepper
4 or 5 onions
2 T. margarine
Parmesan cheese
Croutons

Cook bones (meat) in water with boullion cubes, carrot, Worcestershire sauce, marjoram, celery, bay leaf, salt and pepper for 3 to 5 hours, then strain. Slice onions very thin and separate into strips. Lightly saute' in margarine. Add to stock (with more salt and pepper, if needed) and cook for 30 minutes over medium heat. Serve hot sprinkled with Parmesan cheese and croutons. Serves 4 to 6.

Dr. Charles A. Primer

CAESAR SALAD

2 cloves garlic, peeled
    and quartered
2/3 c. salad or olive oil
1 small head lettuce [iceburg]
1 head endive, romaine or
    other greens [spinach is
    marvelous]

1/2 c. grated Parmesan cheese
1/2 t. salt
1/4 t. pepper
1 egg
3 1/2 T. lemon juice
1 T. Worcestershire sauce
2 c. croutons

Let garlic stand in oil at room temperature for several hours or overnight. Remove garlic. Wash salad greens, drain, and dry thoroughly. Tear into bite-size pieces in salad bowl. Chill until salad time. Then sprinkle the cheese and the salt and pepper over the greens. Drizzle a half cup of the oil over all the salad. With a flourish, drop the raw egg on top and pour lemon juice and Worcestershire sauce onto the egg. Give the salad a good, gentle tossing. For the finishing touch, pour the remaining oil over the croutons, add to the salad, and toss just a bit. Serve immediately. Serves 8 to 10.

John W. Noble

JAMIE'S GREEN SALAD

2 kinds of lettuce [or
  more], broken
1 clove garlic
1 avocado, diced
1 or 2 tomatoes, cut in
  small wedges
1 or 2 green onions and
  tops, finely chopped

1/2 t. Lawry's seasoned salt
1/2 t. lemon pepper marinade
2 or 3 T. Parmesan cheese
1/4 c. Wesson oil [or less,
  if preferred]
1 to 2 T. tarragon vinegar

The key to a good salad is crisp greens. Wash lettuce, roll completely in paper toweling, and refrigerate. Chill 2 to 4 hours. Rub wooden bowl with garlic. Cut avocado and sprinkle with lemon juice to prevent discoloration. Add tomato wedges, lettuce torn into bite-size pieces and sprinkle onion over this. Cover and place in refrigerator until serving time. To toss, add Lawry's salt to taste, sprinkle with lemon pepper and Parmesan cheese. Just before serving, add oil, sprinkle with small amount of sugar; then add vinegar and toss together well.

James Boring

POTATO SALAD

4 c. diced, cooked potatoes
1/2 c. scallions, cut up
1 1/2 c. sliced celery
1/4 c. sliced radishes
2 T. snipped parsley
1 c. mayonnaise

1 T. wine vinegar
2 t. mustard
1/2 t. celery seed
1 1/2 t. salt
1/8 t. pepper

On day before serving, combine all ingredients and refrigerate. Serve on lettuce; garnish with tomato or hard boiled egg wedges, sliced olives, grated carrots or pickles. Serves 6.

Glenn E. Hess

FLAKY BUTTER BISCUITS

2 c. sifted flour
4 t. baking powder
1 t. salt

1/4 c. butter
2/3 c. milk

Sift together flour, baking powder and salt. Add butter and cut in with pastry blender until mixture is like coarse crumbs. Add milk, stir and toss lightly with a fork. Knead dough about 10 times on a lightly floured board. Roll about 1/2 inch thick and cut with biscuit cutter. Bake on lightly greased cookie sheet at 425 degrees until golden brown, about 12 minutes. Makes one dozen biscuits.

Kenneth C. Lust

CHARCOALED ONIONS

6 medium sized onions, peeled   3 t. butter
  [purple variety preferred]   Salt and pepper
6 beef bouillon cubes

    Scoop out small hole in top of each onion. Fill with a bouillon cube and 1/2 teaspoon butter. Add salt and pepper to taste. Wrap each onion tightly in foil. Place on hot coals for about 30 minutes, turning frequently. Unwrap, serve hot. If prepared in the oven, bake at 350 degrees for 30 to 40 minutes. Serves 6.

Buddy Rogers

Cooking time may vary depending upon size of onions used.

CONSOMMÉ ONIONS

1 bunch green onions   Dash cracked black pepper
1 can consomme' [or similar   Pinch of sweet basil
  stock]

    Cut onions so there are 2 or 3 inches of green stem left. Dilute consomme' with 1/2 can of water and cook onions, covered, until tender. If desired, add cracked black pepper and sweet basil to the cooking liquid. Remove onions and boil liquid until thickened. Return onions to pan when ready to serve, heat and coat with thickened consomme'.

Rowland Baldwin, Jr.

Small white onions make a good substitute, but have a different flavor.

HUEVOS ROBERTO

8 eggs   Salt and pepper to taste
1/4 c. half-and-half   3 T. butter [not margarine]
1 jalapeno pepper, chopped   1/4 lb. grated Cheddar cheese
2 shallots, chopped

    Beat the eggs and half-and-half well. Stir in the jalapeno pepper and shallots. Salt and pepper. Melt butter in skillet and scramble to desired doneness. Sprinkle grated cheese on eggs and serve immediately.

Robert D. Jones
Midland, Texas

SHIRRED EGGS

1/4 lb. butter
4 eggs
1 T. Worcestershire sauce
1 T. lemon juice

Dash salt
Dash pepper
Parsley

Melt butter in 2 small flameproof baking dishes at 250 degrees. Place 2 eggs in each dish, add Worcestershire sauce, lemon juice, salt and pepper. Bake at 400 degrees until done. Garnish with parsley and serve. Serves 2.

Francis Kay

MARINATED "EYE-OF-THE-ROUND"

1 "Eye-of-the-round"

Marinade:

1 onion, chopped
3/4 c. catsup
1/2 c. water
2 T. vinegar
2 T. Worcestershire sauce
2 T. lemon juice

2 t. sugar
1 t. dry mustard
1 t. chili powder
1/2 t. salt
1/2 t. paprika
Drop Tabasco

Combine marinade ingredients in a saucepan and boil for 5 minutes. Pour over meat, cover with foil and refrigerate for 24 hours.

When ready to cook, place in 225 degree oven for 2 hours. Then put it on the grill in a shallow foil pan off the fire for 1 hour. This smokes the meat.

R. B. Shelton

Great for a Sunday at home or on a summer afternoon.

STEAKS

2 to 4 heavy beef steaks [8 to 12 oz.]
   or large sirloin [not frozen]
1 can beer

Marinate steaks in beer for 1 to 2 hours; then cook over gray charcoal - not too hot.

Jerry Shelton

GOOD CENTS STEAK TERIYAKI

1 can [8 oz.] tomato sauce
1/2 c. soy sauce
1/4 c. salad oil
1/4 c. sherry

2 T. brown sugar
2 beefsteaks [about
    2 1/2 lbs.]

Combine all ingredients (except steak) in a jar. Shake or stir well to blend. Cover and let stand 4 to 5 hours. Trim steaks, if necessary, and arrange in shallow oblong glass baking dish. Pour marinade over steaks and let stand at least 2 hours. Cook on grill to desired doneness, basting and turning every 5 minutes.

Richard Grainger

FILLET IN BURGUNDY

1 to 3 garlic buds
2 T. butter
4 fillets [6 to 8 oz. each]
Salt and pepper to taste [or
    lemon pepper marinade]
1 c. catsup

Fresh parsley
Fresh mushrooms
1 c. Burgundy [or Chablis]
4 thick slices French
    bread [optional]
Chicken pate' [optional]

In a 10 or 12 inch skillet (preferably copper), saute' garlic buds in butter. Remove garlic and saute' the fillets which have been rubbed with salt and freshly ground pepper (or lemon pepper marinade). In a separate skillet, heat catsup over medium heat until it darkens and thickens. Add parsley to catsup, then thinly sliced mushrooms shortly before sauce is to be used. Continue cooking fillets in butter. When steaks are turned (about halfway through cooking time), add wine to the catsup sauce. For rare steak, cook about 8 minutes over high heat.

A delicious way to serve this is on thick-sliced, toasted French bread which has been spread with chicken pate', with the catsup-parsley sauce over all. If desired, just the steak and sauce may be served. Serves 4.

Dr. Buford Sanders

MEAT SHISH-KABOB

4 lb. top round or sirloin
1 pt. cherry tomatoes
1 can [1 lb.] whole boiled
onions [may substitute
fresh onions]

3 green peppers, cut in
large pieces
16 whole mushrooms [may
be fresh or canned]

Marinade:

2/3 c. soy sauce
1/4 c. sugar
2 T. oil

1 large clove garlic,
minced
3 T. sherry [optional]

Cut beef into 1 inch square chunks - 1/2 inch thick. Combine all marinade sauce ingredients and marinate meat in sauce for at least 20 minutes. Arrange meat chunks on skewers alternately with tomatoes, onions, green peppers, and top with whole mushrooms. Broil over hot charcoal fire or in oven. Turn once. Serves 4 to 6.

Dr. Paul Wick

INDIAN CORN BREAD

Batter:

2 eggs
1 c. milk
1/4 c. bacon drippings
1/2 t. soda

3/4 t. salt
1 c. corn meal
1 can [No. 303] cream
style corn

Prepare batter as for corn bread, adding can of corn.

1 lb. ground beef
Salt to taste
1 or 2 t. corn meal
1/2 lb. Cheddar cheese, grated

1 medium onion, chopped
1 small green pepper,
chopped

Saute' ground meat and salt to taste. Sprinkle 1 or 2 teaspoons corn meal in bottom of hot, greased, 10-inch skillet. Pour half of batter in skillet; add grated cheese, then meat, onion and pepper. Top with remaining batter and bake uncovered at 350 degrees for 45 to 50 minutes.

A. Y. Lewis

EAST TEXAS CHILI

3 T. cooking oil
6 lbs. lean chuck or other
   stew-type meat [trim off
   any gristle and then "chili
   grind" by your friendly
   butcher]
1 or 2 cans tomato juice
2 T. cumin

2 T. oregano
1 T. cayenne pepper
2 T. salt
3 or 4 garlic pods,
   finely chopped
1 T. Tabasco sauce
3 T. Mexene chili powder
4 T. Masa Harina

In a large (8 quart or more) cooking pot, heat cooking oil and add the ground beef, searing it until browned. Add tomato juice and water until the meat is covered by 1 or 2 inches of liquid. Bring to a boil, stirring occasionally; reduce heat and simmer covered for 30 minutes. Add the cumin, oregano, pepper, salt, garlic, Tabasco and chili powder. Simmer for another 30 minutes, stirring infrequently. Add the Masa Harina mixed separately with a little water to make a smooth paste before adding it to the chili. (Do not use flour except as a last resort, in which event mix with corn meal). Simmer for 30 to 40 minutes more, stirring occasionally. Taste the chili for changes in seasoning as one batch will differ from another, depending on variation in meat and seasoning. While simmering, skim grease off, if you prefer. If mixture seems too watery, remove the lid while simmering to permit it to cook down some.

F. Lee Lawrence

To increase the sting and "authenticate" your chili, double the Tabasco and chili powder.

HAM LOAF

Ham Loaf:

2 eggs
4 c. ground ham
1 t. baking powder
1 t. Worcestershire sauce
1 c. bread crumbs
1 c. light cream

Topping:

1/2 c. brown sugar
1 t. flour
1 t. mustard
Vinegar [enough to
   moisten]

Beat eggs. Add ham and other loaf ingredients. Mix thoroughly. Butter a 2 quart loaf pan and line with waxed paper. Fill and spread with topping. Set pan in larger pan of hot water and bake at 375 degrees for about 1 hour. Serves 6.

Hunter Brush

CHINESE BARBECUE RIBS

Pork Ribs

Marinade:

1/4 c. hoisin sauce [available   2 cloves garlic, crushed
    from Oriental food store]   3 T. soy sauce
1/2 c. sugar   6 T. wine [sherry or port]
1 t. salt

     Stir marinade ingredients together, pour over the plates of ribs and let stand at least two hours or longer (overnight is fine).
     To cook, remove ribs from marinade and place in pyrex dish in 325 degree oven for approximately 1 hour and 45 minutes. While cooking, ribs may be brushed with sauce to prevent drying. Serve with chutney or plum sauce dip.

Willis Jarrell

EAST TEXAS SPARERIBS

3 to 5 lbs. pork ribs   1 T. sugar [white]
1 T. salt   1 T. pepper

Barbecue Sauce:

1/2 stick margarine   Dash garlic salt
1 c. catsup   1/8 t. black pepper
2 T. cooking oil   1/8 t. chili powder
1 T. prepared mustard   Pinch crushed red pepper
2 T. Worcestershire sauce   1/4 c. brown sugar [firmly
1/2 medium lemon [juice]   packed]
1 T. vinegar

     Parboil ribs 15 minutes in large pan. Mix salt, sugar, pepper and rub ribs thoroughly with this mixture. To prepare sauce, combine all ingredients and mix well. Brush on ribs and cook on charcoaler over low fire for 1 to 1 1/2 hours. (Bank coals to keep from browning too quickly.) Baste and turn at 20 to 25 minute intervals. Remove to cutting board and slice into individual serving portions. Serves 6.

Edwin Simons

This sauce is also very good on chicken, pork chops and brisket.

SPARERIBS

3 lbs. ribs
2 T. chili powder
1/4 c. brown sugar
1 T. salt

1 t. paprika
2 T. celery seed
1 can [8 oz.] tomato sauce
1/4 c. vinegar

Combine dry ingredients and rub ribs with approximately 1/3 of this mixture. Combine remainder of dry mixture with tomato sauce and vinegar for basting sauce. Cook slowly on outdoor grill, basting frequently with sauce as ribs cook. Tabasco to taste may be added for a hotter sauce.

Bill C. Ross

SPARERIBS A LA JUDY

4 lbs. spareribs, cut into
   2 or 3 rib portions
2 T. Figaro liquid smoke
2 c. catsup
2 c. water
2 T. Worcestershire sauce

1/2 c. brown sugar
1 T. salt
1 clove garlic, chopped fine
1 medium onion, sliced
1/4 c. red wine

Brush ribs with Figaro or any liquid smoke and brown lightly in a 450 degree oven. Pour off grease. Combine all other ingredients and pour over the browned spareribs. Cover and bake at 325 degrees for about 1 1/2 hours or until ribs are tender and well done.

Dr. J. H. Spence

BURGUNDY MUSHROOM SAUCE FOR STEAKS

3 oz. mushrooms, sliced
4 T. butter
2 T. flour
1/2 c. beef bouillon

3 shakes Lawry's salt
1 t. soy sauce
1/2 c. Burgundy
4 t. sugar

Saute' mushrooms in butter. Stir in flour until mixture thickens. Add bouillon; stir until smooth. Add Lawry's salt, soy sauce, Burgundy and sugar. Simmer 10 minutes. Serve over steak.

M. Earl Davis

DRY BARBECUE SAUCE

1/2 c. sugar
1 T. seasoning salt
1 t. paprika
1/4 t. garlic salt

1 t. black pepper
1/2 t. onion salt
1/2 t. dry mustard powder

Combine all ingredients and shake generously over beef, pork, chicken, fish, or game before cooking.

William F. Turner

BAR-B-Q SAUCE

1 onion, chopped
2 cloves garlic, chopped
1/2 c. oil
1/2 stick margarine
1 c. catsup
1 c. vinegar

1 c. water
1 t. red pepper
1 t. chili powder
2 or 3 t. mustard
1 t. salt

Saute' onion and garlic in oil and margarine until onion is soft. Add remaining ingredients and simmer. If desired, sauce may be run through blender for extra smoothness. Makes 1 quart. May be stored in refrigerator several days.

Field M. Davis

Pork and beans may be simmered in this sauce for delicious Bar-B-Q Beans.

OLD TIMER'S BAR-B-Q SAUCE

1 c. catsup
1/2 c. Worcestershire sauce
1 c. water
1 t. salt
1 t. chili powder

1 t. bottled smoke
2 T. brown sugar
Dash of Tabasco sauce
Touch of dried mustard
Dash of garlic powder

Combine all ingredients and mix together well.

Walt Farrington

MEXICAN HOT SAUCE OR DIP

1 can [28 oz.] whole tomatoes
1 pkg. [7 oz.] Good Seasons garlic salad dressing mix [dry]
1/2 can [10 oz.] Rotel tomatoes [or more to taste]
1 t. salad oil
1/2 t. salt

Drain whole tomatoes and pour into blender. Add all other ingredients. Turn on blender for 1 or 2 short spurts. Too much blending makes sauce too watery. Additional blending may be achieved by pouring back and forth from one container to another.

David Boice

RANCHERO SAUCE

1 small or medium onion, chopped
1 or 2 green peppers, chopped
1 1/2 T. olive oil
1 T. flour
1 can Rotel tomatoes with green chilies

1 can [#303] tomatoes
1 clove garlic [or 1 1/2 t. minced garlic]
Salt and pepper to taste
1 1/2 to 2 t. chili powder
1/4 to 1/2 t. Italian seasoning

Saute' chopped onion and green pepper in olive oil for about 3 minutes over low heat. Stir in flour and add Rotel and plain tomatoes which have each been drained and mashed. (Reserve juice in case sauce needs to be thinned). Add garlic and seasonings and continue cooking over low heat for 5 minutes. Serve over scrambled eggs. This amount of sauce will serve about 10. Ranchero sauce may be stored in refrigerator or frozen and reheated (add water when reheating, if necessary).

Dr. Buford Sanders

HOT MUSTARD SAUCE
[Especially for Ham]

1/2 c. vinegar
4 T. brown sugar
2 T. granulated sugar

1/2 c. Coleman's dry mustard
Pinch of salt

Mix vinegar and sugars and boil until slightly syrupy. Stir into sifted mustard until smooth. Add salt. Keeps well in refrigerator.

Frank J. Budde

GARLIC CHICKEN POMPLONA DINNER

Salad:

4 or 5 boiled potatoes
1 jar [med.] stuffed olives
1 can tuna [optional]
3 or 4 hard boiled eggs
Olive oil
Wine vinegar
Salt and pepper to taste

Fruit:

1 glass Malaga wine [or port]
1 shot glass Spanish Fundador
  Brandy [or Triple Sec or
  Grand Marnier]
1 t. cinnamon
2 to 4 T. powdered sugar
Fresh figs, apples, any fruit

Garlic Chicken:

2 whole chickens [2 1/2 lbs.
  each]
6 to 8 garlic cloves
1 T. salt
1 T. freshly ground pepper
1 c. olive oil

After Dinner Drink:

Soly Sombra [anisette,
  Fundador Brandy]

To prepare salad, slice cold boiled potatoes crossways. Place on a deep platter with sliced olives. Place flaked, drained tuna (if desired) over potatoes. Top with sliced hard boiled eggs. Pour on dressing of olive oil, wine vinegar, salt and pepper.

For garlic chicken, cut through breast side of chicken but not backbone. Rub with cut garlic cloves, salt and freshly ground pepper. Flatten chickens, inside cavity up, in shallow roasting pan. Pour olive oil over chicken and into pan. Place coarsely chopped garlic over chickens and into oil. Brown skins over hot fire on top of stove. Roast about 15 minutes in 450 degree oven. Turn skin side up. Baste. Return to oven until done. Baste frequently if chickens appear dry. Cut in half and serve one half per person. Serves 4.

To prepare fruit, make sauce of wine, brandy and cinnamon. Add powdered sugar. Dissolve. Pour over fresh fruit such as figs, apples, oranges, peaches, etc. Sprinkle powdered sugar over top. Garnish with cinnamon sticks.

For Soly Sombra, combine 1/2 anisette and 1/2 brandy. Serve in B & B glass.

Dr. Buford Sanders

A wine tip: serve chilled Chablis or Pouilly Fuisse.

CHICKEN LIVER, ET CETERA, A LA PATIO

8 chicken livers
1/4 c. flour
1/2 t. cayenne pepper
1 1/2 lbs. bacon, thickly
  sliced

2 lbs. mushroom caps
2 lbs. pearl onions [medium
  to large]
2 green peppers, cut in
  chunks

Dust livers with flour and sprinkle with cayenne. Place livers on spit or skewers alternately with bacon (folded in thirds), mushrooms, onions and green pepper chunks. Broil over coals until done.

A. B. Wilson, Jr.

CHICKEN MOLÉ de JUAN

2 fryers
2 c. chicken stock
1 can [18 oz.] tomato juice
1/4 t. cumin
1/4 t. coriander
1/2 t. cinnamon
2 t. chili powder
1/2 t. salt
1/3 c. toasted almonds
1 t. sesame seeds

1 clove garlic, pressed
1 T. crunchy peanut butter, heated
3 T. Hershey's chocolate syrup
1/8 t. cloves
1 t. instant minced onion
1 c. raisins
1/4 of day-old hot dog bun, crumbled

Bake 2 fryers with water in covered roaster for 40 minutes at 350 degrees. Remove bone and skin from chicken and cut in medium sized pieces. Reserve 2 cups stock. Combine all but the last 2 ingredients in skillet and simmer for 45 minutes. Add raisins, crumbs and chicken and simmer 20 minutes more. Serve over rice or plain. Serves 12. Freezes well.

John D. Glass, Jr.

CHICKEN PASTRIES

Pastry for double crust
1/8 c. butter
Pinch garlic powder
1/2 t. sage
1/8 c. flour
1 c. chicken broth

1 t. soy sauce
2 c. diced chicken [or left-over turkey]
Salt to taste [about 1 1/2 t.]
Freshly ground pepper
Paprika or Parmesan cheese

Melt butter, add garlic, sage and flour and cook until bubbly. Add broth and soy sauce. Mix well and cool 1 minute. Add chicken, salt and pepper.

Roll out pastry and cut in circles (about 4 inch diameter). Put spoonful of chicken mixture in each. Fold over (moisten edge, if necessary) and seal by pressing edge with back of fork tines.

Place on greased cookie sheet, spinkle with paprika or Parmesan cheese. Bake at 375 degrees until brown. Serves 8.

Kenneth C. Lust

CHARCOALED DOVES

Breasted doves
Bacon slices

Woody's Bar-B-Q sauce

Wrap 1/2 piece bacon around each dove breast, securing with toothpicks. Marinate in Woody's Bar-B-Q sauce overnight or for several hours.

Charcoal on grill. These are delicious. The bacon keeps them moist.

Watson Simons

COLEEN'S DOVE

Doves
Flour
Lawry's seasoned salt
Pepper
Cooking oil
1 c. bouillon
1 c. claret [or red
    table wine]

1 T. garlic juice
Black pepper to taste
1 scant pinch mixed herbs
1 can cream of mushroom
    soup
1 to 1 1/2 cans water

    Dredge birds in flour with salt and pepper. Fry in deep grease until brown. DO NOT COOK. Remove, drain and place birds in Dutch oven. Add bouillon, claret, garlic juice, black pepper and mixed herbs. Cover and cook 2 hours in 300 to 350 degree oven. Remove from oven; add cream of mushroom soup and water. Adjust seasoning, if desired, cover and cook 1 hour at low heat.

Jesse Johnson

FLAVORED QUAIL OR DRUNK BIRDS

8 quail
Salt and pepper to taste
1 stick butter
2 medium carrots, diced
2 small onions, chopped
4 T. green pepper, chopped

1 c. mushrooms, chopped
6 slices orange peel,
    blanched
2 T. flour
2 c. chicken stock
1 c. white wine

    Rub quail with salt and pepper. Brown lightly in butter. Place in buttered casserole.

    To the skillet in which the birds were browned, add vegetables and orange peel. Cook slowly for 5 minutes. Stir the flour and chicken stock in gradually until the sauce is thickened. Season with salt and pepper. Simmer slowly for 10 minutes until medium thick. Meanwhile, cover quail with white wine and bake 10 minutes in 350 degree oven. Pour sauce over quail and bake, covered, for 20 minutes more.

Mike Ehmans

ROAST DUCK

1 medium sized duck [Wood
duck, Mallard, etc.]
Salt to taste
1 apple, quartered
1 onion, quartered

1 stalk celery, cut in
1/2 inch pieces
3 strips bacon
1/4 c. sherry [optional]

Salt cavity of duck and stuff with apple, onion and celery. Place breast up in roaster and add small amount of water. Lay bacon strips over breast. Pour sherry over duck, if desired. Place in oven, covered, and bake for 2 1/2 hours at 325 degrees. Remove cover to brown for about 30 minutes longer. One or two people may be served per duck, depending on size.

Glenn Collins

ROAST VENISON

5 or 6 lb. venison roast
Salt pork or bacon
2 onions, cut in rings
Salt and pepper
4 whole peppercorns

1 large can tomato sauce
1/2 can consomme'
1/2 can water
1 clove garlic
1 bay leaf

Wipe venison with a vinegar soaked cloth. Lay strips of salt pork or bacon across the roast and fasten with toothpicks. Place onion rings over each toothpick, three to each strip of bacon or salt pork. Salt and pepper to taste.

Roast in 400 degree oven for 30 minutes. Add other ingredients and bake at 350 degrees until tender. Thicken gravy.

Serve with wild rice or mashed potatoes.

William F. Turner

VENISON RAGOUT

3 lbs. boned venison
1 c. vinegar
1 1/2 c. water
Accent
Salt
Freshly ground black pepper
2 c. celery, chopped

2 c. onion, chopped
Rosemary
1/4 c. flour
1/4 c. butter, melted
1/4 c. red Burgundy
1/2 pt. sour cream

Marinate venison overnight in vinegar, 1/2 cup of water, Accent, salt and pepper. Drain venison and place in casserole with celery, onion, a pinch of rosemary and 1 cup of water. Cover and braise in a moderate oven, 350 degrees, for 2 hours. Remove venison. Slice and keep warm in a chafing dish. Strain stock. Stir together flour and butter. Add to stock and cook, stirring constantly, until thickened. Stir in wine and sour cream. Pour over venison and serve from chafing dish.

J. Harold Stringer

Page 371

VENISON CHILI

3 lbs. venison chili meat
   [may use beef chili meat]
1 small can chili powder
1 small can paprika
1 small bottle garlic
   powder

1 T. cumin
1 t. salt
1 T. black pepper
4 T. flour

Brown meat and continue to cook in water over low heat. When tender, add remaining ingredients and simmer for several hours. Serves 15 to 20.

Dr. Merwyn Pickle

BARBECUED SHRIMP

Large shrimp in shells
Melted margarine

Salt
Fine ground black pepper

Wash shrimp in cold water. Blot on paper towel to dry. Arrange in single layer in bottom of broiler pan. Pour margarine over to about half way up. Sprinkle lightly with salt and cover with black pepper - lots of pepper.

Turn oven to broil and put in oven for about 7 minutes. Take out and turn each shrimp over. Sprinkle again with black pepper - return to oven for another 7 minutes or until shell pops when pinched. Serve in bowls with some of juice. Peel shrimp and dip in sauce. Serve with French bread and tossed green salad. Pass "wash 'n dri" or small towels dampened with warm water.

Frank Fite

BACHELOR SHRIMP

Leafy tops from 1 bunch
   celery
1 lb. shrimp
1 onion, chopped
1 clove garlic, minced
4 T. butter

1 c. grated cheese [good
   quality rat cheese]
1/2 t. dry mustard
1/2 t. salt
6 T. dry sherry
1/3 c. shaved almonds

Place celery in salted water and boil. Add shrimp and just barely cook but not fully. Drain shrimp, peel and cut into bite-size pieces.

Saute' onion and garlic in butter until soft. Add cheese, dry mustard and salt and stir over slow heat until cheese is melted. Add shrimp and sherry. When mixture is fully blended, pour into casserole. Top with almonds. Place in oven and broil until brown. Serves 3 to 4.

Dean H. Perry
Cisco, Texas

This dish is complimented by a good dry white wine and a Caesar salad.

FRIED SHRIMP

5 lbs. fresh shrimp, medium
  or jumbo
1 bottle [10 oz.] Worcestershire sauce
1 1/2 c. white vinegar

4 c. pancake mix
3 T. salt
1 T. black pepper
4 T. McCormick Seafood
  seasoning

Remove shell from shrimp, wash and drain. Mix Worcestershire sauce and white vinegar in deep bowl. Combine all dry ingredients separately. Place about 2 to 3 cups shrimp into Worcestershire-vinegar mixture and let soak about 5 minutes. Remove shrimp, drain and roll in dry ingredients to cover thoroughly. Shake off excess and fry in deep fryer at 375 degrees for about 5 to 7 minutes. Repeat process until all shrimp are used. Serves 10.

Jim Arnold

SHRIMP RONNIE

1/4 c. butter
1 lb. fresh mushrooms, sliced
4 lbs. raw or frozen shrimp,
  peeled and deveined
1/2 c. vermouth
1/2 c. rose' wine
1 can [13 oz.] evaporated
  milk [wash out can with
  1/3 can water]
1 lb. Velveeta cheese

3 T. Miracle Whip salad
  dressing
1 t. Lawry's seasoning salt
1/2 t. salt
1/2 t. pepper
1 T. Worcestershire sauce
1 t. curry powder
5 T. cornstarch
2/3 to 1 c. water

Melt butter in large Dutch oven or deep pot. Add mushrooms, shrimp, vermouth, rose' wine, and bring to a slow boil. Simmer about 10 minutes or until shrimp are tender and almost done. Remove from heat and remove all shrimp and mushrooms from sauce. To sauce in pot, add evaporated milk (diluted with the 1/3 can water), Velveeta, Miracle Whip, all seasonings, and cornstarch dissolved in water (not too thick consistency). Stir over low heat until smooth and sauce begins thickening. Add shrimp and mushrooms and simmer slowly on low heat for about 30 to 40 minutes, stirring occasionally. Serve over plain white rice or wild rice. Serves 8 to 10.

Ronald S. Smith

CRAB [OR SHRIMP] GUMBO "CAJUN STYLE"

1/4 c. cooking oil
1/4 c. onion, chopped
1 bell pepper, chopped
1 c. celery, chopped
1 small clove garlic,
  crushed
3 T. brown sugar
3 1/2 qts. water
1 can [medium] tomatoes

1 can [large] Trappey's okra
1 T. file' powder
1 t. salt
1 c. raw crabmeat [or 1 1/2 c.
  small uncooked shrimp]
3 jiggers bourbon
1/4 c. raw rice
1 T. Worcestershire sauce
1/2 t. Evangeline hot sauce

In large (5 quart boiling capacity) pot, heat cooking oil and saute' onions, green pepper, celery and garlic to a light brown, stirring constantly. Add brown sugar, then water, tomatoes (if desired, strain juice to remove seeds), okra, file' powder and salt. Boil, uncovered, over medium heat about 1 1/2 hours. Add crabmeat (or shrimp) and continue cooking for 20 minutes. Add bourbon, then rice and cook 25 minutes more. Last add Worcestershire and hot sauce and continue cooking for 5 minutes.

Chester Wynne

 Extra rice may be cooked separately and served with gumbo at the table. This freezes well.

BAKED FLOUNDER

1 whole fresh flounder
  [2 to 3 lb.]
1/2 c. butter, melted
2 large limes [or 3 small]

Salt to taste
Paprika
Chopped parsley

Place whole fish on buttered foil in low roasting pan or bottom of broiling pan. Melt butter and add juice of 1 large lime or 2 small ones. Pour over fish and salt to taste. Sprinkle paprika over fish. Slice other lime and layer in a strip down the center of flounder. Sprinkle with chopped parsley and bake in a 375 to 400 degree oven for 25 to 35 minutes. Do not overcook. Baste occasionally. Garnish with fresh parsley and extra lime wedges if desired and serve with tartar sauce. Frozen fillets may be used and layered in baking dish.

May also be placed on foil over charcoal grill.

Robert D. Jones
Midland, Texas

BANANAS FOSTER

1 t. butter
1/2 c. brown sugar
1 banana

Dash cinnamon
1 jigger banana liquor
1 jigger rum (151 proof)

Melt butter and add brown sugar. Saute' banana until soft. Add cinnamon, banana liquor and rum. Flame rum. Serve over hard vanilla ice cream. Serves 1.

Maxie H. Wilson

BUTTERMILK ICE CREAM

2 qts. buttermilk
1 pt. light cream
4 c. sugar

3 T. lemon extract
Drops of green food
coloring

Mix and freeze in an ice cream freezer. Makes 1 gallon.

Moliere Scarborough, Jr.

JULIA'S FUDGE

2 c. sugar
2 T. cocoa
2 T. white Karo
1/4 c. evaporated milk
1/4 c. water

1/3 stick butter
1 c. nuts, chopped and
toasted with butter
and salt
1/2 t. vanilla

Mix sugar, cocoa, Karo, milk, water and butter. Boil until a bit of mixture dropped from a spoon forms a soft ball in cool water. Remove from heat for 10 minutes. Place in a pan of cold water and beat until mixture begins to thicken. Add nuts and vanilla and pour into buttered platter or pyrex dish. Cool and cut in 1 inch squares.

Frank Fite

 Plain nuts may be substituted for toasted ones.

QUICK AND EASY SUBSTITUTIONS TO HELP SLIM DOWN RECIPES

- Use cooking spray, instead of oil or grease for frying.

- Instead of using oil, try a small amount of chicken broth or fruit juice when sautéing vegetables.

- Cook vegetables, pastas and rice in chicken or beef broth for loads of additional flavor.

- In place of fatty dairy products, such as sour cream, cream cheese, half and half, and whole milk, use the new low-fat or non-fat versions in your recipes.

- A chilled can of evaporated skimmed milk is a fantastic substitute for whipping cream. Use in sauces, creamed soups and in any other recipes calling for cream.

- Add a great amount of flavor to potatoes, vegetables and grains without adding the fat and cholesterol of butter, by substituting butter flavored seasonings and sprays.

- Fat free egg substitutions may be used in place of whole eggs in casseroles and sauces. If an egg substitute is not available, use two egg whites in place of one whole egg.

- Non-fat yogurts or non-fat sour creams are good substitutions when making vegetable dips and spreads.

- Herb vinegars, as well as balsamic vinegar, add zip to marinades, salads, vegetables and soups.

- Ground turkey breast or ground sirloin have less fat and cholesterol than regular ground beef.

Indexes

FOR EASY PREPARATION

The recipes included in this index have been selected because they require a minimum number of ingredients, create little mess in the kitchen and/or take a short time to cook.

FOR EASY PREPARATION

TO PREPARE IN ADVANCE

An index of selected recipes which may or must have total
or partial advance preparation.

TO PREPARE IN ADVANCE

Recipes in this index have been successfully frozen by our cooks according to the directions which accompany the recipes. Those which do not have freezing instructions may be prepared for the freezer by generally accepted cooking and packaging methods.

FOR THE FREEZER

TO SERVE A CROWD

This index is a guide to recipes which yield more than twleve servings.

TO SERVE A CROWD

SALADS continued
Guacamole Salad or Dip, 13
Ham and Egg Salad Sandwich Loaf, 67
Lime Salad Mold, 55
Shrimp Aspic, 234
Sour Cream Cucumbers I, 76
Tomato-Shrimp Aspic, 70
SALAD DRESSINGS
Lebanese Salad Dressing, 85
Mayonnaise, 86
Poppy Seed Dressing I, 86
Roquefort Dressing, 87
Thousand Island Dressing, 88
SEAFOODS
Crab (or Shrimp) Gumbo "Cajun Style", 374
Gumbo II, 241
Shrimp Aspic, 234
SOUPS
Hearty Vegetable Soup, 50
Weeend Vegetable Soup, 50
VEGETABLES
Basic Rice Casserole, 130
Broccoli Casserole II, 115
Green Bean Casserole I, 112
Harry's Pinto Beans, 114
Mixed Vegetables, 144
Party Rice, 132
Suzanne's Spinach, 136

ALPHABETICAL INDEX

Junior League of Tyler, Inc.
1919 S. Donnybrook Avenue
Tyler, Texas 75701
903-595-5426

Please send me _____ copies of
Cooking Through Rose Colored Glasses @ 18.50 ea. = _____

Please send me _____ copies of *And Roses for the Table*   @ 23.00 ea. = _____

Shipping and Handling $3.00 for one book = _____

Add $1.00 for each additional book = _____

Total = _____

Name _____

Address _____

City _____ State _____ Zip _____

Phone (_____)_____

Make checks payable to Junior League of Tyler, Inc.

Charge to: ___ Visa ___ MasterCard   Account # _____

Valid thru _____   Signature _____

- -

Junior League of Tyler, Inc.
1919 S. Donnybrook Avenue
Tyler, Texas 75701
903-595-5426

Please send me _____ copies of
Cooking Through Rose Colored Glasses @ 18.50 ea. = _____

Please send me _____ copies of *And Roses for the Table*   @ 23.00 ea. = _____

Shipping and Handling $3.00 for one book = _____

Add $1.00 for each additional book = _____

Total = _____

Name _____

Address _____

City _____ State _____ Zip _____

Phone (_____)_____

Make checks payable to Junior League of Tyler, Inc.

Charge to: ___ Visa ___ MasterCard   Account # _____

Valid thru _____   Signature _____

Where did you hear about this cookbook? _____

_____

_____

What local store would you like to see carry this cookbook? _____

_____

_____

Store Name _____

Address _____

City _____ State _____ Zip _____

Phone (_____)_____

Where did you hear about this cookbook? _____

_____

_____

What local store would you like to see carry this cookbook? _____

_____

_____

Store Name _____

Address _____

City _____ State _____ Zip _____

Phone (_____)_____